P9-DFV-242

BOOKS BY LAWRENCE GOLDSTONE

Inherently Unequal: The Betrayal of Equal Rights by the Supreme Court, 1865–1903

Dark Bargain: Slavery, Profits, and the Struggle for the Constitution

The Activist: John Marshall, *Marbury v. Madison,* and the Myth of Judicial Review

The Astronomer

The Anatomy of Deception

Off-Line

Rights

With Nancy Goldstone

Out of the Flames: The Remarkable Story of a Fearless Scholar, a Fatal Heresy, and One of the Rarest Books in the World

The Friar and the Cipher: Roger Bacon and the Unsolved Mystery of the Most Unusual Manuscript in the World

Deconstructing Penguins: Parents, Kids, and the Bond of Reading

Used and Rare: Travels in the Book World

Slightly Chipped: Footnotes in Booklore

Warmly Inscribed: The New England Forger and Other Book Tales

With Vernona Gomez

Lefty: An American Odyssey

BIRDMEN

BIRDMEN

The Wright Brothers, Glenn Curtiss, and the Battle to Control the Skies

Lawrence Goldstone

BALLANTINE BOOKS | NEW YORK

Published in the United States by Ballantine Books, an imprint of
The Random House Publishing Group, a division of Random House LLC,
a Penguin Random House Company, New York.

BALLANTINE and the HOUSE colophon are registered trademarks of
Random House LLC.

All photos courtesy of the Library of Congress

LIBRARY OF CONGRESS CATALOGING-IN-PUBLICATION DATA
Goldstone, Lawrence, 1947–
Birdmen : the Wright Brothers, Glenn Curtiss, and the battle to control
the skies / Lawrence Goldstone.
pages cm
Includes bibliographical references and index.
ISBN 978-0-345-53803-1 (hardcover : alk. paper)—
ISBN 978-0-345-53804-8 (eBook)
1. Aeronautics—United States—History. 2. Wright, Wilbur, 1867–1912.
3. Wright, Orville, 1871–1948. 4. Curtiss, Glenn Hammond, 1878–1930.
I. Title.
TL521.G568 2014
629.130092'273—dc23 2014001424

Printed in the United States of America on acid-free paper

www.ballantinebooks.com

9 8 7 6 5 4 3 2

Book design by Caroline Cunningham
Title page image by Gözde Otman

For Nancy and Emily

CONTENTS

PROLOGUE

Genius Extinguished

At 3:15 A.M. on May 30, 1912, Wilbur Wright died peacefully in his own bed in the family home at 7 Hawthorn Street in Dayton, Ohio, surrounded by his father, Milton; his sister, Katharine; and his three brothers, Lorin, Reuchlin, and Orville. Wilbur had contracted typhoid fever one month earlier from, the speculation went, eating tainted clam broth in a Boston restaurant. At five feet ten and 140 pounds, his body had lacked the strength to fight off an ailment that in the coming decades would be routinely vanquished with antibiotics. He was forty-five years old.

America had lost one of its heroes, one of two men to solve the riddle of human flight, and messages of praise and condolence poured into Dayton from around the world. More than one thousand telegrams arrived within twenty-four hours of Wilbur's death. President William Howard Taft—who at 350 pounds could never himself be a passenger in a Wright Flyer, although his predecessor Theodore Roosevelt had been—issued a statement declaring Wilbur to be the "father of the great new science of aeronautics," who would be remembered on a par with Robert Fulton and Alexander Graham Bell. *Aeronautics* magazine exclaimed, "Mr. Wright was revered by all who knew him, he was honored by an entire world, it was a privilege, never to be forgotten, to talk with him."

Across the nation, newspapers and magazines decried the sad stroke of luck that had robbed the nation of one of its great men. At 7 Hawthorn Street, however, members of the Wright family did not believe Wilbur's death to have been a result of bad luck at all. To them, Wilbur had been as good as murdered, hounded to his grave by a competitor so dishonest, so unscrupulous, so lacking in human feeling as to remain a family scourge as long as any of them remained alive.

Glenn Curtiss.

The bitter, decade-long Wright–Curtiss feud pitted against each other two of the nation's most brilliant innovators and shaped the course of American aviation. The ferocity with which Wilbur Wright attacked and Glenn Curtiss countered first launched America into preeminence in the skies and then doomed it to mediocrity. It would take the most destructive conflict in human history to undo the damage.

The combatants were well matched. As is often the case with those who despise each other, Curtiss and Wilbur were sufficiently alike to have been brothers themselves. Both were obsessive and serious, and one is hard-pressed to find a photograph of either, even as a child, in which he does not appear dour. Wilbur Wright was the son of a minister, Curtiss the grandson of one. Wilbur was the grandson of a carriage maker, Curtiss the son of a harness maker. Each came to aviation via the same route—racing, repairing, and building bicycles—and each displayed the amalgam of analytic instincts and dogged perseverance that a successful inventor requires. Most significant, neither of these men would ever take even one small step backward in a confrontation.

They may have been alike, but they were not the same. Wilbur Wright is one of the greatest intuitive scientists this nation has ever produced. Completely self-taught, he made spectacular intellectual leaps to solve a series of intractable problems that had eluded some of history's most brilliant men. Curtiss was not Wilbur's equal as a theoretician—few were—but he was a superb craftsman, designer, and applied scientist. In physics, he would be Enrico Fermi to Wilbur's Albert Einstein.

After Wilbur's death, Orville attempted to maintain the struggle, but while his hatred for Curtiss matched Wilbur's, his talents and temperament did not. Many subsequent accounts have treated the Wright brothers as indistinguishable equals, but Orville viscerally as well as chronologically never ceased being the little brother. As family correspondence makes clear, his relationship with Wilbur was a good deal more complex than is generally assumed and after his brother's death, Orville was never able to muster the will to pursue their mutual obsessions with the necessary zeal.

Curtiss, who often spoke of his "speed craving," first turned his attention to propulsion. He experimented with motorizing bicycles and in January 1907 set a one-mile speed record of 136.7 miles per hour, for which he was hailed as the fastest man on earth; two years later, he would also be the fastest man aloft. By the time the Wrights, after a three-year delay, finally decided to aggressively market their invention, Curtiss was engineering the most efficient motors in the world. That he would mount those motors on aircraft created a threat to the Wrights' aspirations of monopoly and they brought suit to stifle the upstart. Although the Wrights never ceased to insist that their unrelenting pursuit of Curtiss was a moral issue, it was, as is virtually all such litigation, about money.

But for all the maneuvering and legal gamesmanship, the Wright–Curtiss feud was at its core a study of the unique strengths and flaws of personality that define a clash of brilliant minds. Neither Glenn Curtiss nor Wilbur Wright ever came to understand his own limits, that luminescent intelligence in one area of human endeavor does not preclude gross incompetence in another. And because genius often begets or even requires arrogance, both men continuously repeated their blunders.

Wilbur Wright and Glenn Curtiss might have been the principal players in this tableau, but they were hardly the only ones. Early flyers—"Birdmen," as they were called—were pioneers, heeding the same draw to riches or fame or illumination of the unknown that motivated those who had crossed uncharted oceans centuries before, and so aviation was replete with outsized personalities, brutal competition, and staggering bravery. There were great designers such as Louis Blériot, who flew across the English Channel, the first man to do so, with a foot so badly burned that he had to be lifted in and out of his seat; Thomas Scott Baldwin, "Cap't Tom," inventor of the flexible parachute and incomparable showman, who almost convinced the world that balloons were the future of aviation; John Moisant, who after three failed attempts to overthrow the government of El Salvador took to aviation and within months became the preeminent flyer in the world; Harriet Quimby, an actress and journalist who cajoled flying lessons from her employer to become the first woman to receive a pilot's license and then the first to cross the English Channel; and Glenn Curtiss's most famous flyer, Lincoln Beachey, perhaps the finest aviator the world has ever seen, a man who boasted so many "firsts," "bests," and "never before dones" that his exploits would beggar credibility had they not all been documented by eyewitnesses.

The saga of the Wrights and Curtiss *is* the story of early flight. There was no one and nothing in the remarkable decade of 1905 to 1915 that one or both of them did not touch or affect. Their drama was played out on a stage populated by incomparable characters engaged in a pursuit that had held humankind in its thrall from the dawn of civilization.

BIRDMEN

CHAPTER 1

Fulcrum

On August 9, 1896, a wealthy German engineer named Otto Lilienthal hiked up a hill in Rhinow, thirty miles from his home in Berlin. At the top, he crawled under an odd-looking apparatus, braced himself against a specially designed frame, and stood up wearing a set of wooden-framed fabric wings that measured thirty feet across. He paused at the crest of the incline, made certain of the direction of the wind, took a deep breath, and then began to run down.

To a casual observer, Lilienthal would have made a ridiculous sight: another harebrained amateur convinced that man could achieve flight by pretending to be a bird. Surely, he would end his run with a face full of dirt, perhaps a broken bone or two.

But Otto Lilienthal was no amateur. He was, rather, the most sophisticated aerodynamicist of his day. For thirty years, he had taken tens of thousands of measurements of variously shaped surfaces moving at different angles through the air using a "whirling arm," a long pole that extended horizontally from a fixed vertical pole and spun at a preset velocity, a device originally developed to test the flight of cannonballs. In 1889, Lilienthal had produced the most advanced study ever written on the mechanics of flight, *Der Vogelflug als Grundlage der Fliegekunst*—"Bird-flight as the Basis of Aviation." As Wilbur Wright would later assert, "Of all the men who attacked the flying problem in the nineteenth century, Otto Lilienthal was easily the most important. His greatness appeared in every phase."

In 1891, Lilienthal was finally ready to test his calculations. He fashioned a set of fixed glider wings to the specifications he had developed from his research, strapped them to his shoulders, waited for wind conditions to be right, ran downhill . . . and soared. For the next five years, Otto Lilienthal made more than two thousand flights using eighteen different gliders; fifteen were monofoil and three bifoil. He maneuvered in the air by shifting his weight, usually by kicking his feet and thus altering his center of gravity. He became so adept that at times he could almost float, to allow photographers to gain proper focus. Because dry plate negatives had been perfected in the 1880s, the resulting images were of excellent resolution and soon made their way across the ocean. Lilienthal became a world-renowned figure but he had little use for popular acclaim. Instead, he continued to publish scholarly papers and articles and in 1895 patented his invention.

Otto Lilienthal prepares to go aloft.

But gliding was only an interim step; creating aerodynamic airfoils was only one aspect of what was commonly referred to as "the flying problem."* To achieve the ultimate—self-propelled, controlled, heavier-than-air flight—issues of thrust, force, stability, and weight ratios needed to be addressed. And certainly no sophisticated flying machine would be maneuvered by an aviator kicking his feet. Still, efficient airfoils would expedite resolution of those other issues, so Lilienthal continued to glide, kick, and measure. As sophisticated as anyone living on the vagaries of air currents, Lilienthal was aware that luck had played a role in his continued success. And luck, he knew as well, had a habit of running out.

On August 9, 1896, Otto Lilienthal's did. During his second flight of the day, he stalled in a thermal about fifty feet off the ground, then fell, breaking his spine. The next day, Otto Lilienthal was dead. In his last hours, he uttered one of aviation's most famous epitaphs: "Sacrifices must be made."

Word of his accident spread across the globe, including to Dayton, Ohio, and the headquarters of the Wright Cycle Company, Wilbur and Orville Wright, proprietors. Wilbur had been following Lilienthal's exploits with fascination, and word of his death, as later Wilbur put it, "aroused a passive interest which had existed since my childhood." Lilienthal's passing left a void in the struggle for manned flight and on that day Wilbur decided to fill it.

Wilbur was fortunate in his timing. In 1896, after centuries of stumbles, streams of research and data were about to coalesce to provide final focus for what was to be one of history's most stunning achievements.

The heavens have been the home of the gods in virtually every recorded religion and not a single civilization from earliest antiquity fails to depict men and often women in flight. Sometimes these an-

* Technically, *airfoil* refers only to the cross section of a wing, but it is often used synonymously with *wing* itself, as it will be in these pages.

cient aeronauts are in chariots, sometimes in other odd conveyances, and sometimes, like angels in Christianity even today, they fly by wings sprouting from their bodies. Achieving flight, therefore, might well be considered the oldest and most profound of all human aspirations.

Not surprisingly then, the science of flight has attracted the greatest minds in history—Aristotle, Archimedes, Leonardo, and Newton, to name just a few—but achieving the goal stumped all of them. Learning how to maintain a person or a craft in the air demanded more than a daunting scientific vision and meticulous mechanics; unlike many ground-based scientific enterprises, flight was almost impossible to test experimentally. Not that no one tried. In Roman times, slaves plunged to their deaths when ordered by men of science to leap from great heights with feathered wings strapped across their backs. Others throughout the centuries would fall to injury or death in a variety of quixotic contraptions.

To make the problem even more intractable, air, the medium of flight, is invisible, while for early theoreticians of flight, science was based almost entirely on sensory observation. Unlike modern scientists, they did not have the tools to deal with phenomena they could not see, hear, or touch. For inquiries into the mechanics of DNA replication or the detection of dark matter in the universe, for example, sophisticated instruments and powerful computers are routinely employed to test hypotheses. The ability to test with precision allows theory to precede observation. Einstein's theory of relativity, first advanced in 1905, was not proven until a solar eclipse in 1919 provided the opportunity for astronomers to actually observe through a telescope light bending around a distant star.

Lacking such precision, a scientist can only extrapolate from observations in the natural world. Heavier-than-air flight was possible, of course—one need only watch a bird to appreciate that. So why couldn't man fly as well? Yet as late as 1868, after more than two thousand years of study, the annual report of the Aeronautical Society of

Great Britain lamented, "With respect to the abstruse question of mechanical flight, it may be stated that we are still ignorant of the rudimentary principles which should form the basis and rules for construction."[1]

Achieving human flight, then, turned out to be a giant puzzle, solved over centuries, piece by tortuous piece.

Since air wasn't even yet understood to be an actual substance, the first steps involved fluids. In 350 B.C., Aristotle hypothesized that an object moving through liquid will encounter resistance, and a century later Archimedes developed the first theory of fluid motion. From there, it would take more than seventeen centuries until Leonardo took up the problem and fluid dynamics began to be thought of as a rigorous discipline.

Leonardo's great contribution was based in his observation that when the banks of a river narrowed to constrict its flow, the water in the narrower area speeded up so that the movement of the river remained "continuous." Leonardo could not quantify this function but his observation was eventually generalized into a mathematical relationship between speed and distance and eventually between speed and pressure—the faster a fluid moves over a surface, the less pressure it produces. But as Leonardo was also fascinated with bird flight, he made some effort to apply the principle to gases. That ultimately would result in a device where air moved farther and faster over the top surface of an airfoil than under the bottom, thus creating uneven pressure, which resulted in "lift." He also understood that as an object moved through a medium, it would encounter resistance, friction between the object and the medium, which would slow its progress, later to be quantified as "drag."

It took another century for the next tentative step forward, this in 1600 by Galileo. The great Pisan astronomer was the first to quantify certain relationships in fluid dynamics and thus began to create a mechanical science from what had previously been only speculation. His most significant insight was that resistance will increase with the density of the medium, which would eventually lead to the understanding that as an airplane cruised at higher altitudes, fuel efficiencies would increase.

But with all the advances by science's titans, which later would include Isaac Newton and Leonhard Euler, the applications continued to be solely in fluid dynamics—the resulting equations were then simply assumed to apply equally to gas as to liquid.* In fact, using his equations, Newton hypothesized that powered flight was impossible because the weight of a motor needed to generate sufficient power would always exceed the amount of lift that could be supplied by airfoils that did not weigh more than the motor could support. For those who believed flight was possible, the assumption remained that humans must emulate birds—that is, develop a mechanism to allow for wings that flapped. Devices that attempted to mimic bird flight in this manner were dubbed "ornithopters." A sketch of such an apparatus was found in one of Leonardo's notebooks.

Aerodynamics as a separate science was born in 1799 when an English polymath named George Cayley produced a remarkable silver medallion. Cayley had observed that seagulls soared for great distances without flapping their wings and therefore hypothesized aircraft wings as fixed rather than movable. On the front side of his medallion, Cayley etched a monoplane glider with a cambered (curved) wing, a cruciform tail for stability, a single-seat gondola, and pedals, which he called "propellers," to power the device in flight. On the obverse side of his medallion, Cayley placed a diagram of the four forces that figure in flight: lift, drag, gravity, and thrust. Although actual powered flight was a century away, Cayley's construct was the breakthrough that set the process in motion. In 1853, four years before

* Bernoulli's principle, for example, which measures the relationship of velocity to pressure and which helped airplane builders design wings that would enable lift, was developed solely for fluids. Bernoulli himself had no sense that it would apply to the movement of air as well.

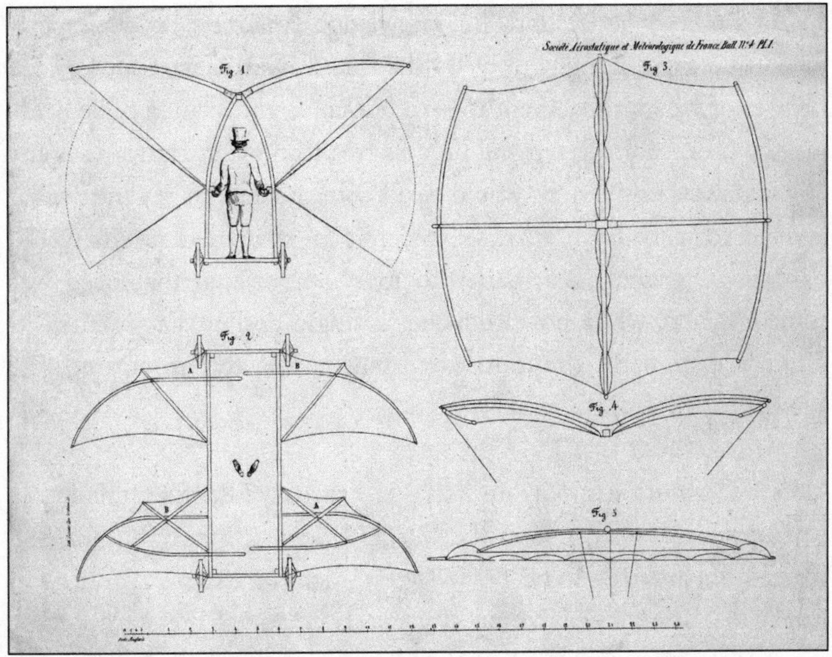

George Cayley's design drawing of a man-powered flying machine.

his death, a fixed-wing glider of Cayley's design was the first to carry a human passenger.*

Cayley's hypotheses did not immediately take root. Not until the 1860s did his work finally spark a rush of interest. The Aeronautical Society of Great Britain was formed in 1866; another was begun in France three years later. Discussions of materials, airfoils, and resistance began to drift across borders and disciplines. Theorizing grew in sophistication and began to take in angle of incidence, the angle at which an airfoil moves through the oncoming air, now called "angle of attack"; and center of pressure, the point on a surface where the pressure is assumed to be concentrated, just as center of gravity is the point at which the entire mass of a body is assumed to be concentrated.

* Cayley, in his eighties, was too old to pilot the device so he recruited his none-too-pleased coachman to undertake the experiment. After one harrowing ride, the coachman begged to be relieved of further flight duty.

As the body of aerodynamic knowledge expanded, serious experimentation grew along with it. By the time Lilienthal strapped on his first set of wings, movement toward human flight seemed to be nearing the inexorable. But if the process was to move forward with any efficiency, experimenters would need some means to separate what seemed to work from what seemed not to—data and results would have to be shared. The man who most appreciated that need was someone who, while not producing a single design that resulted in flight, was arguably the most important person to participate in its gestation.

Octave Chanute was born in Paris on February 18, 1832. His father was a professor of history at the Royal College of France but in 1838 crossed the Atlantic to become vice president of Jefferson College in Louisiana. The elder Chanut—Octave later added the *e* to prevent mispronunciation—moved in 1844 to New York City, where Octave attended secondary school, and, as he put it, "became thoroughly Americanized."[2]

Upon graduation, he decided to study engineering. As there were only four dedicated colleges of engineering in the United States, most aspirants learned on the job, as Chanute chose to do. In 1849, he asked for a job on the Hudson River Railroad at Sing Sing and, when told nothing was available, signed on without pay as a chainman. Two months later, he was put on the payroll at $1.12 per day and four years after that, completely self-taught, was named division engineer at Albany. But with immigrants pouring into Illinois to buy government lands at $1.25 per acre, Chanute instead went west. He gained high repute on a number of railroad assignments and eventually submitted a design for the Chicago stockyards that was chosen over dozens of others. With the successful completion of that project, Chanute was asked to attempt a traverse of the "unbridgeable" Missouri River. Chanute's Hannibal Bridge at Kansas City not only successfully spanned the waterway but elevated the city into a center of commerce, and its designer to national acclaim.

For the next two decades, Chanute continued to push forward transportation engineering. He also perfected a means of pressure-treating wood with creosote that remained state-of-the-art for more than a century. When he retired in 1889, he did so as the foremost civil engineer in the United States and a very wealthy man. For all his personal achievements, however, Chanute never wavered in his commitment to a cooperative approach to problem solving. He attained leadership positions in a number of professional organizations and became active in civic groups in the cities in which he lived. As a result, which might be considered surprising for one so successful, Chanute had no real enemies and was well liked by virtually everyone who came in contact with him.

By 1890, he relocated to Chicago, but he wouldn't pass his remaining days sitting back with his feet up, and gazing out over Lake Michigan. His retirement had been prompted not by a desire to stop working but rather by the intention to pursue a passion that had been percolating for fifteen years. Chanute intended to bring the same skills and approach that had served him so well in his own career to the quest to achieve human flight.

It was not his intent initially to design aircraft but rather to serve as a catalyst, a focal point for the growing streams of theory and data then being generated about "the flying problem." The engineering methodology, he was convinced, the rigorous, thoughtful, step-by-step approach that created a bridge from the idea of a bridge, could be equally applied to heavier-than-air flight. Ideas therefore must be evaluated by peers and, if they showed promise, tested and incorporated in a body of knowledge available to all. Innovation should be rewarded, certainly, and inventions patented, but the process would be best served openly and collegially. Achieving flight for the advancement of humanity must always retain predominance over achieving the goal merely for profit.

Chanute proceeded to correspond with everyone who he could discern was working seriously on heavier-than-air flight and thus thrust himself into the forefront of the ongoing research without

Octave Chanute.

doing any of it on his own. One of his first and most important correspondents was an impoverished expatriate Frenchman living in Egypt named Louis Pierre Mouillard. Mouillard had trained in Paris as a painter but abandoned both the vocation and the city for a peripatetic existence in North Africa observing birds and attempting to replicate their flight. He built gliders and experimented with them in the sand dunes outside of Cairo. Although the test flights achieved very limited success, Mouillard developed some sophisticated and far-reaching insights concerning stability. He and Chanute would exchange letters until Mouillard's death in 1897 and more than once Chanute sent him money, as much for living expenses as to fund research.* Chanute supplied journal articles and perspective gained from other correspondents; Mouillard supplied Chanute with his evaluations of glider mechanics, one of which may or may not have been so significant as to change the course of aeronautical research.

* Mouillard was not unique in this regard. Chanute also sent money to other experimenters with limited funds.

On January 5, 1896, Mouillard wrote from his home in Cairo, "I have not been satisfied, among other things, with the controlling action of my moving planes (annularies) at the tips of the wings. I must greatly increase their importance. This device is indispensable. It was their absence which prevented Lilienthal from going farther; it is this which permits going to left and right." The "moving planes" to which he referred were hinged sections at the rear of each wing, primitive ailerons, which could be manipulated by the aviator to help control flight. Mouillard added, "Steering to the right or left is effected by the bird in many ways, such as a slight bending of the body in the direction desired, a part-folding of the wing on that side, a deformation of one wing-tip, so as to impede the air at that point and to turn upon it as a pivot, etc., etc."[3] Mouillard's theorizing was sketchy and lacked specifics but whether his notion could be described as "altering lateral margins of the wings" was to cause enormous controversy in the years ahead.

The spate of interest in heavier-than-air flight notwithstanding, most, even in the scientific community, continued to deem the notion fanciful at best. (Balloons, which had been around since the Montgolfier brothers soared over Annonay a century earlier, were an accepted public phenomenon, although controlling the contraptions remained a problem.) In 1890, Matthias Nace Forney, an old friend who was a railroad engineer and journalist, asked Chanute to contribute some articles of interest to an engineering journal he had begun editing, *American Engineer and Railroad Journal.* Forney did not specifically request that the articles be about aviation, but he was keen to publish material to help entice sales.

Chanute drew on his correspondence, supplemented with additional research, and submitted to Forney a series of articles on some of the various streams of research and development and aviation, including, of course, Mouillard's. Chanute originally planned six to eight articles "but investigation disclosed that far more experimenting of instructive value had been done than was at first supposed," and the series ran to twenty-seven. Eventually these articles were compiled in book form and published in 1894 as *Progress in Flying Machines*. "Naturally enough the public has taken little heed of the progress really made toward the evolution of a complicated problem, hitherto generally considered as impossible of solution," Chanute wrote in his preface, and "it will probably be surprised to learn how much has been accomplished toward overcoming the various difficulties involved, and how far the elements of a possible future success have accumulated within the last five years."

Chanute was careful to restrict his inquiry to heavier-than-air machines. Unlike many of his contemporaries, Chanute understood that balloons were not corollary but represented an entirely different set of engineering principles and problems. *Progress in Flying Machines* was divided into three sections: "Wings and Parachutes," by which he meant ornithopters; "Screws to Lift and Propel"; and "Aeroplanes," meaning fixed-wings.* In his conclusion, Chanute correctly noted, "The problem of the maintenance of the equilibrium is now, in my judgment, the most important and difficult of those remaining to be solved. . . . Almost every failure in practical experiments has resulted from lack of equilibrium."

The book closed with an appendix by Otto Lilienthal, "The Carrying Capacity of Arched Surfaces in Sailing Flight." Lilienthal was by then the accepted authority on the lift and soaring properties of cambered surfaces, for which there are five key measurements: length from the center of the craft; chord, the distance from the front to the back; surface area, derived by multiplying length by average chord; aspect ratio, which is length divided by average chord and determines shape (thus a wing 10 feet long with a 2-foot average chord would have a surface area of 20 square feet and an aspect ratio of 10:2, where a wing 5 feet long with a 4-foot average chord would have the same surface area but a stubbier aspect ratio of 5:4); and camber, which is the mea-

* Chanute's description of "aeroplanes" was "thin fixed surfaces, slightly inclined to the line of motion, and deriving their support from the upward reaction of the air pressure due to the speed, the latter being obtained by some separate propelling device, have been among the last aerial contrivances to be experimented upon in modern times."

sure of the height of wing curvature against average chord. The tables Lilienthal had produced incorporating these measurements were unquestioned as to accuracy.

Progress in Flying Machines was read by virtually everyone who was experimenting in flight and anyone who was considering it. Its publication in many ways marked the beginning of aviation as a rigorous science and fertilized the soil from which the Wright Flyer sprung nine years later.

So popular was Chanute's work that it almost instantly spawned a rush of correspondence and conferences, and a demand for more literature. In Boston, James Means, a graduate of the Massachusetts Institute of Technology and aviation enthusiast who had made a small fortune marketing low-priced, mass-produced shoes to the average American, decided to go Chanute one better. Like Chanute, Means had retired from industry to join the quest for flight, but unlike the railroad man, he made some formative efforts at design on his own. Means saw the world more broadly than Chanute and was convinced that aviation would reach fruition only with public support and eventual government funding. In 1895, a time when many conducted their researches privately for fear of being labeled cranks, Means decided to generate enthusiasm by proclaiming in a popular medium all the wondrous achievements in aviation either at or just over the horizon. Unlike *Progress in Flying Machines,* whose content was often highly technical, the *Aeronautical Annual* would be aimed at the educated general reader.

Unfortunately, 1895 was a year before the wondrous achievements that Means sought to publicize had actually occurred. Unable to extol tomorrow, Means devoted his 1895 annual to yesterday. He included extracts from Leonardo, articles by George Cayley, a reprint of his own pamphlet *Manflight,* wind velocities for 1892, and even some lines from the *Iliad.* Despite its lack of contemporary content, the *Aeronautical Annual* was a great success.

Means published two more annuals. The 1896 edition was more up to date, with articles by Chanute; Hiram Maxim, who had invented both the machine gun and a better mouse trap before turning his inventiveness to flight; Samuel Cabot, who wrote on propulsion; J. B. Millet, who reported on an engineer from Australia named Lawrence Hargrave, who had developed a "box kite" from which remarkable results had been achieved; and a brilliant young theorist named Augustus Moore Herring, who contributed an article titled "Dynamic Flight."

The 1897 edition, Means's last, was by far his most influential. He was finally able to bring to the public some significant advances, none more noteworthy than a one-mile flight down the Potomac of a motorized, steam-powered, unmanned "aerodrome" launched by America's most famous scientist and photographed by one of its most famous inventors.

CHAPTER 2

Highway in the Sky

While Lilienthal had demonstrated that properly configured airfoils could provide sufficient lift to support the weight of the apparatus and a person, significant obstacles remained to progress from gliding to controlled, powered flight. In addition to the obvious question of accounting for the weight of any motor that would propel the craft, the issue of how the machine would be controlled once a power source was added had yet to be addressed. Controlled flight would have to involve more than simply traveling from one place to another in an unbroken straight line. Those considering the problem of control used as a paradigm one of two other modern marvels, neither of which ever left the ground. The first, by Karl Benz in 1886, was the incorporation of the internal combustion engine into its most notable application, the automobile. The second was the introduction one year later of what was termed the "safety bicycle."

The marriage of the automobile to Lilienthal's glider principles seemed the more manifestly fruitful. Attaching either a steam or gasoline engine to a set of wings and then "driving" it about the sky seemed a goal within reach. The aim, therefore, would be to build a flying machine that was maximally stable—did not roll side to side or dip—and that would require only limited operator intervention to allow it to handle straight and true. Turns, also like 1890s automobiles, would be wide and slow.

In America, the most prominent advocate of the stable motorized glider was Samuel Pierpont Langley. Like Chanute, Langley was a self-taught civil engineer, but his dozen years in the trade were undistinguished and he eventually turned to astronomy. He first built a telescope, then toured Europe to learn the science. Upon his return, he became an assistant at the Harvard Observatory, moved on to a position at the observatory at the United States Naval Academy, and finally went to Pittsburgh, where he was named professor of physics and director of the Allegheny Observatory, where he remained for two decades.

Lacking skills in mathematics or even the theoretical background in his chosen field, Langley's predilections were to the practical; he was a brilliant administrator and a precise observer, and he had fine instincts for experimentation. For his work in measuring solar radiation, for which he took readings with instruments of his own design, he received international acclaim and was offered the post of assistant secretary of the Smithsonian Institution in 1887. With the current secretary near death, Langley would soon succeed to the post and become the most prominent scientific administrator in the nation.

Langley's interest in aviation predated his appointment by only months. As always, he eschewed theory and moved directly to experiment, building an enormous whirling-arm device on the grounds of the Allegheny Observatory and designing instruments to take measurements that would test conventional wisdom. His first notable success was demonstrating as false Newton's hypothesis that flight was impossible. (Newton, as did everyone before Cayley, had theorized using flat rather than cambered surfaces.) This allowed Langley to assert that motorized flight was indeed achievable with existing technology. From there, he set out to achieve it.

Bluff and thick-bodied, Langley was intimidating and imperious. He rarely performed the menial tasks of experimentation himself but instead employed a team of talented young assistants who were charged with adhering to minutely detailed instructions, some of which were contradictory or ludicrous. Langley demanded, for example, that the nuts and bolts of his models be polished as if they were museum pieces. He changed his mind repeatedly, causing much of his assistants' work to be scrapped before it was completed. Langley's overbearing manner created constant friction and would eventually cause a key defection from his team.

As expected, within months of his appointment as assistant secretary, Langley was named to the top post at the Smithsonian Institution. Although he didn't resign his post at the Allegheny Observatory until 1891, he moved to Washington, D.C., where, as an eminent newcomer, he found himself pleasantly in the center of the capital's social swirl. Among the many luminaries eager to talk science with the secretary of the Smithsonian was Alexander Graham Bell, who would become one of Langley's most ardent supporters and closest friends. Even with his notoriety, however, in a position so public, Langley needed to be circumspect about proclaiming his intentions to pursue an end that many still considered the province of the fanciful or the insane.

Proceeding cautiously, Langley set to work to build a powered, stable aircraft that could drive through the skies. He published his early findings in 1891 as *Experiments in Aerodynamics,* which at once illustrated his greatest strengths and most glaring weaknesses. While the data itself did seem to demonstrate that powered, heavier-than-air flight was feasible, his extrapolation of the data to a principle that asserted it took less power to fly fast than slow—which he called "Langley's Law"—proved to be embarrassingly incorrect.

Langley's objective was typically grandiose. He would leap past the aerodynamics—skip the unpowered glider phase—and proceed directly to powered flight. His prototype would be unmanned but if that could be made to work, a manned version seemed simply a matter of increasing the scale and power output of the motor.

Langley's assistants built a series of rubber models, none of which would successfully fly. Rather than analyze the principles under which the models were built, Langley decided that the problem was insufficient power and set to increasing the size of his models to accommodate a larger motor. Beginning in 1891, Langley's team built a series of what he called "aerodromes"; Langley, with no knowledge of Greek, was unaware that an aerodrome is a place rather than a thing. Langley's assistants tried different configurations, considered varying power sources, and attempted to utilize materials that would be both light and strong. Langley employed cambered wings but otherwise considered the aerodynamics of the craft subordinate to weight and power.

The first three aerodromes, numbers 0 through 2, were so obviously overweight and underpowered that Langley did not even attempt to test-fly them. The next two models were improved but still not capable of flight. But Langley's assistants, beleaguered constantly by their punctilious boss, were getting closer. Tandem sets of wings fore and aft of the motor set in a dihedral—in an upward slant from the body, forming a V—did well in simulations and, with a cruciform tail, provided the proper stability.* A light steam engine could generate sufficient power per pound, and the spruce, pine, and silk construction reduced the weight of the craft to thirty pounds. To launch the aerodrome, the team settled on a catapult, which eventually evolved into a complicated overhead arrangement with tackle and pulleys. Langley purchased a flat-bottomed houseboat on which to mount the apparatus and eventually send an aerodrome ranging down the Potomac. All that was left was to get the most advanced aerodrome, number 6, to actually fly. To help find the solution to that final problem, Langley took on two new assistants.

The first, Edward Chalmers Huffaker, a Tennessean who went by E.C., was a forty-year-old slovenly, tobacco-chewing engineer who had submitted a paper in 1893, "The Value of Curved Surfaces in Flight," to the Congress on Aerial Navigation, an event sponsored by

* With dihedral wings, if the craft dipped to one side, the lower side would move more parallel to the air rushing at it, which would increase the lift to that side and right the craft. But lateral stability in a dihedral wing arrangement comes at the expense of maneuverability, restricting the craft to flat turns.

Octave Chanute, who then recommended him to Langley. The always fastidious Langley tried to overlook Huffaker's personal habits, and put him to work on devising the optimal airfoil configuration. The second new assistant came with a reputation for brilliance and would become the most controversial figure in the annals of early flight.

Augustus Moore Herring was also a southerner, born in Georgia in either 1865 or 1867, son of a cotton broker. The family relocated to New York when Herring was a boy. He attended Stevens Institute of Technology, where he later claimed either to have graduated or to have been denied graduation because his senior thesis on aeronautics was too sophisticated for the faculty to grasp. Both claims were false. He was dismissed from school for failing a number of courses and he never attempted to write on aeronautics. Unsubstantiated assertions or outright lies would follow Herring throughout his life.[1]

Audacious and deceitful as he might have been, Herring did not lack either intelligence or talent. Shortly after he left Stevens, he built two Lilienthal-type gliders and showed a remarkable grasp of the German's design principles. He began a consulting engineering practice that failed, so he took a job, as had Chanute, as a chainman on the railroad. Herring wrote to Chanute in 1894 and asked for his help. When Chanute was unable to find Herring work, he hired the young man to develop a more sophisticated manned glider model based on the Lilienthal principles. Chanute by that time had decided that the path to controlled, motorized flight must proceed through the aerodynamics of gliders, opposite the approach that Langley had taken but in accordance with the one that the Wrights would employ six years hence.*

Herring showed great promise, but before the manned glider project could really get started he came to Langley's attention through James Means. Langley offered the young man a position on the aerodrome team at a good deal higher salary than Chanute was paying

* Chanute and Langley, if not personal friends, enjoyed a cordial relationship. Chanute was pleased that Langley was pursuing flight so seriously and Langley was happy to incorporate any of Chanute's findings into his own work.

him. Although Chanute later wrote to Means, "You did me a rather ill turn," he gave his grudging blessing to the move and Herring accepted Langley's offer. He was given a senior assistantship, assigned to improve the aerodrome's overall design.

Two men more likely to clash than Langley and Herring are hard to imagine. It took only five days before Herring wrote to Chanute complaining about the meticulous, rigid perfectionist from whom he had accepted a position. (He also took pains to mention that he was not alone in his dissatisfaction. Huffaker was described as "on the verge of nervous prostration."[2]) One month later, Herring renewed his lament in another letter to Chanute. What irked Herring the most, it seemed, was that while the assistants did all the work, Langley took the credit—as long as things went well. When they did not, the assistants were assumed to be at fault.* Herring endured for eighteen months, until November 1895, and then resigned. The only surprise was that he lasted so long. But during his tenure, Herring had made invaluable contributions to the design of Aerodrome 6, particularly in the wing configuration and tail assembly. Without his participation, Langley would have had no chance.

On May 12, 1896, Langley was finally ready. With Alexander Graham Bell standing on the banks of the Potomac with a camera, Aerodrome 6 was launched. Bell later gave an account of the "remarkable experiment" to the newspapers. "The aerodrome or 'flying machine' . . . resembled an enormous bird soaring in the air with extreme regularity in large curves, sweeping steadily upward in a spiral path, the spirals with a diameter of perhaps 100 yards, until it reached a height of 100 feet in the air at the end of a course of about half a mile."† After the "steam gave out," Bell added, "to my further surprise, the whole, instead of tumbling down, settled as slowly and gracefully as it is possible for a bird to do, touched the water without any damage, and was picked out immediately and ready to be tried again."[3]

* Herring was given to hyperbole and distortion but others made the same charges, although not publicly.

† Bell's Greek was no better than Langley's.

Samuel Pierpont Langley had succeeded in developing the first powered heavier-than-air flying machine. In doing so, he achieved all his goals: He had overthrown centuries of theory and skepticism; flung aviation into the forefront; and established himself among the general public as the nation's foremost scientific mind. The next step was to build an aerodrome sufficiently large and powerful to carry a man. To aid in the endeavor, the War Department, with President McKinley's approval, bestowed on Langley a $50,000 grant, the first ever expenditure of public funds in the pursuit of human flight.

CHAPTER 3

Men in the Dunes

Despite Langley's success, Octave Chanute continued to maintain that development of a successful glider was the real key to flight. He had also decided to become an active participant in the research. One month after Langley's aerodrome corkscrewed down the Potomac, Chanute set up a camp in the sand dunes on remote, windswept Miller Beach, on the shores of Lake Michigan, just east of Gary, Indiana. Unlike Langley, for whom a breeze of five miles per hour was sufficient to deter a launch, Chanute, as would the Wrights four years hence, wanted wind. "No bird soars in a calm," Wilbur would observe. As Chanute later recounted, Miller Beach was specifically chosen because the gliders would need "a soft place on which to alight . . . a dry and loose sand-hill, and there ought to be no bushes or trees to run into. Our party found such sand-hills, almost a desert, in which we pitched our tent . . . about thirty miles east of Chicago."[1]

As had Langley, he had recruited a team of talented younger men. But Chanute's four assistants would have the freedom to pursue their own ideas.* They would also, in theory, receive credit when the ideas

* One of the four was a doctor, as Chanute anticipated a number of crashes during the tests, although medical expertise turned out not to be necessary.

worked, but that was to become a matter of contention as events progressed. The most important of those assistants was Augustus Herring, returned from his misadventure at the Smithsonian. If Chanute bore Herring any ill will, he never showed it.

Herring brought with him his Lilienthal glider but neither he nor Chanute intended to spend a great deal of time on what both considered by then only a formative technology. When the glider was damaged in a crash, they decided not to repair it. "This decision," Chanute wrote, "was most unfortunately justified on the 10th of the succeeding August, when Herr Lilienthal met his death while experimenting with a machine based on the same principle."[2]

Instead, Chanute set Herring to work on his own concept of a "ladder glider," a stack of up to seven airfoils. For this and any other arrangement, Chanute adapted Lilienthal's launching technique.

> The operator stands on the hill-side. He raises up the apparatus, which is steadied by a companion, and quickly slips under and within the machine. He faces the wind. This wind buffets the wings from side to side, and up or down, so that he has much difficulty in obtaining a poise. This is finally accomplished by bracing the cross-piece of the machine's frame against his back, and depressing the front edge of the wings so that they will be struck from above by the wind. His arm-pits rest on a pair of horizontal bars, and he grasps a pair of vertical bars with his hands. He is in no way attached to the machine, so that he may disengage himself instantly should anything go wrong. Then, still facing dead into the wind, he takes one or two but never more than four running steps forward, raising up the front edge of the apparatus at the last moment, and the air claims him. Then he sails forward into the wind on a generally descending course.[3]

The Miller Beach expedition had its share of failed experiments—Chanute's ladder glider was an early casualty—but its one success would change aviation. A collaboration by Herring and Chanute resulted in what was later referred to as the "two-surface glider," described as "the most significant and influential aircraft of the pre-Wright era."[4] The apparatus was bifoil, essentially a Hargrave box kite with two sides removed, the two parallel surfaces held in place by Pratt trussing, a method Chanute had used often in bridge building.* (It had started as a trifoil, but the bottom wing was removed to facilitate control.) The wings were sixteen feet long with a chord of four feet (thus an aspect ratio of four) and covered with varnished silk. The operator, as in Chanute's description, hung supported by bars under his armpits. In the dunes, as well as on the Potomac, dihedral wing placement was employed to create "automatic stability." But rather than the fixed cruciform tail he had installed on Langley's aerodromes, Herring added a tail on a universal joint that could "give" in the wind to help maintain the glider's attitude and avoid the corkscrewing of the Potomac flights.

The design was an immense success. Hundreds of straight glides were made under full control. Difficult to reach as the location was, newspapermen began pioneering their way through the underbrush to report on the great advance. As word of the activities on Miller Beach seeped out, Chanute and his team, especially Herring, became nationally known; not to the extent of Samuel Langley, perhaps, but sufficient to inform the public that the attack on the flying problem was on at least two fronts. While both Langley and Chanute believed the other's approach to be a dead end, for the moment each was content to bask in his own success.

Success, however, has a way of destroying both cooperation and friendship and so it was in Indiana. A dispute arose between Herring and Chanute as to which of them was responsible for the two-surface design. Chanute conceded that Herring deserved full credit for the tail but insisted the remainder of the glider was at his initiative. Her-

* The Pratt truss was developed in 1844 and used when bridges were constructed of iron rather than wood. Its two parallel horizontals are held in place by verticals and diagonals that angle toward the center between the top and bottom planes. The horizontals were sometimes crossed, making an X between the verticals as they were in the glider.

Augustus Herring testing a Herring-Chanute glider, 1896.

ring said the glider was merely a more sophisticated version of a mechanism he had built earlier. When speaking to reporters, he had always referred to the device as his own. Under the headline, "Flying Machine Flies," for example, *The Boston Daily Globe,* while identifying him as "Mr. Chanute's assistant," described the glider as "Mr. Herring's machine."[5]

One prominent historian claims Herring had the stronger case, and agrees that the glider "represented a design that Herring had been evolving over a four- or five-year period." Still, on only one other occasion would Chanute's integrity be questioned—by Wilbur Wright—while Herring's veracity would remain elusive at best for the remainder of his life.

Herring and Chanute differed on another key issue. Herring thought the transition from glider to powered flight was by then a straightforward affair, requiring only extrapolation from previously attained data. He proposed immediately building and testing a machine with either a compressed-air or gasoline motor and propellers.

Chanute was far more circumspect. "I do not know how much further I shall carry on these experiments," he wrote.

> They were made wholly at my own expense, in the hope of gaining scientific knowledge and without the expectation of pecuniary profit. I believe the latter to be still afar off, for it seems unlikely that a commercial machine will be perfected very soon. It will, in my judgment, be worked out by a process of evolution: one experimenter finding his way a certain distance into the labyrinth, the next penetrating further, and so on, until the very centre is reached and success is won. In the hope, therefore, of making the way easier to others, I have set down the relation of these experiments, perhaps at tedious length, so that other searchers may carry the work of exploration further.[6]

Wherever the truth lies, Herring, described as "a bitter and frustrated man," left Chanute shortly thereafter. "For years he had worked in a subordinate role, overshadowed by employers he regarded as less talented than himself. His disappointment festered as Chanute and Langley failed to allow him complete control over their aeronautical research."[7] Herring, the only man to be part of aeronautics' two great triumphs, experimented on his own and sought a new benefactor. He soon found one in the person of Matthias Arnot, a banker and aviation devotee from Elmira, New York. Arnot was fascinated by the glides of almost one thousand feet made by Herring in a triplane glider of his own design that he had tested after leaving Chanute. Even more intoxicating, Herring told Arnot he had designed a compressed-air motor to power the glider and so, for only a modest outlay of funds, Arnot could participate in one of history's seminal events.

As always, Herring started well. He built another model of the two-surface glider, this time called the "Herring–Arnot glider," and tested it at Dune Park in autumn 1897. To show no hard feelings, he invited Chanute to attend. The old man arrived to a much more frenzied scene than when he ran the camp. Where Chanute saw excessive publicity as ultimately harmful to the overall goal, Herring seduced the press. He even allowed a reporter from the *Chicago Times-Herald* to experience soaring firsthand and write of his experiences for the paper:

> Any man endowed with an average amount of nerve, a cool head and a quick eye and a fair muscular development can soar through the air nowadays, provided he is equipped with a machine like the one being used by A. M. Herring among the sand dunes near Dune Park, Ind. All that is necessary for him to do is to seize the machine with a firm grasp, say a prayer, take a running jump into space, and trust to luck for finding a soft place when he alights. His chances of getting hurt are about one in a thousand in his favor, while having more sport to the second than he ever dreamed possible.

The unnamed reporter's account—the article is without byline—reflects the childlike joy of those early glider days:

> The wind grows stronger . . . one takes four or five running steps down the plank and jumps off, expecting to drop like a stone to the sand. To his surprise and pleasure he experiences about the same sensations felt by a man when taking his first ascension in an elevator. . . . As the machine mounts in the air one sees the ground sinking beneath. He imagines he is a hundred feet in the air, and begins to wonder if he will ever come down and be able to see his folks again in this world. The thought no sooner comes when the machine suddenly begins to descend with lightning speed. The machine settles down slowly and steadily, and to the disappointment of the operator his feet strike the sand. His experience in the air is over. He turns around and looks up the side of the hill, feeling that he has traveled at least a thousand yards. When the tapeline is brought out, however, he is somewhat disgusted to find that he is only 110 feet away from his starting point. He wonders how

this can be, when he was up in the air at least ten minutes. Then he receives another shock, when he is told that his flight lasted just five seconds.[8]

Camping in the dunes to experiment took significant funding, however, and expenses mounted. By the time Herring claimed to be ready for the powered glider, Arnot was no longer ready to pay for it. Herring solicited Chanute and then William Randolph Hearst, neither of whom was willing to put up the $7,000 Herring said he needed. He filed for a patent for his design but was turned down because the examiner saw no practical application for his invention.* With no one willing to underwrite the construction, Herring used what money he had to begin on his own. He had a wife and two children, so funding the project personally was an enormous risk. But whatever else one might say of Herring, he never lacked for conviction.

In October 1898, Herring finally launched his craft at St. Joseph, Michigan, a biplane powered by a three-horsepower, compressed-air motor turning propellers both pusher—mounted at the rear of the machine—and tractor—mounted at the front.† He flew fifty feet on his first try, seventy on his second. In both, the underpowered craft was barely aloft, skimming so close to the ground that Herring had to tuck his legs under him to avoid them dragging along the flight path.

Herring would later claim that these two hops were the breakthrough that aviation was looking for, but few agreed. He continued to be unsuccessful in attracting investment, although both Chanute and Arnot remained supportive of his research. (Herring could be charming when it suited him and a number of those with whom he

* The patent office was inundated with requests, most from cranks, for aviation patents and turned a harsh eye to anything that hadn't already flown. The Wrights would encounter the same problem in 1902.

† The distinction would hold through the first decade of flight when most biplanes were pushers and most monoplanes were tractors. Eventually, of course, both pushers and biplanes would disappear.

ended formal associations were willing to vouch for him with others. Chanute would later do so with the Wrights.)

In 1899, Herring lost all his equipment and materials in a fire and, feeling bitter and unappreciated, left aviation, determined to use his skills to make some money. He would return to the field with the same ambition.

CHAPTER 4

To Kitty Hawk

Wilbur Wright's decision to join in the quest for manned flight did not result in an immediate rush to build and test-fly gliders. With a business to attend to and no real knowledge of even the formative aerodynamics of the day, he began by reading everything on the subject available at the Dayton Library, which wasn't much, and—taking a cue from Lilienthal—spending endless hours watching birds in flight. Buzzards, with their immense wingspan, were his favorites.*

After three years of self-education, Wilbur had gained some theoretical knowledge of aviation and was ready to move on. On May 30, 1899, thirteen years to the day before he succumbed to typhoid fever, he wrote a letter to the Smithsonian Institution in which he noted that he had "been interested in the problem of mechanical and human flight since [he] was a boy," and announcing his intention "to begin a systematic study of the subject in preparation for practical work." He

* Although in later years, Wilbur and Orville would both claim they had come to the flight problem together, Orville had little or no input before the first visit to Kitty Hawk in autumn 1900. Wilbur, while he was alive, always publicly spoke of the two of them as a unit and after Wilbur's death, Orville added himself to incidents in which he took no part. But that, according to Tom Crouch, was merely to assuage Orville's sensitivity to not being included as an equal in every step of the process.

asked "to obtain such papers as the Smithsonian Institution has published on this subject, and if possible a list of other works in print in the English language." Wilbur felt the need to add, "I am an enthusiast, but not a crank."[1]

Richard Rathbun, one of Langley's assistants, replied three days later, sending a list that included Chanute's *Progress in Flying Machines,* Langley's *Experiments in Aerodynamics,* and James Means's three editions of the *Aeronautical Annual.* Chanute's book was priced at $2.50 and the others at $1 each. Rathbun also sent Wilbur four pamphlets from the Smithsonian reports: one by Mouillard, one by Lilienthal, one by Langley, and one by Huffaker. Wilbur remitted one dollar for Langley's book and obtained the others on his own.

That Wilbur devoured the literature and became thoroughly versed in the principles of flight as they were then understood there is no doubt. What would be a question of immense significance is to what degree the work of others, in some cases patented work, such as Mouillard's, affected his thinking and contributed to the ultimate design of the Wright Flyer. No one would ever accuse Wilbur of stealing an idea—his insights were too fresh and groundbreaking—but whether his ideas were totally without precedent or even to some small degree extensions of previously enunciated theories would determine the breadth of any patent he and Orville might be granted for a flying machine of their design.

Wilbur Wright was defined by both his brilliance and an upbringing that would first support his genius and then undermine it.

He was born in 1867, the third son of Milton and Susan Wright. His father was a pastor and ultimately became a bishop, one of six ruling elders in the Church of the United Brethren in Christ. The sect had its origins in the Great Awakening in the mid-eighteenth century and began as a loose-knit group of German-speaking churches in Pennsylvania, Virginia, Maryland, and Ohio. By 1800, it had grown sufficiently that the elders organized, instituted an annual meeting, and began sending preachers to ride circuit and spread the faith.

Members were socially progressive and personally ascetic. From the time of the Missouri Compromise, the church preached abolition and women's rights. In the 1830s, it expelled any member who owned slaves. The Brethren were also pacifist and forbidden to drink alcohol, work on the Sabbath, or become members in secret societies such as the Freemasons. In 1847, the church established Otterbein College in Westerville, Ohio, named after one of its founders and the first college in the United States to include women as both faculty members and students. Two decades before the ratification of the Fourteenth Amendment, Otterbein accepted African Americans into the student body.

Milton joined the church in 1846 at age eighteen and became a lay preacher a few years later. He was fierce in his devotion to learning—Milton Wright would show himself to be fierce in all of his beliefs—and eventually accepted a teaching post at Hartsville College, where he met Susan Koerner, his future wife. They married in 1859 after Milton returned from an extended church assignment in Oregon.

The Wrights had seven children, two of whom died in infancy. Orville was born in 1871, four years after Wilbur; Katharine, the baby of the family and the only surviving daughter, was born in 1874.

Through dedication, an unyielding spirit, and high intelligence, Milton rose through church ranks. In 1869, he became editor of the sect's official newspaper, the *Religious Telescope,* and used the forum to promote strict adherence to the church constitution, which more liberal Brethren read as being adaptable to social change. Freemasonry, for example, had lost much of its stigma and a majority of church members sought to broaden their appeal by relaxing the strict prohibition against admitting Masons and members of other secret societies. In this and other matters, Milton stood firm in opposition and found himself increasingly marginalized.

Most of the Brethren would have accepted compromise, but in no small part as a result of Milton's intransigence these policy disputes escalated into a full-blown rift that ultimately tore the Church of the

United Brethren in Christ in two, and provided an eerie precursor to Wilbur's war with Glenn Curtiss.[2]

Although possessed of a fast wit, which Milton lacked, in temperament and worldview Wilbur was very much his father's son. Milton was described by the Wrights' most thorough and sympathetic biographer as "isolated and combative . . . not adept at the skills required to make friends and influence people. . . . His limitations as a politician were apparent. Reconciliation, negotiation, and compromise . . . were foreign to him."[3] That description would apply equally to Wilbur. In addition, both were extremely litigious and acutely sensitive to perceived injustice. Wilbur fought at Milton's side as the Church of the United Brethren in Christ split and on occasion became almost his father's alter ego. In this and a subsequent battle within the church, Orville took no part.

Most biographers agree that a childhood accident was pivotal in Wilbur's life. By all accounts outgoing and gregarious growing up, in the winter of 1885 Wilbur was struck in the mouth playing a game akin to ice hockey and lost some of his front teeth. Although he recovered quickly from the physical injuries, he unaccountably sank into a depression that lasted almost three years. He left high school before graduation, abandoned plans to attend Yale, and spent most of his time nursing his mother, who had become ill with tuberculosis.

What returned Wilbur to vibrancy was Milton's war with the Brethren. In 1888, after almost two decades of increasing animus, the struggle between the liberal faction of the church, by now the vast majority, and the intransigent conservatives, dubbed the "Radicals," finally neared resolution. A vote of the members had been called to permanently settle the issues in dispute. Campaigning was furious and Wilbur, still only twenty-one, wrote pamphlets and scathing editorials, spoke at public meetings, confronted his father's attackers, and attempted to influence wavering Brethren by force of personality. He demonstrated a flair for debate, keen insight, and a bent for lacerating sarcasm. But there would be no tipping of the scales. In the end, convinced the rules for the vote had been rigged, Milton and Wilbur called on other conservatives to boycott the election in an attempt to deny the liberals the three-fourths participation required to make the result binding.

When the votes were counted, Bishop Wright's faction was soundly defeated as expected, but the three-quarters requirement had not been met. In a general conference, however, five of the six bishops and most of the members voted to ratify the result regardless. Milton Wright was the one dissenter and formally split with the majority.

There were now two Churches of the United Brethren in Christ, one called "Old Constitution," and the other "New."* Disposition of church property—buildings, land, and possessions—was now at issue and the liberals sued to gain control. Since the lawsuits were filed at each venue where the church owned property, Milton Wright was forced to defend each one separately, which meant hiring lawyers, giving depositions, and participating in the court proceedings. He threw himself totally into the task. In a moment described as "the one time in his life that work came before family," Milton, "in addition to heading the defense team, remained the leading Churchman of the Old Constitution branch, participating in virtually every phase of the rebuilding process. He traveled incessantly, visiting congregations and organizing new conferences."[4] Once again, Wilbur was at his father's side or helping in the effort from the family home in Dayton. With it all, however, Milton's branch of the Brethren lost all but one of the lawsuits, which left the Radicals without property and nearly destitute.

The church schism left deep scars on Milton as well as Wilbur, Orville, and Katharine, the three Wright siblings still living at home, and drew them inward. "They came to believe in the essential depravity of mankind. The world beyond the front door of their home was filled with men and women who were not to be trusted. . . . An honest person was well advised to expect the worst of others."[5]

* Bishop Wright's sect survives and information about its history and activities can be found at ub.org. The New Constitution sect merged with and is now part of the United Methodist Church.

Wilbur Wright in 1905.

With that jaundiced view of human interaction, Wilbur, by then in his twenties, was left to find a vocation of his own. The problem was not simple because Wilbur never considered the church and seemed to lack passion for anything else. His brother provided the answer; Orville was fascinated by printing. He spent two summers as an apprentice and then, instead of finishing high school, decided to start a business of his own. (Katharine, who served as surrogate homemaker after her mother's death in 1889, would eventually enter Oberlin College, from which she graduated in 1898.) Orville was a master craftsman and built a press from scavenged scrap metal. He took on local jobs at cut-rate prices and did the printing for the church. After he turned a profit, he began a weekly newspaper, the *West Side News,* and when Susan Wright finally succumbed to her illness, he drew Wilbur into the business with him.

The brothers were hardworking and inventive, and their business thrived. Orville kept the machinery in such superb running order that he and Wilbur received contracts to design and build presses for other firms. Although the brothers were known to "scrap" from time to time—voices were often raised in the shop as they argued out a design point—they were fiercely loyal to each other and almost a subset of the larger Wright family. It seemed to family and friends that Wilbur and Orville would pass their days as successful, modestly wealthy, valued members of the Dayton community.

Then, in 1892, they took up bicycling.

They rode the "safety bicycles" that had been introduced in 1887 to replace the unstable "high wheeler," a difficult machine to get on and off and even more difficult to control. The safety bicycle looked a good deal like the modern version, with pedal-sprocket chain drive, a braking system, pneumatic tires, and equal-sized front and back wheels.

The safety bicycle became an immediate rage and along with the automobile helped remake the American landscape. It is nearly impossible to overestimate the societal impact of personalized mechanical transport on a population that could not previously move about for any distance without a horse. The prospect of traveling where one desired whether or not a railroad stopped there or a steamship docked there was intoxicating.

Although the automobile would have a greater long-term impact, the bicycle's popularity was more immediate. Because it lacked an engine, a bicycle was priced within the means of most Americans. Bicycles could be ridden to work during the week and then for recreation on Sunday. Enthusiasts could form clubs to explore and socialize. Young men could race. Bicycles soon became a popular means of allowing young gentlemen and ladies to pass wholesome time together. Of course, both automobiles and bicycles needed roads—or sometimes just an open field—but, bumpy and rutted though they might have been, there was no shortage of either. Given the freedom that personal mechanical transportation imparted, a few jolts and the occasional sore bottom seemed a small price to pay.

Millions of the two-wheelers were sold in little more than a decade and hundreds of small manufacturers rushed to enter the booming field. Bicycle construction was not child's play, as it involved welding, stamping, and other industrial processes, but nor was it so complex that anything beyond a small building or even a dedicated back room was required to set up a shop.

Wilbur and Orville were bitten with the cycling bug and they often rode together, sometimes for hours. In a rare exhibition of sociality, they even joined the local YMCA cycling club. But like all mechanical devices, bicycles break down and the Wrights, the most mechanically adept of the group, soon found themselves giving hours over to alignments and adjustments. Always quick to discern a business opportunity, they were soon augmenting their printing income with bicycle repair and soon after that left printing entirely. By 1896, they decided they could build better bicycles than they were repairing. As with everything Wilbur designed and Orville constructed, Wright Cycle Company bicycles contained innovations unavailable elsewhere, like an oil-retaining wheel hub and coaster brakes.

Young Orville Wright.

By chance, Wilbur and Orville had stumbled into the very profession that would best prepare them for experiments in aviation. For unlike Langley, Wilbur understood almost by instinct that stability, not propulsion or even lift, was the crucial element of flight and that the safety bicycle, not the automobile, was the most appropriate vehicle from which to extrapolate control principles. Although he would not yet see it in such terms, to be stable, particularly in a turn, a bicycle had to be controlled in two of the three axes of motion—side to side (yaw) and laterally (roll). The third axis, "pitch," front to back, only applied to bicycles during a crash. If a bicyclist did not slightly bank his machine in a turn—employ "roll"—he would likely end up in the bushes or on the ground.

Wilbur was not the first to see the parallels between bicycle travel and flight. In the 1896 edition of the *Aeronautical Annual,* James Means included an article of his own, "Wheeling and Flying." Although he did not refer directly to issues of stability, Means did write, "It is not uncommon for the cyclist, in the first flush of enthusiasm which quickly follows the unpleasantness of taming the steel steed, to remark, 'Wheeling is just like flying!' This is true in more ways than one. . . . Both modes of travel are riding upon the air, though in one case a small quantity of air is carried in a bag and in the other the air is unbagged. . . . To learn to wheel one must learn to balance; to learn to fly one must learn to balance."[6] From that essential truth, Wilbur Wright embarked on a course of hypothesis and brilliant intuition.

Receipt of the Smithsonian materials set Wilbur to work in earnest. Orville, as noted, did not share his brother's enthusiasm for the project; the Smithsonian letter had been written by Wilbur in the first-person singular.

Within weeks, Wilbur had his first great epiphany, a counterintuitive deduction. He came to understand that the best way to achieve stability in flight was to make an aircraft inherently *unstable*. Whether Wilbur came to this insight from whole cloth or based on the writings of others, he had made a leap of enormous significance.

Obsessed with creating a machine that would remain perfectly stable in the air, Langley had employed the dihedral wing arrangement to prevent his aerodrome from dipping to one side; Herring added the cruciform tail and universal joint.

Instead of avoiding roll, Wilbur embraced it. Legend has it that one day he noticed that when he twisted an empty bicycle inner-tube box to one side, the other side would twist in the opposite direction. The resulting "warping" was similar to the way he surmised birds twisted their wing tips to maintain lateral control, rather than by shifting their weight. But it's more likely the breakthrough was the result of more banal activities. As he would later write to Octave Chanute, "My observation of the flight of buzzards leads me to believe that they regain their lateral balance, when partly overturned by a gust of wind, by a torsion of the tips of the wings. If the rear edge of the right wing tip is twisted upward and the left downward the bird becomes an animated windmill and instantly begins to turn, a line from its head to its tail being the axis. It thus regains its level even if thrown on its beam ends, so to speak, as I have frequently seen them. I think the bird also in general retains its lateral equilibrium, partly by presenting its two wings at different angles to the wind, and partly by drawing in one wing, thus reducing its area."[7]

By July, Wilbur had built a prototype kite to test his theory. The design, with wings roughly six feet across, was similar to the two-surface Herring–Chanute glider, which in turn was a derivation of Lawrence Hargrave's box kite. Wilbur's addition was four cords that he could manipulate like a puppeteer to create a primitive wing-warping effect. For the first time, wings became flexible rather than rigid surfaces. He flew the kite for some local schoolboys in late July while Orville was on a camping trip.* Initial results were good—Wilbur seemed to be able to control the stability of the kite by twisting the sets of wings in opposite directions. From there, the next step

* Here again, the brothers later claimed to have built the kite together, but it is hard to accept that Wilbur would have tested this watershed invention with his collaborator not present.

was to refine the arrangement and then build a kite large enough to carry a man.

In order to achieve success with a more complex apparatus, Wilbur had to move beyond theory and teach himself both aerodynamics and engineering. The materials from which he was working were filled with formulas, ratios, coefficients, and terminology with which he was completely unfamiliar. For the initial structure of the airfoil—its length, chord, and camber—he could rely on Lilienthal's tables that measured the lift and drag of various configurations; any alterations, however, would involve concepts new to him, such as center of pressure and center of gravity, and he would therefore be forced to undertake a painstaking process of trial and error. There is no overstating the magnitude of Wilbur's achievements given such a primitive starting point.

By spring of 1900, Wilbur felt sufficiently comfortable with his level of knowledge to write to Octave Chanute. His letter of May 13 began without preamble. "For some years I have been afflicted with the belief that flight is possible to man. My disease has increased in severity and I feel that it will soon cost me an increased amount of money if not my life. I have been trying to arrange my affairs in such a way that I can devote my entire time for a few months to experiment in this field."

From the first, Wilbur was largely unconcerned with the aspect of the problem on which Langley had obsessed—propulsion—and therefore told Chanute that he intended to experiment without motors. Those, he asserted, would be an easy appendage to add once the aerodynamics had been perfected. "What is chiefly needed is skill rather than machinery. . . . It is possible to fly without motors, but not without knowledge & skill." He asked Chanute to forward details on "to what extent similar plans have been tested and found to be failures."

Wilbur also noted, "I make no secret of my plans for the reason that I believe no financial profit will accrue to the inventor of the first flying machine, and that only those who are willing to give as well as to receive suggestions can hope to link their names with the honor of its discovery."

He described his proposed methodology in detail.

> I shall in a suitable locality erect a light tower about one hundred and fifty feet high. A rope passing over a pulley at the top will serve as a sort of kite string. It will be so counterbalanced that when the rope is drawn out one hundred & fifty feet it will sustain a pull equal to the weight of the operator and apparatus or nearly so. The wind will blow the machine out from the base of the tower and the weight will be sustained partly by the upward pull of the rope and partly by the lift of the wind. The counterbalance will be so arranged that the pull decreases as the line becomes shorter and ceases entirely when its length has been decreased to one hundred feet. The aim will be to eventually practice in a wind capable of sustaining the operator at a height equal to the top of the tower. The pull of the rope will take the place of a motor in counteracting drift.

Wilbur asked Chanute to suggest the "suitable locality."

Chanute, by then sixty-eight years old, turned out to be the perfect correspondent, especially for one as committed to science for science's sake as Wilbur Wright claimed to be. He responded to Wilbur's letter with encouragement and enthusiasm, although he was wary of the light tower idea, and described his success using the box kite. He suggested San Diego and Pine Island, Florida, as locations but added that since they lacked sand hills, "perhaps even better locations can be found on the Atlantic coasts of South Carolina or Georgia."

On June 1, Wilbur wrote again to Chanute and said, "For the present I have but little time for aeronautical investigations, in fact I try to keep my mind off this subject during the bicycle season as I find that business is neglected otherwise. Later in the year I think I shall be able to give several months of my time. Just now I am content with trying to settle upon a general plan of operations, and find a suitable location." Orville continued to remain uninvolved; Wilbur's correspondence was again in the first-person singular and the wording of the letters leaves little doubt that he saw himself as working alone.*

But Wilbur could not keep his mind off flying. Two months later, at the peak of bicycle season, he demonstrated that he had been working nonstop on the glider when he wrote to Chanute, "It is my intention to begin shortly the construction of a full-size glider. Hitherto I have used pine in the frames, but for the large machine I wish to use spruce, a wood not obtainable in Dayton yards. It would oblige me greatly if you would give me the name of a Chicago firm of whom I could get the timber I need. Also I would be glad to have your advice as to a suitable varnish for the cover. I have been using shellac."

Wilbur had also found his location. The United States Weather Bureau had recommended obscure, isolated Kitty Hawk, North Carolina, as one of the few places in the nation with sandy stretches and steady prevailing winds of about fifteen miles per hour. Wilbur contacted the head of the local weather bureau and confirmed Kitty Hawk as the place to test his full-sized glider. He then prepared the materials in Dayton, again alone, "cut, steamed, and bent the ash ribs that would give shape to the wings, and carefully fashioned the fifty or so additional wooden pieces. Components that could not be obtained at Kitty Hawk, including metal fittings and fasteners and spools of 15-gauge spring steel wire for trussing the wings, were purchased at home and packaged for shipment. Yards of glistening sateen fabric were cut and sewn into the panels that would cover the finished wings."[8]

Wilbur left in early September and discovered that getting to Kitty Hawk was something of an adventure that included a bone-rattling ferry ride across Albemarle Sound. When he arrived, he boarded with a local family and began construction. Orville, who had finally signed

* Orville, in a deposition for the Wrights' case against Glenn Curtiss taken after Wilbur's death, stated, "After reading the pamphlets sent to us by the Smithsonian, we became highly enthusiastic with the idea of gliding as a sport." He went on to describe the entire process that led to the construction of the first glider, and in fact all the work that preceded the letter to Chanute, as having been done by them both.

on, joined him at the end of the month and brought materials to allow them to live in a tent at the site of their test flights. "Trying to find Will at Kitty Hawk," he wrote to Katharine from Elizabeth City before he embarked on the ferry, "reminds me very much of a relief expedition to some lost Arctic explorer."[9] He arrived safely and from that point forward, the "I" in Wilbur's correspondence was replaced by a "we."

The Wright brothers' first season at Kitty Hawk lasted only three weeks, in which they experienced success and disappointment. The derrick arrangement that Wilbur had described in his letter to Chanute was a failure, as Chanute had predicted, and the camber of the wings—at 1:23 only half what Lilienthal had used—made high winds a necessity for flight. But the brothers learned proper positioning of the elevator, an airfoil in the front of the craft to provide additional lift and help control pitch; that the operator should lie prone rather than in a sitting position; and to change the dihedral of the lower wing to an anhedral (a downward angle from the center) to decrease stability

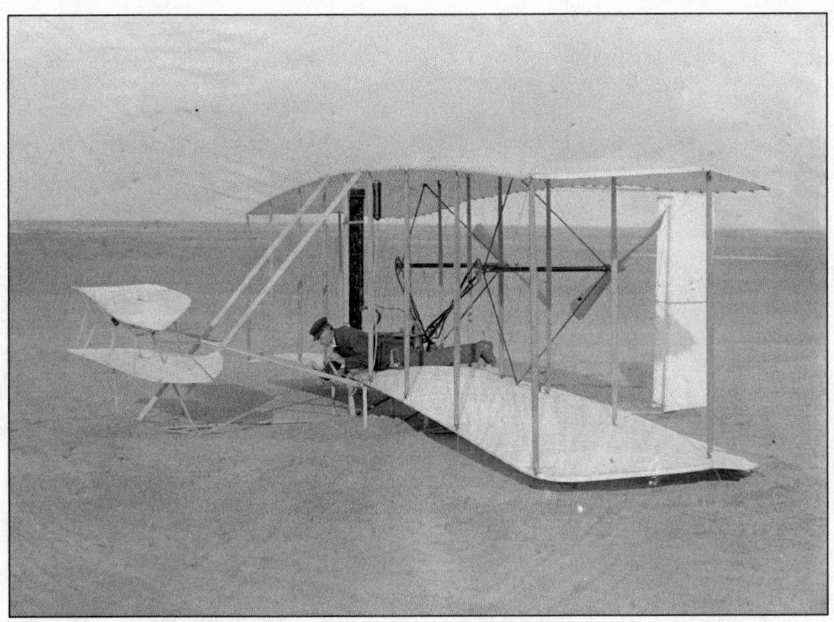

Wilbur in prone position, just after landing a glider.

and make the glider more maneuverable. By the time they left in the last week of October, Wilbur, who did all the flying, had succeeded in achieving a number of low, short, but significant glides.

Back in Dayton, they wrote to Chanute, telling him of their progress and the innovations they had incorporated into their glider. Chanute was particularly impressed with the prone operator's position, which he estimated "diminished head resistance by ⅔." He added, "A magnificent showing provided that you do not plow the ground with your noses."[10]

Wilbur and Orville were already planning to return to Kitty Hawk in 1901, prepared to take a giant step forward.

CHAPTER 5

Sophomore Slump

Unaware that his thesis had come under threat in the North Carolina dunes, Samuel Langley maintained his conviction that propulsion was the only vital element in moving from an unmanned to manned aerodrome. Octave Chanute, in an 1897 article, had given a sense of how undeveloped the ideas of thrust were. "All sorts of contrivances have been proposed; reaction jets of steam or of compressed air, the explosion of gunpowder or even nitro-glycerine, feathering paddle wheels of varied design, oscillating fins acting like the tails of fishes, flapping elastic wings like the pinions of birds, and the rotating screw."[1] Langley had always favored the "rotating screw"—the propeller—which seemed to have analogous application from use on ships. To drive the screw, a motor more powerful than anything with which Langley had experimented would be required and preliminary calculations indicated steam would not produce the required weight-to-horsepower efficiencies. Gasoline seemed like the best choice; to build such a motor, Langley cast about for an assistant with the proper expertise. He wrote to Robert Thurston, a professor of engineering at Cornell, asking for a "young man who is morally trustworthy ('a good fellow') with some gumption and professional training." Thurston recommended a senior engineering student named Charles

Manly and Langley hired him to oversee the design and to eventually fly the finished product.

Langley also engaged Stephen Balzer to adapt a five-cylinder rotary automobile engine to power his aerodrome, but it soon became clear that Balzer's designs would not be up to the challenge. Manly, the junior man on the team, took on the task. He would spend much of the next two years developing the fifty-horsepower gasoline motor that would drive the manned aerodrome.

The Wrights were so excited to return to Kitty Hawk for the 1901 tests that instead of waiting once more until September and the end of peak bicycle season, they left for North Carolina in July. To watch the bike shop they hired a young machinist and mechanic named Charlie Taylor, a local man they'd known since high school.

When they departed, they brought with them a glider they saw as improved in every way. The wing surface had been almost doubled to provide sufficient lift in lighter winds and they had refined the front elevator. The camber of wings had been increased from the relatively flat one inch of height for every 23 inches of width to Lilienthal's formula of 1:12. After a series of positive tests, they would be able to add a motor—which Orville and Charlie Taylor could build—and achieve powered flight the following year. So confident were Wilbur and Orville in the season's triumph that they invited Octave Chanute to visit them in Dayton before their departure and then to Kitty Hawk to witness their achievement. Over dinner, Chanute suggested they bring with them Edward Huffaker, who was described as being in the final stages of building a glider of his own, and a flight-obsessed physician named George Spratt.

The brothers arrived in Kitty Hawk on July 11, but the 1901 stay in North Carolina turned out to be not a triumph but rather a study of failure, frustration, and torment, the latter inflicted by a combination of the slovenly Huffaker and a predatory swarm of mosquitoes that "came in a mighty cloud almost darkening the sun."[2]

When the glider finally flew at the end of July, it exhibited a ten-

Wilbur, Orville, Chanute, and E. C. Huffaker in the work shed at Kitty Hawk, 1901.

dency to plunge straight down into the sand unless Wilbur (who once again did all the flying) pushed himself all the way back in the middle to alter the center of gravity and then reached all the way forward to move the elevator in a full-up position. Even with these contortions, the glider flew erratically, sometimes threatening to plummet from twenty feet up or more. To go aloft in a machine that behaved so unpredictably was to invite serious injury or death. Orville wrote to Katharine that they now seemed at the same juncture Lilienthal had reached just before he was killed. Wilbur did discover that manipulating the forward elevator could bring some control to the craft, but not nearly enough to make the glides safe.

The Wrights made sufficient modification to the elevator and the camber to correct the pitch problem, but then discovered that the wing-warping system, of which they had been completely confident, seemed also to create instabilities. The system was operated by a hip cradle that Wilbur wore while lying prone on the bottom wing. He would shift from one side to another to twist the wings in the direction he wanted, something of a next-generation Lilienthal kick, but rather than even out the glider, on one occasion the right wing shot downward into the sand, sending Wilbur out the front into the elevator. Unlike the first difficulty, this problem seemed intractable. In fact, Wilbur had experienced a phenomenon at low altitude that would plague early designers and cause much more serious, often fatal accidents at greater elevation. If not properly designed and flown, there was a disquieting tendency for an aircraft to increase its bank until it went into a spiral dive.*

Chanute, who had come to visit (fortunately for him, after the mosquitoes departed), left the camp in early August with George Spratt. The Wrights had enjoyed Spratt's company, finding him intelligent, good-natured, and eager to help. They loathed Huffaker, thinking him inept professionally and revolting personally. "Some things are rather more amusing to think about than to endure at the time," Wilbur noted later.

When Wilbur and Orville left North Carolina at the end of August, their mood was far different than it had been the year before. Instead of vaulting forward, they had taken a step back. Even worse, the problems they were encountering seemed without solution; they cut to the core of Wilbur's hypotheses. Wilbur was unaccustomed to being so completely wrong. And for once, home would not provide respite. Milton Wright, it seemed, had gotten himself embroiled in another fractious church legal dispute, this time with members of his own already splintered sect. And once more, Wilbur would be enlisted to see him through it.

The head of publications for Milton's Old Constitution sect was a preacher named Millard Keiter. Publications were a major source of church revenue and Milton began to suspect Keiter of embezzlement. He prompted an audit that seemed to confirm his fears and Keiter was removed from his post by church elders. But Keiter convinced a num-

* As was subsequently discovered, this is because the bank angle starts the aircraft turning, which speeds up the wing on the outside of the turn (the high wing). The faster wing produces more lift, which rolls the aircraft into a steeper bank.

ber of board members that the audit discrepancies were oversights or honest errors. Milton launched a pamphlet war, the tracts written by Wilbur. When the written word did not have the desired impact, Milton brought in the civil authorities without consulting other church elders and had Keiter arrested for forgery.

At a subsequent hearing, the charges against Keiter were dismissed, albeit on technicalities, and Bishop Wright was ostracized for acting unilaterally. Milton, as always, upped the stakes and Wilbur was right there with him, auditing the books, writing letters and pamphlets, and jawboning church officials. Keiter's supporters succeeded in turning a significant number of elders against Bishop Wright and then having him brought before a special church commission in Huntington, Indiana, on a variety of charges, including "insubordination" and "maligning" Millard Keiter. Huntington was the home of the new church college, which Milton had been instrumental in helping to establish, and the commission hearing was an embarrassment for the entire Wright family. Orville wrote to Wilbur, urging him "have someone . . . use his influence to keep notices out of the papers."[3] The hearing dragged on through the summer and Milton was ultimately found to have overstepped his authority and ordered to admit his error and apologize to Keiter. Predictably, Milton refused. The elders then stripped him of his post, although there was no formal mechanism for physically expelling him from church functions.* Most significant for Wilbur, here was another occasion where justice—and injustice—were seen as absolute, where right and wrong were without nuance and therefore closed to compromise.

While the Keiter incident simmered, Wilbur had a business to run and a problem to solve. With typical thoroughness, he went back to the beginning. He assumed nothing and looked at everything with a fresh eye. As he studied the problem, he began to suspect more and

* The order was reversed in 1905 and Milton Wright was restored to his post. Millard Keiter moved to Kentucky, where he was eventually indicted for land fraud.

more that the fault lay in the data on which he had based his design, specifically Otto Lilienthal's lift and drag tables.

Lilienthal, Langley, and virtually everyone who had researched aerodynamics had utilized a whirling-arm device. But a whirling arm was an "open" system and inaccuracies were inevitable. Lilienthal had attempted to account for discrepancies by running multiple tests, the theory being that inaccuracy could be factored out by repetition. Still, there was no avoiding that the method was slapdash.

In 1871, a remarkable English marine engineer and Aeronautical Society member named Francis Herbert Wenham built the first wind tunnel, a "closed" system, to test how different airfoil shapes would react to air currents. Wenham had a variety of interests and would make contributions to many fields, but none more than aviation. He was the first to note that the camber of a wing should not necessarily be uniform, an arc of a circle, but should be thicker at the front and trail off at the rear, similar to the birds he watched soar across the skies in locales as far flung as Egypt. He had contributed an article for the first *Aeronautical Annual,* titled "On Aerial Locomotion and the Laws by which Heavy Bodies Impelled through Air are Sustained," a reprint of a paper he presented upon founding the Aeronautical Society in 1866. Eventually, Wenham attempted to build a glider of his own and when it failed to fly, resolved to determine the cause by taking more precise measurements of airfoils than any previously achieved. Aware of the deficiencies of a whirling arm, he began to experiment with air rushing through an enclosed box.

Wenham's design, however, suffered deficiencies of its own and turned out to be of limited utility. Subsequent versions were improved but still unable to guarantee accurate measurements. Few were willing to eschew the whirling arm for an unproven technology. But Wilbur and Orville realized that a wind tunnel was precisely what they needed to move past Lilienthal's inaccuracies and obtain measurements that would allow them to correct the design flaws of the 1901 glider. They simply needed one that worked. So they set to build an improved model, bringing to the task their combination of incisive reasoning and flawless craftsmanship, spiced as always with a touch of Wilbur's genius.

Wilbur described the product.

> My brother Orville and I built a rectangle-shaped open-ended wind tunnel out of a wooden box. It was 16 inches wide by 16 inches tall by 6 feet long. Inside of it we placed an aerodynamic measuring device made from an old hacksaw blade and bicycle-spoke wire. We directed the air current from an old fan in the back shop room into the opening of the wooden box. In fact, we sometimes referred to one of the two open ends of the wind tunnel as the 'goesinta' and the other end as the 'goesouta.' An old one-cylinder gasoline engine (that also turned other tools in the shop, such as our lathe) supplied the power to turn the fan. This was because there was no electricity in our shop. In fact, even the lights were gas lights.
>
> It took us about a month of experimenting with the wind tunnel we had built to learn how to use it effectively. Eventually we learned how to operate it so that it gave us results that varied less than one-tenth of a degree. Occasionally I had to yell at my brother to keep him from moving even just a little in the room because it would disturb the air flow and destroy the accuracy of the test.

Their wind tunnel was the most sophisticated ever constructed and the Wrights experimented with their invention for two months, testing two hundred airfoil shapes and configurations. They were obsessively precise and their measurements were more accurate than any previously achieved. When they concluded their testing just before Christmas 1901, they had confirmed that Lilienthal's tables were "full of errors." The brothers were exhilarated by the result. "From all the data that Orville and I accumulated into tables, an accurate and reliable wing could finally be built." And Wilbur understood the import.

"As famous as we became for our 'Flyer' and its system of control, it all would never have happened if we had not developed our own wind tunnel and derived our own correct aerodynamic data."[4]

The return to Kitty Hawk in 1902 resulted in the explosive leap forward the brothers had expected the year before. They arrived in late August with a radically new design for the glider. The wing had an aspect ratio of 1:6, doubled from the previous incarnation, which meant a longer and narrower design. The camber was 1:20, not far from the 1:23 that Lilienthal had employed but, as Wenham had hypothesized, it was not an arc but rather had its peak near the leading edge.

The 1902 glider featured another significant change, the addition of a fixed two-pane rudder at the rear to compensate for the tendency Wilbur had encountered for the wings to dip too severely when the warping mechanism was employed.

Still, with the Keiter business unresolved, Wilbur's focus continued to be divided. To aid his father's cause, he studied every detail, participated in setting the finest points of strategy, and on three occasions traveled to Huntington to participate in the defense.

Once at Kitty Hawk, however, the Keiter matter was forced into the background as the new design was tested. There were days when the brothers—Orville was by now going into the air as well—might make as many as seventy-five glides, some as far as three hundred feet. The only remaining issue was that the strange "skidding" that Wilbur had experienced the previous year had not been eliminated by the fixed rudder. Orville hypothesized that perhaps the rigidity of the rudder was contributing to the problem and that a hinge might improve the glider's response. This was Orville's first significant theoretical proposal and "he would raise the issue carefully. All too often, he suspected his older brother reacted against his suggestions on principle."[5] But Wilbur reacted well. They also decided that a single pane would work as well as the double and rebuilt their glider with a movable rudder linked to the wing-warping hip cradle.

The rudder was the last piece of the puzzle. The Wrights had created a three-axis system that could turn an aircraft efficiently and maintain a constant position relative to the ground. The new model soared with complete control and the brothers took turns feeling the exhilaration of their invention. By the time they left North Carolina three weeks later, they had completed perhaps one thousand glides, attaining distances of as much as six hundred feet.

On October 5, the day before the new glider was completed, Wilbur and Orville had visitors. Octave Chanute showed up at Kitty Hawk and brought with him Augustus Herring.

Herring had been as unsuccessful out of aviation as in. Once again out of money, he had contacted Chanute, who seemed to have a limitless capacity to give people one more chance, and asked for patronage for another glider. Chanute had agreed and suggested Herring test his design at Kitty Hawk, where great things were afoot.

Herring's glider failed and, as he could see for himself, the Wrights' did not. More significant, he saw why the Wrights had been so much more successful than he. Herring slunk away after ten days but he left with at least a cursory notion of what it would take to successfully fly a heavier-than-air craft.

Wilbur and Orville had their biggest successes after Herring and Chanute departed, making more than 250 glides in "any kind of weather," including a 30-mph wind. The control issues had been solved. They had created a craft that could fly. At that point their research became congruent with Langley's—all they needed was a means of propulsion.

But while Langley and the Wrights raced to be the first to achieve fixed-wing flight, another sort of aviation was capturing the public's imagination.

CHAPTER 6

Gas Bag

The press, many scientists, and most government officials remained skeptical of the prospects for heavier-than-air flight. There were even periodic calls to investigate the $50,000 given to the incorruptible Langley. Lighter-than-air flight, however, was an exciting new technology that seemed to many the obvious solution to the flying problem. The fascination with balloons was largely the work of one man with the courage of a tightrope walker (which he was) and the audacity of P. T. Barnum (whom he rivaled).

Thomas Scott Baldwin was born either in Missouri in 1854 or in Illinois in 1857, although he later claimed to have begun life in a log cabin in 1861. His parents seemed to have died when he was about twelve, either together or separately. Baldwin later told reporters he had seen them gunned down before his eyes by Confederate renegades during the Civil War, which was mathematically impossible for whatever birth date was correct, although no one ever seemed to notice or care. His schooling ended when he ran away from an orphanage with his older brother Samuel, probably when he was about fourteen.

As an adult, Baldwin favored titles. In the 1880s, despite his limited education, he dubbed himself "professor," once again with the acquiescence of the press. He changed "professor" to "captain" in the ensuing decade—an appellation he retained until 1917, when he actually acquired military rank, commissioned in the army as a major.

According to Baldwin's own recollections—apocryphal, certainly, although no one knows to what extent—he began his professional career as a tumbler in the W. W. Cole circus but soon took his skills to the trapeze and the wire. "What I acquired in these days helped me as an aeronaut," Baldwin said later. "I learned in walking the tightrope that it is not so much a matter of practice or of any peculiar muscular movement or strength as it is in keeping at it until you have the 'feel' of confidence, and when once this comes to a man, he is equally at home on wire, rope or ground."[1]

Baldwin soon tired of circus life, or perhaps he couldn't abide being someone else's employee. He had his own ideas about what people would pay to see and by age twenty had set out on his own. One of the things he was convinced people would pay to see was a man floating off to an uncertain fate, so he began dabbling in ballooning in 1881.

Manned balloons of that time were either "captive," attached by a long tether to a fixed point on the ground, or "free," left to the mercy of the prevailing winds. The only means of control for either sort was varying the altitude by manipulating the hydrogen gas in the bag.

Although there was good money in public demonstrations of either of those methods, Baldwin saw the future as being in "airships"—balloons as a conveyance. But if balloons were to take you where you wanted to go, they would need a mechanism to make them "dirigible"—steerable. And of course for round-trips it wouldn't do for a dirigible balloon to sail at the mercy of air currents, so a means would be required to maintain forward thrust against the wind.

At first Baldwin admitted that he accepted the conventional wisdom that "balloons had little to do with aerial navigation," but as he studied the subject he concluded "the popular notion of balloon manipulation was entirely incorrect. A balloon does not 'go up,' but rather is forced up by the closing of the air below it as it rises, and this pressure forces it higher and higher as a wedge—the content of the balloon is a cork and the air is the water. Hydrogen being thirteen-fourteenths lighter-than-air—by displacing so many feet of air—the air served as a brace to the balloon, as there is normally seven tons of air pressure on a man's body. It was getting this fact firmly fixed in my mind that I felt I would some day make a dirigible balloon a success."

In 1885, Baldwin took his talents and his ambitions to the boomtown of San Francisco. He first got the city's attention by walking a tightrope from the balcony of Cliff House to Seal Rocks and back, a round-trip journey of nine hundred feet over pounding surf one hundred feet below.[2] In his quest for both adulation and riches, the first only as a means to the second, he decided to add a wrinkle to the standard balloon demonstration. He would rise up in a captive balloon and then parachute out. Parachutes had also been around for almost a century but they were stiff, rigid, and extremely unreliable; if positioned incorrectly, they would fail to catch the wind and carry their unfortunate passengers straight—and quickly—to their deaths. Baldwin decided to vent the silk canopy and attach flexible ropes, an arrangement that would better allow the contraption to right itself in the air. Like most daredevils, Baldwin rigorously tested his theories before risking his life on them.

"I studied the matter for months. I experimented with sand bags just my own weight and did not venture a jump until I had the 'feel' that it could be safely done. I made most of my jumps in water, and if it had not been that every particle of my body was hard as iron from former training as a gymnast and taking of all kinds of jolts, I would not have lasted through these early experiments."

While Baldwin's canopy seemed safe enough, remaining attached to it promised to be a challenge. He had built no harness or any other means of tethering himself to the apparatus. As the parachute descended, Baldwin grasped a ring that held the cords, trusting that a gust of wind would not jerk the ring out of his hands.

Finally ready for a public exhibition, Baldwin offered to prove the efficacy of his invention by a public test jump—assuming, of course, someone was willing to pay him to do it. "I went to Mr. Morton of the

Market Street Cable Line and told him I thought I had an exhibition that would be a good feature for the Golden Gate Park, and he asked me what it was, and I told him a parachute jump. I said I would jump for a dollar a foot, and he answered: 'Go ahead and jump a thousand feet!' "

In January 1887, Baldwin did precisely that, floating gently to the ground below and his thousand-dollar prize.

Baldwin soon took his parachute show on the road, venturing higher and higher for greater prize money. In May 1888, in Minneapolis, "Professor Baldwin" performed his greatest feat. He allowed the balloon to take him five thousand feet into the air, then parachuted to a predetermined spot on the ground for his usual dollar-a-foot fee.* Not content to restrict his fortunes to the domestic market, Baldwin crossed both oceans, performing across Europe and in Asia in venues as exotic as Siam.

But Baldwin had not given up his "visions of an airship." While in Germany, he met with Count Zeppelin and kept himself abreast of developments in aerodynamic research. As he studied the problem, he correctly surmised that control, both of altitude and direction, were offshoots of propulsion and center of gravity. Ultimately, he turned to the same devices that provided inspiration to fixed-wing inventors. "As the bicycle and automobile developed, they revealed to me a way of overcoming the one vital difficulty, that of providing power for an airship, and now aerial navigation has become merely a mechanical proposition." Baldwin decided internal combustion engines provided the closest approximation of the power source he sought. To provide the actual thrust, Baldwin "spent many months at the Santa Clara College, studying the law of fluid movement, for air is a fluid, the only difference being in matter of density." He concluded that a propeller had to be of a particular design. "We found by a series of experiments that the air in striking a blade of a parabolic curve at a certain angle—

* While Baldwin is generally credited as the inventor of the flexible parachute, he never bothered to take out a patent, a practice he would continue in his research with airships.

say forty-five degrees—goes up over the blade instead of down as commonly believed."

In October 1901, while Baldwin was still attempting to devise the proper configuration of propulsion and directional control for his airship, Alberto Santos-Dumont, a young Brazilian coffee heir living in Paris, stunned the world—and won 100,000 francs for himself—by successfully navigating a motorized balloon around the Eiffel Tower before returning to his starting point.* Santos-Dumont was a fixture in Paris *haute société*. Barely one hundred pounds, he wore only the best clothes, dined nightly at Maxim's, and counted among his many intimates Gustave Eiffel—the tower's designer—the jeweler Louis Cartier, and members of any number of royal families. On his trip around Eiffel's tower, he used bicycle pedals to start a small gasoline engine that turned his propeller at 180 revolutions per minute. For his achievement, he received notes of congratulations from Jules Verne and H. G. Wells.

Although Santos-Dumont had developed a dirigible airship, the propulsion was weak and control problematic. There were many who thought the Eiffel Tower circuit was based more on a fluke of wind currents than in efficacy of design. (In one of his many previous attempts, Santos-Dumont had drifted helplessly into the wall of a hotel and was left hanging from the roof after the gas bag exploded.) In order to gain sufficient thrust to give him control in more than a light breeze, Santos-Dumont tried a bigger motor but that added so much weight as to defeat the purpose. Neither he nor anyone else seemed to know quite how to proceed.

Baldwin was stumped as well; according to a later magazine ac-

* At first, Henri Deutsch de la Meurthe, who put up the prize, balked at paying because Santos-Dumont had finished ten seconds over the allotted thirty minutes to complete the circuit. But the time included a one-minute-forty-second delay in grasping the rope to secure the airship. After Santos-Dumont shrugged off the prize, claiming that he had intended to give it to the poor anyway, Deutsch de la Meurthe paid up. Santos-Dumont split the prize money between the poor and the workmen who built and maintained the craft.

count, he removed a 24-horsepower engine from an automobile, but the result was an uncontrollable hash.[3] Then in 1904, he "chanced to see a new motorcycle, the motor of which seemed to be exactly what he wanted to propel his new airship."[4] Upon examination, Baldwin saw that the machine and its lightweight two-cylinder motor had been fashioned by the G. H. Curtiss Manufacturing Company of Hammondsport, New York. He had never heard of the company but telegraphed and asked to purchase a motor not attached to a frame. The message was received by the owner, a twenty-six-year-old mechanical whiz named Glenn Hammond Curtiss.

Glenn Curtiss was born in Hammondsport in 1878, his middle name given to him by parents who thought the small town on Keuka Lake in western New York State was paradise. His father died when Glenn was four. In school, where he completed only eighth grade, Curtiss showed high proficiency in mathematics, a good deal less in spelling.

From the time he was a small boy, Curtiss was a tinkerer. At ten, he made a camera out of a cigar box; at twelve, he built a telegraph out of spools, nails, tin, and wire. While in his early teens, he was often hired to wire neighbors' houses for telephones or electric light. When the family lived in Rochester so that his sister could attend a school for the deaf, Curtiss, still a teenager, got a job at the Eastman Dry Plate and Film Company and there invented a stenciling system that allowed the backs of film to be stenciled one hundred times faster. Like Wilbur Wright, Curtiss was always thoughtful and analytic when taking on a mechanical problem and even as a young boy seemed serious to the point of being glum. Despite his outward demeanor, however, he was said—again like Wilbur—to have a sharp, biting wit.

Young Glenn Curtiss's other passion was speed. Like the Wrights, he was bitten by the bicycle bug but preferred racing to touring. The local pharmacist noted, "He had tremendous endurance. He was never a quitter. He would do anything that was fair to win."[5] Curtiss put what he later called his "speed craving" to practical use as a bicycle messenger for Western Union.

Word of Curtiss's mechanical acumen got around and he was often solicited by local bicycle owners to perform tune-ups or make repairs. In 1897, when he was not yet twenty, he sold all the leftover stock from his father's harness business and used the proceeds to take over a bicycle repair shop. He soon opened a second shop and acquired sales licenses for a number of national brands. In March 1898, Curtiss married Lena Neff. The two would remain devoted to each other for more than three decades.

By 1900, Curtiss was building bicycles and, as with the Wrights, his designs were superior to most other machines on the market. At that point, however, Curtiss decided to mount a gasoline engine on one of his bicycles. "Motor cycles"—the name had been recently coined—were a newly invented hybrid of the automobile and the safety bicycle. The first one had been offered for sale in the United States only five years earlier and only a few thousand were in existence, most poorly balanced jerry-built affairs.

In 1901, Curtiss obtained a mail order engine casting from the only company selling such items for motorcycles, but it came unfinished and without instructions so Curtiss cobbled together the rest. There was no carburetor, so he employed a tomato can "filled with gasoline and covered over with a gauze screen, which sucked up the liquid by capillary attraction. Thus it vaporized and was conducted to the cylinder by a pipe from the top of the can."[6] Although the finished product functioned, it was underpowered, so he ordered a larger motor. That one was a "terror" but misfired constantly and Curtiss realized he could build a better engine than he could buy. The result was a reliable motor that achieved a better horsepower-to-weight ratio than any other for sale. He traveled to nearby fairs to race his own machines and orders began to roll in.

Within two years, Curtiss had acquired a reputation for brilliance at engine design and his motorcycles were purchased by enthusiasts across America. He opened a factory to try to keep up with demand and was continually adding capacity and employees as word of G. H.

Curtiss motorcycles spread. But no matter how big the business got, Curtiss never ceased being a fixture on the factory floor, overseeing production and making improvements to the product. In January 1904, he traveled to Ormond Beach, Florida, and set a world ten-mile speed record, finishing the run in 8 minutes, 54.4 seconds, a mark that held for seven years. Six months later, he received the telegram from Thomas Baldwin.

Curtiss found Baldwin's request for a disembodied motor strange, especially since Baldwin hadn't mentioned to what use he intended to put his purchase. Still, an order is an order, so Curtiss pulled a motor off a used motorcycle, polished and tuned it, then sent it off to California.

Curtiss's used two-cylinder V-shaped motor was the last piece of Baldwin's puzzle. He attached it to scaffolding installed underneath a balloon filled with hydrogen gas and christened the finished product the *California Arrow.* Baldwin later provided a description of the apparatus:

> The *Arrow* consisted of a bag of Japanese silk, seventeen feet in diameter and fifty-two in length, covered with ten coats of varnish, inside and out, and outside of all a netting of number sixty cotton seine, with six-inch square mesh. The keel or rudder of the ship is forty feet in length, made of laminated spruce, and forms an equilateral triangle, the strongest curve known to modern science and the one that is used in bridge construction. The *Arrow* only weighs 300 pounds and is sixty feet in length, and has a rail on top, with two rails on either side, three feet apart.

In October 1904, Baldwin took his Curtiss-powered dirigible east to the Louisiana Purchase Exposition in St. Louis. The fair had opened the year before to mark the purchase's centennial, but the planned aeronautics exhibition with its whopping $100,000 prize for the most successful flight had been put off in an attempt to attract competitors.* To help stage the extravaganza, the exposition's organizers had appointed Octave Chanute and Alberto Santos-Dumont to an advisory board in 1901. With the Wright glider achieving spectacular results and motorized flight perhaps imminent, in January 1902 Chanute contacted the Wrights and urged them to participate.

Wilbur was tempted but, aware that "a power machine . . . is the only kind that could hope to be awarded a prize of any kind," he was uncertain that he and Orville could complete such an aircraft in time. Therefore, he added, "Whether we compete will depend much on the conditions under which the prizes are offered. I have little of the gambling instinct and unless there is reasonable prospect of getting back at least the amount expended in competing I would enter only after very careful consideration."[7] In the end, however, he declined, deciding that regardless of what he and Orville offered, Santos-Dumont would ensure that the competition would be skewed to favor airships. Wilbur informed Chanute, "As there are no consolation prizes provided for flying machines . . . we would have to win the grand prize or nothing."

In early fall 1904, Santos-Dumont, the most famous balloonist in the world, shipped his balloon to St. Louis and stored it in a shed where it was promptly vandalized; unknown saboteurs slashed the gas bag repeatedly. Santos-Dumont was certain that jealous competitors were the culprits but, as he had suffered a similar incident in London, American authorities were dubious. Police intimated that members of the Frenchman's own crew were responsible. Outraged at the suggestion, Santos-Dumont withdrew from the competition and returned to Paris.

With the field thus left open, Baldwin anticipated leaving St. Louis with a triumph and $100,000. He arrived with "a small flat trunk containing a silk balloon and netting, a small crate containing a motor-

* Equal to $2.5 million in today's dollars.

cycle engine, and a long crate containing the propeller shaft." The propeller and framing would be fashioned on-site.

One of the other balloonists he encountered at the fair was a twenty-eight-year-old from Toledo named Augustus Roy Knabenshue. Knabenshue, who went by his middle name and whose father was editor in chief of the *Toledo Blade,* had been bitten by the ballooning bug as a child. By his early twenties, he was appearing at fairs and charging attendees for ascensions. Initially, he purchased balloons, some from Baldwin's factory, but had since taken to fabricating his own. Ballooning was still something of an avant-garde pastime, so to spare his straightlaced family embarrassment, Knabenshue registered at fairs as "Professor Don Carlos."

Knabenshue and Baldwin immediately hit it off. The younger man couldn't wait to see the famed globe-trotting "Cap't Tom," as Baldwin had taken to billing himself, achieve the first dirigible flight in the United States, and Baldwin had found a man to help with the extensive preparations. Knabenshue agreed to build the propeller and the undercarriage and ultimately he assembled the *California Arrow* himself.

All seemed in readiness but when Baldwin attempted to test-fly his airship, he made a troubling discovery—the *Arrow* couldn't lift off the ground with him at the helm. Baldwin was near fifty and fat in a thin young man's game. Knabenshue, however, was small and reedy, one hundred pounds lighter. Although Knabenshue knew nothing of steering and controlling the airship, Baldwin asked him to pilot the craft and offered basic instructions in direction and attitude, the latter of which involved scrambling forward and backward along the catwalk under the scaffolding. Baldwin was charging a thousand dollars for each flight in addition to the prize money and he offered his young apprentice 50 percent of the profits after expenses. On October 25, Roy Knabenshue took the *California Arrow* aloft.

Knabenshue later recalled that before the flight, Baldwin, ever the promoter, "walked me beyond earshot and repeated his instructions. If

Roy Knabenshue on the catwalk of Cap't Tom Baldwin's airship at the Louisiana Purchase Exposition in St. Louis.

anything happened to cause the loss of the balloon full of gas, it would ruin our prospects of making a profit on the first flight. The only sensible thing to do would be to go over the fence and come down immediately. We would then tow the ship back and be ready for a flight the following day."[8]

Baldwin had been prescient. The motor had been fed a poor mixture of gasoline and oil and Knabenshue, handling the *Arrow* inexpertly, was forced to land in a cornfield. But to the surprise of both pilot and designer, the voyage was a huge success. The *Arrow* had traveled fifteen miles, remained aloft for more than an hour, and newspapers were filled with breathless accounts of the voyage.

On October 31, the pair achieved an even greater triumph. Knabenshue traveled a three-and-a-half-mile oval course at an altitude of two thousand feet on a windy day. Spectators cheered and threw their hats in the air as the *Arrow* made its return against the strong current of air. Afterward, they hoisted Knabenshue on their shoulders and carried him around the field. Baldwin had proved his contention that an airship could maneuver and make headway against the wind. The only mitigating factor was discovering the $100,000 prize was a fantasy, the money having been used by the promoters as operating expenses for the fair.

Whether he was hoodwinked or not, the St. Louis flight brought Baldwin national attention. Requests for exhibitions abounded, each offering more money than the last. Knabenshue returned to California and flew for Baldwin before adoring crowds.

Cap't Tom went east to Hammondsport to meet the man who had built the motor that powered the *Arrow*. Baldwin said afterward that he expected to encounter a stuffy businessman in his forties or fifties, well dressed and self-important. Instead, he found himself opposite a quiet, painfully shy young man dressed in overalls who had to wipe his hand free of grease in order to offer a handshake. This unlikely pair struck an instant friendship, each drawn by admiration to qualities in the other that he lacked. They set into an extended discourse on the best way to improve airship propulsion. Within days, Curtiss had refined his designs, making them even lighter and more efficient to suit the needs of airships, the same needs that would later present themselves in fixed-wing aircraft.

Baldwin remained in Hammondsport for a few weeks, most of the time as a guest in the Curtiss home. He charmed everyone in sight with his bluff, open manner, his unflagging good humor, and his tales of far-off climes. When he left, Baldwin had concluded a long-term arrangement with the Curtiss Manufacturing Company to supply propulsion for the fleet of Arrows he planned to build.

When Baldwin arrived in California, Knabenshue announced that he was leaving Baldwin's employ and striking out on his own. The exact circumstances of the parting are unclear—it was described merely as a "disagreement"—but six months later Knabenshue would exhibit his own airship, the *Toledo,* at an Independence Day celebration in his hometown. Knabenshue's craft, also powered by a Curtiss motor, was sleeker and more aerodynamic than the *California Arrow* and Knabenshue began to grab headlines Cap't Tom thought reserved for him.

Baldwin resolved to return to preeminence. He hadn't lost any weight during his weeks as a Curtiss houseguest so he needed a replacement pilot. With bookings to be honored, he was likely prepared to accept anyone who could fly, certainly someone less adept than Knabenshue, who even Baldwin admitted had become expert in controlling the airship.

Instead, he found someone better. Early in 1905, a brash, fearless teenager named Lincoln Beachey walked into his office and within minutes Baldwin knew he had struck gold.

Beachey was born in San Francisco on March 3, 1887. His father, W. C. Beachey, was a blind Civil War veteran who could not work, so his mother, Amy, took in laundry to make ends meet. Although Amy Beachey worked from morning until night, the family was always strapped for funds. Eventually she placed her husband in a soldiers' home and in 1902 unsuccessfully sued for divorce, claiming her husband had failed to provide for her because his pension was not large enough to contribute to the family's support.

Lincoln Beachey had a keen mind—like Glenn Curtiss, he was especially adept at mathematics—but left school at age twelve or thirteen. He later said that he immediately began to learn the mechanics of airships but the evidence is that he restricted his activities to ground-based vehicles for the next three or four years.* In 1902, he was registered in a two-mile bicycle race; by 1904, he had graduated

* Beachey gave a number of interviews beginning in his late teens in which he recounted some details of his early life. While the essentials seemed to have been true, he was as addicted as his employer to exaggeration.

to motorcycles. Beachey's competitiveness was quickly established. In June of that year, he finished first in a five-mile race but was "disqualified on the ground of professionalism." In addition to temperament, Beachey's body type was ideally suited for flying. At a stocky five feet seven, he could be quicker and surer along the treacherous undercarriage than even Roy Knabenshue.

Beachey arrived just in time for Cap't Tom to send him north to Portland and the Lewis and Clark Exposition. Once again, prize money was offered for successful flights, but this time the money had been kept separate from operating expenses. Baldwin constructed two new airships for the July event. The first, much larger than the *Arrow,* he dubbed the *Angelus;* the second he named the *City of Portland.*

Although the *Angelus* was plagued by a series of mechanical problems and eventually ruined, Beachey's handling of the giant ship garnered raves. A feature article by the Associated Press lauding the "Boy Aeronaut" made the rounds in newspapers across America. Described as a "blue-eyed lad of eighteen of retiring disposition who makes daring flights in the big Baldwin airship," Beachey was asked what it felt like to fly.

"There's really nothing to it. It's just the same as being on the ground so far as nervousness is concerned. I stand on this two-inch beam along the under side of the frame work, walk along it when I want to reach some other part of the ship, and think nothing whatever about being 2,000 feet up in the air; all my thoughts are centered on how to make the ship operate as we expect it to do. It's just as safe up there as it is down here if you don't get scared, and scary people have no business in an air ship."[9]

After he switched to the smaller *City of Portland,* Beachey continued to amaze, making the balloon "do practically everything but turn somersaults," until September 26, when he made what the Associated Press called "perhaps the most remarkable flight ever made in an airship."[10]

As reported in the *Los Angeles Herald:*

> Beachey navigated the huge vessel with wonderful dexterity and precision, at all times having it under perfect control. He made one stop on top of the Chamber of Commerce building, where he delivered a letter written by President Goode of the exposition to the chamber of commerce relating to the efforts of that body and the commercial clubs of the city to secure an attendance of 100,000 at the exposition next Saturday—Portland Day. Beachey once more ascended and headed his airship toward the office of the *Oregon Journal,* where he dropped another letter by President Goode. From the *Journal* the airship swiftly made its way to the Oregonian building, where another letter addressed to the *Evening Telegram* was dropped on the roof. From the Oregonian building, Beachey headed westward toward St. Vincent Hospital, maneuvering high in the air for a few minutes. Beachey then headed the airship for the exposition grounds, where he landed safely.[11]

Shortly after the fair closed, the Boy Aeronaut and Cap't Tom had a falling-out, likely over money, and Beachey traveled to Toledo to join Roy Knabenshue as his "assistant." The two began appearing in exhibitions across the nation, splitting large fees. Knabenshue was an excellent pilot, but no one could look good compared to Beachey. He demonstrated such preternatural control of an inherently uncontrollable airship that he could actually maneuver down a narrow street between two rows of tall buildings. Not yet twenty years old, the Boy Aeronaut became a regular feature in newspapers and magazines.

Beachey's burgeoning fame wasn't hurt by a series of near disasters. In one instance, while he was "several hundred feet off the ground," the gasoline tank for the motor sprung a leak and caught fire, threatening to ignite the remaining gasoline and the hydrogen in the balloon. After trying in vain to smother the fire, Beachey leaned over the flimsy rail and opened the relief valve, allowing the remaining gasoline in the tank to run out. With only what "little vapor remained in the engine," Beachey then guided the ship to its ascension point, where the ground crew secured it. When he alighted, both of Beachey's hands were burned.[12] The following year, a broken propeller landed him in the treacherous currents near Hell Gate in New York, where he made his way to a buoy until he could be rescued by a passing boat.[13]

In between mishaps, Beachey set records for altitude and speed, astonishing the thousands who regularly came to see him perform. Beachey's showmanship outdid even Baldwin's. In 1906, just eleven days after he had narrowly escaped death in Cleveland when a propeller cut the gas bag and sent him plummeting one thousand feet to the ground, Beachey drove his airship over the Capitol in Washington, D.C. Congress suspended business for an hour "in joyous, neck craning contemplation." Later, Washingtonians took to pinning a paper to their lapels that read, "Yes, I saw it." Beachey then proceeded to the White House, where he landed on the lawn. After determining President Roosevelt was not at home, Beachey returned to the Capitol, landed nearby, and was treated to lunch by some senators and representatives.

But Thomas Baldwin never backed away from a fight. With Beachey and Knabenshue now his competitors, Baldwin pushed forward with his airship fleet to win back the headlines. After the earthquake destroyed his San Francisco factory in April 1906, he journeyed east to talk over the idea with Curtiss. The talks went so well that Baldwin decided to relocate his manufacturing facility to Hammondsport.

So successful were airships that Baldwin convinced some substantial portion of the general public and an even larger percentage of congressmen that military balloons were the future of aviation, and they began to lose interest in fixed-wing aircraft entirely.

CHAPTER 7

Where No Man Had Gone Before

As Langley and Baldwin had discovered, creating thrust in the air was another problem for which there was no practical model. Wilbur also thought initially to adapt the sort of short, stubby propeller that powered ships, but, like Baldwin, he soon realized that propulsion was one of the areas in which fluid dynamics and aerodynamics diverged.[1] An aircraft would need a longer, thinner device, essentially an airfoil turned to the vertical where lift was converted to thrust. So only weeks after the Wrights returned to Dayton in fall 1902, Orville was at work fashioning an even more precise wind tunnel from which to obtain measurements to design their propulsion system. Eventually, the brothers constructed a cambered pair of propellers out of laminated spruce and then mounted them on sprocketed bicycle chains, twisting one of the chains so that the propellers spun in opposite directions.

The motor seemed to them the simplest part of the puzzle. Any engine that could generate what they had calculated was the minimum eight to nine horsepower and weigh less than 160 pounds would do just fine. The motor would be water cooled and have no carburetor.

Gasoline would drip into the cylinders from a tank mounted above the motor and then mix with air and vaporize due to the heat of the engine. Although the basic design was Orville's, to do the actual machine work and construction the Wrights used their mechanic, Charlie Taylor.

Wilbur Wright's relationship with Octave Chanute during this period remained cordial but also evidenced growing evasiveness. Chanute seemed to have realized that in Wilbur, he was dealing not with a malleable youngster but instead with a confident, strong-willed man who might well be reluctant to share research with anyone he considered a potential competitor or in fact to follow any course that conflicted with his own plans. So, while urging Wilbur to patent his and Orville's invention—which the brothers had every intention of doing anyway—he tried to find ways to bring their work into the light. At their first meeting in 1901, he had convinced Wilbur to write two short articles, "Angle of Incidence," which was published in *Aeronautical Journal,* and "Die Wagerechte Lage Wahrend des Gleitfluges," ("The Horizontal Position During Gliding") published in *Illustrierte Aeronautische Mitteilungen*. Neither of these was particularly elucidatory but they did enter Wilbur in the lists of aviation experimenters.

In September of that year, Chanute asked Wilbur to address the Western Society of Engineers on the gliding experiments. Chanute was president of the group and Wilbur agreed. Although this talk was a good deal more expansive than either of the articles and Wilbur went into some detail about the errors he suspected in Lilienthal's tables, he sloughed over the most important feature of the Kitty Hawk experiments, noting merely, "Our system of twisting the surfaces to regulate the lateral balance was tried and found to be much more effective than shifting the operator's body." The talk was reprinted in the group's journal in December 1901 and then in the Smithsonian Institution Annual Report for 1902.

At this point, as Wilbur's voluminous correspondence bears out, he continued to trust Chanute and exhibited not the slightest hesitation in sharing knowledge. In 1901, for example, Wilbur wrote nearly two dozen letters in which he gave extremely detailed explanations of his theories, experimental results, attempts to solve remaining problems, and even the measurements from which he and Orville were working. Wilbur went so far as to agree to publish results of their wind tunnel tests, the most significant and proprietary data they had produced. The only hesitancy he showed had little to do with aviation. "As to the presence of ladies [at the Western Society of Engineers meeting], it is not my province to dictate, moreover I will already be as badly scared as it is possible for man to be, so that the presence of ladies will make little difference to me, provided I am not expected to appear in full dress, &c."[2]

Chanute for his part provided details of other experiments as well as translations of articles and scientific work by French and German experimenters. On January 10, 1902, Wilbur wrote, "You will understand that your generosity and kindness is appreciated more than I can well express. We thank you most heartily." Although Wilbur declined to appear at St. Louis, that he even considered going public with his work at that point is certainly a testament to his loyalty and to his belief that Chanute was offering productive counsel.

But after the 1902 tests, when Wilbur and Orville were certain success lay just ahead, cracks appeared. On March 23, 1903, the Wrights applied for a patent for a "flying machine," using the 1902 glider as their model. The motor had yet to be built, but the brothers were interested in protecting the means of control, not the power source. Their application was quickly denied; the patent office was not about to grant a patent for a flying machine that had not flown. In his correspondence with Chanute, although Wilbur continued to discuss technical matters in great detail, he specifically avoided mentioning both the application and the rejection.

Chanute gave lectures in Europe, one in which he referred to the Wrights as "his pupils" and "devoted collaborators," and wrote articles on the Wrights' work, none of which met with the slightest objection from Wilbur. In fact, Wilbur expressed gratitude that Chanute had become their conduit to experimenters across the Atlantic. After his return, Chanute visited the brothers in Dayton and Wilbur agreed to once again address the Western Society of Engineers.

In a letter of July 24, 1903, however, after the motor had been built and the propeller problem solved, Wilbur became more assertive. In response to a query as to whether the rear rudder was operative, Wilbur replied, "The vertical tail is operated by wires leading to the wires which connect with the wing tips. Thus the movement of the wing tips operates the rudder. This statement is not for publication, but merely to correct the misapprehension in your own mind. As the laws of France & Germany provide that patents will be held invalid if the matter claimed has been publicly printed we prefer to exercise reasonable caution about the details of our machine until the question of patents is settled. I only see three methods of dealing with this matter: (1) Tell the truth. (2) Tell nothing specific. (3) Tell something not true. I really cannot advise either the first or the third course." That he was following the second course with Chanute himself he did not feel the need to point out.

Chanute's response was a partial retreat. "I was puzzled by the way you put things in your former letters. You were sarcastic and I did not catch the idea that you feared that the description might forestall a patent. Now that I know it, I take pleasure in suppressing the passage altogether. I believe however that it would have proved quite harmless *as the construction is ancient and well known*." Wilbur was having none of it. He reacted with uncharacteristic harshness, telling Chanute in early August he had "entirely mistaken" the objections to making the rudder arrangement public. "The trouble was not that it gave away our secrets, but that it attributed to us *ancient methods we did not use*."[3] Wilbur was particularly adamant that Chanute not mention "the warping of the wings" to anyone.

With Chanute put off, the Wrights attacked the final logistical problem: how to launch the craft. For gliding, the apparatus was dragged to the top of a hill or sand dune and then run down, allowing a combination of gravity and wind to provide the force to lift the glider off the ground. But with the motorized craft weighing in at more than 650 pounds, lugging it up a hill was out of the question. Also, if the Wrights were to gain a patent for having flown "unassisted," launching downhill might invalidate their claim. So Wilbur and Orville settled on a track, eventually sixty feet long, on which the craft, guided by two bicycle wheel hubs, one fore and one aft, would travel until sufficient thrust had been attained to become airborne.

The Wrights arrived at Kitty Hawk in late September and walked into a series of frustrations. The propeller shaft cracked twice and with no means of repair in their desolate surroundings, new equipment had to be brought from Dayton; the motor failed its first tests, not producing sufficient revolutions per minute to get the craft off the ground; the sprockets on the chain connecting the motor to the propellers continued to come loose; the weather turned stormy, precluding any attempt at flight for weeks.

While they waited for their fortunes and the weather to turn, they received word that Langley and Manly were preparing to fly.

On October 7, 1903, with great ceremony, before a gaggle of reporters, scientists, army officers, and government luminaries—but not Langley, who was "detained" in Washington—Langley's manned aerodrome was hoisted to a track laid along the length of the houseboat from which it would be slung by catapult down the Potomac. Charles Manly, who had fashioned a sophisticated, lightweight motor that would generate 50 horsepower, sat in the center, prepared to soar into history. Onlookers stood on the banks of the river, waiting to throw their hats into the air and break into wild cheering. Finally, the stays were removed and a counterweight flung the machine toward the river.

The aerodrome barely cleared the track before it proceeded to drop straight into the Potomac's icy waters. So precipitous was its descent that Manly was lucky to free himself from the wreckage and bob to the surface in the cork vest he had worn to insulate him from the cold.

Langley was eviscerated in the press, front-page fodder across the nation. The *New York Times* headline read, "FLYING MACHINE

FIASCO; Prof. Langley's Airship Proves a Complete Failure. Prof. Manley [*sic*], in the Car of the Aerodrome, Escapes with a Ducking in the Potomac."[4] *The St. Louis Republic* agreed. "Flying Machine Built by Langley an Utter Failure." The San Francisco *Call* added, "Langley's Flying Machine Fails Completely." The following day, the *Times* continued the assault on the editorial page. Under the headline "Flying Machines Which Do Not Fly," the editor wrote, "The ridiculous fiasco which attended the attempt at aerial navigation in the Langley flying machine was not unexpected, unless possibly by the distinguished Secretary of the Smithsonian Institution who devised it, and his assistants."[5]

Undeterred, at least publicly, Langley insisted the principle was sound and that a flaw in the launching mechanism was to blame. He released a statement that said, "The machinery was working perfectly and giving every reason to anticipate a successful flight when this accident, due wholly to the launching ways, drew the aerodrome downward at the moment of release and cast it into the water near the houseboat."[6] Manly stated categorically that he had felt a catch in the

The Langley aerodrome just after takeoff, October 7, 1903. It is already heading into the water.

mechanism at the point of release, which must have been responsible for the aerodrome hitting the water like, as one reporter described it, "a sack of mortar."

The team set to work once more, this time with the perfectionist Langley determined that no flaw in any mechanism would cause him embarrassment. They went over every inch of the aerodrome, the launching track, and the catapult, checking, adjusting, and polishing. Langley also announced he would only launch if the wind was ideal, which meant five miles per hour or less. What the team did not do was reexamine the assumptions under which the aerodrome had been constructed.

On December 6, Langley tried again. Newspapers across the nation once again reported on the attempt and once again the result was a disaster. "A complete wreck," as *The New York Times* observed.

"On the signal to start, the aeroplane glided smoothly along the launching tramway until the end of the slide was reached. Then, left to itself, the aeroplane broke in two and turned completely over, precipitating Prof. Charles Manly, who was operating it, into icy water beneath the tangled mass." Once again Manly was threatened with drowning, and another of Langley's assistants leapt in the water to help drag him to the surface. Langley, who had chosen to be present this time, "was crestfallen when he saw the fruit of months of study, labor, and a great expenditure of money disappear beneath the water, close to where he was standing aboard a tug."[7]

Langley again tried to pass off the failure as a technical defect in the launching mechanism, easily correctable, but this time there were dissenting views. Army engineers who finally studied the design realized that the aerodrome was fatally flawed, lacking both sufficient power and sufficient lift. Going from a model to a full-size aircraft involved computing weight-to-thrust ratios that aerodynamicists had yet to formalize; with no background in mathematics and scant in engineering, Langley had ignored computations of scale and had never realized that it requires eight times the lift to keep a craft double the volume in the air. While the secretary insisted he would conduct another test within days, the army decided they had spent $50,000 on a boondoggle. Joseph Taylor Robinson, a congressman from Arkansas, was quoted as observing, "The only thing [Langley] ever made fly was government money."[8] Langley abandoned aviation and died a defeated man only three years later, never able to discern why he had been so stunningly unsuccessful.

While the press and the public came away from the aerodrome's spectacular failures with renewed doubts about powered flight, the Wrights were nearing the moment that Langley had so desperately craved.

The only good news the Wrights had in October was Langley's debacle. "I see that Langley has had his fling and failed," Wilbur wrote to Chanute on October 16. "It seems to be our turn to throw now, and I wonder what our luck will be."

Whether the motor, at 12 horsepower, would be strong enough to lift the machine off the ground was very much at issue. Chanute, who visited for a week in November at Wilbur's urging, said that according to his calculations the Wrights' propulsion system would lose so much power as it transferred through the elements that what remained might not generate sufficient thrust. Chanute was not being an alarmist; Wilbur had come to the same conclusion. After Chanute left, Wilbur and Orville fine-tuned the motor and the drivetrain as best they could until they felt confident that the machine could achieve the needed thrust. Before they could run a test, however, the propeller shaft suffered its second crack, sending Orville back to Dayton.

Virtually at the moment Orville finished repairing the shaft, Samuel Langley's aerodrome suffered its second ignominious plunge into the Potomac. Three days later, December 11, Orville arrived at Kitty Hawk.

On December 14, 1903, the Wrights made their first attempt. Wilbur had done all the initial tests previously but for this historic event the brothers flipped a coin. Wilbur won. He and Orville grasped their hands together but said nothing. Wilbur then took his prone position on the lower wing, slipped into the hip cradle, pushed the lever to engage the magneto that would start the motor, and waited as Orville stood at the end of one of the wings, steadying the craft for its run down the track.

The machine picked up speed too quickly for Orville to keep up—they had chosen a slight downhill for the attempt—and once free of the track, it nosed up, stalled, then came down, less than fifty feet away. An elevator support was damaged in the crash but there was little other damage and, most important, Wilbur was unhurt.

Despite the failure of the first attempt, the brothers both knew the problems were minor. Three days later, they tried again. Orville was up, so just after ten thirty in the morning, he took his place on the lower wing. An icy wind was blowing from the north—optimal to generate lift but less so for lying in a machine moving into the teeth of it. Orville had set up a camera at the near end of the track and asked John Daniels, one of the local men who'd helped them for three years, to snap a picture at the moment of launch.

First flight. One of the best-known photographs in the world.

Once again the motor was started and Wilbur ran along holding one of the wing tips to steady it. This time there was no glitch. The aircraft took off at the end of the track and flew; only 120 feet perhaps, but those forty yards were the first ever traveled in a controlled, powered, heavier-than-air flight by a human being. Even the photograph was perfect. Daniels caught the machine just as it left the ground, Wilbur in mid-stride at its right. No image is more famous.

The Wrights made three more flights that day, the last of which was a remarkable 852 feet by Wilbur. After they had finished, a gust of wind blew over the world's first airplane, the Flyer, as they named it, damaging it sufficiently that the Wrights decided not to waste their time on repairs. As Wilbur and Orville saw it, their prototype was already obsolete. Their plans called for a model vastly improved and they intended to lose no time in creating it.

CHAPTER 8

Patent Pioneering

To what degree the Wrights wanted to inform the public of their success has always been a matter of confusion, shared perhaps by Wilbur and Orville themselves. On December 17, the day of the flights, Orville sent a telegram to his father. "Success. Four flights Thursday morning all against twenty-one mile wind. Started from level with engine power alone. Average speed through air, thirty-one miles. Longest 57 seconds. Inform press. Home Christmas."* But Wilbur also sent a curt telegram to Octave Chanute on December 28 that said merely, "We are giving no pictures nor description of machine or methods at present."

Upon receipt of the December 17 telegram, Bishop Wright sent his son Lorin to *The Dayton Journal* but the editor did not consider a fifty-seven-second flight newsworthy. "If it had been fifty-seven minutes, then it might have been a news item," the editor sniffed. The following day, however, a report appeared in the *Virginian-Pilot* that was later picked up by newspapers across America. The *Pilot* reported

* Orville also wrote an undated note to Milton that read, "Misjudgment at start reduced flight to hundred and twelve. Power and control ample. Rudder only injured. Success assured. Keep quiet." But this was almost certainly written after Wilbur's aborted flight on December 14.

that on a machine with "two six-blade propellers, one arranged just below the frame so as to exert an upward force when in motion and the other extending horizontally to the rear from the center of a car, furnishing the forward impetus," Wilbur Wright "flew for three miles in the face of a wind blowing at a registered velocity of 21 miles per hour, then gracefully descended to earth at the spot selected by the man in the navigator's car as a suitable landing place." There were no photographs of the craft, which of course did not exist, nor any real detail of the flights. Many of the more prominent newspapers such as *The New York Times* and *The Washington Post* ignored the story altogether.

By the beginning of 1904, a corrected account appeared in *The Cincinnati Enquirer*. This version, supplied by Wilbur and Orville, provided an accurate version of the events in North Carolina and included photographs of the brothers and of the glider (but not the powered craft) in flight. The story was also picked up by a number of newspapers from Virginia to Hawaii, along with Wilbur's statement verbatim, but it was generally treated in a low-key fashion.[1] Why the Wrights' achievement did not receive the sort of triumphant headlines that would have greeted Langley's success remains a mystery. Perhaps the spectacular assertions were difficult to take seriously after the aerodrome's equally spectacular failure. *The New York Times,* for example, continued to ignore the Wrights and at the end of January 1904 was still reporting on the Langley machine as if it were still the big news in aviation; at the end of February, *The Washington Times* reported on the Wrights' machine as if it were a glorified Lilienthal glider.

There were those, however, who took the story very seriously indeed. On December 26, the Wrights received an extraordinary letter from Augustus Herring. "I want to congratulate you on your success at Kitty Hawk," he began, "and I want to write you a frank, straightforward letter."

What followed was anything but. "To begin with," Herring observed, "I do not know the construction of your power machine any more than you know the details of my latest but since it too is operative and represents a gasoline driven two surface machine reduced to near its simplest form it seems more than probable that our work is going to result in interference suits in the Patent Office and a loss in value of the work owing to there being competition." Even by Herring's standards this statement was astonishing in its mendacity. There was, of course, no "latest"; Herring had not succeeded in powered flight since his compressed-air model five years before, and he had no design with even a vague hope of satisfying a patent examiner. "I don't think litigation would benefit either of us if we can come to agreement otherwise," he added, "because there will be enough money to be made out of it to satisfy us all." Herring could not have realized how laughable was an attempt to threaten the litigious Wrights with a lawsuit. He went on to detail the "long and faithful" work he had devoted to the "problem" and how he "spent my fortune and all my earnings on it almost to my last dollar."

Herring then attempted to convince Wilbur and Orville that despite anything Octave Chanute might have said, he had designed both the Chanute glider and a powered machine that had traveled seventy-two feet and could be "reconstructed and flown." Here was the first example of a gambit Herring would employ repeatedly and with great success to hoodwink future business partners—that he had applied for and in some cases been granted a series of patents that could be used to obtain licensing fees from virtually anyone who subsequently succeeded in powered flight.

Finally, Herring came to it. "Now the point is this: If you turn your invention into a company, I want to be represented in it—not solely because it is in my interests but because it would probably be equally much in yours." Herring then listed six points in which he asserted that although the machines were similar, his was designed with a more efficient engine, "more reliable for long flights," and that he had developed an "efficient means for keeping the equilibrium automatically." This is one boast that was at least partly justified. Herring had long advocated the use of a gyroscope as a controller to achieve automatic lateral stability. Of course, Herring claimed to have *built* a machine with automatic lateral control—yet another claim that was patently false. As far as anyone could tell, he had never even tested the concept in a prototype.

Herring concluded, "Would you consider joining forces and acting as one party in order to get the best terms, broadest patent claims and to avoid future litigation?" He proposed a two-thirds and one-third split, generously offering Wilbur and Orville the larger share.

The Wrights dismissed Herring's proposal out of hand. They had seen for themselves that Herring's designs didn't work. As Wilbur wrote to Chanute, "This time [Herring] surprised us. Before he left camp in 1902 we foresaw and predicted the object of his visit to Washington, we also felt certain that he was making a frenzied attempt to mount a motor on a copy of our 1902 glider and thus anticipate us, even before you told us of it last fall. But that he would have the effrontery to write us such a letter, after his other schemes of rascality had failed, was really a little more than we expected."[2]

Uncertainty about publicity aside, what is not at issue is the Wrights' plans for their invention. They had decided to seek not only to protect their invention with a patent, but to establish a monopoly under which every manner of controlled flight would fall.[3]

Their patent application in 1902 demonstrated the need for expert help, so two weeks into 1904, they contacted Harry A. Toulmin, an experienced patent attorney in Springfield, Ohio. Toulmin's initial reply to the "Wright Cycle Co." was perfunctory. A second letter, on January 19, this time to Wilbur, set his fee at eighty dollars and advised that the patent be sought as a "soaring machine," not a "flying machine." If the Wrights wanted to apply for the latter, meaning a machine with a motor, "there will be all possible objections raised, a working model, and a demonstration of the operativeness of the device as a flying machine will be insisted upon, and the matter will probably require our personal attention at Washington. For this kind of work we shall be obliged to charge you, in addition to traveling expenses, our per diem rate of $30 for such time as we shall give to the matter."[4]

So the decision was made to pursue a patent for the glider and control system only, avoiding mention of any power source, although later Toulmin modified his view to file "in such a way as to not exclude its being construed as covering a flying machine." Wilbur also engaged Toulmin to apply for patents in England, France, Germany, Austria, Italy, Russia, and Belgium.

The application Harry Toulmin filed with the United States Patent Office in March 1904 would set the course of American aviation for the next thirteen years. Rather than simply specify the elements of Wilbur's wing-warping system as a mechanical construction, Toulmin expanded the notion of wing warping to cover any system where the angle of any device at the wing tips varied the "lateral margins" in opposite directions from the angle of wings at the center.[5] Thus Toulmin altered the patent from seeking exclusivity for a *device* to seeking exclusivity for an *idea,* the principle of lateral control itself. If such a patent was granted and ratified by the courts, it would apply to configurations that the Wrights themselves had not employed or even conceived of and so virtually no aircraft could subsequently be flown

Orville making a right turn, demonstrating the warping of the wings.

without licensing by Orville and Wilbur, precisely the breadth they were seeking.

Ten years earlier, Toulmin's audacity would likely have resulted in a rejection or at least a drastic narrowing of scope. But in 1898, patent law had undergone a profound change; a new and special category of license called a "pioneer patent" had been created by the Supreme Court. In *Westinghouse v. Boyden Power Brake Co.,* Justice Henry Billings Brown had written that "a patent covering a function never before performed, a wholly novel device, or one of such novelty and importance as to mark a distinct step in the progress of the art . . . is entitled to a broad range of equivalents."* Brown did not find "pioneer patent" in the law—no such designation has ever been stipulated in any American statute. Brown's ruling was "jurisprudential," applied or simply created by judges based on their interpretation of either the Constitution or the common law. "Pioneer patents," it was further decided, could not be granted to anyone who merely improves or refines an idea nor can it be the first such patent published in the national registry. But those successful in attaining pioneer status would enjoy an enormous advantage in any subsequent legal action, as a court would generally rule that the patent has been infringed even by a product whose character seems only peripherally related to the plaintiff's design.

Patents are widely accepted even among fierce advocates of free trade as necessary to protect innovation, the lifeblood of economic progress, and Brown's opinion came in a period where corporate and monopoly rights were protected by the Court to a degree never seen

* 170 U.S. 537, 561-62 (1898). The case involved braking systems used to slow railroad trains. The opinion upheld the Westinghouse patent in its broadest application; Justice Brown had been an attorney for the railroads before being named to the bench. Brown added, "Most conspicuous examples of such patents are the one to Howe, of the sewing machine; to Morse, of the electrical telegraph; and to Bell, of the telephone." Two years earlier, Brown had written the opinion for which he is best remembered in *Plessy v. Ferguson,* which upheld the doctrine of "separate but equal" and ushered in the era of Jim Crow.

before or since in American history. Twelve years before *Westinghouse,* in *Santa Clara v. Southern Pacific Railroad,* Chief Justice Morrison Waite first indicated that a corporation enjoyed the same Fourteenth Amendment protections as an individual citizen. In 1905, in *Lochner v. New York,* the Court struck down a state law that attempted to limit bakery workers to a ten-hour day, which ushered in three decades of the justices voiding laws attempting to regulate conditions in the workplace on the vague and since discredited notion of "liberty of contract." Toulmin never discussed whether he had filed his application based on *Westinghouse,* but since it was the most important patent case decided in the previous decade, he could hardly have been unaware of how fertile the possibilities it presented to his clients.

The stakes for the Wrights increased exponentially. While working to improve and refine their machine to create a salable model from the prototype, they needed not only to protect against the copying of their wing-warping construction, but also to prevent anyone else from developing a similar device before their patent was granted. Pioneer status was not retroactive.

As with the tests at Kitty Hawk, Wilbur and Orville set to work not in secrecy but wrapped in an odd cloak of invisibility. Rather than return to North Carolina, they secured the use of a hundred-acre meadow called Huffman Prairie to experiment and test-fly improved variations of the Flyer. This they did in full view of the local population, answering questions of any newspapermen who happened along—there were few—while still being largely ignored by the popular press. Once more, they neither shunned attention nor sought it.

The Wrights' decision to pursue the Flyer's development in twilight deepened their conflict with Octave Chanute. When Chanute had encouraged them to seek a patent for their invention, he assumed they would seek protection merely for the mechanics of the wing-warping system. He complained to a friend that the Wrights had become "secretive," and wrote to Wilbur, "You talked while I was in camp of giving your performance, if successful, all the publicity possible, and you knew that I would not divulge the construction of your machine as I have never disclosed more than you yourself have published. Your telegram indicated a change of policy which you can more fully impart when I see you."[6] Chanute, having experienced what he considered a deceitful grab for credit by Herring, began to suspect that Wilbur would behave in the same fashion. "In the clipping which you sent me you say: 'All the experiments have been conducted at our own expense, without assistance from *any* individual or institution.' Please write me just what you had in your mind concerning myself when you framed that sentence in that way."[7]

Chanute was more than a bit disingenuous here, seeing how he called the Wrights his "pupils" in Europe and added that Wilbur and Orville were bringing "his designs" to fruition. And in an article in *The St. Louis Republic* on January 4, 1904, announcing his appointment to the coming fair, it was said that "the Wright brothers of Dayton, O., who have recently made the first real flight ever made with a machine not employing gas and heavier-than-air, profited by and followed up to a successful conclusion the experiments originally made by Mr. Chanute."

Although Chanute would continue to insist that he had never intended to deny the Wrights full credit for their invention—and perhaps he was just an old man guilty of overstatement—there is little doubt that he saw his role as far more than fatherly inspiration.

Wilbur's reply bore similar disingenuousness.

> The object of the statement, concerning which you have made inquiry, was to make it clear that we stood on quite different ground from Prof. Langley, and were entirely justified in refusing to make our discoveries public property at this time. We had paid the freight, and had a right to do as we pleased. The use of the word "any," which you underscored, grew out of the fact that we found from articles in both foreign and American papers, and even in correspondence, that there was a somewhat general impression

> that our Kitty Hawk experiments had not been carried on at our own expense, &c. We thought it might save embarrassment to correct this promptly.[8]

Despite this exchange, correspondence between Wilbur and the man who would be his mentor remained frequent, with the pleasant tone that had characterized their previous letters. But Wilbur had made his course clear and Chanute was now powerless to influence the two most important people in the field in which he had toiled selflessly for more than a decade. He visited Dayton later in January and once more urged Wilbur to participate in the St. Louis Exposition. The air show, after all, had been put off a year and Wilbur's previous objection that a glider would be maneuvered out of a prize by Santos-Dumont was moot. Wilbur gave Chanute the courtesy of accompanying him, with Orville, to St. Louis to inspect the fairgrounds, but then once more declined to participate.

Instead, Wilbur and Orville repaired to Huffman Prairie to pursue their monopoly, confident the groundbreaking innovations in their design would keep them well ahead of any potential competitor. The race might be against time but the time, as the Wrights saw it, was long and their lead insurmountable.

Yet, like their second season at Kitty Hawk, 1904 turned out to be a frustrating muddle. They began with great confidence; Orville had built a second, more powerful motor and the Wrights modified the design of the wings, the bracing, and the elevator. But as Langley had discovered, moving from a successful prototype to a machine that could sustain flight sufficiently to interest buyers—especially military buyers—proved more difficult than they anticipated.

Their troubles began almost immediately. Rumors of their activities had continued to surface, generally accompanied by either incorrect or fanciful descriptions of their machine. In May, perhaps to set the matter straight or in response to Chanute's prodding but more likely in a reflection of their own uncertainty, the Wrights invited the press to a demonstration of powered flight. But they chose to do so without first testing the newly designed Flyer; public flight would be the craft's inauguration.

The result was a boondoggle. On the first day, with about forty reporters present—no photographs were allowed—the Flyer refused to leave the ground in calm winds. After two days of bad-weather delays, the brothers succeeded into coaxing the Flyer into a jaunt of only thirty feet. "Then the Machine Dropped to Earth," read the headline in one of the few newspapers that reported the event. Most of the remaining reporters left muttering that these Dayton boys were no better than Langley.

Throughout the season, the Wrights found themselves less successful than with the Kitty Hawk machine. Huffman Prairie lacked the steady winds of the Outer Banks but did possess enough bumps and ruts to make laying a track for launch almost impossible. By the summer, the sixty feet along the North Carolina sand had stretched to 240 feet across uneven Ohio meadowland. And if the wind shifted, as it often did, the track had to be shifted along with it. When Wilbur or Orville was successful in getting the Flyer into the air, the results were maddeningly inconsistent. Sometimes the craft would soar, sometimes it would drop.

The May fiasco turned out to be serendipitous; the Wrights were free to experiment and try to solve problems without their every failure reported in the newspapers. The first order of business was to change the launch mechanism. Two hundred feet of track was unworkable, so they set up an awkward, complicated pulley and weight system to replace it.* A twenty-foot-high pyramid-shaped scaffold held a 1,600-pound weight at the pinnacle. A forty-foot track ran from the base of the scaffolding with ropes and pulleys going from the weight to the bottom of the scaffolding, then out to the end of the track and back. The Flyer was positioned at the base of the pyramid and attached to the rope. When the weight was dropped, the aircraft

* At this point, the Wrights, despite their bicycle background, never considered wheels. The Flyer was fitted with skids for landing.

The Wrights' derrick launcher. This cumbersome mechanism would be supplanted by Curtiss's wheeled takeoff.

was pulled down the track and launched. Unwieldy as the arrangement sounds, it worked. From September when it was first employed to year's end, the flights became much longer.

Although the flying remained unpredictable, there was progress—and with progress came a decision. Newspapermen would no longer be welcome at Huffman Prairie. Wilbur wrote to Chanute on October 5, "Intelligence of what we are doing is gradually spreading through the neighborhood and we are fearful that we will soon have to discontinue experiments. As we have decided to keep our experiments strictly secret for the present, we are becoming uneasy about continuing them much longer at our present location. In fact, it is a question whether we are not ready to begin considering what we will do with our baby now that we have it."

The American press might have decided they were likely frauds, but the Wrights were not dismissed everywhere. Chanute's drumbeating had aroused a good deal of interest in Europe, particularly in his native France. The French considered themselves proprietary founders of aviation science. French experimenters raised a patriotic call for their nation not to cede supremacy in powered flight to uncultured Americans.

Wilbur and Orville seemed to understand that the risk from the Continent exceeded anything that existed at home. Their correspondence with Harry Toulmin during the second half of 1904 is almost entirely devoted to the various European patents they were pursuing. Finally, France, Great Britain, and Belgium approved their applications but German requirements were more stringent and the process was delayed. With patents in hand in two of the three biggest overseas markets, Wilbur and Orville decided not to wait until the Flyer had been perfected to pursue the main goal of their plan.

CHAPTER 9

The Vagaries of the Marketplace

On January 3, 1905, the Wrights visited their congressman, Robert Nevin, at his Dayton home. At his request, they followed with a letter on January 18. In it they claimed their machine had been "fitted for practical use," that it "flies through the air at high speed." They did admit that their "experience in handling the machine has been too short to give any high degree of skill," but noted that "toward the end of the season" they made "two flights of five minutes each," in which they "covered five miles at thirty-five miles an hour." They then asserted, "Flying has been brought to a point where it can be made of great practical use in various ways," suggesting "scouting and carrying messages in time of war." While the details were accurate, the letter implied a degree of consistency and technological advancement that the Wrights had yet to achieve. The Flyer was not at all ready to be employed as a military asset. Nonetheless, the potential revenues from any nation that saw the wisdom of obtaining a monopoly on motorized flight were vast and, with their American patent still pending, the temptation for Wilbur and Orville to try to cash in on their invention with one giant stroke must have been irresistible.

Nevin promised to deliver the letter personally to Secretary of War William Howard Taft. The congressman took ill, however, and his aide passed the letter on to the army's Board of Ordnance and Fortification. But the army had no further interest in writing checks on the vacant assurances of would-be inventors. "The Board has found it necessary to decline to make all allotments for the experimental development of devices for mechanical flight," the commanding general wrote back, and the Wrights' machine "has not yet been brought to the stage of practical operation." The army response has been held up as the model of shortsightedness in most accounts of the period, but the general was correct. The Wrights might one day produce a machine with practical military application, but they were not there yet. Nor had they included any proof that their assertions were rooted in fact. And while the Wrights had not requested funds for development, it was clear in their letter that they were not offering their machine to their country out of patriotism.

The British, however, were not in a similar rush to issue a "flat turn down," as Wilbur put it. Once he received what he considered an insulting reply from the army, Wilbur plowed ahead. An official at the War Office asked for terms and Wilbur offered a machine that would fly at least ten miles, perhaps as far as fifty. Of course, the Wrights hadn't approached even the low number. The War Office replied that the terms were acceptable but they could not consider a machine that went less than fifty miles. In late April, the British offered to send an attaché to observe the Flyer in Dayton. Wilbur accepted, though it is uncertain what he intended to say when the Flyer could stay in the air for only twenty seconds and then more often than not crashed. A new model was in the works but had yet to be tested. While he waited for the attaché to arrive, Wilbur wrote to Chanute, "We would be ashamed of ourselves if we had offered our machine to a foreign government without giving our own country a shot at it, but our consciences are clear."

In the end, the issue was moot; the attaché wasn't coming. Without communicating the change of plan to the Wrights, he left for an extended assignment in Mexico and would not return until October.

But the delay turned out to be fortuitous. The 1905 model, despite a number of improvements and modifications—the most important of which was to separate control of the tail rudder from the wing-warping harness—achieved no better results than the previous year's. If anything, the crashes and damage to the Flyer had gotten more severe. By the end of August, a good deal of tinkering had borne no fruit.*

In early September, they identified the problem. The size and placement of the forward elevator was changed and the Flyer suddenly began to live up to its name. Flights became longer, more graceful, and more controlled. By early October, they were staying in the air for thirty minutes, covering more than twenty miles, and landing not because of problems, but because they ran out of gas.

With the British attaché still unaccounted for, Wilbur and Orville once more looked to their own government. Four days after Wilbur flew for forty minutes, the Wrights wrote directly to the secretary of war. Without mentioning that they had already offered the Flyer to the British, they referred to their "informal offer" of "some months ago," then asserted, "We do not wish to take this invention abroad, unless we find it necessary to do so, and therefore write again, renewing the offer." They proposed a series of trials in which the Flyer would travel up to one hundred miles (but at least twenty-five) at thirty miles per hour or more, with price on a sliding scale based on performance. Once again, Wilbur and Orville included no photographs nor proof that they had created a machine that actually flew.

They received a two-paragraph reply from the Board of Ordnance and Fortification, the first of which was a rejection virtually

* The only positive development for the Wright family, and even that was mixed, was the clearing of Milton Wright's name. Wilbur had prepared a detailed, scrupulously researched paper that demonstrated that virtually everything his father had said about misuse of church funds and the duplicity of Millard Keiter was true. At a general conference of the Old Constitution sect, the Wrights' position was accepted and the matter was closed. But although Bishop Wright was restored to his previous position, he was by then seventy-seven and effectively retired from church leadership.

verbatim to that of the previous January. The second paragraph was equally dismissive. Before a contract could be entered into, the board wanted to know the cost and date of delivery "with such drawings and descriptions thereof that are necessary to enable its construction to be understood and a definite conclusion as to its practicability to be arrived at." Wilbur and Orville, who already believed the board was populated by dolts, declined to tip their hand. Instead, virtually the day after they received the letter from Washington, they rekindled their offer to Great Britain and also offered the Flyer to the French.

To the British, they guaranteed a fifty-mile minimum. To interest the French, the Wrights wrote to Ferdinand Ferber, a French army officer and aviation pioneer with whom they had been in touch after an introduction from Octave Chanute. Ferber had built successful gliders based on the Wright model and, encouraged by Chanute, had inquired about purchasing a Flyer three months before. By November, Ferber had conducted some preliminary experiments in motorized flight.

Although the Wrights were aware that Ferber's designs would fail, they heaped praise on his efforts, adding, "France is indeed fortunate in finding a Ferber." Although "France already has reached a high degree of success," they added, "it may wish to avail itself of our discoveries, partly to complement its own work; or perhaps partly to accurately inform itself of the state of the art as it will exist in those countries which buy the secrets of our motor machine." They then offered the Flyer to France at what they described as the bargain price of one million francs, or $200,000, more than they had asked of either the United States or Great Britain.

That the Wrights would indulge in such uncharacteristic fawning seems to indicate a growing need to interest *someone* in their invention. But they had made another decision that would make a sale only more difficult. After the October flight, increasingly concerned that their design would be stolen, they decided to do no more public flying. A signed contract would be prerequisite to a demonstration. The

Wrights were willing to forgo payment if the machine did not perform as advertised, but anyone who bought either an airplane or the design would be forced to do so without having first seen the airplane in flight.

That chimerical decision coincided with the return of the British attaché from Mexico, by then prepared to recommend purchase of a Flyer after the demonstration he had been promised months earlier. When Orville explained that the rules had changed, offering statements of witnesses and photographs of the Flyer in the air in lieu of an actual flight, the attaché was flummoxed. "Many people, you tell me," he wrote, "have seen flights on Oct 3, 4 & 5. I only want to see one too."[1]

But the Wrights were as always uncompromising and ultimately the British government declined to accede to the Wrights' terms. As 1906 began, the Wright Flyer remained the only successful airplane and the brothers' technological advantage was vast, but neither Wilbur nor Orville seemed to grasp that no lead is insurmountable if you stop running before you've reached the finish line.

CHAPTER 10

The Inexorable Progression of Knowledge

On January 1, 1906, the *New-York Tribune* noted in passing: "The Wright Brothers, of Dayton, Ohio, are said to have made no less than fifty short flights with [an aeroplane]." One week later, *The New York Times* ran a feature article in which "two young brothers . . . sons of a minister now residing in Dayton, Ohio . . . [who had been] experimenting in strict secrecy for several years" had succeeded constructing a flying machine "propelled by its own power, without any aid of balloon or gas bag." The article went into great detail about both the machine and its performance and was atypical of those generally written about the Wrights in that it was largely accurate.

These articles and a number of others were the result of a different story about the Wrights, one that was printed in newspapers from Washington, D.C., to San Francisco. "France to Buy Yankee Airship," the headline read. A private consortium of French industrialists using government financing offered a $5,000 option on the agreed $200,000 purchase price. The syndicate would have until April 5, 1906, to deposit the remaining funds at Morgan Bank's Paris office, at which time the Wrights would produce their airplane for testing. Even bet-

Close-up view of the Wright Flyer, including the pilot and passenger seats.

ter, Wilbur and Orville would not be precluded from also selling the machine to the United States military.

The conditions were significant because the Wrights had learned that their patent application was near to being approved. Minor changes to the drawings and descriptions were all that were left of the patent examiner's two-year string of objections.*

Unwilling to deposit $195,000 on a promise, the French sent a three-man commission to Dayton to see a demonstration without first asking permission of the Wrights. Incredibly, Wilbur and Orville refused even to show the delegation the aircraft, once again offering only witness testimonials and photographs to prove their claims.

Although the members of the delegation were convinced the Wright airplane could fly, the French ministry refused to move for-

* Toulmin had been correct: The Wrights had asked that references to motorized flight be reinserted and the examiner ordered them removed.

ward without some notion of how far, how fast, and how high the Flyer could go. The Wrights, it seemed, had competition. Another article appeared in American newspapers in early January, one that the brothers apparently missed. "Santos-Dumont has abandoned for the present the gas bag type of airship, of whose possibilities he has given the world the most striking demonstration. He is now working on the principle in which Maxim, Langley, Chanute, and the Wright brothers have had such faith."

Santos-Dumont was revered in France, thought a genius. His balloon trips down the Champs-Élysées had become legendary. He had returned to France from St. Louis muttering of skulduggery, and at home in Paris, once more a hero, he changed his focus from gas bags to the box kite.

He was also intimate with the elite in every corner of French society, including the government. If Santos-Dumont intended to create a flying machine similar to the one under consideration, he should certainly be given the opportunity. And if he was successful, he would hardly charge his government one million francs for its design.

The ministers sent a telegram to Dayton adding conditions to the sale, such as a requirement that the airplane reach an altitude of one thousand feet, be delivered by August 1, 1906, and be exclusive to France, which the Wrights "at once rejected." Instead, they proposed extending the option period one year if the French would extend the delivery date until October 1 and waive the exclusivity provision with regard to the United States entirely. The option lapsed. Soon afterward, the Wrights agreed to France's terms but the war ministry refused to reopen negotiations. Wilbur and Orville got to keep the $5,000 but lost the opportunity for a far greater payday. Even worse, despite what seemed irrefutable proof that they had actually flown, whisperings began that they were simply a couple of bluffers who were attempting to perpetrate an elaborate hoax.

But for every skeptic, there was a convert. In April 1906, *Scientific American,* which had earlier scoffed at the Wrights' claims, ate a good bit of crow:

> When the list of their flights given above was first announced last December in France, it was incredible to many people both there and here that so novel a device as a flying machine could be operated frequently for nearly six months in the vicinity of a large city without the fact becoming generally known. The Wrights refused to make a statement, and they gave the names of but a few persons who had seen them fly. With the communication recently sent by them to the Aero Club, however, they sent a list of names of seventeen men who were eye-witnesses of their experiments. In order to dispel any lingering doubt regarding the flights, the reported accounts of which the leading German aeronautical journal, *Illustrirte Aeronautische Mitteilungen,* characterized as "ein Amerikanischer bluff," a list of questions was sent to the seventeen witnesses. In all we received eleven replies.

The editor eventually wrote, "In all the history of invention, there is probably no parallel to the unostentatious manner in which the Wright brothers of Dayton, Ohio, ushered into the world their epoch-making invention." The magazine expressed the hope that the Wrights would share their invention with an eager world. But rather than respond with a public flight, Wilbur and Orville dug in their heels. Wilbur wrote to Chanute on April 28, "Our position is constantly becoming stronger in other countries and we will soon find a sale somewhere. The French will buy eventually and probably under less favorable circumstances than today." Whether this was bluff or self-delusion is not clear, but in no other country was a sale in the offing and the Wrights would never receive as much money from the French as they lost on this deal. In that same letter, Wilbur informed Chanute that their U.S. patent application finally had been approved.

That the Wrights' achievements could exist in such uncertainty is not surprising; the news media of the early 1900s were fragmented and often contradictory. Rumor and falsehood often masqueraded as fact; two opposing versions of the same story appearing in different newspapers in the same city would arouse no curiosity from readers. Thus while the paucity of hard evidence of the Wrights' flying would arouse skepticism in some, a wealth of anecdotal evidence would persuade others, particularly those with some knowledge of aviation. The Aero Club of America, for example, a group of wealthy and influential balloon enthusiasts who had established their organization as an offshoot of the Auto Club, attested to the Wrights' claims.

Sufficient was the word of mouth about the brothers from Dayton that in May 1906, Glenn Curtiss wrote to the Wrights in an attempt to persuade them to mount a Curtiss motor on the Flyer. As he was scheduled to be in Columbus for a balloon exhibition with Baldwin, he offered to travel to Dayton to discuss the matter. Although the light and powerful Curtiss motor would make the Flyer more attractive to the military, the brothers were not about to deal with outsiders. They declined.

In early September 1906, Curtiss and Baldwin returned to Ohio for another balloon exhibition, this time at the Dayton Fair. The Wrights were curious about Baldwin and the four met at the fairgrounds. Wilbur and Orville even helped Baldwin retrieve his airship when a wind blew it from its mooring. The Wrights and Curtiss were each impressed with the intelligence and acumen of the other. Wilbur and Orville invited Curtiss to visit their shop. What followed was the most important and controversial meeting in early aviation history.

Not in dispute was that Wilbur and Orville showed Curtiss photographs of their machine in flight—the same photographs that had been offered to the British and the French—but not an actual airplane. The three also had a long and amicable discussion in which they exchanged a good bit of expertise. Curtiss was justly proud of his lightweight motors and the Wrights of their Flyer. But was Curtiss pumping the brothers for technical information that he could then use to create his own airplane? Had he even considered trying his hand at fixed-wing flight? Or did the discussion never go beyond means of propulsion? None of those questions has ever been definitively answered and in the dispute that followed the fault line runs directly through whichever interpretation of that meeting one ascribes.

On September 22, Curtiss wrote to the Wrights from Hammondsport, noting that he had achieved efficiencies by cutting away a bit of the inner surfaces of propellers "so as to reduce the resistance and allow it to speed up." Wright advocates claim this suggestion was gleaned from the Wrights, although it would appear from the wording that Curtiss was experimenting on his own. They also cite this letter as proof of Curtiss's nefarious intent, evidence that he was contemplating a move to fixed-wing aircraft, although, again, nothing in the letter gives any such indication. What is more, Curtiss supporters assert that had his intention been to steal the Wrights' ideas, he certainly wouldn't have rushed to inform them of it. And Curtiss also wrote, "Mr. Baldwin spoke of you yesterday and mentioned that he meant to write you and thank you for interest and services at his first opportunity. Expect that he will be pretty busy, however, for a few weeks yet." And Curtiss closed, "Hoping to hear from you at your convenience."[1]

It would seem that the most that can be inferred from this letter is that the Wrights and Curtiss discussed propeller design, which no one has questioned, and that Curtiss wanted to keep the channel of communication open. He viewed the Wrights at that point as potential customers and so his tone was polite and as warm as possible for men who had known one another only briefly. The claim that Curtiss was announcing a theft of ideas, in effect declaring war, seems absurd.

But, as future events would bear out, Curtiss must have walked away from that meeting with *something*. That over the next two years he would simply conjure up the designs that were to make him one of the world's preeminent figures in aviation without any impetus from what he saw and heard in Dayton seems equally absurd.

The difficulty here has been the propensity of aviation historians to extrapolate from the later feud and assume an equally adversarial relationship in 1906. Far more likely, what took place in the wake of the Dayton meeting was grounded in the same clash of philosophies that manifested itself in the patent wars. The Wrights were convinced they owned lateral stability and that anyone who developed any system based on the notion of redirecting airflow in opposite directions on either side of the aircraft—"altering lateral margins"—had stolen from them. Curtiss believed, as did most others at the time, that fundamental ideas, even great scientific insights, were public domain and that only mechanical devices or specific applications were proprietary. Curtiss doubtless learned of the fundamentals of lateral control from the Wrights, perhaps even the details of wing warping, but believed that he had every right to create a system that was competitive—or superior—even though based on the same abstract principles. Unlike some of the other great pioneers, Curtiss never employed wing warping, never even experimented with it. Thus both Curtiss and the Wrights could be equally convinced of their own rectitude and, at least to this point, no deceit or malfeasance need be assumed.

Baldwin remained above the fray, convinced at least for the moment that the future of aviation lay in balloons. For his shortsightedness, Cap't Tom was rewarded when the War Department bought a dirigible for the U.S. Army Signal Corps for $10,000.

Baldwin's belief in dirigibles was a mixture of the fanciful and the prescient. "It is no idle dream to prophesy that in future years people will have their airships, just as they have had their bicycles and automobiles, for a period of practical development is at hand when the construction of airships will be so simplified that the cost will be greatly lessened. I have a son twelve years of age, and I believe he will live to see the day of airships under perfect control, floating over the cities. What a revolution all this would make in industrial projects, and what a revolution it would make in our roads—no one can obtain title deeds in the blue sky or right of way to the milky way, it will be free alike to the poor man, as well as to the wealthy autocrat, a universal byway of communication between the countries of the whole world." Although he may have had the vehicle wrong, his view of the future was correct. "I am led to believe that within the next quarter of a century great things will be achieved in the line of aerial navigation, and that we shall have not only airships for rich men's pleasure, but that they will also be utilized as a means of transport for both passengers and goods, utilizing a right of way in the sky and the 'high seas' of the infinite space."[2]

CHAPTER 11

The First Brazilian Aloft

Aviation had become the rage in France, and any number of young engineers and mechanics built gliders and even tried motorized devices, but it was to fall to Alberto Santos-Dumont to again capture the imagination of Europe. On October 24, 1906, five years after his Eiffel Tower triumph, before an adoring crowd of socialites and reporters, he persuaded an awkward, lumbering aircraft called *14-bis* to rise three meters off the ground and remain in the air for sixty meters. (Like Langley, Santos-Dumont numbered his efforts. His first twelve were balloons, as was fourteen. Number thirteen was his first heavier-than-air machine and it didn't leave the ground.) The ungainly apparatus, which either he or the newspapers giddily dubbed "Bird of Prey," was a glorified box kite with an engine thrown on, but Santos-Dumont was nonetheless hailed as the first man to achieve heavier-than-air flight.* He even won a $10,000 prize for doing so. Three weeks later, he once more dazzled onlookers by flying his contraption two hundred meters across the Bois de Boulogne, this time adding a rudder that he maneuvered with his shoulder.

* He was initially reported to have flown a one-kilometer loop at ten meters, but the report turned out to be substantially inflated.

French pride soared and deep satisfaction permeated the war ministry, where they saw themselves as not only saving almost one million francs but also as showing faith in an adopted countryman over a pair of arrogant Americans.

Unlike the Wrights' Kitty Hawk flights, Santos-Dumont and his "perfected airplane" were reported on in virtually every newspaper in America. Octave Chanute used these accounts to renew his urging that the Wrights go public. He wrote to Wilbur, "I fear he is now very nearly where you were in 1904." Unlike his correspondent, however, Wilbur knew precisely what Santos-Dumont had and hadn't done. "From our knowledge of the subject, we estimate that it is possible to *jump* about 250 ft. with a machine that has not made the first steps toward controllability and which is quite unable to maintain the motive force necessary for flight." Wilbur scoffed at the initial report of a one-kilometer flight. He told Chanute that from what he and Orville had read of *14-bis,* "We predict that his flight covered less than 1⁄10 of a kilometer," an estimate that turned out to be accurate. But Wilbur was less accurate about the future. "When someone goes over three hundred feet and lands safely in a wind of seven or eight miles [per hour] it will be important for us to do something. So far we see no indication that it will be done for several years yet."

In addition, what Wilbur failed to appreciate was that even if Santos-Dumont's aircraft was a technological dead end and might not compare to the Wrights' vastly superior design, its very presence provoked a threat to the brothers' already questionable strategy of playing a pat hand. Santos-Dumont's success was certain to further inspire other designers and with sufficient knowledge of aerodynamics now available, competing machines that could compare might be completed quite a bit sooner than the Wrights' estimates. In fact, when he decided to move from balloon technology to fixed-wing, Santos-Dumont had consulted with a talented young French engineer named Gabriel Voisin. After working for a few months with Santos-Dumont in 1905, Voisin continued to explore the technology on his own, eventually teaming up with another engineer, Louis Blériot. The two formed an aviation company but split up after Santos-Dumont's flight in *14-bis* and Voisin joined his brother Charles. Blériot continued to experiment independently.

Fixed-wing aviation was suddenly big news in America as well, but Wilbur and Orville, rather than dominating the headlines—which they could have done with ease and thereby made sales a good deal simpler—chose to remain shadowy figures. The general situation was summed up in an article that ran in *The New York Herald* on November 24, 1906. "The mystery of the Wright brothers and their doings has been considerably increased by the interviews this week, which have been widely quoted all over the country. 'We must suspend judgment on the Ohio inventors till we actually know more of their doings,' said a member of the Aero Club of Great Britain. 'Some people discount the doings of the Wrights, others swear by them, but no one seems able to prove anything on their behalf.'" In a greater irony, the Bureau of Ordnance and Fortification was reported the following week to have contacted the Wright brothers "with great interest" because the army believed their "aeroplane experiments were on the verge of success." In fact, newspaper reports almost always mentioned the Wrights in a way that virtually begged for the brothers to provide some verification of the rumors of their success. The nation was eager to make them heroes. But Wilbur and Orville would not be moved. They had decided on their strategy, and that, as far as they were concerned, was that.

Others, however, were eager to seize the opportunity. Five days after the *Herald* article appeared, the Wrights were visited by Ulysses Eddy, a stringer for Charles Ranlett Flint, a venture capitalist who had negotiated so many mergers and acquisitions that he was later called "the Father of Trusts."* Eddy arranged a meeting in New York with

* Flint's greatest coup would come in 1911, when he merged three data processing companies to form the Computing-Tabulating-Recording Company, which would later become International Business Machines, or IBM. In his last years, however, Flint became tabloid fodder. In 1927, when he was seventy-seven years old, he married a woman in her mid-thirties. He declared before departing for his honeymoon that

Flint & Company and on December 17, three years to the day after the first Kitty Hawk flights, Orville went east. The Wrights had still not sold a single Flyer and when Orville returned to Dayton, he told Wilbur that they should hear Flint out.

The Wrights were, as always, deeply distrustful of anyone proposing to become their partner, but Charles Flint was equally leery of engaging in business with two men who refused to demonstrate their product. Flint wrote to Octave Chanute, whom he had met professionally, and asked for a character reference. Chanute, whom the Wrights had begun to view with suspicion, wrote back, "From somewhat intimate acquaintance, I can say that in addition to their great mechanical abilities I have ever found the Wright brothers trustworthy. They tell the exact truth and are conscientious, so that I credit fully any statement which they make." On the strength of Chanute's words, Flint decided to move forward. He sent a senior member of the firm to Dayton to make a deal.

Negotiations went on for almost four months. The Flint Company made a number of proposals to represent the Wrights in Europe; United States representation was never discussed. First, they offered to buy the rights, which the brothers refused, and then tried to find an agency and royalty arrangement that would satisfy both sides. Even if a formula were found, sales would not come easily. Flint's European agent, Hart Berg, requested one or both brothers sail to the Continent to establish subsidiary companies and help impress potential customers. Wilbur asked to stay home and work on improvements to the Flyer but Orville insisted that his older brother was more fit for the task. So in May 1907, Wilbur crossed the Atlantic.

"greed was the impelling force that made millionaires go on after more money. Ambition and thirst for power have a part but greed and greed alone is the reason for a man wanting to swell his ward." After his return, his behavior became erratic and at one point, he disappeared for twenty-four hours, wandering about in bathrobe and slippers. At his death in 1934, Flint's fortune was estimated at between $100 million and $200 million, roughly $3 billion in current value.

CHAPTER 12

Langley's Legacy

Samuel Langley's health deteriorated after his failures on the Potomac and in two years he was dead. The aerodrome had gone from being a scientific marvel to epitomizing the crackpot invention. One of the few serious members of the scientific community who did not lose faith in Langley was Alexander Graham Bell.

Bell had his own theories of flight, which, like Langley's, saw propulsion as the key. Obviously, the heavier the craft the more robust the power source required, so Bell's formula revolved around massive kites constructed of thousands of small "tetrahedral cells." Bell was fascinated by these three-dimensional pyramids, thought them one of nature's miracles. The tetrahedron was particularly suited to flight as the weight-to-strength ratio was such that massive airfoils could be constructed with a minimum of bracing and thus create maximal lift per pound. In 1903, three months before Langley's aerodrome made its first dive into the Potomac, Bell published an article in *National Geographic,* "Tetrahederal Principle in Kite Structure," in which he wrote, "Of course the use of a tetrahedral cell is not limited to the construction of a framework for kites and flying machines. It is applicable to any kind of structure whatever in which it is desirable to combine the qualities of strength and lightness. Just as we can build houses of all kinds out of bricks, so we can build structures of all sorts out of tetrahedral frames."[1]

Also like Langley, Bell thought aerodynamics the tail to propulsion's dog. Bell conducted a number of experiments with tetrahedral kites but all were unmanned and unpowered.

Late in 1906, Bell decided to assemble his own team of talented young men to attack the flying problem. He was convinced flight could be achieved by merging Langley's notions of propulsion with his tetrahedral kite.

His first recruit came from an unlikely source. In February 1907, he received a letter from a young United States Army lieutenant, Thomas Selfridge, who sought to meet with Bell to discuss both his experiments and manned aviation in general. Selfridge, grandson of an admiral and graduate of West Point (where his classmate was Douglas MacArthur), had an impeccable reputation and was by all accounts one of the brightest young officers in the army. He was also one of the few who saw military aviation as an essential component of future warfare and had gotten himself assigned to the Signal Corps' fledgling aeronautical division.*

Before communicating with Bell, Selfridge had solicited the Wrights. He had written to Wilbur in January, asking permission to "come to you next summer and work as a mechanic under your supervision and instruction." Selfridge was aware that Wilbur would "at first probably regard [the proposal] with a great deal of suspicion." But Selfridge insisted his motives were simply to learn about the new science of aviation since "there is no one in the United States Service who has yet made a specialty of this subject" and observed to Wilbur that "it would be to your advantage, as I think you'll admit, to have a government officer in a position to report intelligently on your work provided you intend to submit your machine to the War Dept." Selfridge added, "Of course any secrets that I may learn I should consider

* The Signal Corps, which had funded Baldwin's dirigible, was far more forward-looking than the Bureau of Ordnance and Fortification.

as given me in confidence and need hardly assure you would never be divulged without your permission."

Wilbur did not reply for six weeks and then penned a curt letter refusing Selfridge's request. "As Americans," Wilbur wrote, "we naturally feel a national as well as a personal pride in having mastered the art of flight, and therefore greatly regret the relations now existing between the war department and ourselves, for which we are in no way to blame, but which prevent the first use of the art at home." By this, of course, Wilbur meant the army's refusal to buy the technology for $100,000 without witnessing a demonstration.

By the time Wilbur's letter arrived, Selfridge had met with Bell in Washington. Bell was so impressed that he wrote to President Theodore Roosevelt and asked for the young lieutenant to be assigned to him. Roosevelt, an old friend, agreed.

Also in January 1907, Bell met Glenn Curtiss, then en route to Florida to attempt to become the fastest man on earth. Weeks before, Curtiss had received a request from a crackpot inventor from Detroit for an immensely powerful eight-cylinder motor for a flying machine of dubious design.* Curtiss didn't take the idea seriously but the man paid, so he built the engine. The inventor decided it wouldn't work after all, so, out of curiosity, Curtiss mounted the massive contraption on an elongated bicycle frame. With that, he had the world's largest motorcycle—and the fastest. Curtiss intended to prove that on the flat, water-packed sand proving ground at Ormond Beach.

Bell had initially intended to use Manly's motor design, but after speaking with Curtiss he changed his mind. Bell asked Curtiss to join him in Nova Scotia for the kite project and Curtiss agreed to consider it. Curtiss continued on to Florida, where his eight-cylinder monster completed a measured mile in 26.4 seconds, or 136.3 miles per hour, setting a land speed record that lasted until 1930.

After he returned to Hammondsport, Curtiss agreed to leave the

* When recounting the story two decades afterward, Curtiss could not remember the man's name, only that his plan was to build an airship shaped like an enormous stovepipe that sucked air in the front and blew it out the back.

factory for the summer and become a member of Bell's team. In addition to Selfridge and Curtiss, Bell had recruited two Canadian engineers, Frank W. "Casey" Baldwin (no relation to Cap't Tom) and J. A. D. McCurdy. While Bell was aware of the Wrights' work and certainly of their patent, he viewed the patent, and all patents, as limited to specific mechanisms.* He also did not take their designs seriously.

For the most part, Europeans seemed to agree. Even with Flint & Company's representation, as in the United States, government officials were unwilling to commit funds to purchase a machine they had never seen, and in many cases, particularly in Santos-Dumont's France, they questioned whether it had ever flown at all.

The Wrights tried to counter the suspicions without altering their stance. They agreed to submit an article to the inaugural June 1907 issue of *Aeronautics* magazine, a splashy new journal devoted exclusively to aviation, which featured detailed scientific tracts, news of the various aero clubs that were springing up nationwide, and reports on air shows and fairs. Balloons occupied a good deal of space in the early issues but were quickly squeezed out by news of fixed-wing machines. Along with the Wrights, Octave Chanute submitted an article to the first edition and virtually every balloonist and manufacturer took out an advertisement. The Curtiss Manufacturing Company had a full page on the reverse side of the cover, offering motors of 3½ to 40 horsepower in two, four, and eight cylinders. Thomas Baldwin had a full page toward the back of the magazine extolling the *California Arrow*.

* Bell had no small experience in patent law. He had been a party in perhaps the most famous and contentious patent suit in American history. Elisha Gray, a serious inventor in his own right and the founder of the Western Electric Company, had sued Bell, claiming that Bell had stolen his design for what would become the telephone. The two inventions had reached the patent office on the same day, February 14, 1876. Each insisted he had been there first, although Bell's application was logged in before Gray's. Charges and countercharges were exchanged for years and suggestions of skulduggery involving bribery, influence peddling, and drunken patent examiners persist to this day. The Supreme Court finally settled the matter, at least legally, by deciding for Bell in 1888.

The Wrights offered details of their flights—length, duration, and average speed—without any discussion of aeronautics, simply noting that "the favorable results which have been obtained have been due to improvements in flying quality resulting in more scientific design and to improved methods of balancing and steering." Chanute's article, while positing the "now acknowledged success of the Wright brothers," also observed—ominously for Wilbur and Orville—that "some 30 or 40 European aviators have built or are building 'de toutes pieces,' motor equipped flying machines on wheels in the hope of speedily accomplishing mechanical flight." Even at this formative stage, an improvement to the Wrights' derrick launching system was in the works.

With competitors closing the gap, the Wrights finally got a bit of good news from home. Cortlandt Field Bishop, president of the Aero Club, had impressed on a New York congressman who was also his brother-in-law the importance of the Wrights' invention and the obstinance of the army in giving them a fair hearing. The congressman spoke to President Roosevelt, who instructed Secretary of War Taft to take a fresh look. Taft referred the matter to the Wrights' old nemesis, the Board of Ordnance and Fortification. After meetings and an exchange of correspondence, the Wrights offered to sell the army a Flyer that would carry two men and enough fuel for a 200-kilometer flight, neither of which they had yet approached in their tests, and to train an army aviator to operate the machine. For this they asked $100,000. Orville handled these negotiations since Wilbur had already left for France. He also agreed to a public trial after the contract was signed but before any money was paid, in which they would fly at least fifty kilometers at fifty kilometers per hour. Other than the specifications, this represented much the same conditions that had borne no fruit two years earlier.

The board replied that the price was so high as to require a special appropriation by Congress, which could not be obtained until autumn, and questioned whether the Flyer would be sold to the United States on an exclusive basis. They once again asked to see a demonstration flight, noting that it would be of "material assistance . . . in reaching a conclusion." Orville replied that the sale would in no way be exclusive to the United States, then added, "In view of the abundant evidence already available, we do not regard the actual sight of the machine a prerequisite to the formulation of terms of contract."

The army disagreed. Orville received a curt reply in which the board promised to take up the matter at its next meeting, and then another in October, three months later, in which they promised to take it up after Congress met. After that, nothing. Once again, the opportunity to sell the Flyer to the United States government had been squandered.

Wilbur insisted on the same conditions in Europe with an equal lack of success. Even with the powerful Flint & Company at his side, one by one, governments refused to consider entering into a contract to purchase a product they hadn't seen, even for no money down. The only country in which there was some interest was aviation-obsessed France, but getting to the right people involved navigating through a morass of government officials, financiers, industrialists, and palm-greasers. Wilbur and Hart Berg could never be certain that the people to whom they were speaking had any authority at all.

Eventually, Wilbur proposed to fly fifty kilometers at one thousand feet, after which the French government would purchase a Flyer for one million francs and, as had become standard, agreed to a demonstration after signing as a condition of sale. Different from the offer at home, however, was that if the deal was consummated, France would enjoy a period of exclusivity before the private consortium that would manufacture the Flyer could sell airplanes to other nations.

Accustomed to making family decisions that were not later questioned, he cabled the details to Orville as a courtesy. To Wilbur's shock, the usually acquiescent Orville refused to endorse the deal, balking at the exclusivity clause. Subsequently, the French refused as well. A stung Wilbur wrote to Orville, "So I am turned down on both sides after both sides had, I thought, indicated approval quite definitely. . . . I confess that I am a little hurt that you should refuse to take this job yourself and then turn down my recommendations after I supposed you had given your assent to every important point in the proposition submitted."[2]

The strain of continued failure began to wear on both. As would be the Wrights' pattern, each blamed everyone but himself. To Wilbur, Ferdinand Ferber went from a man France was lucky to have to "the man largely responsible for the failure of the final negotiations in March 1906," someone "double faced" and "bitterly hostile."[3] In July, Orville complained about Flint & Company. "I am so completely disgusted with them that I would like to sever our connection . . . they have been *so* tricky that it keeps us busy watching them."[4]

Acrimony turned internal as well. In the same letter, Orville complained of Wilbur's scanty communications, and Wilbur responded by carping that Orville didn't understand the pressures he was under. He complained to his father in a long and bitter letter on July 20. "You people in Dayton seem to lack perspicacity," he began. But most of his vitriol was saved for Orville. "Instead of tending to his own work and letting me attend to mine, he seemed to have no responsibility as to his own work, but the whole responsibility as to mine. . . . So far as his letters indicate, he spent his time on things of no use in the present situation, and left the necessary things undone."

This last reference was, bizarrely, to the lack of a Flyer in Europe with which to fly the very demonstrations that Wilbur had categorically refused to make. Neither brother had been off the ground in two years. Now, with the strategy of nonflying falling apart, Wilbur asserted to Milton, "If a serious mistake has been made, it lies in the assumption that the machine would be available quicker than now seems possible. I am not to blame for this." As the difficulties mounted, the two-way "scrapping" in the shop became one-way abuse, with Wilbur foisting blame on Orville for any problem that came up.

So Orville ordered a machine crated up and shipped across the Atlantic and then he left for France himself. He arrived in time to submit another proposal to the French minister of war. The matter moved with glacial speed through the French bureaucracy, compounded by the exodus for August vacations. Sick of waiting, Wilbur left for Berlin to attempt to make a sale to the Germans. But German bureaucrats worked no more quickly than the French and Orville's reticence with regard to granting any exclusivity to the French applied to the Germans as well. In August, Wilbur once more took out his anger on his younger brother. "I have *no letter whatever* from you since I left. You must keep me informed. It will not do to telegraph me to do nothing in Germany without giving an opinion of the terms. . . . We must have an offer in shape to present immediately once it is decided to make one. It is as important for me to know everything that happens in Paris as for you to know what is going on here. I have kept you informed but you have sent me nothing."[5] That same day, Orville did send a letter to Wilbur suggesting they suspend negotiations until they could make arrangements to demonstrate the Flyer to their potential customers but the airplane continued to lie in its crates at French customs in Le Havre.

Wilbur and Orville remained in Europe until late fall, shuttling either together or separately between Germany, France, and England in a fruitless crusade to obtain government commitments to purchase their product. Skepticism was so widespread as to whether they achieved anything approaching what they had claimed that two German officers traveled to Dayton in October to interview Bishop Wright and some locals to confirm the accounts. Even when they reported back favorably to their government, no one was willing to sign on.

In October, Wilbur admitted defeat. He wrote to Katharine, "We doubt whether an agreement will be reached before we have really made some demonstrations somewhere and stirred up some excitement." Within weeks, out of options, Wilbur returned to the United States, heading to Washington to negotiate terms for a demonstration flight that, if successful, would result in a sale. Orville sailed for New York a month later.

In his new negotiations with the government, Wilbur dropped virtually all the Wrights' initial demands and the army responded almost immediately. On December 5, 1907, Wilbur received a communication from the Board of Ordnance and Fortification. It noted that "Mr.

Wright . . . said the offer therein contemplated [in their previous letters] disposal of certain secrets, but they were now prepared to furnish an operative machine capable of carrying two persons for the sum of $25,000." All subsequent machines would be purchased for $10,000 and, as before, included the offer to train an officer.

Official specifications were forthcoming within a month. Bidders would be required to submit drawings and descriptions of all parts of their machines, although this was modified to allow the Wrights to "maintain their secrets"; prove they held patents on all proprietary features; demonstrate that the airplane was capable of carrying two persons with a combined weight of 350 pounds and sufficient fuel for 125 miles; travel at least forty miles per hour average with and against the wind, with deductions from the price for less, bonuses for more; fly at least one hour and then land the airplane so that it could immediately take off again; steer in all directions without difficulty and at all times be under perfect control and equilibrium; provide a simple and transportable starting device; and instruct two men in its operation. Although not specified, it was understood that both operator and passenger would be seated rather than lying prone.

These were precisely what Wilbur had agreed to in their talks with the board. The Wrights had gone from feeling as if the world were conspiring against them to having the deck stacked in their favor, assuming only that they could deliver what they had promised. Still, the government could not simply hand money to one manufacturer without first soliciting bids, so it opened the trials to anyone who could produce an airplane that met the specifications. The Wrights were unconcerned. Nobody else could—and what was more, anyone bidding would be required to post a certified check for 10 percent of their bid. The trials would be at Fort Myer, Virginia, and bids were due February 1, 1908.

On January 27, the Wrights submitted their bid for $25,000 for the first machine and $10,000 each for anything more, along with a certified check for $2,500. As in any open auction there were a number of other bids, most from cranks and one from a convict. With one of the other bidders, however, it was difficult to determine into which category he fell. Offering to sell the army a flying machine for $20,000 was none other than Augustus Moore Herring.

Herring had recently resurfaced in interviews but as far as anyone could determine, he had done nothing in aviation for years; nor did he seem to hold any patents. But his name was well-known, as were his successes with the Herring–Chanute glider, so once he posted his $2,000 he was an official bidder.

The Wrights' experience with Herring at Kitty Hawk had led them to assume that the bid was a bluff, as they had done with a remark he had made the month before about having learned the secrets of the Wright machine. They were, as they saw it, the only real bidders.

Then in March, as if to demonstrate that 1908 would be very different from 1907, Hart Berg informed Wilbur and Orville that they had a deal in France, not with the government but with a private consortium. The terms, which the Wrights would have rejected three months earlier but which they now welcomed, included a series of demonstrations before pen was put to paper. But if the Flyer performed as advertised, the Wrights would receive $100,000 on delivery of the first machine, $4,000 for each of four additional airplanes, as well as 50 percent of the stock of the new company, some of which would be used as working capital.

Although they had done significant work in the shop, particularly on the motor, the army requirements included a number of milestones that they had yet to achieve. To the Wrights' credit, although their most recent model Flyer was three years old, they never exhibited a wisp of doubt that they would fulfill even the highest expectations for their machine.

Still, to ensure that the Flyers that would take to the skies over Fort Myer and in France would represent the pinnacle of their efforts, they repaired to test and improve their product. And that couldn't be done properly in Ohio, so the Wrights returned to the scene of their original triumph, Kitty Hawk.

CHAPTER 13

Closing Fast

When Chanute tried to warn Wilbur that the French were making great strides and might soon produce machines to rival his, Wilbur replied on January 1, 1908, "I still hold to my prediction that an independent solution to the flying problem would require at least five years." If anything, Chanute had understated the case. French designers had been experimenting furiously, some with radically different designs. Both Louis Blériot and another engineer, Léon Levavasseur, built monoplanes, but could not initially make them fly. (Levavasseur named his airplanes after his financier's daughter, Antoinette, and formed a company under that name in 1906.) The Voisin brothers had teamed with a young enthusiast named Henri Farman, son of an English father and French mother, who had flown an unstable but airworthy craft more than two kilometers in October 1907. The following month, steering with his rudder alone and making essentially flat turns, Farman flew in a one-kilometer circle.

While Wilbur was correct that none of these craft could match the Flyer, improving the handling of an airplane that could stay in the air for kilometers was a good deal easier than making one fly in the first place. The gap was closing. But in the early days of 1908, few would have predicted that the biggest threat to the Wrights would emanate not from Europe but rather from a small town in central New York.

On September 30, 1907, while the Wrights were bouncing from one sales misadventure to another, Alexander Graham Bell officially established the Aerial Experiment Association (AEA). For reasons never fully explained, his wife, Mabel, supplied the $20,000 to capitalize the venture. The camp, at Beinn Bhreagh, Bell's estate in Nova Scotia, was a combination of think tank and old man's vanity play. From the first day, the group had meetings, kept minutes, and signed a formal agreement that began "Whereas the undersigned Alexander Graham Bell of Washington, D.C., U.S.A., has for many years past been carrying on experiments relating to aerial locomotion at his summer laboratory at Beinn Bhreagh, near Baddeck, N.S., Canada, and has reached the stage where he believes a practical aerodrome can be built on the tetrahedral principle driven by an engine and carrying a man, and has felt the advisability of securing expert assistance in pursuing the experiments to their logical conclusions and has called to his aid Mr. G. H. Curtiss." Bell listed the other members of the group, then went on for two more pages without inserting a period into his remarks. Although any prior inventions of the members would remain their property, anything developed by the group would belong to the association.

Bell had no sons of his own and the AEA lads quickly became surrogates.[1] Selfridge seems to have particularly caught the fancy of both Bell and his wife. The tetrahedral machine was to be the group's first project and Bell assumed that his charges felt the same enthusiasm for the project as did he. While it would be an overstatement to assert that the younger members were merely humoring the older man, none of the other members of the group held out much hope for the contraption. In fact, it became clear early on that their benefactor would contribute little to any practical progress. Nonetheless, they built his motorized kite, a forty-two-foot-wide enormity called the *Cygnet,* which contained 3,393 of his treasured tetrahedrons, each made of red silk, open in the front to allow for airflow, with a section in the middle cut out for a pilot.

On December 6, 1907, the giant kite with its forty-two-foot wingspan was hauled out on a scow to the middle of Bras d'Or, the lake abutting Bell's home. Curtiss had built a motor but Bell wanted to test it first as a glider, so the *Cygnet* was tethered to a motorboat. Selfridge had been chosen as pilot and, like the Wrights, he lay prone in a cutout in the center. Bell had been correct about lifting power; a gust of wind took the kite into the air, where for seven minutes Selfridge took readings. But the *Cygnet* was inherently uncontrollable and at a shift of the wind, the kite hurtled downward, crashing into the lake. Selfridge was pulled from the freezing water unhurt but the fragile kite with its thousands of cells was severely damaged.

Bell wanted to rebuild the *Cygnet* and try again but according to the terms of the agreement the members had signed, they could move on to a design of one of the others. Everyone by this time had ideas he wished to try. Selfridge, by virtue of his adventure in the water, was chosen to be first. The group also decided to relocate to Hammondsport, a far more convenient location, and where the facilities of the Curtiss Manufacturing Company would be at their disposal.

By March 1908, Selfridge had designed and the group had built a bi-wing craft dubbed *Red Wing,* named for the red silk fabric left over from the *Cygnet.* The wings bowed from the center "like horizontal parentheses," and narrowed at the ends. The upper wing had a span of forty-two feet and came to a point; the lower was six feet shorter and truncated at the tips. The wings had an average chord of slightly more than five feet. Curtiss, as he did with all AEA constructions, designed and built the motor. The *Red Wing* was fitted with a fixed, single-pane rudder and no mechanism for pilot control. Selfridge himself wrote, "This was the virgin attempt of Aerial Experiment Association to construct a motor driven aeroplane and hence we were not over-sanguine of success at the first trials." To the surprise of everyone, however, on March 12 the machine actually went airborne, taking off from the frozen surface of Lake Keuka and flying more than three hundred feet in a wide arc before clipping its right wing and crashing on the ice. Such was the continued mystery surrounding the Wrights that the *Red Wing*'s short hop was billed in a number of newspapers as "the first public flight in America."

The group considered it a great success. The next venture should have been assigned to Baldwin, who had piloted the craft, but he decided to work jointly with Curtiss. Using data from the *Red Wing* flight, the two designed *White Wing,* another biplane, this one with a front elevator and movable rear rudder. Curtiss suggested a steering wheel instead of levers and supplied a three-wheel system copied from motorcycle sidecars rather than skids. But the most significant feature was the addition of movable structures at the end of the wings, what would later be called ailerons.*

The group had all realized the necessity of addressing lateral control. There was no suggestion of wing warping. By all accounts, the aileron system was Bell's suggestion, although where he originally came by the idea was never firmly established.[2] But a number of experimenters—perhaps even Mouillard—had either hypothesized about movable wing tips or had even experimented with them.[3] Subsequently, a number of designers claimed to have been the source of the idea, including the ubiquitous Augustus Herring, who insisted he had employed ailerons in his 1894 glider, an assertion that appeared another fabrication. Herring's gliders never got off the ground far enough to make lateral stability an issue. And if he had attained lateral stability, why would he have abandoned ailerons on later models?

Herring notwithstanding, the design of the *White Wing* is cited by Wright proponents as further evidence that Curtiss stole from them. But in addition to the fact that the idea was almost certainly not Curtiss's, there was an exchange of letters between the Wrights and Curtiss a few months before that become odd if Curtiss harbored larcenous intent.

* The word literally means "fin" or in some translations, "little wing."

On December 30, 1907, he wrote to the brothers on AEA stationery, which listed him as "Director of Experiments." After noting that he had been following the development of their aircraft, he said, "I just wish to keep in touch with you and let you know that we have been making considerable progress in engine construction." Curtiss then went into great detail, far more than the Wrights would have done, on the specifications of his motors, which varied from 15 to 40 horsepower and "embody the same design as our cycle motors which, as you have heard, develop more power for the cylinder capacity than any others." He then offered Wilbur and Orville a motor at no cost "as we have great confidence in them." Then Curtiss said something even more curious for one man purportedly planning on stealing from another. "The writer has been getting rather deeply mixed in Aeronautics and Hammondsport is getting to be quite a headquarters for this class of work." Curtiss concluded by inviting both to visit and "to make you guests as long as you would care to stay."

While it is possible that this was all a ruse designed to put the Wrights at their ease while Curtiss hatched his plot, or that Curtiss only decided to steal from them after it was written, far more likely is that the letter was written by a man who saw himself innocent, both then and in the foreseeable future, of any act that might be considered improper. This is not to say that he *was* innocent—that again depends on how one views the limits of innovation—simply that he believed he was.

The Wrights had no interest, but their response was warm. "We remember your visit to Dayton with pleasure," the two-paragraph letter closed. "The experience we had together in helping Captain Baldwin back to the fair grounds was one not soon to be forgotten. When you see the Captain, please remember him to us."

In any event, the rudimentary system, fashioned by Curtiss and controlled by body motions of the pilot, was installed on the *White Wing* for its first flight on May 22, 1908. With Curtiss at the controls, it flew at a height of about ten feet for nineteen seconds, covering a measured 1,017 feet. Similar flights followed until *White Wing* was wrecked when the ailerons were shifted incorrectly by McCurdy. The system worked so well that Bell filed for a patent on the aileron system jointly with the other members of the AEA.

The success of *White Wing* threw open the doors of powered flight. With French aviators already covering five, then six, then ten kilometers, with Léon Levavasseur refining his lightweight Antoinette motor, and others such as Blériot nearing success, the entry into competitive aviation of a brilliant designer such as Curtiss did not bode well for the Wrights' long-term preeminence.* Unless, of course, they could successfully make everyone else pay them for the privilege of being in the business.

* The May 1908 edition of *Aeronautics* featured a full-page advertisement of a man carrying an eight-cylinder, 120-horsepower Antoinette motor on his shoulder.

CHAPTER 14

Vindication

For this trip to Kitty Hawk, the Wrights were not alone.

After years of disdaining public media, Wilbur and Orville had finally learned that perception could not be ignored. They allowed, even encouraged, a number of reporters to follow them to the Outer Banks and report on their progress. Then they penned a long article for the June 1908 edition of *Aeronautics* in which they gave details of both the refinements to their machine and the results of each test. That article was followed by another written by Byron Newton, a reporter for *The New York Herald*, one of the journalists who had witnessed the Kitty Hawk tests, who extolled in a long, laudatory piece, "I did not believe they had made conspicuous progress in sustained flight and I did not believe they had made a record of twenty-four miles as claimed by them. I believe all these things now and more."

The Wrights might have continued to be doubted by some in Europe, but in America they were approaching celebrity status and their upcoming flights at Fort Myer were as eagerly awaited as a visit by President Roosevelt.

But the Wright brothers' achievements were not the only ones that received coverage in the June *Aeronautics*. Following Newton's piece was another, copiously illustrated with photographs, "The Work of the

Aerial Experiment Association." It appeared over Alexander Graham Bell's byline but was actually culled from Associated Press dispatches and submitted by Glenn Curtiss. Curtiss's flight of 1,017 feet was billed, correctly, as "the longest ever made in a heavier-than-air machine by an aviator on his first trial." No immediate threat to twenty-four miles perhaps, but a thrown gauntlet all the same. The article contained a lengthy description of the lightweight Curtiss V-8 motor used on both of the AEA's models. It should have been clear to Wilbur and Orville that Curtiss was building power plants far superior to anything they could produce. They had already contracted to have motors on their French machines supplied by an outside firm. Had they made the same arrangement domestically with Curtiss, the course of world aviation would have been altered.

There were two other articles of interest in that issue of *Aeronautics*. The first was a short item that noted, "Work is progressing on the aeroplane A. M. Herring is building under contract for the U. S. Army Signal Corps. . . . Details of the machine are being kept secret to a great extent, but we have reason to believe that it will be of the Herring–Chanute bi-plane type . . . the two engines have been specially designed by Mr. Herring . . . with a maximum of 17 horsepower for each." Wilbur said of this, "It is my opinion he will never go to Washington."[1]

The second was a long feature on Thomas Baldwin. Despite the rush of interest in fixed-wing flight, dirigibles continued to be seen by many, both in the military and among the civilian population, as the true future of aviation. Baldwin would also be at Fort Myer as part of his deal with the Signal Corps and balloons had already begun to be tested in scouting missions by other nations.

Dirigibles remained a public phenomenon and air shows featuring the gas bags continued to draw large crowds. Ballooning therefore attracted any number of young, aggressive aeronauts, drawn to adventure, danger, and fame. Other than Beachey, the most notable of these was Charles Keeney Hamilton, a tiny, wiry daredevil with a wild shock of red hair who always seemed to have in his mouth either a drink or a cigarette, sometimes both. Dirigibles might have seemed like a nearly obsolete technology by the more forward-looking, but in May 1908 they were a training ground for the aviators who would help shape the futures of the Wright brothers and Glenn Curtiss.

By the time the articles appeared, Wilbur was across the Atlantic. Before he left, he visited Flint & Company offices in New York, and after that meeting he gave Orville two pieces of disquieting news. The first was that "our French business is not in very good shape," owing to the withdrawal of one of their French partners. "It is evident we will have a hard pull over there but I think things will go better with someone to steady Berg." The cause of the trouble was the "excitement over recent flights by Farman & Delagrange."* The second was even more ominous. "One of the clippings which I enclose intimates that Selfridge is infringing our patent on wing twisting. It is important to get the main features originated by us identified in the public mind with our machines before they are described in connection with some other machine." Whether Wilbur's choice of words was significant can only be surmised, but neither he nor Orville would use the narrow phrase "wing twisting" again when referring to their patent but rather the more inclusive "lateral margins," or "lateral balance."

When Wilbur arrived in France on May 28, the crated Flyer that Orville had sent the previous summer was waiting for him. When he opened the crates three weeks later, he had an unpleasant surprise. He immediately turned on his brother. "I . . . have been puzzled to know how you could have wasted two full days packing [the crates]. I am sure that with a scoop shovel I could have put things in within two or three minutes and made fully as good a job of it. I never saw such evidence of idiocy in my life. . . . Ten or a dozen ribs were broken and as they are scattered here and there through the surfaces it takes almost as much time to tear down and rebuild as if we had begun at the be-

* Léon Delagrange was a sculptor who purchased an early machine from the Voisin brothers, made a series of spectacular flights, and set records for distance, outdoing even Farman.

ginning." The damage was pervasive to almost every piece of the construction: fabric, coil, radiator, magneto, and axle. Fasteners were missing entirely. For the next two days, Wilbur complained in his diary of working morning until night fixing the mess Orville had made of things.

The only problem, as Orville later pointed out, was that when they had arrived in France, the crates had been packed perfectly with not one piece broken or missing. The crates had been opened at the customs house in Le Havre, the contents examined and then replaced by gorilla-pawed customs officials in the jumble Wilbur found them. After Wilbur's error was pointed out to him, he made no further mention of the incident, but did not apologize and continued to bark orders in letters to the brother he had described to his sister as "not as careful" as he was.

Wilbur's abuse became so incessant and harsh that finally Katharine wrote back to him, "Orv looks perfectly terrible—so pale and tired. . . . I wouldn't fuss at him *all* the time. You have troubles too but I can't see any sense in so much complaining at him."[2] After he received the letter, Wilbur backed off.

At Hammondsport, Curtiss had designed the third of AEA's aircraft, which Bell dubbed *June Bug*. This version was almost identical to *White Wing* except for a box tail instead of pane rudder, stronger bracing, and varnished muslin on the wings instead of silk. The major difference was human, not mechanical; Curtiss showed that he would be as adept a pilot in the air as he had been on the ground. With a deft touch on the shoulder harness that controlled the ailerons, Curtiss coaxed longer and longer flights out of *June Bug* and early in July decided to try for the first publicly offered prize for fixed-wing aviation in the United States.

Scientific American, by this time Wright enthusiasts, had decided to offer a trophy to commemorate powered flight. The statuette was an elaborate affair, silver over an onyx base, featuring an eagle with flared wings sitting atop a globe that was suspended in clouds at the head of

Curtiss at the wheel of June Bug.

a pillar, flanked by three winged horses on each side. North and South America appeared on the rear surface of the globe; on the front, incongruously, was the image of Langley's aerodrome.

To win permanent possession of the trophy, an aviator—or two brothers—would have to win a competition three times in three separate years, with each test devised to test the limits of aviation for that year. The 1908 prize would go to the first airplane that completed a straight one-kilometer flight. An added stipulation was that the aircraft had to take off under its own power, which meant wheels instead of a derrick and track. The Wrights, unwilling to refit the Flyer for wheels, refused to enter and so Curtiss had the field to himself. On July 4, 1908, he flew 5,360 feet (1.634 kilometers), witnessed by a slew of dignitaries and Aero Club members, including Charles Manly. Another interested spectator was Augustus Herring, who had taken to popping up whenever something of importance was going on. On a subsequent flight, Curtiss tried to maneuver in the air, but the tiny ailerons at the ends of the wings were not sufficient to effect turns.

June Bug was too much for the Wrights. Orville, who had previously reacted to a rumor that the AEA intended to sell the *Red Wing* for $5,000 by declaring, "What cheek!" and "Some nerve!" notified Curtiss that he was infringing their patents, in language that would indicate Orville had consulted Toulmin, although no actual written communication exists. "I learn from *Scientific American* that your *June Bug* has surfaces at the tips of the wings, adjustable to different angles on the right and left sides for maintaining lateral balance." Orville then referred to the Wright patent, assured Curtiss that they had not given permission for use of any proprietary features "for exhibitions or in a commercial way," and then asserted that "Claim 14 of our patent No. 821,393 specifically covers the combination which we are informed you are using."[3] In furtherance of their aspirations to monopoly, Orville added, "We believe it will be very difficult to develop a successful machine without the use of some of the features covered in our patent." He then offered to discuss a licensing arrangement with Curtiss.

Curtiss's reply was somewhere between an evasion and an outright lie. Rather than address what he saw as the differences between the Wright patent and his arrangement, he simply assured Orville that "contrary to newspaper reports, I do not expect to do anything in the way of exhibitions," that his flights were simply part of the AEA's work and that he referred the "matter of patents to the secretary of the organization," who happened to be Thomas Selfridge. Selfridge had earlier written to the Wrights asking for advice and been referred to the patent.

But events were moving so fast for the Wrights on both sides of the Atlantic that infringement issues were soon shunted aside. On August 8, Wilbur made the first public flight of a Wright Flyer at Hunaudières race track near Le Mans, 125 miles from Paris. By the time he landed, aviation had been changed forever. The French, who had been so smug after the successes of Farman, Delagrange, and Santos-Dumont, were stupified. Although his first flight lasted less than two minutes and Wilbur was using the stick control for the first time, the grace and control of the Flyer left onlookers literally gasping. Over the next two weeks, Wilbur made about ten more flights, none of them more than eight minutes. He flew easily and gracefully, turning in deep banks, carving circles and even figure eights in the sky, all with control of the aircraft far beyond anything seen before. "Frenchmen seemed to vie with each other in giving the praise and credit so long overdue," *Aeronautics* reported, "and all hasten to say 'never had any doubts.'"

On September 6, after a flight of almost twenty minutes, Wilbur wrote Orville that "the newspapers continue exceedingly friendly and the public interest and enthusiasm continues to increase." While Wilbur noted that some in the French aviation community "do all they can to stem the tide," others, such as Louis Blériot, "are very decent."

Success had a good effect on Wilbur. His tone in these letters of early September 1908 is uncharacteristically lilting; after a decade of experimentation, success, and then frustration, the battle to create a monopoly was nearly won. The only difficulties seemed to be an endless flow of dinner invitations from French luminaries, the inability to find anyone to work on the Flyer who could understand what Wilbur was saying, and a cranky motor that he could not get to work properly for any length of time.

The motor problem, while never totally solved, became moot on September 16, when Wilbur made headlines around the world by keeping the Flyer in the air for nearly forty minutes, covering twenty-nine miles at an average speed of forty-six miles per hour. All three marks represented official records. Also significant in these letters were Wilbur's change in tone toward his brother; he now leapt on the tales of Orville's prowess.

"The newspapers for several days have been full of the stories of your dandy flights," he wrote to Orville on September 13, "and whereas a week ago I was a marvel of skill, now they do not hesitate to tell me I am nothing but a 'dub,' and that you are the only genuine champion skyscraper." Wilbur was equally gushing to his sister. "When I made my first flight over here, the sudden change from unbelief to belief raised a furor of excitement I had not expected . . . but the news from America seems to have been sufficient to repeat the stir."

Nothing, not riches nor fame, meant more to Orville than praise from his older brother. And Katharine, in a letter of September 12, added, "We are simply ready to explode and the town is crazy." It is difficult to imagine Orville being any happier or more fulfilled than he was at that moment in mid-September 1908.

And Orville had earned the praise. On September 9, he shattered all records by flying, albeit unofficially, for fifty-seven minutes over the Fort Myer parade ground, traveling an estimated forty miles, landing only to perform minor maintenance to his motor. He then returned to the air, this time staying aloft for sixty-two minutes and reaching speeds of perhaps fifty miles per hour. A third flight lasted only six minutes but was made with a passenger sitting next to him. During the practice runs at Fort Myer, Orville flew higher, farther, and faster than anyone had before. His banked turns elicited the same awe in the United States as had Wilbur's in France. "He drove his ship down the field far past the aerodrome and into the broken country beyond. Over the roofs of the post buildings he sailed, and he looked down on the graves in Arlington through the tree tops ninety feet beneath."

All that remained was the official test. "There is no doubt," *Aeronautics* reported in the issue that went to press just before the trial, "that the contract speed of forty miles per hour will be met easily."

But even the best fortune can be fleeting.

CHAPTER 15

Orville and Selfridge

Glenn Curtiss was at Fort Myer as well. He had arrived in mid-August with Thomas Baldwin for the dirigible trials. Baldwin's entry, dubbed Signal Corps Dirigible No. 1, was twice the size of the *California Arrow* and powered by a 25-horsepower Curtiss motor with a propeller designed by Thomas Selfridge. While Orville's achievements were grabbing the headlines, Baldwin's high-flying air-ship also impressed army brass and had, to many senior officers, more immediate application for scouting and communication. Although some considered Baldwin's creation inferior to Count Zeppelin's massive airships, Baldwin's was smaller, more maneuverable, and thus would be "far more effective in time of war." In the trials at Fort Myer, the dirigible easily stayed in the air for more than two hours, although it was clocked at 19.61 miles per hour instead of the contracted twenty. As in Europe, ten- to twelve-hour flights were anticipated.

But Baldwin also had his difficulties. On their practice runs, Cap't Tom piloted the craft and Curtiss handled the motor. The size of the balloon initially caused navigation problems and at one point after Curtiss returned to Hammondsport, the motor turned balky, necessitating his return. Orville recounted his difficulties with glee in a letter to Wilbur. "Curtiss was here Thursday and Friday," he wrote on September 6. "They have not been able to make the motor on the dirigible run more than a minute or two without missing about half its explosions. Ours runs without a miss. Selfridge has been trying to find out how we do it!" In fact, Curtiss repaired the motor and it then ran without a hitch.

That Tom Selfridge would be accused of skulking about attempting to appropriate the secrets of propulsion from Orville is an indication of the depth of distrust and enmity that had already built up between the Wrights and the AEA members, particularly Curtiss and Selfridge. For Orville and Wilbur to deduce that Curtiss had tried to steal their ideas concerning lateral control was reasonable; but Glenn Curtiss built the best-running, most efficient motors in the world. Even the Wrights had admitted that theirs were inferior, and as Orville well knew, a Wright-approved motor was giving Wilbur fits in France.

And Orville didn't stop there. "I will be glad to have Selfridge out of the way. I don't trust him an inch. He is intensely interested in the subject, and plans to meet me often at dinners, etc. where he can pump me. He has a good education, and a clear mind. I understand that he does a good deal of knocking behind my back." He added in a letter to his sister, "Selfridge is doing what he can behind our backs to injure us." To which Katharine replied, "I observe that Lt. Selfridge is always in the front row when it comes to wringing your hand! He makes me sick."

Orville seems not to have expressed those sentiments to Curtiss, with whom he spoke regularly. "I had some talk with Mr. Wright," Curtiss wrote to Bell, "and nothing was said about his patents on adjustable surfaces. He has nothing startling about his machine and no secrets." Curtiss, however, had a view of the Wright motor similar to Orville's of his. "The engine is the same as they had four years ago, being rather crude and not exceptionally light."

Although no one publicly questioned Orville's skill or experience as an aviator, particularly after his record-breaking flights in early September, he was flying an airplane at Fort Myer with a new set of lever controls that Wilbur had designed specifically for the trial. They gave him some early trouble. Curtiss also wrote to Bell, "The first flight was rather short as Mr. Wright said he was unaccustomed to the machine and the levers seemed awkward for him. He made a wrong move and headed for the tent [into a dive], which necessitated immediate landing."

As the trial approached, an officer was needed to ride with Orville as a passenger. The Signal Corps had appointed a five-man "Aeronautical Commission" to oversee the test and, for the infant science of aeronautics, three of the five were young lieutenants. The most experienced of the three was Selfridge, the only man in the United States military to have personally flown an airplane.[1] As a result, Selfridge was chosen as Orville's passenger, a decision that left Orville none too pleased, but Selfridge was far too well thought of for him to make his displeasure public.

On September 17, 1908, before two thousand spectators, both men took their places in the Flyer. At just after 5 P.M., the counterweight was dropped and the airplane sprung down the track. The Flyer made three circuits of the field more than one hundred feet off the ground, Orville stolid at the controls and Selfridge barely able to contain his excitement. He had flown *June Bug,* but that experience was nothing like this.

According to W. S. Clime, a photographer on the scene to record the flight for the army, "There was a crack like a pistol shot coming from above. I saw a piece of a propeller blade twirling off to the southward. For a brief period it kept on its course, then swerved to the left and with a swoop backwards, but in an almost perpendicular manner it fell for half the distance to the ground. Then suddenly righting itself regained for an instant its normal position only to pitch forward and strike on the parallel planes in front for altering the elevation, raising an immense cloud of dust that momentarily hid it from view."[2]

There was a rush to the wreckage, and those arriving first saw that while both men were grievously hurt, Selfridge's injuries were far more serious. The fuel tank and motor had broken loose in the crash and pinned him underneath. He was unconscious and seemed to be choking on his own blood. With mounted cavalry positioned to keep spectators away, both men were removed from the wreckage and rushed to Fort Myer Hospital. Although Orville had broken his femur and four ribs and dislocated his hip, doctors from the first knew he would recover. Selfridge had two fractures of the skull in addition to internal injuries. He was wheeled into the operating room as soon as he arrived at the hospital but never regained consciousness. Just before 9 P.M., he died.

Powered flight had its first fatality, Thomas Selfridge, an exceedingly bright and almost universally respected officer, only twenty-six years old, for whom everyone who knew him had only the highest regard, except perhaps for the man who had sat next to him in the crash.

The accident was minutely dissected. Orville later said that he ini-

Tending to Orville or Selfridge after the crash at Fort Myer.

tially heard or felt two thumps and then a louder one that shook the craft violently. He cut his engines and turned for the derrick and seemed for a moment to have control of the airplane, but then the nose suddenly turned upward and the craft began to drop. The rudder lever would not respond and soon they pitched forward into the ground below. Orville said that he was regaining control in the second before the crash and if he'd had another twenty-five feet of altitude, he might have righted it.

Examination of the wreckage showed that one of the new, longer propellers Orville had mounted for the test flight had cracked lengthwise and lost thrust, causing a disequilibrium that caused the second propeller to strike a support wire to the tail, which then wrapped around and snapped it.

There was a rush to dismiss the crash as the freak occurrence that it almost certainly was. An article appeared in newspapers across the nation saying only that after the propeller snapped, "the machine turned over in the air and fell to the ground." It quoted Charles White, "a mechanical expert," as discounting "any serious defect in the machine," but "merely want of better construction of the propellers." White added, "The aeroplane was under perfect control and the accident was not due to any fault of operation."

The army agreed. An official inquiry absolved Orville of any blame and concluded the crash was an unavoidable accident, a fluke, and should not interfere with the Wrights' returning to again demonstrate the Flyer whenever they were able. The deadline for meeting the contract specifications was extended for nine months.

There were, however, whispers that the real story might be different. Bell asserted that if they had used one propeller shaft instead of two, the craft could have been controlled and landed safely. Bell also noted, "When the accident at Fort Myer occurred, Mr. Wright did not know exactly what had happened, for the rudder and propellers were behind him, and therefore out of his sight. He did not dare to look round very much, for the operation of his controlling levers demanded all of his attention at the time."[3] Hinted at but never said was that

Orville's handling of the new lever system might have slowed his reaction time and lost him the seconds he needed to ease the Flyer into a controlled glide; also that his irritation at having to make the flight with a man he considered a thief and a spy had been a distraction. Finally, in a gesture the Wrights could only have considered a rank betrayal, Octave Chanute examined the wreckage and told reporters "if the Wrights had used one propeller instead of two, the result would not have been as serious."[4]

But the most damning criticism of Orville came from his brother. In a letter to Milton, Wilbur lamented that the crash was "a great pity, a great pity." He assured his father that he felt "sure we can keep such a thing from happening again." Then, with damning offhandedness, Wilbur wrote, "I think the trouble was caused by the feverish conditions under which Orville had to work. His time was consumed by people who wished to congratulate and encourage him."

To Katharine, he was more blunt. After telling her, "The death of poor Selfridge was a greater shock to me than Orville's injuries," he wrote, "I cannot help thinking over and over again, 'If I had been there, it would not have happened.' The worry over leaving Orville alone to undertake those trials was one of the chief things in almost breaking me down a few weeks. . . . It was not right." As if in recognition of what he was implying, Wilbur hastened to add, "I do not mean that Orville was incompetent to do the work itself, but I realized that he would be surrounded by thousands of people who, with the most friendly intentions in the world, would consume his time, exhaust his strength, and keep him [from] having proper rest. When a man is in this condition, he tends to trust more to the carefulness of others instead of doing everything and examining everything himself." Wilbur surmised that if Orville had not delegated the fastening of the screws to Charlie Taylor, but had done it himself, "he would have noticed the thing that made the trouble whatever it may have been."

Katharine's animus toward Selfridge had not seemed to have lessened in the wake of his death. In letters to her family immediately after the events of September 17, Katharine at no time expressed regret for earlier remarks or even mentioned Selfridge. She wrote as if Orville had been in the airplane alone. Finally, Selfridge rated two sentences in a letter to Wilbur, when she noted simply that his burial was to be the next day and that she sent a condolence card to his parents when they arrived in Washington and flowers to the funeral, which no member of the Wright family attended. By the time Selfridge was buried, discussion among the Wrights centered entirely on Orville's injuries and rescheduling the trial for the Signal Corps.

But if the Wrights stayed away, members of the AEA did not. Curtiss—although he had again returned to Hammondsport before the crash—McCurdy, Bell, and Baldwin were named as honorary pallbearers, as was Octave Chanute. After the service, another in the odd events that surrounded the Wright patent claims occurred. As Bell, Baldwin, and some of the others were walking past the tent that held the remains of the Flyer, Bell walked in and measured the chord of the wing. Later, although the sergeant guarding the wreckage confirmed that the measurement was innocently done, simply a matter of curiosity and that the AEA members left afterward, the Wrights accused Bell and the others of using Selfridge's funeral as an opportunity to take detailed measurements and steal their secrets.

The destruction of the Flyer should have left the field open for the only other entrant in the trials. But instead of an airplane, Augustus Herring delivered a series of weak excuses. First he asked for a month's postponement of his August 15 date because a weight fell to the ground while he was testing his motor and the vibration threw it out of tune. He promised to fly rather than transport his machine to Washington. Then he was granted a second month's grace to complete the lightest and most efficient motor ever. Finally, on October 12, with no further adjournments possible, he showed up at Fort Myer—arriving by train—with two large suitcases and a wardrobe trunk in which were a few disembodied parts of the aircraft he claimed was not quite ready but when completed would dwarf the accomplishments of all who had come before. The army accepted this as a "technical delivery" and gave Herring an additional month to produce an actual product. In November, Herring assembled the press to report that he had indeed flown his two-surface machine on Long Island with excellent results, but because it sustained minor damage on landing it would not be available to be flown at Fort Myer until the next series of trials in 1909.

Herring's claims to flight were reported but greeted with skepticism and some amusement. In fact, by the time he and his suitcases had left the nation's capital, everyone associated with the trials saw him as little more than a flamboyant liar.* Or almost everyone. One man was sufficiently naïve to continue to take Herring's claims seriously and he would pay dearly for doing so. The man was Glenn Curtiss.

* *The New York Herald* wrote, "The Herring airship is packed in a suit case. This is the safe way to use it."

CHAPTER 16

The Toast of France

Orville remained bedridden in Fort Myer Hospital for six weeks and Katharine was with him every day. "Your sister has been devotion itself," Chanute wrote to Wilbur. "Fearing that he might lack something she stayed up at the hospital every night and deprived herself so much of sleep that I ventured to remonstrate with her about it. She then said that, as the danger of complications seemed to be over, she would take better care of herself, go down to Washington to sleep, and return to Dayton as soon as she felt that she could do so."

His injuries would cause him great pain for the rest of his life, but Orville was determined that neither discomfort nor infirmity would slow him down. He left the hospital in late October in a wheelchair. By sheer force of will, within days he was walking with two canes, within weeks with one. In January 1909, despite being sensitive even to slight vibrations, he set sail for Europe with Katharine to join Wilbur. During the voyage, the ship rolling and bouncing on the waves, he charmed his fellow passengers with his affability and good spirits.

Wilbur had intended to return by Thanksgiving, then by Christmas, but finally realized he would need to remain in Europe well into 1909. His and Orville's dream was finally coming true and he simply could not abandon it. In this he had Orville's full support.

If Wilbur's achievements had inspired awe before Orville's crash, in the wake of the accident he became positively Olympian. Four days after his brother was taken to the hospital, he flew for more than ninety minutes, covering more than forty miles. Three weeks after that, he flew for more than an hour with a passenger. He set an altitude mark in November, flying to ninety meters. Scientists, government officials, other aviators, and royalty were among those who witnessed the incredible exploits of Wilbur Wright and his flying machine. He was given gold medals, honors, and testimonials; he won prizes and received congratulations from luminaries across Europe. He dined with Paul Painlevé and Auguste Rodin. Photographs, descriptions, and caricatures—most emphasizing his emaciated frame—filled the newspapers. Through it all, Wilbur never ceased being Wilbur. He was gracious but modest; appreciative but unimpressed. He tolerated the attention but was never either swayed or spoiled by it. Royalty impressed him not in the least. He wrote to Orville on October 9, "Queen Margherita of Italy was in the crowd yesterday. Princes and millionaires are as thick as thieves on the 'Flyer.'"

What pleased Wilbur more than the accolades was the rush of business. The impediments that had beset the contract with the French syndicate evaporated and in late October Wilbur began to train his first pupil, a French-Russian aristocrat, Charles Alexandre Maurice Joseph Marie Jules Stanislas Jacques, count de Lambert, whose family could be traced back to 1287. The following month, an official French subsidiary was established, La Compagnie Générale de Navigation Aérienne (CGNA). Initial indications were that more than one hundred airplanes could be sold for at least $5,000 each. The Germans, who had resisted establishing a syndicate, now solicited Wilbur, money bulging from their pockets. "Herr Loewe . . . offered $25,000 and a ¼ interest in the business for our German interests. I merely smiled," he wrote to Orville.[1] Italians, Russians, and Britains sought Wilbur out. Officers of the Spanish and even the Argentine military made their introductions. In November, the Wrights were offered $500,000 by an Italian syndicate and Wilbur finally realized he was not coming home for the holidays. Instead, he decided to establish a winter training facility in the resort city of Pau, in the south of France near the Spanish border.

Soon afterward he asked Orville to join him in Europe "for a couple of months." Ten days later, he became more insistent. "I very strongly suggest that you and Kate, and Pop if he will, should come over to Europe immediately. It is important to get machines ready for the spring business. . . . I do not see how I can get home, and yet I am crazy to see some of the home folks and to have some consultation with you. I believe it would be the best thing you could do."

Orville and Kate booked passage immediately. Milton, who had just turned eighty, could not make the trip. On January 11, 1909, they landed in Plymouth, and they were in Paris the following day.

Working with the AEA convinced Curtiss that the future was in fixed wings, not balloons. Although he and Baldwin would remain close, Curtiss threw his energies and vision to improving airplanes. His first idea was to rig an airplane to take off and land on water. The Wrights had made a cursory experiment with a water takeoff in March 1908 but quit after the initial attempts failed badly. Curtiss decided to use *June Bug* as a vehicle for real experimentation. He attached pontoons of various weights and configurations to the undercarriage and tried lifting off from Lake Keuka. The *June Bug*, now renamed the *Loon*, failed to become airborne. The pontoons, even at their lightest, added too much weight for the thrust generated by the motor. But Curtiss had a baseline from which to work and he would soon revisit hydroplanes.

Toward the end of 1908, the AEA produced its fourth and final design, this one McCurdy's, which was dubbed *Silver Dart*. The craft did not contain any great innovations, but featured a water- rather than air-cooled engine, larger ailerons, and sturdier construction. It was test-flown constantly, perhaps for as many as one thousand miles.

The AEA weren't the only ones making strides in aircraft design. Santos-Dumont had moved from the lumbering *Bird of Prey* to a light, exquisitely designed monoplane he called *Demoiselle* (Damsel). Constructed of bamboo and silk and with a two-cylinder motor, the *Demoiselle* had a span of only seventeen feet, was nineteen feet long, and weighed only 265 pounds. In his tiny craft, Santos-Dumont made speeds of more than fifty miles per hour. Henri Farman, flying a craft designed with the Voisin brothers, continued to make impressive shows of speed and distance. Louis Blériot, short and dumpy with a wide handlebar mustache and a shambling demeanor suitable to the Comédie Française, had entered the lists as well. After making a good deal of money by inventing acetylene headlamps for automobiles, Blériot had begun to dabble in flight in 1903. His first construction was an ornithopter that could not get off the ground; his glider collaboration with Gabriel Voisin had met with an equal lack of success. Finally, in 1907, he built a monoplane, the *Blériot VII,* a clumsy, poor-handling affair that nonetheless could more or less sustain flight. By late 1908, he had moved four models further on and his untested *Blériot XI* seemed to hold great promise.

The Wright patent seemed to deter no one. Early in 1909, Glenn Curtiss proceeded to take the very steps he had assured the Wrights he would not—exploit aviation commercially and in exhibitions. To facilitate his move, he joined forces with a man who assured him that together they could not only produce the most advanced airplanes ever seen but also keep any legal maneuvers by the Wrights at bay.

Having been repeatedly shunned by the Wrights, Augustus Herring had initiated a telegram exchange in which he persuaded Curtiss that he held patents on airplane stability that preceded the Wrights' and insisted that the time was ripe to enter the market "before the Wrights took to the courts with their patent and tried to monopolize the business." To sweeten his ultimate offer of partnership, Herring told Curtiss that he had financial connections in New York who were just itching to capitalize on the commercial possibilities of airplane production. At one point, Herring wired, "Best possible backing. Small company first. Way clear to million each."[2] It took Curtiss almost a month to decide but the deal seemed simply too good to pass up. And so, on March 3, 1909, the new partners met the press and announced that the G. H. Curtiss Manufacturing Company would become the Herring–Curtiss Company.

It was a colossal blunder. In order to obtain Herring's patents, or rather the promise of Herring's patents since Curtiss didn't ask to see paperwork in advance, Curtiss put up almost all of the money, and the corporate structure was so ill-considered that Herring ended up with most of the stock. When asked at the press conference why he had yet to fly publicly, Herring replied that he could not make public demonstrations because his patents were only pending, but even then Curtiss did not feel the need to demand more details.

Curtiss wasn't alone in his stunning gullibility. Cortlandt Field Bishop became a stockholder and director of the company, although his $21,000 investment was a good deal less than Curtiss's outlay of more than $82,000, which represented almost his entire net worth.[3] Bishop's brother invested an additional $16,000 and the Bishops were supposed to attract other New York millionaires, which never happened. Thomas Baldwin was made a director and would head the "airship division," which would never exist. Curtiss assigned plant, property, and goodwill of the G. H. Curtiss Manufacturing Company to the new venture. Herring's outlay, as can best be determined, was less than $6,000 and might not have exceeded $1,000.[4]

The arrangement, of which Curtiss had not informed his AEA partners in advance, strained his relations with the other members, although, oddly, Bell himself always remained on good terms with the man who walked out on him. McCurdy and Baldwin released a statement just after the announcement in which they speculated with obvious irony that Herring must have provided some very strong evidence that he wasn't a fraud to get Curtiss to team up with him. The Herring–Curtiss Company was incorporated on March 19; on March 31, the Aerial Experiment Association officially disbanded in a solemn little ceremony in Bell's home. Glenn Curtiss, who had been entreated by Bell to make the final trip to Baddeck, was not in attendance.

Before the ink was dry on their agreement, Herring was off, supposedly dividing his time between preparing his airplane for the 1909 Fort Myer trials and rounding up customers and investors for Herring–Curtiss. As Curtiss would later learn, he was actually doing neither.

Orville and Katharine joined Wilbur in Pau, where large, opulent living quarters and workspace had been specially built for the famed Americans at a cost to the city of $15,000. In return, the Wrights made the city the official site of their training school. There Wilbur and Orville were "inundated" with requests from Europe's elite. They flew for Edward VII of England, former prime minister Arthur Balfour, and King Alfonso of Spain. (Alfonso had wanted to be the first monarch to make a flight himself, but his wife had wheedled a promise from him to remain on the ground. The king kept to his vow but muttered while he watched Wilbur fly figure eights that airplanes were safer than automobiles. Katharine later praised Alfonso for being "a good husband" for not breaking his word and going aloft.)

The Wrights were the most noted Americans in Europe, written about in newspapers across the Continent, often either in hyperbole or outright fiction. But unlike articles in previous years, these exaggerations were all flattering, or would have been if Wilbur, Orville, and Katharine hadn't found them so silly. That none of the Wrights had their head turned would be an understatement. "Kings are just like other nice, well-bred people," Katharine remarked to a reporter.[5]

At the end of March, Wilbur traveled to Italy in response to an offer of $10,000 to fly demonstrations and train two aviators. He spent almost the entire month of April flying on a plain outside Rome before the likes of King Victor Emmanuel and J. P. Morgan. As the month drew to a close, the Wrights were forced to return home to prepare for the Fort Myer trials. Wilbur had not set foot in the United States for almost a year. Instead of sailing from France, however, the brothers made a stopover in Great Britain, where there had been a good deal of discussion at the War Office about developing an air fleet. They left without coming to a licensing arrangement but instead contracted with a private firm to produce six airplanes for sale with the possibility of a good many more in the future.

The three Wrights sailed into New York Harbor on May 11, 1909, as national heroes. Of far more importance to them, they seemed to be on the verge of becoming as wealthy and powerful as Rockefeller or Carnegie.

Also in May 1909, Curtiss produced a radically new airplane. Dubbed the *Gold Bug* for the color of the varnish used over the "Baldwin rubberized silk" wing fabric, the craft was a biplane, with parallel wings instead of the AEA's bows, a twenty-nine-foot span and 4.5-foot chord, and a double front elevator and double vertical rudder with a horizontal panel halfway up. Control was generated by a movable steering wheel rather than a lever, and the landing gear was Curtiss's usual tricycle design with a brake on the front wheel. But the feature that made the *Gold Bug* unique was the placement of "movable surfaces at either extremity of the main planes, each movable surface being half within the main cell and half without." In other words, Curtiss had for the first time devised a system of true ailerons, independent surfaces that would enhance stability and maneuverability. For speed, always a Curtiss priority, he produced a newly designed motor, lightweight, four cylinder, and water cooled, which Curtiss claimed "develops more power per square inch of piston area than has ever been secured in a gas engine."[6] An eight-cylinder motor was under construction.

The *Gold Bug,* which Curtiss renamed *Golden Flier,* had an additional distinction. After failing to buy a machine from the Wrights, the Aeronautical Society of America, a group of wealthy aviation aficionados, had ordered the airplane from Curtiss and had agreed to pay $5,000 for it, the first commercial sale of an aircraft in the United States.* The deal included the training of two men. As Herring had

* The Aeronautical Society was not affiliated with the Aero Club and was generally dismissed by the older organization as being filled with dilettantes.

insisted that his "contract" with the Signal Corps predated their agreement and was thus his alone, Curtiss applied the same standard to the Aeronautical Society sale. When the Wrights learned of the transaction, which they viewed most correctly as a blatant violation of Curtiss's promise, they immediately began to lay the grounds for a lawsuit. But with an aileron patent pending of his own and Herring's patents now at his disposal, Curtiss was confident he could withstand any legal assault.

Also in May 1909, Augustus Herring was granted yet another extension on delivery of his airplane to the Signal Corps, one month, this time because "public exhibition might invalidate two of his foreign patents." Still, Curtiss pushed on, remaining oblivious to the possibility that Herring would offer him no protection at all.

In mid-June, as a condition of the sale, he flew the *Golden Flier* at Morris Park in the Bronx, the first public flight of an airplane in New York City. The machine handled wonderfully and Curtiss decided to make a run for the second leg of the *Scientific American* trophy, which would go to the entrant making the longest flight during the calendar year of at least twenty-five kilometers. The magazine's editors and the Aero Club officials had expected the *Silver Dart* to enter, but McCurdy and Bell pulled out.* The Wrights once more declined, particularly since as they now saw it they would be competing against their own invention.

On July 17, at Mineola, Long Island, Curtiss made nineteen circuits of the 1⅓-mile course, more than forty kilometers, to claim the prize. Anyone with knowledge of airplanes would have noticed something else of significance about Curtiss's flight. His system of ailerons was more efficient than the Wrights' wing warping. (Later, opponents of the Wrights' patent claims would wonder why, if the Wrights had actually anticipated ailerons, they hadn't used them.)

For the Wrights, the Mineola flight was the final indignity. Only

* Bell objected to a change in the rules. Originally the prize would go to the first airplane to travel twenty-five kilometers. When the magazine decided to keep the competition open for the entire year, Bell withdrew under protest.

weeks later, Wilbur would meet with attorneys in New York to file suit. At about the same time, the army refused Herring's request for yet another extension and canceled his contract.

Upon their return from Europe, the Wrights, who had yet to sell a single airplane in their native country, were treated like conquerors. On June 10, President William Howard Taft personally presented them with the Aero Club medals and the following week they were feted with a huge two-day presentation in Dayton. Bishop Milton Wright gave the invocation on the first day and in a grand ceremony on the second, General James Allen of the Signal Corps presented the brothers with a Congressional Medal, Governor Judson Harmon presented them with the Ohio Medal, and Mayor Edward Burkhart presented them with the Dayton Medal. Through it all, Wilbur and Orville stood in obvious discomfort at the spectacle and not at all pleased that they had been drawn away from their work. In fact, they were in the shop both mornings, leaving only to take part in as little of the hoopla as possible. Both brothers' speeches were restricted to "Thank you, gentlemen." The following day, they left for Washington to complete the Fort Myer trials.

The Wrights remained at Fort Myer for more than a month. Despite constant hectoring that they get on with the tests—at one point, the Senate adjourned to watch, only to have Orville refuse to go aloft in a 15-mph wind—the Wrights were determined to be cautious, thorough, and painstaking, and that there be no repetition of the 1908 disaster. They tested, they fine-tuned, they monitored the weather as never before. As *Aeronautics* delicately phrased it, the Wrights' approach "certainly should serve as an object lesson in patience and perseverance to both inventors and experimenters." When they finally felt comfortable that the conditions were right, both brothers decided that Orville should do all the flying. There was perhaps no activity that would be more painful for him than being launched down a rail and then sitting in front of an airplane motor, but Orville intended to bury the previous year's crash forever.

On July 27, Orville took army lieutenant Frank Lahm as a passenger on a record-breaking flight of more than one hour, twelve minutes. Ten thousand spectators crowded the airfield to watch, including President Taft and most of his cabinet. Taft personally congratulated Orville after he landed. With the army's requirement for a one-hour, two-man flight fulfilled, all that remained was a five-mile flight with a passenger at forty miles per hour, which Orville undertook three days later. With the 130-pound Lieutenant Benjamin Foulois next to him, Orville flew to Alexandria and back, almost ten miles, averaging 42.58 miles per hour, and thus earned a $5,000 bonus for the additional two miles per hour, bringing the army contract to $30,000.

Gone was the whispering about the Wrights' years of silence and their month of delay at Fort Myer. Orville and Katharine returned to Dayton the following day while Wilbur remained in Washington to finalize the contract to sell airplanes to the army and train aviators, an agreement that they had sought for four years.

But before Wilbur could sit down with the generals, even before Orville's two brilliant test flights, the Wrights' dream of dominating aviation had been smashed. The culprit was not Glenn Curtiss. Such was the progress of aviation that a forty-kilometer flight around a set course was no longer exceptional. But on July 25, an event occurred whose immense significance not even the Wrights could deny. On that day, in a monoplane of his own design, with a foot so badly burned that he had to be helped into the cockpit, Louis Blériot flew across the English Channel.

CHAPTER 17

Trading Punches

Nine months before Blériot's flight, in October 1908, inspired by Wilbur's demonstrations, Lord Northcliffe, owner of the English newspaper *Daily Mail,* had offered a prize of £1,000 ($5,000) to the first man to achieve the crossing. Northcliffe was in awe of the Wrights and as with most everyone involved in aviation expected Wilbur to immediately declare his intention to claim the prize. He even offered Wilbur an additional $7,500 under the table to undertake the flight.* But unwilling to risk failure in the harsh Channel winds, especially after Orville's crash at Fort Myer, Wilbur declined to make the attempt. He chose instead the safer option of the Coupe Michelin, also worth $5,000. He was awarded that prize after a remarkable two-hour-and-nine-minute flight in intense cold at Le Mans in which he officially traveled seventy-three miles but "counting the wide curves" might have flown ninety.† He waited until the final day of the year to make certain that his effort would not be bested. "I

* After Blériot's feat, Orville would write to Wilbur that "the *Daily Mail* is against us."

† The prize had been initiated by André Michelin earlier in 1908, to be awarded each year until 1915 to the aviator who flew the farthest on a predetermined course. Michelin intended to award a "grand prize" at the end of the eight-year competition, but after 1914 French aviators were no longer flying for sport.

am sorry that I could not come home for Christmas," he wrote to his father on New Year's Day of 1909, "but I could not afford to lose the Michelin prize, as the loss of prestige would have been much more serious than the direct loss. If I had gone away, the other fellows would have fairly busted themselves to surpass any record I left."[1]

Wilbur could certainly have then attempted the twenty-three-mile Channel flight, less than a third of the distance he'd already flown, but again he declined. He missed an enormous opportunity. Crossing the Channel in 1909 was like crossing the Atlantic in 1927. The prestige that would accrue to the man who succeeded in traversing the most famous geographical barrier in Europe spurred a rush of activity and innovation. By summer 1909, three French aviators had airplanes they thought equal to the task.

The first, Hubert Latham, whose father was the son of a wealthy English indigo trader and whose mother the daughter of an even wealthier French banker, was a fearless motorboat racer and big-game hunter and had already floated across the Channel in a balloon at night. Latham was tall, handsome, urbane, and equally facile in French, German, and English. He was never seen in less than the latest fashion and a cigarette in a long white holder was a constant companion. Latham would attempt the crossing in the *Antoinette IV*, Léon Levavasseur's latest, a monoplane that had the look of a giant insect. The second was Wilbur Wright's pupil, Count de Lambert, who had purchased two Wright Flyers and brought them to the French coast. The third was Blériot. After witnessing Wilbur's exhibitions, Blériot abandoned the ailerons that he had stuck on the ends of the wings and adopted wing warping. Although here was a blatant appropriation of the Wrights' patent, neither the Wrights nor the French company that was manufacturing Flyers under a Wright license took immediate action.

Smart money and sentiment were with Latham. The Wrights' achievements notwithstanding, the *Antoinette* seemed the most advanced aircraft and the French/English Latham could boast supporters on both sides of the Channel. Latham did take off first, early on July 19. With huge, cheering crowds on both coasts and motorboats and yachts dotting the water, Latham got about a third of the way across before his engine stalled and he was dumped into the rough Channel waters. When the warship that had been dispatched for just such an eventuality reached him, Latham was sitting placidly on the fuselage of the crippled *Antoinette,* puffing on a cigarette. As soon as he stepped out on dry land, he ordered another *Antoinette,* the *VII,* this one also with warped wings instead of ailerons.

The next day, Count de Lambert became a casualty without ever clearing land. He crashed both of his newly purchased Flyers and was forced to drop out. That left Latham and Blériot to sit in their rooms in Calais and wait for the howling winds to sufficiently subside to allow them to fly in safety. Blériot was nursing a left foot with third-degree burns, suffered on an earlier flight of the *XI* when the asbestos insulation on his exhaust pipe had shaken loose. Blériot needed crutches to walk and intended to strap them to the fuselage so that he might make his way about when he reached England.

Finally, just after midnight on July 25, the wind abated. Blériot and his wife were awakened at two in the morning. He ate breakfast, tested the aircraft, and waited for both sunrise and Latham. But Latham never appeared. An associate had forgotten to wake him. Blériot took off at 4:30 A.M., doubtless reveling in his luck. After six years, a string of failures, and countless crashes, he was flying uncontested to celebrity and renown—assuming he didn't end up in the water.

For the Channel flight, Blériot had purchased a three-cylinder, 25-horsepower Anzani motor, light but not particularly powerful. Ten minutes after takeoff, he disappeared into the mist. His wife stood terrified at the railing of the warship as it steamed to where her husband might be if he had gone down. Even with the cork lifebelt Blériot wore, with his foot bandaged and the water particularly rough, there was little chance of survival if he were forced into the waves. But ten minutes later, the *Blériot XI* emerged from the clouds. Cheering on the English side told those aboard ship that the monoplane was still airborne.

Shortly after 5 A.M., Blériot landed in a field marked by supporters waving *tricoleurs*. Oil thrown from the engine covered his face and he complained that the wind over the Channel had stung, but he was helped out of the *XI,* unstrapped his crutches, and limped into immortality.

Told of his competitor's plight, Blériot agreed to split the prize if Latham followed him across that day, but Blériot's luck was complete. Heavy wind and rain appeared almost as soon as he landed and Latham was left near Calais, "sitting with his head on his monoplane, weeping."[2] Blériot, on the other hand, became an instant international icon. He was awarded the Legion of Honor and mobbed in London and Paris. Among the attendees at the luncheon in his honor to receive his £1,000 check was Ernest Shackleton, recently returned from the Antarctic.

Orville Wright, when told of Blériot's feat at Fort Myer, agreed it "was a great flight," and that the Frenchman was one of the most daring of all aviators. But Orville also hastened to note that Blériot's was a personal triumph and not "an advancement in the art of flying" as "the monoplane has not as good a method of control as the biplane we use." Orville also noted that Blériot had "added movable wing tips to his machine."[3] But no backhanded praise could obscure that the Frenchman had stolen headlines out from under him. Blériot's flight, noted a Wright biographer, "was one of those rare moments when the entire world sensed that something extraordinary had occurred."[4] Told of Orville's comments, Glenn Curtiss also congratulated Blériot and added, "He has demonstrated beyond a doubt that he has built a monoplane that is serviceable and trustworthy."[5]

As well as gaining him personal glory, Blériot's crossing had restored French national honor. To mark the return of aviation supremacy, a consortium of champagne growers led by Marquis de Polignac, chairman of Pommery, decided to host the world's first-ever "air meet," a

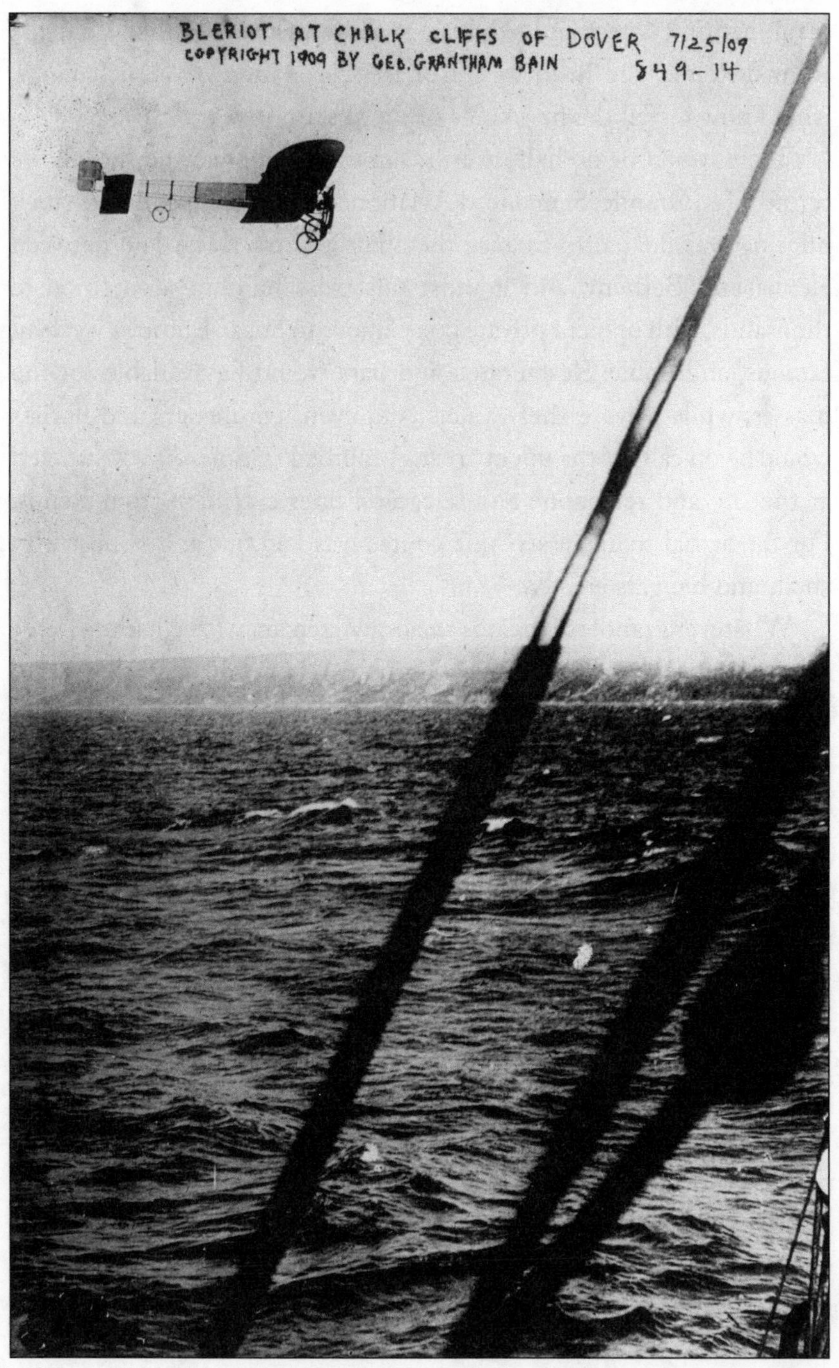

BLERIOT AT CHALK CLIFFS OF DOVER 7/25/09
COPYRIGHT 1909 BY GEO. GRANTHAM BAIN
849-14

Louis Blériot over Dover. His flight across the English Channel would bring worldwide acclaim, to the consternation of the Wrights.

combination contest and exhibition in the fields of Bétheny, outside Reims. Reims, the historic site of the coronation of French kings, would now install the first kings of the skies.

There would be no half measures in what Polignac and his fellows termed La Grande Semaine d'Aviation de la Champagne. A stock offering was floated to finance the affair, rail track was laid between Reims and Bétheny, and grandstands were built to accommodate thousands, with opulent private boxes above to house Europe's wealthy, famous, and noble. Restaurants and bars would be available for the masses, while private chefs, valets, and even hairdressers and florists would be on call for the upper crust. A railroad station was constructed at the site and telephone and telegraph lines extended from Reims. For the actual flying, a six-mile course was laid out and almost fifty sheds and hangars erected.

Whatever grandiose dreams the organizers may have harbored, reality outdid them. Tickets were grabbed up almost as they were printed, every hotel room in Reims was quickly booked, and a thriving spare-bedroom market grew up among private homeowners. When even that proved insufficient, city fathers erected temporary shelters to house the crowds. Eventually, so many spectators descended on Reims that an area large enough to hold forty thousand was hastily built to supplement the grandstand.

In the program, daily prizes and 200,000 francs would be awarded for a variety of performance criteria, including distance, speed, duration, and altitude. By far the most prestigious event would be the Coupe Gordon Bennett, awarded to the aviator who completed the fastest two laps of a ten-kilometer course that was longer than any man had flown publicly just one year before.* France was betting on its new Legion of Honor recipient, Louis Blériot.

Although the organizers very much wanted the meet to be "international," only one of the more than twenty competitors who had

* Bennett was the expatriate publisher of *The New York Herald* and a longtime air enthusiast who put up a $5,000 prize to go with the trophy.

agreed to come to Reims was not French—George Cockburn, a Scot. The Wrights easily could have participated. Orville was already in Europe, having sailed over with Katharine in August to set up the Wright subsidiary in Germany. There he dined with Kaiser Wilhelm and Count Zeppelin and proceeded to stun the Germans as had Wilbur the French. Seeing how the Wright exploits had prompted all this aviation hysteria, it would have been a coup to journey to Reims and walk away with the big prize.

But the Wrights once again refused. In this case, it was not timidity but pique; their competitors, after all, were a bunch of patent infringers. Still, Orville wrote Wilbur that he had been told, "Our machines will take 75% of the prizes at Rheims unless something unexpected happens."[6] So Orville remained in Germany to generate sales, conducting demonstrations before huge crowds, which included almost every member of the royal family, and Wilbur stayed put in America. With the Wrights unavailable, Cortlandt Field Bishop, Aero Club president and Curtiss partner, asked Curtiss to represent American aviation at Reims. Although Curtiss later claimed to have "been chosen," he in fact knew he was Bishop's second choice.[7]

Nonetheless, Curtiss accepted instantly. Like Blériot, he focused on the top prize, the Gordon Bennett trophy. "Without letting my plans become known to the public, I began at once to build an eight-cylinder, V-shaped, fifty-horsepower motor. This was practically double the horsepower I had been using. Work on the motor was pushed day and night at Hammondsport, as I had not an hour to spare."[8]

Curtiss also designed an airframe for the event, made it as small, light, and maneuverable as he could, then as with the *Golden Flier* placed ailerons at the end of the wings on the last front bracing between the two airfoils. He dubbed his entry the *Rheims Racer*.* He finished with so little time to spare that "in order to get to Rheims in time to qualify, we had to take the aeroplane with us on the train as personal baggage." When Curtiss arrived he was stunned to learn that

* "Rheims" was the accepted spelling in 1909.

Blériot had mounted an eight-cylinder, 80-horsepower motor on his refurbished *XI,* and Latham, who was back in the *Antoinette IV* after another failed attempt to cross the Channel on July 29, had been reported as flying as fast as sixty miles per hour. Curtiss, whose "personal hopes lay in my motor," then thought his chances "very slim indeed."

Almost forty fixed-wing airplanes were entered but only three aviators were in Wright Flyers, five of which had been purchased from the Wright Company French affiliate.

As the meet opened, Curtiss was informed that the Wright brothers had filed a patent infringement suit against the Aeronautical Society of America in New York City and against Herring–Curtiss Company and him personally in Buffalo. He replied, "I should like to ask the Wrights if they really believe my machine is an infringement of their patents. It is quite absurd to say so."[9]

The infringement suit seemed to be the first in a series of omens. Curtiss suffered a badly sprained ankle in a practice flight and in another barely avoided a midair collision with an *Antoinette* by quickly gaining altitude and flying over the other aircraft. The maneuver earned applause from the thousands who lined the practice area and a sigh of relief from Curtiss. Unlike most of the French, he had brought only one plane with him and if that was damaged he was out of the competition. He therefore avoided many of the early events, resulting in some grousing from an American contingent that included former first lady Edith Roosevelt and eleven-year-old Quentin, the ex-president's youngest son.

Although spectators and aviators were forced to contend with weather that was often uncooperative, the actual flying overwhelmed any inconvenience. *The New York Times* called the Reims meet "a week of miracles."[10] Hundreds of thousands who had never seen a plane in the air, many of whom did not even believe that flight was possible, witnessed three, five, even eight airplanes in the sky at once. On one occasion, seven aircraft flew against the backdrop of the 275-foot-tall towers of the famed medieval cathedral that heretofore had been the city's most magnificent attraction. Huge crowds gasped at crashes and cheered success. Standing marks for distance, duration, speed, and altitude—Latham soared to a heady 508 feet—were beaten and then beaten again. Hubert Latham, Henri Farman, and a newcomer, Louis Paulhan, played leapfrog in the record books. Farman eventually stayed in the air a stunning three hours and fourteen minutes, traveling 112.41 miles, obliterating Wilbur Wright's distance record and winning $10,000, the biggest single prize awarded. Farman also won the $2,000 prize for flying with passengers, which had been expected to go to an aviator in a Wright.

By the time the Coupe Gordon Bennett was run, crashes and mechanical mishaps had eliminated all but five qualifiers. Glenn Curtiss went first and set a blistering time of 15:50.4, or 45.73 miles per hour.[11] The three flyers who went next, Latham, Cockburn, and Eugène Lefebvre in a Wright Flyer, could not come close to Curtiss's time, but the last competitor was Blériot. With a more powerful engine, Blériot outstripped Curtiss on the straightaways, but the aileron-

Curtiss besting a competitor at the first Gordon Bennett Race, Reims, France.

equipped *Rheims Racer* was far more efficient in the turns. Curtiss, watching from the staging area, was certain Blériot had won but when the times were taken, Blériot had finished six seconds behind. The huge crowd, which had been screaming Blériot's name, was stunned when the Stars and Stripes was run up and the band played "The Star-Spangled Banner." The two thousand Americans in the crowd cheered wildly and Quentin Roosevelt told Curtiss his victory was "bully."* With his victory, Glenn Curtiss had established himself as the fastest man on earth and in the air. That same day, Wright Company lawyers served papers on Curtiss's wife in Hammondsport.

On the last day of the meet, Curtiss won another speed race, this one thirty kilometers, and became, with Blériot, one of the two most celebrated aviators in the world.

The Wrights, despite a fast start—their airplanes set duration records on the first day and Lefebvre set a speed record on the second—did not have a successful meet. In the final tally, none of three aviators in Wright Flyers—Count de Lambert, Lefebvre, or Paul Tissandier—placed first in any category; their score stood at one second, one third, and four fourth places, whereas Curtiss won two of the three events he entered and finished second in the other. As Orville observed to Wilbur, "We were completely flaxed out. The machines like the *Antoinette*, with long fore and aft dimensions, are much steadier in winds—that is, do not pitch. . . . Lefebvre was the only one that did anything to uphold the reputation of our machines."[12] Orville would soon transmit even worse news. Soon after the meet ended, Eugène Lefebvre was killed in a crash, the second aviation fatality, both coming in Wright Flyers.

Losing as they did at Reims left the Wrights angry and confused, especially since, as Orville put it, "If I had gone in [the races], I think we would have taken everything." Orville also noted to Wilbur, "But I

* Quentin Roosevelt, his father's favorite, would die in air combat in World War I, shot down over France on Bastille Day, 1918. He was twenty years old.

did not enter, having received the telegram saying you were displeased with my competing."[13] Where there was no disagreement was on their view of Glenn Curtiss. In addition to the *Scientific American* trophy, the man whom Orville had described as "frightened" at Reims had now employed stolen technology to win the Gordon Bennett prize. Curtiss in two short years had gone from an obscure fabricator of motorcycle engines to Wilbur and Orville Wright's most loathed and feared competitor. That he flew to acclaim seemingly oblivious of his crimes must have incensed the rigidly moral Wrights all the more.

Curtiss, now a major attraction, packed up the *Rheims Racer* and headed to Brescia, Italy, where a group of promoters had put together another air meet. Brescia, at the time Italy's third-largest city, was a noted racing center, first for bicycles, then automobiles. Many of the French aviators, including Blériot, journeyed south as well, although Blériot would be less of a threat as he had burned both his hands after an explosion on the last day at Reims. Not as opulent as Reims and plagued by the same spotty weather, Brescia nonetheless attracted hundreds of thousands of spectators, including King Victor Emmanuel and Princess Letizia, Giacomo Puccini, and the poet Gabriele d'Annunzio. A young Franz Kafka attended the meet as a reporter.

As they had at Reims, French-made planes dominated, but the $10,000 grand prize for speed went to Curtiss. He also won the quick-start prize and finished second in altitude. Wright Flyers were again shut out. After the competition was completed, Curtiss took d'Annunzio aloft, the first time he had carried a passenger. The poet exclaimed, "Until now, I have not really lived." He later announced that he was rewriting the protagonist of the novel on which he was working to make him more resemble the redoubtable American.

When Curtiss crated his airplane to head for home, he did so as an American hero. Few newspapers devoted more than a line or two of copy to note that he was being sued by two other American heroes who accused him of being a thief. On September 22, just days after he disembarked from the *Kaiser Wilhelm* in New York, the Aero Club of

America hosted a luncheon honoring the *Rheims Racer*'s victory, for which Wilbur Wright was invited to share the head table. Wilbur declined to attend.*

But Wilbur gained retribution only days later at a venue every bit as lavish and ostentatious as Reims or Brescia, except this one was in the largest and most important city in the United States.

In 1905, a commission made up of New York's most elite began planning a celebration of the three-hundredth anniversary of Henry Hudson's discovery of the river that bore his name and the centennial (plus two years) of Robert Fulton's sailing a steamboat on it. Members included Andrew Carnegie, William Rockefeller, William Van Rensselaer, Andrew Dickson White, Grover Cleveland, Joseph H. Choate, J. P. Morgan, Oscar Straus, and Seth Low.

The occasion was as much to celebrate the rise to preeminence of the only recently incorporated New York City as the accomplishments of two men.† Hudson–Fulton would be celebrated in all five boroughs; hundreds of thousands of incandescent bulbs would light the streets and the masts of ships; millions of yards of ribbon would stream from lampposts, doorways, and buildings; fifty-two American warships would take part in an international naval parade up the Hudson that would stretch for ten miles. Exact replicas of the *Half Moon* and the *Clermont* would be built, manned, and sailed. On the ground, a military parade would march up Broadway, extolling the might of a nation that had recently joined Europe in the race to empire. There would be a historical parade, a carnival parade, a children's festival, and dedicated museum exhibits; Brooklyn would host a series of auto races. The extravaganza would attract more than one million visitors, including dignitaries from virtually every nation on earth.

* Curtiss was presented with a gold medal at the luncheon, at which 150 were in attendance, including Guglielmo Marconi, inventor of the wireless. The Gordon Bennett trophy, which Curtiss had also received, was topped with a facsimile of a Wright Flyer.

† Until 1898, New York City consisted of Manhattan and the West Bronx. On January 1, 1899, the east Bronx, Richmond, Queens, and Kings County (the city of Brooklyn) were merged to form Greater New York City.

Initially, the organizers had envisioned an airship display over the Hudson as one of the centerpieces of the weeklong event. Thomas Baldwin signed on early and would be the featured balloonist. As the months played out, however, it became clear that no spectacle would be complete without an exhibition of America's acclaimed new invention, the airplane.

In early August, the committee contacted Wilbur Wright and offered $15,000 for a flight of at least ten miles or one hour, with as many trials as were needed. At first, Wilbur hesitated. New York Bay and the Hudson were considered particularly treacherous to airplanes because of unpredictable crosswinds and updrafts caused by the Palisades on the New Jersey side. A crash at such a prominent venue would be a professional as well as a personal disaster. Finally, however, the opportunity to demonstrate the Flyer's capability to an immense domestic audience proved too tempting to refuse. Wilbur told Orville of the contract in the same August 21 letter in which he informed his brother that he had "met Mr. Toulmin at Washington for the purpose of starting suit against the Curtiss crowd."[14]

After word of the Reims meet reached America, the committee cabled Curtiss and offered him $5,000 for a flight from the staging area on Governors Island to Grant's Tomb at 122nd Street and back, a distance of about twenty miles. It is uncertain if Curtiss was aware he was being paid only a third of what had been offered to the Wrights for a flight of twice the distance but, in any event, Curtiss accepted, intending to use the *Rheims Racer*. Only after he returned to the United States, however, did he discover that Herring had accepted $5,000 from Rodman Wanamaker to display the *Racer* in Wanamaker's department store.

Having nothing to fly, Curtiss returned to Hammondsport immediately after the Aero Club luncheon for a replacement airplane, this one untested and with a good deal less horsepower than the *Racer*'s V-8. It did not arrive until September 27, leaving just a day to assemble and prepare the craft, and then make the flight. Curtiss had also accepted an offer of $5,000 to help commemorate St. Louis's centennial the first week of October, a schedule that would have been workable if the *Rheims Racer* had been available when he docked. The Wrights had been invited to St. Louis as well, but had refused.

Two adjacent hangars had been built on Governors Island, so for the first time since the Wrights filed suit, Wilbur and Curtiss were forced into proximity. Neither of the combatants exhibited animosity in public. When Curtiss arrived, he made a point of popping into the Wright hangar to say hello and Wilbur made a point of asking a number of questions about Reims. Newspapers dutifully reported that "no ill feeling exists because of the suit which the Wright brothers have brought against the Herring–Curtiss company for alleged infringement of patents. Wright asked Curtiss if he found the information given him by the Wrights before he sailed for France of any value to him. Mr. Curtiss replied that he had and further pleasantries were exchanged."[15]

Grover Loening had a much better view and saw things differently. "Wilbur was furious at this controversy," he wrote later. "[He] openly despised Curtiss, was convinced he was not only faking but doing so with a cheap scheme to hurt the Wrights, and here on this very occasion was the first public appearance of that vicious hatred and rivalry between the Wright and Curtiss camps."[16]

Loening, who would spend a lifetime in aviation, went to the Hudson–Fulton while still an engineering student at Columbia University. Because of family connections and his knowledge of aeronautics, he was allowed to loiter in areas generally reserved for the aviators and so witnessed behavior hidden from public view. Curtiss treated him civilly but Wilbur took to the twenty-one-year-old, even putting him to work on the Flyer. The Wrights subsequently hired Loening after his graduation and within four years he was the Wright Company's chief engineer.

Predictably, as a lifelong Wright supporter, Loening was no friend of Curtiss. In his memoirs Loening described him as merely "a promoter," rather than "an engineer or scientist," as opposed to Wilbur and Orville, who were both. He attributed Curtiss's notoriety solely to a coterie of clever "publicity men." Loening related an anecdote from the Hudson–Fulton exhibition to prove his point. "On a flying field, I once found Curtiss standing near one of his new planes. I asked him a simple question about the approximate area of the tail surface. Curtiss answered, 'Oh, I don't know, but if it isn't right the boys will fix it.' And in that answer is the evidence that Curtiss was a promoter and not an engineer or even his own designer, excepting in a vague way. But if Orville was asked a similar question, he would bring out of his pocket a little memorandum book he always carried and tell you exactly, not approximately, the figures inquired about."[17]

Leaving aside for the moment that when this encounter took place members of the Wright and Curtiss camps were hardly likely to be expansive with each other, the notion that the man who designed and built the most efficient motors on earth—and the machine that had just beaten the world at Reims—did not know the specifications of his own aircraft is absurd.

Loening's recollections of the Wrights are more elucidatory. "One of the interesting things about Wilbur . . . was the hours of practice he would put in on the controls of the plane, sitting in the seat, hangar doors all closed, no one around, quietly sitting there imagining air disturbances and maneuvers and correcting the rudder and warping wings and elevator to suit."

But where Loening's reminiscences are most valuable are in his discussion of early flight:

> The modern aviator has no conception of what those early planes were like. The stability was nil—flying them felt like sitting on the top of an inverted pendulum ready to fall off to either side at any moment. The speed range was nothing at all. High speed, landing speed, climbing speed were all within one or two miles an hour, because the planes got off into the air with no reserve whatever, and only because of the effect of the ground banking up of air

Wilbur examining the canoe attachment he designed for his first flight over water at the Hudson-Fulton Celebration in New York.

> which was not then understood. . . . Turns had to be most carefully negotiated because the excess power was so low that the plane would often sink dangerously near the tree-tops.[18]

As the appointed time for the air exhibitions grew near, the weather again refused to cooperate. On September 28, both Wilbur and Curtiss waited in vain for the 20-mph gusts to lessen, but they did not. Each had a particular reason not to chance his first flight in marginal conditions. Curtiss, using an untested machine of limited power, couldn't be certain if his airplane would respond in a crisis. Wilbur had attached a canoe sealed with canvas to the underside of his aircraft to add buoyancy in case of a crash on the water; he feared the airplane might flip over without it. As the canoe might alter the aerodynamics, he wanted to be certain of full control during his maiden flight.

After it became clear that no one would fly on the twenty-eighth, Wilbur returned to his hotel in Manhattan, but Curtiss remained on Governors Island and slept in the hangar. He woke early the next morning to discover that the winds had abated but fog had settled in over the bay. From there, what he did or did not do became a source of controversy.

Curtiss, according to later press reports, took off, disappeared into the fog, then returned to Governors Island sometime later to land. It turned out, however, that none of the reporters had actually been present for the flight. Loening later insisted Curtiss hadn't flown at all. "Curtiss never got off the ground," he wrote. "The required run into the wind would have brought him right by where I stood. . . . Also Curtiss never could, in my opinion in that morning fog, again have located the landing area on the island."[19]

When Wilbur arrived shortly after 9 A.M., Loening told him that Curtiss had fabricated the story. While Wilbur never personally accused Curtiss of lying, neither did he dissuade anyone else from doing so. That the Wright camp openly scoffed at Curtiss's claim was duly transmitted to the press but no reporter chose to print the allegation.

Of all the reporters covering the event, perhaps the most knowledgeable was another twenty-one-year-old, Jerome Fanciulli. Fanciulli had studied aerodynamics in college, joined *The Washington Post,* and then moved to the Associated Press, where he became their expert on aviation. Fanciulli had covered the trials at Fort Myer and witnessed Selfridge's death. Both the Wrights and Curtiss respected him, but Curtiss had taken to him as Wilbur Wright had taken to Loening. Fanciulli, on the other hand, thought Curtiss "rather naïve and badly needing someone to manage his affairs, especially his public relations."[20]

Fanciulli was about to be married and was content to remain with the AP, but Tom Baldwin urged Curtiss to lure him away to perform the very functions in which Fanciulli had discerned Curtiss as weak. Curtiss took Baldwin's advice and pressed Fanciulli to head the exhibition team Curtiss foresaw developing, as well as to establish a flight school and oversee sales and marketing of Curtiss airplanes. Fanciulli was tempted but unwilling to have anything to do with Herring, whom he considered a "four-flusher and a fake."

During their meeting, Fanciulli was blunt and direct, and Curtiss, rather than bristling at criticism from an upstart, left convinced that the young reporter was just what he needed. Eventually, Curtiss set up a separate corporation, the Curtiss Exhibition Company, and named Fanciulli vice president and general manager.

After Curtiss's brief flight—or nonflight—the winds once again picked up and he wheeled his airplane back to the hangar and left for his hotel. Wilbur found the temptation irresistible. First he took his Flyer with the canoe affixed underneath for a brief spin around Governors Island to see how it handled. Satisfied even in 15-mph winds, soon afterward he ascended once more, this time flying toward and then around the Statue of Liberty. Before returning to land, Wilbur banked the aircraft toward the huge ocean liner *Lusitania,* which would dominate headlines for a different reason six years hence, and flew across the bow. Thousands cheered onshore and foghorns were cacophonous in the bay. In the afternoon, Wilbur made a third flight, this time venturing into the Hudson River crosswinds.

Even then, Wilbur wasn't done. After he and Curtiss were grounded by weather for the next two days and Curtiss was forced to leave for St. Louis, his contract with the Hudson–Fulton commission unfulfilled, Wilbur decided he would fulfill not only his obligation but also Curtiss's.* On October 4, Wilbur catapulted his Flyer aloft, American flags affixed to the elevators and the canoe, and flew up the Hudson.

A newspaper reported, "An aeroplane flashed past the white dome of Grant's tomb today, then turned gracefully in midair over the Hudson shot like a falcon back to Governors Island, 10 miles away. Wilbur Wright of Dayton, O. thus placed his name in the ranks of Hudson and Fulton today in one of the most spectacular feats in the history of aeronautics."[21]

With Wilbur's tour de force and Orville setting records before

* The commission balked at paying the $3,500 Curtiss asked to defray expenses. Only the threat of a lawsuit got them to fork over $2,500. But Wilbur was never fully paid, either; he received only $12,500 of the promised $15,000.

hundreds of thousands of exultant Germans, Curtiss's victories in France and Italy were finally pushed from the headlines. But the Wrights were also attracting attention of a different sort. In October 1909, *Aeronautics* engaged a New York patent attorney named Thomas A. Hill to analyze the Wrights' suit. Hill knew as much as any attorney anywhere about aircraft design and subsequently served on the board and as president of the Aeronautical Society. To demonstrate impartiality, the *Aeronautics* editors felt it necessary to include a preliminary note that was certain to elicit a volley of guffaws on both sides of the Atlantic. "All interested in the advancement of aviation have welcomed the suit brought by the Wright Brothers, and aviators all over the world should commend the Wrights for taking the initiative towards establishing 'the limits to which other inventors may go' with respect to their particular patent."

Of course, aviators all over the world were furious with the Wrights. In his memoirs, Grover Loening noted that by bringing suit the Wrights had "turned the hand of almost every man in aviation against them."

"I have carefully inspected the file wrapper at Washington," Hill wrote, "and also their bill filed in [United States District Court] and am at a loss to find the motive for such a suit at this time." The crux of Hill's argument was that nothing in the Wrights' patent made reference to or seemed to incorporate "supplemental structures" (ailerons) that in no way altered the "lateral margins" of the wings. To buttress his opinion, Hill cited the Wrights' own letter to the patent examiner appealing the initial rejection of their application. "The twist is in the [wing] surface itself," Wilbur had written, "and has no reference to a variation in the angular inclination of a plane to a car or body suspended beneath it." As ailerons were planes (surfaces) suspended beneath the top wing, Hill considered this demonstrable proof that the Wrights had not conceived of ailerons as a means to lateral stability and therefore could not be seen to have included them in their patent. Hill then cited Harry Toulmin, who, in appealing yet another rejection of the patent application (there were many), wrote, "The lateral balance of the machine is controlled by the twisting of the ends [of the wings]. . . . This is the main feature of the applicants' invention."

Hill concluded, "It is impossible to find under the most liberal interpretation of said claims the particular construction characterizing the Curtiss machine. The use of supplemental surfaces appears to be indisputably a public right."*

It was, however, going to become more difficult for Curtiss to prove that in court; Wilbur and Orville had decided to accept serious investment money and with the money would come all the resources that money buys. The first solicitation had come from Fred and Russell Alger, majority stockholders in the Packard Motor Car Company and sons of a former governor of Ohio. The Algers had corresponded with Orville for a year, expressing interest in forming a corporation. Orville had been noncommittal. In July 1909, Russell Alger suggested bringing in other automobile manufacturers, including Henry Ford. The Wrights still gave no encouragement. In August, the Algers finally made a firm offer. Their group would put up $65,000, for which they would receive 65 percent of the stock. The Wrights would get 35 percent for their patents and also be paid 10 percent of the gross of each airplane sold. Wilbur wrote to Orville, "I replied that we would not care to let so large a proportion of the business go on so ridiculously low prices, but that we might consider letting a small block, say

* Hill was hardly a Curtiss sycophant. In 1914, he initiated a patent infringement suit against Curtiss far more questionable than that of the Wrights. After Curtiss had succeeded in designing an aircraft that could take off and land on water, Hill represented one Albert S. Janin of Staten Island, described in the New York *World* as a "poor cabinet maker" or "an obscure and almost penniless carpenter" who had filed a patent application on the very day Curtiss had first taken off from the water. Janin's concept, for which he had been trying to raise money for years but which was never built nor tested, was to attach small side floats to either side of the aircraft to maintain stability while it rested on the surface of the water. Hill succeeded in obtaining an initial judgment for Janin, who quit his five-dollar-a-day job the day it was handed down, but the ruling was ultimately overturned by an appeals court that characterized Janin's creation as "a mere description."

twenty-five percent, go at a rather low price." The Wrights felt strapped for cash and, as Wilbur wrote to Orville, it was "not going to be easy getting a big cash bonus because the French company has made such a mess of things."*

But help was on the way in the unlikely person of a baby-faced twenty-four-year-old at Morgan Bank. Clinton R. Peterkin had begun as an office boy nine years earlier and worked his way up to a junior loan position. Peterkin proposed to Wilbur that he be allowed to put together a roster of investors. Wilbur admired brashness and so, probably with more than a dose of skepticism, he let Peterkin go ahead—but only if the backers he attracted were well-known and powerful.†

To what was likely everyone's surprise but his own, Peterkin succeeded in doing that very thing. He first ran the idea past old man Morgan himself. Morgan not only pushed in some of his own chips but brought in Elbert Gary, chairman of United States Steel. With those two on board, attracting additional investors was easy. Soon the investor list included Cornelius Vanderbilt, August Belmont, Howard Gould, and an assortment of mine owners, rail magnates, and steel company executives. The Wrights asked to include the Algers and publisher Robert J. Collier, who had been supportive in the pages of his magazine.

But ironically, Morgan could not remain on the board. The other investors feared the titan of 32 Wall Street would overshadow the rest of them, as might Gary for that matter—quite a sentiment coming from men such as Vanderbilt and Belmont. Difficulties were averted

* Why Wilbur and Orville felt that they needed cash is a mystery. Orville had recently sent Lorin, who was keeping the books, a draft for $40,000 from the German affiliate.

† Peterkin might have been young but he was hardly inexperienced. Before approaching Wilbur he had helped finance mines in Mexico, ranches in the Dakotas, and orange groves in Florida. He had been following the Wrights since 1905, a time when most American businessmen didn't know they existed. Eventually, he would earn the nickname "the Harriman of the Air" and enjoy a long and successful business career until his death in Los Angeles in 1944. He was a man of varied interests; in 1906 he wrote a letter to *The New York Times* in which he extolled fresh air and a good diet as a cure for respiratory ailments.

when the two agreed to step aside. Morgan's uncharacteristic gesture of diplomacy was not popular with everyone. When Wilbur sent the details of the new roster to his brother, Orville cabled back, "I prefer J. P. Morgan."

But Morgan remained out and it was soon agreed that Wilbur would be president of the new Wright Company and Orville a vice president, along with financier Andrew Freedman. Clinton Peterkin would also be rewarded with a vice presidency.* The offices of the new company would be in New York but the factory would remain in Dayton.

The financial arrangements were immensely favorable to Wilbur and Orville. The Wright Company would be capitalized at $1 million, quite a step up from the Algers' offer. The Wrights would receive $100,000 in cash, one-third of the stock, and the same 10 percent royalty on sales. (In return, the Wrights agreed to hire the Algers' nephew Frank Russell to run the factory.)

With everyone agreed on particulars, the legal niceties were concluded with dispatch and on November 22, 1909, the Wright Company was incorporated in Albany under the laws of the state of New York. The *New York Times* headline read, "Big Men of Finance Back the Wrights."

One of the primary goals of the new company was to permanently neuter competition. The Algers had been urging Wilbur and Orville to hire a prominent patent attorney for months, but they had stuck with Toulmin. Now, although Toulmin would continue to play a role, higher-powered legal talent would be brought to bear. DeLancey

* Peterkin's stay with the Wright Company would be brief. On November 29, 1909, Andrew Freedman wrote to Wilbur and Orville, "By reason of the actions of Mr. Peterkin since your departure, I have come to the same conclusion that you had already formed, and I do not desire to be associated with him here in connection with management of the company." The nature of the "actions" was never made clear other than that Peterkin had been "indiscreet" with reporters, probably meaning he aggrandized his role in getting the company off the ground. In a subsequent letter to Wilbur and Orville, Freedman noted that Peterkin was very junior at the Morgan Bank and that Vanderbilt agreed that the company would be better without him.

Nicoll, the company's Wall Street lawyer, asserted, "There is not a machine that pilots the air that doesn't infringe the Wright patents." Peterkin told the newspapers that it was "the purpose of the Wrights and the Board of Directors to maintain and defend the Wright patents against all comers . . . and that one of the main purposes in forming the corporation with such a strong Board of Directors was to assist the Wrights in every way to maintain their patent rights."

The long-term corporate vision was as ethereal as the wealth of its investors. "The members of the company are confident that in three years, at least, the aeroplane will be as popular as the automobile," Andrew Freedman observed. To that end, the corporation would open a training facility in Florida, and research would be undertaken to develop passenger service—the Wrights believed a twenty-passenger airplane was already feasible—as well as mail and freight service. Another specific stipulation of the corporate agreement was that Orville and especially Wilbur be left free of any burdensome administrative details so that they could spend their time on research and innovation.

Even worse for Curtiss, at the very moment the Wrights solidified their business, the Herring–Curtiss partnership was descending into chaos. At an October 23 emergency board of directors meeting, Herring was instructed to produce all patents and inventions. The matter could no longer be put off; Herring–Curtiss was being sued and those patents were its best and perhaps only defense. But Herring, of course, could not comply, there being no patents or inventions to produce.* Perhaps of equal importance, the company had almost no money. The only income was what Curtiss earned in prize money and from the sale of motors. Herring–Curtiss had sold only one airplane and the purchaser was being sued by the Wrights, which made further sales in the immediate future problematic.

Curtiss waited two months while Herring stalled, prevaricated,

* Herring, in his later lawsuit against Curtiss, denied that any specific request had ever been made.

and worked behind the scenes to either take control of the company himself or quietly dispose of his stock. Finally, another board meeting was called on December 18, for which Herring showed up with a lawyer. The board voted to seek an injunction compelling him to turn over his patents and inventions. After the vote, Herring asked to leave the room for a few moments to consider his response. A bit later, his lawyer left as well to confer with his client. Neither returned. After a time, Jerome Fanciulli was dispatched to find the two men but both had vanished. Herring, in fact, hid in the woods while his lawyer snuck off to telephone for an automobile. The two then cajoled lodgings for the night and in the morning made their way to the railroad station and eventually New York before their partners could catch up to them.

Curtiss got his injunction the following day but had no one on whom to serve it. Herring had gone into hiding. When he emerged, it was with legal action of his own. Herring accused Curtiss of stealing *his* inventions, of losing Herring's money through mismanagement, and of manipulating the board of directors at Herring's expense. Herring, it seemed, was not about to go quietly—if he would go at all.

The Wrights merely watched with amusement and satisfaction. The contrast between the elite, qualified partners they had taken and the shady, self-promoting proto–confidence man with whom Curtiss had thrown in could not have been more acute. With such a juggernaut at their backs and with Herring–Curtiss on the verge of self-immolation, Wilbur and Orville had every reason to believe that the monopoly they had been seeking for more than five years could now simply be plucked from the trees.

CHAPTER 18

Best-Laid Plans

The stir over fixed-wing aircraft had not diminished the enthusiasm for dirigibles, particularly for the vast majority of Americans who had never seen either in the air. Baldwin, Knabenshue, and Beachey, therefore, did quite well touring the country and either competing for distance or speed or putting on exhibitions, sometimes soaring in tandem. Balloonists would open the St. Louis centennial, although three days had been set aside for Curtiss to fly. Other features of the event included the "appearance of mysterious veiled prophets," and a number of talks by Frederick Cook, an Arctic explorer who at the time was considered to have been the first man ever to reach the North Pole.*

* Cook's claim to have reached the pole in April 1908 has never been either definitively verified or disproved. The following April, Robert Peary claimed to have reached the pole and that Cook was a fraud. Cook was also embroiled in a controversy over a possibly spurious claim to have been the first man to summit Mount McKinley. Peary and his supporters orchestrated a campaign to have Cook discredited, often bringing celebrities to support the Peary cause—Wilbur and Orville Wright, for example, attended a dinner in his honor. Eventually, Cook was declared a fake and Peary was given credit for the achievement. Years later, research demonstrated that Peary's claim was likely bogus as well.

Curtiss shone in St. Louis, flying to the accolades of thousands, but that seemed scant consolation after being humiliated by Wilbur Wright in New York. Curtiss and Knabenshue began to discuss mounting a major international air meet, similar to those in which Curtiss had achieved acclaim in Europe. Jerome Fanciulli thought it an excellent suggestion. The Wrights had demonstrated distaste for such affairs and Curtiss could therefore have the headlines more or less to himself.

Knabenshue, as it turned out, had previously talked of the idea with Charles Willard, a twenty-five-year-old Harvard-trained engineer who had taught himself to fly on the *Golden Flier*, the very airplane that Curtiss had sold to the Aeronautical Society and prompted the Wrights' suit against them. Baldwin and Beachey were keen for an air meet as well. Sentiment seemed to favor the West, where no heavier-than-air craft had yet flown. Knabenshue had been told that Los Angeles city officials were as anxious to find a way to celebrate the growth of their city in size and sophistication as the aviators and aeronauts were to find a venue for their meet. They had already discussed bidding for the 1910 Gordon Bennett trophy race, which would be held in the United States since the 1909 winner, Curtiss, had been an American.

Knabenshue was designated as the group's representative; he went to California and contacted a flamboyant Los Angeles promoter named Dick Ferris. Ferris was something of a Barnum of the West. He had produced everything from opera to automobile processions to "all Indian theater"; he put on plays with horses racing across the stage; in early October, he had promoted a "nightinee," a night baseball game between the Los Angeles Angels and San Francisco Seals of the Pacific Coast League. He also happened to be president of the local balloon club.*

Ferris was off and running. He recruited his friend Max Ihmsen,

* Two years later, he would be implicated in a plot to foment a revolt in Baja California to install a government more amenable to the American tourist trade.

publisher of the *Los Angeles Examiner*, and in early November after one rejection—city fathers were under the impression that Ferris wanted them to put up the money—the City Council endorsed the meet, to be held January 10–18. (It would ultimately run until the twentieth.) A strict stipulation was that no city funds would be required.

Dick Ferris didn't need politicians; he knew how to raise money. Within two days, he wired $10,000 to Curtiss and the meet had its first star. Ferris solicited the Wrights as well but was ignored. Wilbur and Orville, flush with their new corporate articles, had no intention of sullying their hands in the exhibition business. What was more, they intended that no one else did, either, as Ferris was soon to find out.

For international appeal, Ferris swung high. He cabled Blériot, Latham, Count de Lambert, and Louis Paulhan. Paulhan combined superb flying skills with European panache and had been one of the most popular flyers at Reims. He had set an altitude record that Latham had bested and Los Angeles seemed to Ferris the perfect place for Paulhan to try to return the favor.

Ferris was in the headlines virtually every day, touting the meet's importance to the city. "I am in receipt of frequent telephone calls and written messages approving the idea as a great boost for Los Angeles, and in fact all California. It shows people the way to keep up with aeronautical progress nowadays and that we are not behind the rest of the world in this regard."[1] To help stoke the fires, he announced—prematurely as it turned out—that Latham and Lambert had "as good as accepted." Neither came. But Paulhan did agree—as long as he was paid $25,000. On December 1, Henry Huntington, president of the California Aviation Society, cabled $25,000 to Edmund Cleary, Paulhan's manager.

The Los Angeles Merchants and Manufacturers Association promised to raise $100,000 for operating expenses and prize money. As a local newspaper noted, "If this is done, it will make the rest of the world stare at Los Angeles, for other cities have been struggling for months to raise an equal amount for an international aviation meet next summer."[2]

All that was left to find was a suitable setting for the spectacle. Organizers eventually chose Dominguez Hill, a mesa approximately thirteen miles south of central Los Angeles that was part of Rancho San Pedro, a 43,000-acre land grant. Daughters of Manuel Dominguez, the original owner, made the property available without a fee. In addition to its ideal topography, the mesa, renamed Aviation Field, was only a half mile from a Southern Pacific railroad terminal and near a Pacific Electric trolley line as well.

Dick Ferris supervised the construction of a grandstand that would hold 25,000. A 2½-mile course was laid out, marked by towers, and an "aviation camp" of large tents was set up to house the airplanes and dirigibles. The meet would be replete with a sideshow featuring carnival barkers and Siamese twins, ample concessions, and a medical station installed to patch up the wounded—of which everyone expected there to be many. Then, of course, there was the $80,000 that had been set aside for prize money.

As December drew to a close, it seemed to all concerned that Ferris had brokered a huge success. Tickets were sold up and down the west coast and attendance for the ten-day event promised to approach a quarter million. That Ferris was forced to admit that only Paulhan and two assistant pilots would arrive from across the Atlantic dampened spirits not at all.

Curtiss, it seemed, had hired Jerome Fanciulli at just the right time—there would be a Curtiss Exhibition Team after all, although at first it was an ad hoc affair consisting solely of one aviator of questionable sanity who operated without any supervision whatever.

Curtiss's flyer was Charles Hamilton. Hamilton, who demonstrated a remarkable ability to survive crashes, be they in gliders, dirigibles, or fixed-wing aircraft—he would have sixty-three—thrust himself on Curtiss in October 1909 and simply pestered him into submission. When Curtiss finally acquiesced and agreed to teach Hamilton to fly, he discovered that he had stumbled on a natural, a man capable of wowing audiences and keeping Curtiss airplanes in the headlines. Curtiss signed Hamilton to an exhibition contract—which included a provision absolving Curtiss of all liability for Hamilton's mishaps—then turned Hamilton loose on a breathless and eager public.

Within weeks, Hamilton in the *Rheims Racer* had flown in a gale and in a blinding snowstorm, won a race with an electric automobile, sped across the sky at record-breaking 62.72 wind-aided miles per hour, crashed twice, barely missed telegraph wires on another occasion, and once had to dive from the airplane as it careened across the ice, landing face-first on a frozen lake.[3] The crowds, which began in the hundreds and grew to thousands, loved him.

When Charles Willard decided to bring his *Golden Flier* to Los Angeles, the Curtiss "team" had its third member.

All Dick Ferris and his investors needed to do was wait for the deluge of spectators to arrive. Even the weather promised to cooperate, as it generally does in California. Unfortunately, the Wrights did not.

On January 3, 1910, one week before the air meet was to begin, federal district court judge John R. Hazel granted the Wright Company's request for an injunction enjoining the Herring–Curtiss corporation and Glenn Curtiss and Augustus Herring personally from manufacturing, selling, or flying airplanes for profit. Hazel, with no training in aerodynamics, nonetheless went into great detail in an opinion that accepted every assertion of the Wrights and none of Curtiss and concluded that it was "not improbable they may succeed at final hearing, and therefore a preliminary injunction be granted." Harry Toulmin wrote to Wilbur and Orville, "You have much to be thankful for . . . his opinion follows our brief in reasoning and conclusions; much of it adopts our language."[4] Although the writ was aimed only at one competitor, as the Wright Company had announced that every airplane currently in use infringed on their patent, similar orders were soon to follow.

For Curtiss, and every other airplane manufacturer, Hazel's decision was a potential death knell. Patent infringement cases, fraught with technical specifications that puzzle even experts, often stretch out for years. During that period, the defendant is generally free to continue to compete with the plaintiff, understanding that crippling retroactive damages will be assessed if he loses. Here, however, Hazel was preempting the decision, effectively putting Curtiss out of business in advance, denying him the opportunity to sell his airplanes and thereby perpetuate the income stream necessary to defend himself in court. As one law professor noted, "Maintaining patent rights through litigation can be so expensive that unless it is funded by rapidly expanding production of the invention, the patent holder [or defendant] can be bankrupted by litigation costs alone."[5]

Judge Hazel himself was a questionable character. A high functionary in the political machine of United States senator Thomas Collier Platt and characterized in the newspapers as a "political henchman," Hazel had been named to the bench at Platt's behest by Ohio's own William McKinley. The federal judiciary's Western District of New York had been established by Congress on May 12, 1900, and Hazel, who openly sought the appointment, was tapped for the post five days later. Hazel had helped secure McKinley's election four years earlier and was energetically engaged in a similar pursuit at the time of his nomination.

The appointment was greeted with derision. The New York Bar Association "by an overwhelming vote" had declared him unfit for the bench, after an exhaustive search of judicial records that "could not find any reported law case in the argument of which Mr. Hazel took any part," nor had he ever "at any time appeared in any Federal court on any question and had never taken part as a lawyer in any matter involving admiralty, *patent,* revenue, or bankruptcy law." Even worse, he was found to have lied under oath concerning a $5,000 commission he'd received for brokering the sale of an overpriced yacht to the federal government after the outbreak of the Spanish-American War. The bar association, confirming the obvious, concluded that his nomination was simply "a reward for political service."[6] Hazel himself admitted that "he had not paid much attention to the law . . . he has been busy organizing victories for the Republican Party."[7]

Unconcerned with such niceties, Platt rammed Hazel's confirmation through the Senate in executive session (so that no vote would be recorded), and he was sworn in on June 9, 1900.

Not infrequently, a judge will be thrust in the middle of a great controversy ill-equipped to grasp the nuances but where his ruling would nonetheless become a vital part of jurisprudence. So it was with John R. Hazel, when the man who had never been part of a patent infringement case in his life sat on an action that would help determine the future of one of the most important technological innovations in human history.

The automobile.

In 1878, George Selden, a patent attorney, part-time inventor, and son of a prominent Republican judge in Rochester, New York, had succeeded in designing a one-cylinder internal combustion "road engine." Although Selden's construct was based on an earlier, inferior design, he filed for a patent that covered not only his creation, but any gasoline-powered internal combustion engine used on what would later be defined as an automobile. Selden was fully aware that his patent had no immediate application and so, without ever attempting to build an automobile himself, he repeatedly filed amendments to his application or took the full two-year allotment to reply to examiners' inquiries, all to keep the process in limbo so that his patent would not expire before he could put it to use.

Finally, in 1895, with automobile technology yielding practical results, Selden completed the process and was granted a patent. Four years later, the year after the Westinghouse case, still with no intention of ever building an automobile or even the engine specified in his patent, he sold a percentage of the rights to a consortium that called itself the Electric Vehicle Company, which proceeded to file infringement actions against every independent automobile manufacturer in sight. One of the suits, against the Winton Motor Carriage Company et al., was eventually heard in Buffalo by newly seated district court judge John R. Hazel. The defendants asserted that Selden did not, in fact, have a "patentable invention," since by the time he finally allowed his application to go through, motorcars were being built in both Europe and the United States with an engine based on different design principles than Selden's, which would prevent Selden from securing pioneer status.

Hazel dismissed the defendants' claims and, despite grounds that many experts in the field thought dubious at best, upheld Selden's application of his patent to every internal combustion engine then in use. In the wake of the decision, most automobile manufacturers capitulated, thinking it cheaper to obtain licenses than fight the ruling.[8] A group of them banded together as the Association of Licensed Automobile Manufacturers and paid a license fee on each vehicle sold—and George Selden became a wealthy man almost overnight. Selden even formed his own automobile company, but again did not attempt to produce an automobile.

Some independents, however, refused to knuckle under. One of them was Henry Ford, at the time a small operator with a vision of affordable mass-produced machines. Where most of the others tried to keep a low profile, Ford openly flaunted Hazel's ruling. He went so far as to take out advertisements promising to reimburse anyone who purchased a Ford product if the higher court's decision went against him, for which he was widely hailed as a David standing up to Goliath.

In 1906, Selden filed suit and in September 1909, just two weeks after Glenn Curtiss raced to victory at Reims, a federal circuit court in New York ruled against Ford and confirmed that legally George Selden was the true inventor of the automobile. The judge wrote that Selden's patents "are so fundamental as to cover . . . every modern car driven by petroleum vapor as yet commercially successful."[9]

The Selden circuit court decision broadened the pioneer principle and almost certainly had direct impact on the terms under which the Wright Company was formed. Clinton Peterkin was simply too clever not to see the implications of a highly charged patent ruling handed down less than a mile from where he worked, and men such as J. P. Morgan and Cornelius Vanderbilt would well have understood the vast potential multiples to their investment engendered by a ruling of such sweep.

Though the automobile fight was nowhere near over, Judge Hazel, political henchman though he may have been, seemed vindicated by the circuit court. And the ruling caused no public outrage. Theodore Roosevelt's trust-busting notwithstanding, the mood of the day was hardly antimonopoly. The vast fortunes amassed by the very people who had invested in the Wright Company were widely seen not as the fruits of greed, but rather as engines of economic growth. Hazel's decision, therefore, to grant a preliminary injunction to the Wright Company was neither surprising nor unpopular, except among the Wrights' competitors.

The very day Hazel issued his order in Buffalo but before it was published, Wright Company lawyers met Louis Paulhan as he stepped off the gangplank of the *Bretagne* in New York City. During the Hudson–Fulton meet, the Wrights had asked for an injunction to prevent Farman or Blériot planes from being brought into the country. The issue was unresolved—Blériot and Farman, who was by then designing, had sold planes to American enthusiasts, each of whom was fighting the Wright action—but Wright lawyers served Paulhan with a subpoena ordering him to appear in court on February 1 on the same suit. Paulhan had shipped two Farmans and two Blériots, which had arrived in advance. The subpoena would not prevent Paulhan from flying but would make him liable for royalties if the Wrights gained their order. The marshal didn't speak French and Paulhan spoke no English, so at first the aviator thought he was being arrested.

If Paulhan was annoyed at the misunderstanding, the following day he would be furious. Armed with Hazel's newly issued injunction, Wright lawyers served Paulhan with another order, this one on January 14 to show cause on why he should not be restrained from making any flights in the United States. Paulhan, prototypically French, pulled himself up to his full five feet four, gave a dismissive wave, and stalked off, announcing that his American lawyers would handle everything. He then boarded a special Pullman car with Mme. Paulhan, Edmund Cleary, aviators Didier Masson and Eduard Miscarol, eight mechanics, and Escapade, his poodle, and headed for Los Angeles. Curtiss had left days before and so could not be served until he arrived on the west coast.

Suddenly, the Los Angeles air meet, and the sizable sums invested by the city's most prominent citizens, were very much at risk. Judge Hazel's order seemed preemptory and absolute.

There was near panic among the organizers but they had no choice but to push on and hope that some resolution could be found. Dick Ferris made certain that Los Angeles newspapers continued to report on the preparations and the arriving aviators as if Hazel's order did not exist, and the public bought in. Thousands upon thousands made plans to attend and the air meet was big news in the entire western half of the nation. Meanwhile, Wright Company lawyers issued a statement that Curtiss and Paulhan would be in contempt of court if they flew.

The Wright Company's legal attack might have been good business but it was abysmal public relations.[10] It was one thing to try to prevent thieves from profiting from their crimes, if that was in fact what was going on, but it was quite another to cause enormous financial hardship to citizens of a city who had acted totally in good faith, to say nothing of depriving potentially hundreds of thousands of Americans of the chance to see an airplane for the first time. That the Wrights themselves had refused to fly in Los Angeles, as they had refused to fly in St. Louis, made them look all the more venal.

Outrage stretched across the Atlantic. In France, Wilbur Wright was transformed overnight from hero and adopted son to scoundrel. "Aviators here characterize it as unsportsmanlike," *The New York Times* reported, using a word with damning implications.[11] Louis Blériot was quoted as saying, "It is regrettable that at the beginning of a science toward the development of which all the world should bend its efforts, inventors should put forth such unjustifiable pretenses in an endeavor to monopolize an idea, and instead of giving loyal aid to their collaborators to seek to trammel them as much as possible."

Henri Farman, who had just won the 1909 Coupe Michelin with a flight of 144 miles, echoed Blériot's criticism, and also gave a hint of how French aviators intended to fight the Wrights in French courts. "The device for warping the wings of an aeroplane was used by Lilienthal in his gliding flights, by Herring and Chanute in America, and by [Clement] Ader in France before the Wright patents were obtained. The only exclusive feature the Wrights can claim is the simultaneous control of the torsion and rear rudder by the same level, and this is not possessed by our machine."[12] Blériot's and Farman's comments were met with almost universal acclaim in aviation circles.*

The French captured the public fancy in America as well. On January 7, when his train was passing through El Paso, Louis Paulhan endeared himself across the United States when he declared, "I am going to Los Angeles to fly."

The pressure finally got to the Wrights. The next day, January 8, after "a conference of attorneys," Judge Hazel agreed to lift his injunction. Curtiss and Paulhan needed only to deposit $10,000 bonds with the court as security for the Wrights against future damages.[13] The deposits were made and the meet was on.

Wilbur also felt the need to make a public statement. Even then, he could not help but be inflammatory. Wilbur made it clear "that there would be no letup on the part of the Wright Company in pros-

* Curiously, Grover Loening wrote an article for the January 1910 issue of *Aeronautics* magazine, titled "Description of Successful Types of Aeroplanes," which provided detailed descriptions of the Farman, Curtiss, Blériot, Voisin, Wright, and Antoinette machines. The issue went to press before Judge Hazel's injunction and nowhere did Loening, who would later be vehement in insisting that the Wrights' competitors were all infringers, indicate that the means of "transverse control" were based on the same principles. Rather, he described the systems in a manner that would indicate they were independent in concept and construction. In the February issue, he wrote a follow-up article in which he again treated the Curtiss and Wright methods of transverse control as completely different.

ecuting these actions," and added, "We made the art of flying and all the people in it have us to thank for it." Then he said, incredibly, "We spent every cent we had accumulated by years of savings, and we worked day and night for years amid the laughter of the world."[14] That Wilbur believed this fantasy, one he echoed often, is certain. But never in their years at Kitty Hawk or Huffman Prairie had they approached financial ruin and the world could hardly have laughed at experiments conducted in secret. Worse, while perhaps Octave Chanute had overstated his role in the Wrights' experiments, for Wilbur to imply that he and his brother had worked without support was simply so false as to be insulting—as Chanute would soon point out, precipitating a rift that would endure until Chanute's death. Wilbur then denied that either he and Orville or "the men of vast wealth" who invested in them had any interest in forming a trust, an assertion that flew in the face of their own previous statements. Although neither Wilbur nor Orville had ever spoken of their monopolistic aims to the press, they had expressed such sentiments widely both to friends such as Chanute and to associates in the affiliates with whom they had contracted overseas. That Wilbur would allow himself such ridiculous overstatement is testament to his indignation at having to back down in the face of adverse public opinion.

To further fuel his anger, the Los Angeles air meet was an immense success.

Although only some sixteen of the promised forty airplanes and airships were actually present and a number of those fell firmly into the crackpot category, including a five-winged monstrosity cobbled together by a science teacher at Los Angeles Polytechnic High School and an ornithopter constructed by a different teacher from the same school, the genuine aircraft that were present awed the quarter million spectators.* Lincoln Beachey's older brother Hillery arrived with a

* Although science classes at Los Angeles Polytechnic must have been fascinating, neither of those nor any other of the amateur inventions actually flew.

"Gill-Dosch," supposedly an exact replica of a Curtiss, but had difficulty rising off the ground.

On opening day, Curtiss made the maiden flight and thus became the first man to fly an airplane on the west coast. But the crowd belonged to Paulhan. Making a surprise appearance on day one, Paulhan made three flights, the last of which stretched for almost thirty miles. He gave "a remarkable exhibition of control over his machine, gracefully making sharp turns, dipping almost to the ground, and scattering a group of frightened officers and skimming over the grandstand only a few feet above the heads of the spectators." After a perfect landing, "Paulhan was cheered madly. Men shouted themselves hoarse while women applauded and waved handkerchiefs. Paulhan danced gaily into his tent."[15]

The next day and for the remainder of the meet, Paulhan and the Curtiss aviators dazzled spectators with feats most would have thought impossible. "Here, on historic ground," *Aeronautics* trumpeted, "world's records were broken and cross-country flights were undertaken that demonstrated beyond the question of a doubt the practicability of the aeroplane."[16] Among the many highlights: Curtiss flew fifty-five miles per hour with Jerome Fanciulli; Paulhan took up the army observer, Lieutenant Paul Beck, and dropped sandbags as simulated bombs; Paulhan, Curtiss, Hamilton, and Willard took off and flew together in an informal squadron; the three Curtiss aviators went aloft and chased one another around the field, dipping and diving over the grandstand; Paulhan succeeded in recapturing the altitude record by ascending to 4,164 feet; Paulhan made a cross-country flight, amazing the spectators by heading off to the Santa Anita race track and then returning, a distance of forty-five miles for which he won $10,000; he made a twenty-mile flight over the Pacific with Mme. Paulhan in the passenger seat; Mme. Paulhan ascended in a balloon; and Paulhan took Dick Ferris, Mrs. Ferris, and William Randolph Hearst up as passengers.

On the final day, Curtiss and Paulhan staged a duel. Paulhan was flying for the endurance prize, Curtiss for speed. Paulhan started first in a Blériot, and Curtiss, in the smaller *Rheims Racer,* took off after him. By the third lap Curtiss had overtaken the Frenchman, the two airplanes coming over the grandstand "with the speed of express trains." Curtiss easily won the speed prize, and also for quick starts, maneuverability, and perfect landings, but Paulhan won for altitude, endurance, and cross-country flying. In the end, Paulhan walked off with $19,000 in prize money, the Curtiss team more than $10,000. After the planes had landed, the meet ended with a parade featuring a wizened Oregon Trail veteran named Ezra Meeker in an ox-drawn prairie schooner, followed by "cowboys, burros, carriages, automobiles, balloons, dirigibles, and finally the various aeroplanes."[17]

Curtiss had one more show to perform. He told reporters that he was prepared to demonstrate that his airplanes did not rely on the same three-axis combination the Wrights had patented and he would prove it. He sent Hamilton aloft with the tail frozen and Hamilton, according to newspapers, "flew successfully . . . with the vertical rudder tied, demonstrating that the use of such a thing in the Curtiss machine was not necessary to its flight in order to produce an equal balance. It was pointed out . . . that even though there may be some similarity in the vertical rudders of the Curtiss and the Wright machines, Curtiss can successfully maintain perfect equilibrium, even though the vertical rudder be eliminated."[18] Lieutenant Beck, the army's representative and Selfridge's successor, later testified that the Curtiss system and that of the Wrights differed both technically and functionally and that therefore Curtiss airplanes did not, in his opinion, fall under the Wright patent.

With the closing of the meet, exhibition requests poured in. The next day Paulhan departed for a tour that would take him first to San Francisco and then east with stops all through the southern half of the United States; Hamilton would take the *Rheims Racer* to San Diego and up the California coast; Willard would head to Oregon and Curtiss back to Hammondsport.

Beachey and Knabenshue had performed brilliantly in their exhibitions as well. They soared together and showed incredible control of the giant gas bags. Beachey won the dirigible race and Knabenshue finished second. The spectators were appropriately appreciative and the press appropriately fawning. But to Knabenshue and especially to Beachey, the realization that airships would soon be an outmoded technology was distinct.

CHAPTER 19

Bowing to the Inevitable

The Los Angeles meet left the Wrights and their investors in a quandary they could hardly have anticipated. With a corporation capitalized at $1 million, their arch-competitor's business in disarray, and a sympathetic judge issuing a ruling all but lifted from their business plan, they had nonetheless been outflanked. Public opinion was against them, the French were furious with them, and the opportunity to use the courts as a means of intimidation to halt future air shows had largely evaporated. With the injunction withdrawn and the legal issues and aerodynamic concepts so complex that even those in aviation did not fully grasp them, years would likely be required to fully adjudicate their claims. Thousands if not millions of Americans were willing to pay to witness the miracle of flight; exhibitors would be all too willing to risk the future buffets of the judiciary while they stuffed their wallets.

Unwilling to surrender to the unpalatable option of sitting on the sidelines and watching patent infringers steal profits that should rightfully be theirs, and under pressure from their investors, Wilbur and Orville decided to mount an exhibition team of their own. Andrew Freedman wrote to Wilbur on December 21, 1909, urging him to "get underway as soon as possible." In a subsequent letter, he suggested that "it would be a good thing" to secure the services of the "Curtiss outfit" even "if they were paid very handsomely for their work, so we could get into the field at the earliest possible moment."[1]

Working with Curtiss was unthinkable, of course. On January 17, even before the Los Angeles meet had concluded, Wilbur sent a telegram to Roy Knabenshue inviting him to Dayton to discuss managing the Wright team. Knabenshue's expertise was to that point solely with balloons but his experience with the mechanics of booking and appearing at exhibitions fit the requirements. Knabenshue and the Wrights had corresponded for almost two years, mostly letters from Knabenshue seeking to lease Wright airplanes for exhibition purposes, a proposition Wilbur and Orville had politely declined to consider. Knabenshue had even come to Dayton in 1909 to press the idea. While the Wrights had continued to refuse, they had been impressed with Knabenshue's sound judgment and solid family values.

Knabenshue had run his own business for four years and was reluctant to become an employee, even of the Wrights, but by March he had signed on. Soon afterward, the Wright Exhibition Team was incorporated as a wholly owned subsidiary of the Wright Company.

Wilbur and Orville made the decision to join what they called "the mountebank game" in the midst of an explosive breach with Octave Chanute. After Wilbur's disparaging comments appeared in *The New York Times,* Chanute granted a January 17 interview to its rival, Joseph Pulitzer's New York *World,* in which he stated categorically that the Wrights had not been the first to understand that "adjusting lateral margins" was the key to stability, but that they had extrapolated from others, especially Mouillard. Chanute acknowledged that the Wrights had been the first to "successfully" adopt the principle but said they had hardly achieved their success without assistance.

Wilbur was livid. Not only did he consider Chanute's assertion a lie, but it also cut to the heart of the infringement suits, which Wilbur assumed the old man had done intentionally. Just two weeks earlier, Wilbur had written warmly to Chanute, agreeing to travel to Boston for a dinner in his honor.[2] Now his correspondence took a far different tone. On January 20, he posted what has since become a famous letter to his erstwhile friend and confidant. Referring to the New York *World* article, he noted:

> You are represented as saying that our claim to have been the first to maintain lateral balance by adjusting the wing tips to different angles of incidence cannot be maintained, as this idea was well known in the art when we began our experiments. As this opinion is quite different from that which you expressed in 1901 when you became acquainted with our methods, I do not know whether it is mere newspaper talk or whether it really represents your present views.

After scoffing at the notion that Mouillard or anyone else "anticipated our methods," Wilbur, at his most acerbic, concluded:

> It is our view that morally the world owes its almost universal use of our system of lateral control entirely to us. It is also our opinion that legally it owes it to us. If however there is anything in print which might invalidate our legal rights, it will be to our advantage to know it before spending too much on lawyers, and any assistance you may be able to give us in this respect will be much appreciated, even though it may show that legally our labors of many years to provide a system of lateral control were of no benefit to the world and a mere waste of time, as the world already possessed the system without us.[3]

Whatever his tone, Wilbur was on firm ground. To imply that the Wrights had merely extended the work of others was at the least a gross understatement. None of those whom Chanute—or Farman and Blériot—suggested predated the Wrights' discovery had come anywhere close to solving the problem or even proceeded beyond some vague conception that wing tips might have something to do with lateral stability. But Wilbur, with unshakable conviction of his own righteousness, failed to countenance that his own behavior might have contributed to Chanute's rather silly allegations. Nor would he attempt to find a middle ground. Octave Chanute would become just another of the many people who, because of jealousy or some other flaw of character, turned away from his brother and him.

Chanute responded on January 23. He tried to soften his remarks to the *World,* but did not retract them, continuing to insist that he had made Wilbur aware of other theorists who discussed altering the "angle of incidence" of wing tips. "When I gave you a copy of the Mouillard patent in 1901, I think I called your attention to his method of twisting the rear of the wings," he wrote. Then he went on the attack.

> If the courts will decide that the purpose and results were entirely different and that you were the first to conceive the twisting of the wings, so much the better for you, but my judgment is that you will be restricted to the particular method by which you do it. Therefore it was that I told you in New York that you were making a mistake by abstaining from prize winning contests while public curiosity is yet so keen, and by bringing suits to prevent others from doing so. This is still my opinion and I am afraid, my friend, that your usually sound judgment has been warped by the desire for great wealth.[4]

Accusations of avarice had a particular sting and Wilbur responded with a long, bitter letter on January 29, to which Chanute, in failing health, did not respond. Wilbur would write again in April, seeking rapprochement without concession.

> I have no answer to my last letter and fear that the frankness with which delicate subjects were treated may have blinded you to the real spirit and purpose of the letter. . . . My object was not to give offense, but to remove it. If you will read the letter carefully I think you will see that the spirit is that of true friendship. I think the

differences of opinion which threaten trouble are not so much in regard to facts as in regard to forms of expression and manner of statement. That is why I have suggested that a joint statement should be prepared which would do justice to both and injustice to neither. We have not the least wish that your helpfulness to us should be kept from the public, as one of the interviews attributed to you seemed to intimate. Our gratitude and our friendship are genuine. It is our wish that anything which might cause bitterness should be eradicated as soon as possible.[5]

But there would be no joint statement. Chanute replied in May that he would sail for Europe and attempt to regain his health. The two did not correspond again.

Even as Wilbur and Orville made plans for their exhibition team, the Wright Company continued the injunction strategy. On February 17, federal district court judge Learned Hand, sitting in New York City, specifically citing the Westinghouse case, affirmed Judge Hazel's January 3 ruling and issued an injunction against Louis Paulhan, who was triumphantly touring through the west and south. If Paulhan wanted to continue to fly, he must post a $25,000 bond.*

Paulhan had taken in thousands and was dazzling spectators wherever he went. As superb as was his flying, his panache was its equal. The little Frenchman with the mustache was a national sensation, traveling by rail from one city to the next, then soaring, swooping, and diving in a manner most who saw him could not have dreamed possible. On January 25, for example, the San Francisco *Call* reported, "Paulhan Rivals Birds in Cross Country Flight," that his Farman biplane "Conquers Storm; Rises Easily in Half Gale with Daring Frenchman in the Saddle." The *Call* also dutifully ran a column on

* Where Hazel's judicial qualifications might have been hazy, there were no such questions with Hand. He is generally regarded as one of the preeminent legal theoreticians ever to sit on the American bench and would enjoy a highly distinguished thirty-five-year tenure as a circuit court justice in New York.

page one purportedly written by Paulhan, although the paper neglected to mention the aviator's unfamiliarity with English. On February 1, in Denver, Paulhan had a "Close Call for Life: Machine Crashes into Fence, but Daring Aviator Comes Up Smiling."[6] And on it went.

Finally, in Oklahoma City the marshal who had been trailing Paulhan caught up with him and served him with Judge Hand's injunction. Paulhan balked at the outrageous sum asked as a bond. He canceled the remainder of his tour, loaded his entourage into their private railroad car, repaired to the Hotel Knickerbocker in New York, and booked passage on the next ship home. Although the judge later stayed the injunction and reduced the bond to $12,000, Paulhan continued to refuse to either pay or fly. Edmund Cleary denounced the Wrights as "cuckoos of the atmosphere."[7] After Paulhan sailed for France, the marshal seized the two Farmans and the two Blériots. Paulhan was unconcerned. The airplanes were not his, but had been loaned to him for promotional purposes by the manufacturers.

Although their investors had wanted to leave them free to supervise production and develop new aircraft, both by necessity and inclination Orville and especially Wilbur began to become immersed in the legal process. Both submitted depositions in Dayton on March 7, after which Wilbur left for New York to submit an affidavit on March 12, then continued to Buffalo to submit another affidavit on March 19. Wilbur's willingness to absent himself from research, the one activity that might provide insurance against the vagaries of the legal system, would prove a good deal more costly to Wright Company fortunes than would Curtiss or any other competitor.

While Wilbur was filing legal papers, Charles Hamilton was tearing up the skies, and often the ground as well. He flew in high wind, over mountains and water, testing the limits of Curtiss's airplane to the thrill of ever-larger audiences. In San Diego, for example, he made "some wonderful flights through the canyons, over the ocean, and into the wilds of Old Mexico . . . the daredevil feats made the hearts of the spectators stand still."[8] But in Seattle, he dove from three hundred feet to the surface of a pond in the *Rheims Racer* with the intention of skimming the surface. Instead, one of his wing tips touched the water and the aeroplane "turned a somersault and fell, a mass of wreckage, into the water." Hamilton broke no bones—a rarity for him—but collapsed after he was rescued and taken to the hospital with "a serious head injury."[9] He was back flying within the week.

Although he was not billed as specifically flying for Curtiss, that Charles Hamilton flew Curtiss aircraft was in every news article. But Curtiss's casual approach to team management allowed the headstrong Hamilton to assert an increasing degree of independence. Hamilton took the view that the aviator was a good deal more important than the airplane and that therefore the contracted percentages he was obliged to turn over to Curtiss were exorbitant. (Of course, as will be seen, if he had flown for the Wrights, he would have received much, much less.) Hamilton began his rebellion by becoming inconsistent in reporting his earnings to Hammondsport. By the end of April, he had ceased filing reports at all. Once again Curtiss had chosen to go into business with a partner who turned out to be difficult, egocentric, and unreliable. Unlike Herring, however, at least Hamilton could do his job.

Distasteful as Wilbur and Orville may have found it, Paulhan and Hamilton—and Curtiss—had helped create an atmosphere bristling with commercial promise. The growing public obsession with exhibition flying could not help but spur the sale of airplanes. Unlike Curtiss's peek-over-the-shoulder approach with Hamilton, the brothers' commitment to the Wright team was rigorous and planned in detail. In April, Wilbur returned to Dayton to build "aeroplanes for exhibition purposes." Although the Wrights had "twenty-five to fifty machines on orders already booked," those sales would have to wait. "The first lot of biplanes to come through will be turned over to Orville Wright, Roy Knabenshue, and other aviators employed by the exhibition company."[10]

Immediately after he joined up, Knabenshue offered Lincoln Beachey a place on the team. Beachey had never flown a fixed-wing aircraft in his life, but that didn't stop him from insisting on a good deal more money than the Wrights were willing to pay. The Wrights never negotiated with employees, nor in this case did they have to. By May, they had twenty-five applicants from whom to choose. Some were recruited from close to home. Walter Brookins was a local product whom Wilbur and Orville had watched grow up. As a boy, he had been a student of Katharine's at Central High School and now became a student of her brothers, the first man taught personally by Orville to fly. With Beachey out of the picture, Knabenshue signed up two other Californians, race-car driver Archibald Hoxsey and bicycle trick rider Ralph Johnstone, who were more amenable to Wilbur and Orville's terms.

How Hoxsey came to the team is illustrative of the mood of the times. "I'd been selling automobiles out in California," recalled Beckwith Havens, who would later fly for Curtiss. "I managed to make quite a bit of money selling Haines cars. Out on the coast, I would run into Arch Hoxsey and he was driving racing cars for John W. 'Bet-a-Million' Gates.* I met him on the street one day in Pasadena and he said, 'I've lost my job. I'm looking for a new one.'"

Havens asked Hoxsey to give him a hand preparing a Stanley Steamer he was getting ready to race. "All Hoxsey could talk about was the [Dominguez Field] air meet. He said, 'Did you hear about the prizes? My heavens, they give $10,000 for a prize. I don't think it would be any harder to fly those things than to drive a racing car. That's for me.' Of course, his old boss had put up some of the original money for the Wright brothers, so he just went to the boss and the boss slid him in on the Wright team. Things worked fast in those days, and within a few months, he was their top flyer."

As always, Wilbur and Orville intended to maintain total control

* Gates was born in Illinois in 1855. He made a fortune selling barbed wire in the dying days of the open range, parlayed that into a bigger fortune in land speculation, then in 1902 struck oil in Texas and founded the company that would become Texaco. Gates's penchant for wagering enormous sums on horses prompted an English newspaper to refer to him as "Bet-a-Million" Gates, a sobriquet he despised. He had been an early investor in United States Steel and came to know Elbert Gary, who let him in on the Wright Company incorporation.

of the product. "We propose to train enough men in aviation to make us independent of the foreign contestants in case they do not respond to the invitation to participate in our meets," Wilbur stated in a newspaper interview. Aviators would be trained in the Wright method of flying both in Dayton and in a training facility Orville had established in Montgomery, Alabama.

The terms under which Wright team members signed on were severe. "The Wright Company," related aviator Frank Coffyn, "sent the members of the exhibition all over the country . . . to make money for the Wrights. And I'll tell you why." Coffyn's father was vice president of a New York bank who had participated in financing the Wright Company and had obtained an introduction to Wilbur for his son. Young Coffyn joined the team early in 1911. "The Wright Company gave us a base salary of $20 a week, and $50 a day for every day we flew." This was when the Wrights were receiving $1,000 per day for each aviator who performed. "In those days, I was able to do quite a lot of exhibition dates for them and I was able to make six or seven thousand dollars a year." Team members were forbidden to drink, smoke, or swear, and there was no flying on Sunday. The Wrights provided the equipment, of course, which few of the team members could afford.

While the Wright Exhibition Team was training, Wilbur and Orville were the objects of a rising wave of hostility throughout the aviation community. They were surprised at how widespread the bitterness was, although they should not have been. Where Thomas Hill's article in *Aeronautics* might have been passed off as steeped in self-interest, Octave Chanute's criticisms could in no way be viewed in a similar light; Chanute was perhaps the most universally beloved figure on the aviation scene. In March, all the European aero clubs informed Cortlandt Field Bishop that no European aviator would agree to appear in the United States until the Wrights' suit against Louis Paulhan was settled. Promoters stood to lose hundreds of thousands of dollars in the boycott.[11] The Wrights' proposal to cover the shortfall in famed European aviators with their own newly trained flyers—at $1,000 per day—did not endear them to exhibition sponsors.

The following month, Wilbur announced a solution—or, more accurately, a victory. In a deal brokered by Andrew Freedman, although Wilbur didn't say so, the Aero Club of America agreed to refuse to sanction any meet or exhibition in which the promoters had failed to obtain a license under the Wright patents.[12] Foreign aviators would thus be allowed to fly in sanctioned meets. Once again, the terms were steep—the Wrights demanded 10 percent of the gross receipts of any meet with an Aero Club sanction. Since few meets would clear that much, Wilbur and Orville had more or less ensured that anyone promoting an exhibition would be working for them.

During the negotiations with Freedman, Aero Club officials floated the idea of a major international air meet—to be sanctioned—at Belmont Park in Jamaica, New York, near the current site of John F. Kennedy International Airport. Freedman was enthusiastic as the fees would be hefty, a windfall for the Wright Company. He agreed to help with the financing and asked Wilbur to help with organization, logistics, and the invitations to British and French aviators. "We need your assistance here," Freedman wrote Wilbur, "to lay out this plan very big and imposing, at the same time to have no reckless waste. . . . I do not question, if the weather is good in our week, but that we will have from 200,000 to 300,000 people at our Meet." Wilbur grudgingly agreed, although his only specific response was an emphatic insistence that no foreign aviator receive more than $2,500 in appearance fees.

Attracting flyers was not a certainty, since the Wright lawyers were active across the Atlantic as well, ensuring that resentment would be spread across the entire aviation community. Infringement suits were filed against both manufacturers and aviators in France and Germany, including Farman and Blériot. While some of those named had certainly expropriated the Wrights' wing-warping system, many, as did Curtiss, employed ailerons and independent lateral and rudder control. In France in particular, the accusations of cheating against a national hero like Blériot further turned the Wrights into pariahs.

Although Wilbur and Orville rarely saw the need to court popular approval—or *any* approval—Wright Company investors understood that to effectively secure the preeminent place in the market they sought, some effort to mollify the howls of a growing population of critics was required. Otherwise public opinion just might bleed into legal opinion. In May 1910 a remarkable exchange took place in the pages of *Aircraft* magazine. *Aircraft,* whose maiden issue had appeared only three months earlier, had published an article by George F. Campbell Wood, secretary of the Aero Club, titled "The Wright-Curtiss-Paulhan Conflict." In it Wood hinted that the Wrights' three-axis provision of its patent was not as applicable to other aircraft as the brothers claimed. In the April issue, another article, over Louis Paulhan's signature, insisted that his rudder operated independently of the ailerons, which of course Curtiss had asserted as well. Although neither judge who had ruled on the case had discussed this separation of two axes of control, that the Wrights' patent would apply to machines that did so seemed increasingly questionable. That the Wrights themselves had disengaged the rudder from the wing-warping control only bolstered the argument.

The May exchange in *Aircraft* was in two consecutive articles, each by a lawyer. The first was by the Wrights' patent attorney, Harry Toulmin. Given this unique forum to explain why Wilbur and Orville actually did invent a system from which others appropriated fundamental principles without which their own devices would not fly, to justify the breadth of the Wright patent to an increasingly antagonistic peer group, to explain the science, Toulmin chose appeals to, of all things, patriotism and sympathy.

In an article titled "Attacks on Wright Brothers Wholly Unjustified," after acknowledging that "those interested in aeronautics have drifted into two camps—one pro-Wright and the other anti-Wright," Toulmin expressed surprise that such a division could exist "among the countrymen of the Wright brothers, or among those having a sincere interest in the progress of aviation." Toulmin's surprise was not directed to "the few who are in haste to commercialize aeronautics and make money as showmen"—omitting for the moment that his clients were now engaged in both of those pursuits—but rather to the "genuine opposition to the attitude of the Wrights, or to the judgments of the courts," which he deemed "incredible."

The crux of Toulmin's argument was that the term of the patent, seventeen years, was not a particularly long time. "Who can say, with justice or honesty of purpose, that the Wright brothers or their assignees should not have the exclusive use and control of this marvelous invention for this brief period, after which it passes to the public by operation of law?" Toulmin went on to note that the Wrights had made "expenditures almost to the exhaustion of their resources," and then evoked the United States Constitution to again plead for exclusivity during "this brief period." Those opposed to the court's decision, Toulmin insisted, "were expending no money, were giving no time and, indeed, no thought to production" while "the Wrights were working with loss, in obscurity, and without moral or financial aid or encouragement." Toulmin then asked, "Do these opponents, be they few or many, realize that, when all is said and done, the real essence of their attack is not against the Wrights merely, that it is an attack on property and is opposition to the statutes and to the provisions of the Constitution?" All this justifies the Wrights being paid "some share of [aviation's] very handsome proceeds."

Seventeen years, of course—thirteen of which remained when this astonishing article appeared—was a lifetime in a formative industry such as aviation, where initial demand for a groundbreaking product can be at its most intense. And while the Wrights certainly devoted personal resources to the quest for flight, at no time were they near the end of their financial rope. And of course, the royalties they were asking were not merely "some share of very handsome proceeds"; they were sufficiently high as to be almost confiscatory. To assert that others were not risking both their fortunes and their lives in similar pursuit was both ludicrous and insulting to a readership who knew that neither was remotely true. That the Wrights had received both encouragement and support from Octave Chanute, among others, was hardly a secret, and of course, they had not worked so much in obscurity as in secret. Finally, questioning the patriotism of any who would oppose the Wright monopoly was unlikely to persuade doubters. But most conspicuous in Toulmin's article was the absence of any explanation of why the Wrights *deserved* their sweeping patent; that, pioneer patents or no, the granting of exclusivity hadn't been simply an error by a judge who knew nothing of aeronautics. There was no mention of the three-axis question.

In the article immediately following, the response to Toulmin was ferocious and scathing. The author was Louis Paulhan's attorney, Israel Ludlow. Unlike Toulmin, who had no experience in aeronautics before the Wrights, Ludlow's credentials were unquestioned. He was a charter member of the Aero Club of America and beginning in 1905 had built several large gliders flown by the very same Charles Hamilton who now flew for Curtiss. But Ludlow's talents lay in the law, not engineering. None of his designs sustained flight, and on April 14, 1906, he went aloft himself and fell two hundred feet when his glider's canvas and bamboo frame cracked in a strong wind. Ludlow broke his spine in the fall. He was pinned for a time under the wreckage and at first not expected to live. He survived but lost the use of his legs and spent the last fifty-four years of his life in a wheelchair. Despite his infirmity, Ludlow remained active in aviation and was a fixture at air shows and Aero Club functions. And as a *mutilé de guerre,* he was the object of respect and affection.

Ludlow characterized the Wright patent as "a power of injunction, a possible monopoly, which, owned by a covetous and rich corporation, might threaten the very life of aviation, stifle development in this country and bar out the fruits of foreign progress." He added acidly, "Is not the attitude of the Wright Corporation that 'there is not enough profit in aerial navigation for all, but just enough for the Wrights'?" Ludlow then took issue with Wilbur and Orville's claim to be sole inventors of the aeroplane, calling the device "the result of the inventive genius of the mechanical age." Ludlow contended that the approximately $700,000 spent by Curtiss, Farman, and Blériot in developing aircraft while the Wright invention remained secret was "prima facie proof that these aeroplanes are not slavish copies, but are the result of independent development."

While not as outrageous as Toulmin's contentions, Ludlow took liberties with the truth as well. Implying the Wrights had merely extended the work of others was, as with Chanute, simply untrue. His further assertion that the Wrights had invalidated their patents by attempting to sell them to foreign governments was equally spurious, as was another accusation, that the drawings in the Wright patent applications had been intentionally falsified and, if copied by a designer, would be "suicidal."

But in his reiteration that the "Wright patent fundamentally is a combination claim between the rear vertical rudder and the side control," he was on firmer ground. "If one element of the combination is missing there can be no infringement under the present interpretation of the Courts," was also a correct statement as far as it went. The courts, of course, were free to interpret the scope of the Wright patent any way they chose.

Finally Ludlow attacked the severity of the Wrights' proposed remedy and by inference its chilling effect on technological progress. "The Wright Company's modest demand in the Curtiss and Paulhan suits was that their opponents' machines be delivered over to them that they may destroy them and that all profits and three-fold damages in addition be paid to it." He added, "The Wright Company is attempting to impose an exorbitant tax . . . and is claiming a monopoly for selling, making, working, using, or exhibiting aeroplanes, under the pretense that such monopoly is the reward due the Wright brothers for making public . . . a practical aeroplane."

May ended as badly as it began for Wilbur and Orville. On the twenty-ninth of that month, Glenn Curtiss completed the first true cross-country flight in the United States and he did it with the full participation of the nation's largest newspaper, *The New York Times.*

CHAPTER 20

Team Sports

As part of the Hudson–Fulton exhibition, the New York *World*, the same newspaper that published Octave Chanute's interview critical of the Wrights, offered $10,000 to the first aviator who replicated Fulton's journey from Governors Island to Albany, or flew the reverse route from Albany to New York. The flight, 150 miles, was considered too far for a heavier-than-air machine. It was, in fact, longer than the distance Henri Farman would fly to win that year's Michelin cup. Only a dirigible, it was believed, could complete such a journey, and during the Hudson–Fulton two airships, one piloted by Thomas Baldwin, did try for the enormous prize. Each was done in by a combination of atmospheric conditions and mechanical failures.*

When the Hudson–Fulton was done and the prize unclaimed, the *World* extended the offer for a year and Curtiss became interested. In addition to the glory, with both the Herring fiasco and the infringement suit far from settled, he was constantly in need of money. By early spring of 1910, aviation had advanced sufficiently that an air-

* Baldwin, who took off whooping, "Albany or Bust!" was in the air less than ten minutes before a piece of wood snapped off in the high wind and jammed his steering apparatus, sending Cap't Tom unceremoniously into the river. He was rescued by a navy cutter.

plane was more likely to complete the journey than a dirigible. Not wanting potential competitors to know his intentions, Curtiss undertook his preparations in secrecy.

But one of those competitors would not be Wilbur Wright. While $10,000 would seem irresistible to most flyers, once again Wilbur Wright chose to eschew ostentation and focus on sales—still refusing to understand that the two were interrelated.

Because of the distance, terrain, shifting winds, and treacherous air currents, the trip would require intricate planning. Curtiss's first decision was to begin from Albany rather than Governors Island because "there were convenient spots where one might land before getting well under way, should it become necessary," while "there are very few places for an aeroplane to land with safety around New York City."[1]

Next, a special airplane would be designed for a trip spent either over or in proximity to water. While not exactly creating a hydroplane, Curtiss, as had Wilbur, made provision for an emergency landing in the river. He filled a canvas-covered box with corks and attached it to the underside of the airplane, mounted an angled plane on the front to deflect water, and placed pontoons under the lower wing. The craft would also carry a large fuel tank and therefore require a V-8 engine powerful enough to handle the extra weight. In spring 1910, Curtiss had built his airplane, which would be christened the *Hudson Flyer.*

The flight plan also required great care. Realizing that he might be forced down short of his final destination, "I wanted to know of another place on the upper edge of the city where I might come down if it should prove necessary. I looked all over the upper end of Manhattan Island and at last found a little meadow on a side hill just at the junction of the Hudson and Harlem rivers, at a place called Inwood. It was small and sloping, but had the advantage of being within the limits of New York City. It proved fortunate for me that I had selected this place, for it later served to a mighty good advantage."[2]

Toward the end of May, as the *Hudson Flyer* was being assembled on Rensselaer Island, Curtiss journeyed by steamboat from Albany to New York and peppered the captain with questions about topography and weather. Among the obstacles he encountered was a bridge at Poughkeepsie. "I began to deliberate whether it would be better to pass over or beneath it in the aeroplane." Curtiss also chose Poughkeepsie as a place to land the *Flyer* to refuel and check the machine out. Although the director of the State Hospital for the Insane offered his lawn, Curtiss chose an open field called Camelot on the east side of the river.

On Sunday, May 29, 1910, at 7:03 A.M., Glenn Curtiss took off from Rensselaer Island. *The New York Times* was determined to outdo its rival, the *World*, and so chartered a special train to make the run parallel with and sometimes under the *Hudson Flyer.* Passengers included a slew of *Times* reporters and photographers and Lena Curtiss. They relayed updates to hotels and clubs by telegraph, so thousands were kept abreast of Curtiss's progress and were able to run to the roofs of their buildings to see the *Hudson Flyer* pass. Hundreds of thousands of others stood along a river dotted with sail and power boats of every size and description, all awaiting a glimpse of the intrepid aviator making his historic flight.

In ninety minutes, Curtiss reached Camelot. When he landed, he discovered to his annoyance that replacement fuel had not been delivered. Had he chosen West Point for his refueling stop, fuel would have been plentiful, but this was farmland. Fortunately, any number of automobiles had driven to the spot and their owners were thrilled to donate eight gallons of gasoline and a gallon and a half of oil to the cause. During the stopover, the *Times* train pulled off on a siding and Lena Curtiss had time to give a hug and kiss to her husband before he ascended for the run to Governors Island.

But the last stretch would also be the most dangerous. Just north of West Point, the river narrows and runs through the cliffs of Hudson Highlands, a narrow pass dominated by Storm King Mountain on the west bank, before widening out ten miles to the south. The topography creates a wind tunnel effect through the pass and fierce downdrafts in the air above.

Curtiss ascended to two thousand feet to safely clear the mountain but was unprepared for the maelstrom. He hit the air currents and the airplane almost instantly dropped fifty feet, lurching to the side at the same moment. Curtiss was lifted from his seat like a bull rider in a rodeo and only his grip on the controls kept him from being thrown from the airplane.

He was asked later by reporters if he had been scared. The newspaper account fit well with Curtiss's public image. As the *Times* reported, "'Well, I can't say that I was scared, but it upset me a little,' said Curtiss with a smile. 'It was the worst plunge I ever got in an aeroplane, and I don't want to get another one like it soon. After that I went lower, because the variations in the air currents were not so great near the ground or the water.'"[3] Privately, he was less self-possessed. "My heart was in my mouth," he said. "I thought it was all over."[4]

Just north of Manhattan, Curtiss noticed his oil gauge showed near empty. His scouting trip to Inwood turned out to be fortuitous because he headed for an estate built on a rise just off the Hudson whose lawn sloped gently toward the river. He landed there with ease, was welcomed by the occupants, once again replenished fluid by accepting donations from the automobilists, took off, and landed soon afterward on the very spot that had been the scene of his greatest humiliation not ten months before. A representative worked his way through the crowd to present Curtiss with a check for $10,000.

Curtiss's flight down the Hudson was the most publicized feat of aviation in history, outstripping even Blériot's jaunt across the Channel. *The New York Times* devoted no less than twelve separate articles to the flight on May 30. The main headline read, "CURTISS FLIES, ALBANY TO NEW YORK, AT THE SPEED OF 54 MILES AN HOUR; Travels Faster Than Twentieth Century Limited, but *Times* Special Train Keeps Pace." Other articles contained Lena Curtiss's expressions of confidence in her husband, Curtiss's own commentary, an interview with the pastor who emptied his church to watch, and even the impressions of a West Point cadet who was inspired to take up flying himself. The spread contained numerous photographs, including a spectacular shot taken from the train of Curtiss soaring over Storm King Mountain. The *Times* had never devoted this much space to a news story, even during the Civil War. As a result, the account was splashed on front pages across America and Glenn Curtiss was once again lauded as the most accomplished aviator in the United States.

Not just the Wrights failed to be overjoyed by Curtiss's notoriety. On the very day the *Hudson Flyer* took off from Rensselaer Island, Byron Newton, editor at *The New York Herald*, wrote to Andrew Freedman about "an interesting talk" he'd had with Charles Hamilton. When Hamilton heard that Curtiss would try for the *World* prize, he had rushed to New York from Jacksonville, Florida, hoping to use Curtiss's own *Rheims Racer* to steal the $10,000 out from under his employer, but the airplane did not arrive in time. Newton described the diminutive daredevil as "destined to be one of the greatest aviators in this country, possibly the world," and that Hamilton "may soon be detached from Curtiss." Newton offered to arrange for Hamilton to make flights for the Wrights as Hamilton was "eager to do some stunts that will make the N. Y.–Albany flight look like the hop of a toad."[5]

The day after Curtiss landed on Governors Island, *The New York Times* announced an offer of $25,000 for the first man to fly from New York to Chicago. Hamilton immediately announced his intention to win the money. Hamilton had already suggested a New York to Chicago flight to Byron Newton, an offer Freedman had passed along to Wilbur, noting that "under every condition you ought to engage this man . . . at any price or percentage he may demand for his work." Freedman added, "It is absolutely essential that the Wright machine be shown in its true capacity," particularly in view of the public image of Curtiss's airplanes.[6] But if there was a paradigm for the type of man the Wrights would *not* employ, the hard-drinking, profane, and insubordinate Hamilton was it. Wilbur categorically refused. Freedman wrote back that while he understood Wilbur's decision, he regretted it.

Those regrets would multiply in the weeks ahead.

In early June, the Wright Exhibition Team, supervised personally by Wilbur, made its debut at an air meet at the Indianapolis Speedway. Curtiss may have gotten the glory in New York but the Wright Company would make the money in Indianapolis, as Wilbur was quick to point out to Freedman. He noted that the Wright team would receive half the gross receipts with a $25,000 minimum guarantee. Knabenshue, who cut the deal, was described as "a good hustler."

Eleven aviators participated, six of them Wright team members. One of the remaining five was former aeronaut Lincoln Beachey, registered in a "Beachey monoplane," which was actually borrowed from a Los Angeles Aero Club member and previously flown—and crashed—by Beachey's older brother Hillery. After Knabenshue had been unable to meet his price, Beachey had remained in California and taught himself to fly fixed-wing aircraft. Whether he chose Indianapolis to make his debut specifically to impress Wilbur Wright is not known, but if he did the choice was in vain. Beachey was far too independent for the Wrights' taste and, as with Hamilton, Wilbur wanted nothing to do with him.

In truth, there seemed to be little need for either man. To inaugurate the Wrights' entry into exhibition flying, Walter Brookins set a new altitude record of 4,384 feet. To make the achievement sweeter, the previous mark had been set in Los Angeles by Louis Paulhan, who was by then launching a steady stream of attacks on the Wrights' patent suits. The straightlaced, teetotaling Brookins also set an unofficial record by rising to 1,000 feet in less than seven minutes. Two days later, he broke his own record flying to 4,503 feet and, when his engine conked out on the way down, glided to a landing in a wheat field.

Of the five other entrants, four, including Beachey, never got airborne; the fifth, G. L. Baumbaugh, crashed just after takeoff, never getting higher than ten feet off the ground. After Wilbur had again declined to hire him, Beachey continued east, to Hammondsport, to meet with Curtiss. Like the Wrights, Curtiss had established a formal flight school with the intention of expanding his exhibition team. Although Beachey crashed the first two planes he took up, Fanciulli persuaded Curtiss to keep him on.

Regardless of the Wrights' success, Indianapolis was not New York, and in the wake of the *New York Times*'s beatification of Curtiss for his flight down the Hudson, the Wrights' reluctance to aggressively embrace the exhibition phenomenon in the media centers of the East—and to employ the brilliant Hamilton—began to try the patience of their partners.

It didn't help that on June 10, again in a Curtiss machine, Hamilton had won $10,000 for a round-trip from Governors Island to Philadelphia, another of the prizes hastily offered by newspapers in the wake of Curtiss's Hudson flight.* Then, on June 15, a federal appeals court in New York vacated Judge Hazel's preliminary injunction, ordering that Curtiss's $10,000 bond be returned, thus allowing Curtiss to fly unencumbered until the case was actually decided. Wilbur immediately left for New York to help plead for a reinstatement of the bond, a task that should have been left to the lawyers. Wilbur's presence did not help; the court stuck to its decision.

On July 8, 1910, Freedman's patience ran out. He wrote to Wilbur: "I have heard very little mention of the Wrights or their progress. Had expected to hear that you had a machine down here for the Atlantic City Meet, but so far have heard nothing of it." Then Freedman took a tone that Wilbur had likely only previously experienced from his father. "I think that in justice to the men who have gone into this enterprise with you that you should give a demonstration of some kind in this section of the country before long. Our people here will lose interest in the Company for the reason that flights of all descriptions are being made by everybody, excepting the Wrights. Some little consideration is due them for the practical endorsement of the Company."[7]

* The sponsors were *The New York Times* and the Philadelphia *Ledger.* Curtiss and Hamilton must have had at least a temporary rapprochement as Curtiss removed the propeller from the *Hudson Flyer* and loaned it to Hamilton when Hamilton's propeller was discovered to have a crack.

Freedman was particularly irritated because the Wrights had signed a contract to participate at Atlantic City, for which they would receive a guarantee of $20,000 against 20 percent of gross receipts, and the meet had been widely advertised as "the first contest between the Wright and Curtiss machines." (The advertisement noted, "It is also expected that Charles K. Hamilton, the great long distance aviator, will be present and race from July 7 to July 11.") If the Wrights were unrepresented at the meet, observers might well interpret their absence to a fear of competition.

Wilbur replied to Freedman's chiding with uncharacteristic contrition. He explained that he hadn't been certain a Flyer could be prepared in time for the Atlantic City meet but now he would promise to "overhaul one of our newest machines so as to have it in first class condition and will send it next week."[8]

The decision turned out to be sound. In Atlantic City, in front of 100,000 spectators, Walter Brookins bested the altitude mark he had set in Indianapolis, soaring to 6,175 feet, thus winning the $5,000 prize promoters had put up for anyone who could ascend a mile or more. The promoters were stunned at having to fork over the funds; ascensions of that altitude were widely considered impossible. Of course, Brookins did not get to keep the money; he had to turn all but the regular $50 daily stipend over to the Wrights. Brookins was so loyal to Wilbur and Orville that he never stated publicly where the prize money actually went.[9]

"The Wright Company never let us keep any of the prizes we won," Frank Coffyn noted. "The company kept them and we just got our $50 a day. No bonuses. Nothing. It was a very sore kind of project with us because the Curtiss Company allowed their pilots to keep fifty percent of all the prizes they won. We used to get furious about it but it didn't do us any good. The Wrights wouldn't let us have it."

When asked if the Wright aviators might have done better as a group if they'd been paid prize money, Coffyn replied, "Maybe so, but it didn't make any difference to me because I used to try and do the best kind of flying I could anyhow." But Coffyn also admitted that, without incentive to make extra money, he was extremely conservative. "I did my flying in a careful manner. [The other flyers] did stunts and things. I was just careful enough not to overtax the strength of the plane and that's how I got through it, I think."

Curtiss had a successful meet as well. He won $5,000 by flying fifty miles in the *Hudson Flyer,* virtually all of it over water. He also won prizes for the quickest start and the quickest climb to one thousand feet. But with money being thrown about so loosely, exhibition flying was about to become both a good deal more competitive and a good deal more dangerous.

CHAPTER 21

Mavericks

Among the two thousand Americans who witnessed Glenn Curtiss win the Coupe Gordon Bennett at Reims in September 1909 was one Joseph Jean Baptiste Moisant, the fourth and youngest son of French Canadian parents who had emigrated from Quebec to Illinois. Determined to be American to the core, the boys, although not their three sisters, had anglicized their names and so "Joseph Jean Baptiste" became "John Blevins." John Moisant was something of an international celebrity and had come to Reims after a rather busy year. Just one month before, he had narrowly evaded capture and possible execution after a third failed attempt to lead an invasion of El Salvador.

By any standard, the Moisant family was exceptional. They left Illinois for California in the 1880s and within ten years had amassed a fortune in lumber, real estate, mining, and a variety of other enterprises. In 1895, led by eldest son Alfred, the Moisants bought a sugarcane plantation in El Salvador so vast that it was a day's ride from one end to the other. Alfred also oversaw the purchase of a salt mine and a bank.

For more than a decade, the Moisants, tightly knit and fiercely protective of one another, extracted enormous profits from Central America, ensured by Alfred's willingness to provide financial support to friendly governments. In 1907, however, an old-fashioned jefe, General Fernando Figueroa, was elected president of El Salvador, although vote counts in military dictatorships are always subject to question. Figueroa took a dim view of the gringos who had become accustomed to telling Salvadorians in power how to behave. That the Moisants supported his opponent, Prudencio Alfaro, was also not in their favor. Finally, and likely most important, Figueroa owed a good deal of money to the bank Alfred owned and had no real desire to pay it back. He began to put pressure on the Moisants to forgive the loan and perhaps even cede a portion of their empire to the government.

Alfred Moisant was content to work through official and unofficial diplomatic channels to outflank Figueroa, but for John, described by a biographer as "driven by an uncontrollable desire for adventure and wealth and an almost adolescent need to be seen as a swashbuckling hero," only direct action would do.[1] John traveled to Nicaragua to meet with its president, General José Santos Zelaya, who at that moment was attempting to make his dream of reuniting Central America a reality.* Not surprisingly, Zelaya saw himself at the head of the proposed five-nation federation. The idea did, in fact, enjoy a good deal of support in the region, but not in El Salvador. Zelaya and Figueroa were not mutual admirers.

John proposed ousting Figueroa by landing an expeditionary force on the beach that would then fight its way to the capital. The force would consist of Nicaraguans and Salvadorian dissidents, including two generals, one of whom would be installed as puppet president. Zelaya agreed and left John to make the arrangements. Left unclear was which of the two generals would sit in the president's chair and also whether Moisant would be subordinate to them in the invasion or their superior.

When Figueroa heard of John's plotting in Managua, he clapped the two middle Moisant brothers in jail for inciting revolution and demanded a hefty indemnity for their release. Alfred refused and in-

* A federation had been established in 1824, only to collapse fifteen years later.

stead persuaded a reluctant United States counsel to summon the navy. Figueroa gave in to gunboat diplomacy and freed the brothers.

On June 11, 1907, just when tensions were easing slightly, John's expeditionary force landed at Acajutla, the coastal city nearest the Moisant plantation. After initial success, the two Salvadorian generals took to bickering, which halted their advance sufficiently to allow government troops to regroup and force a retreat and then a rout of John Moisant's army.

This political theater went on for two more years. John Moisant was jailed, hunted, and threatened by both Salvadorian officials and the U.S. State Department, all the while establishing a reputation ordinarily reserved for the likes of Captain Kidd. His third and last invasion took place in April 1909. His forces never reached shore, intercepted by two U.S. Navy cruisers who promised to fire on him if he attempted to land. Moisant steamed away, this time facing arrest by his own government as well as by Figueroa, although only one of the two would have had him put to death. After yet more diplomatic wrangling, John B. Moisant, plantation owner, gun runner, mercenary, and impeccable dresser, was allowed to return home a free man if he foreswore Central American politics. In July, John Moisant stepped off an ocean liner in New York and never visited Central America again.

Forced to eschew leading invasions of foreign nations, John was left desperate for an outlet for his obsessive audacity. On a whim, he traveled to the Reims meet and instantly turned his attention to aviation. Exhibition flying seemed perfect for his idiom, something he could attack with a buccaneer's flair.

John Moisant might have been headstrong and narcissistic but he was far from stupid. Along with his sister Matilde, he had long observed birds in flight, and tried to grasp the same principles that Wilbur Wright had deduced. After Reims, he stepped up his efforts and when he thought he had solved the problem, before he had ever flown, he set to designing and building an airplane. His plan was to become the world's greatest exhibition flyer in an aircraft of his own creation.

It is typical of the Moisants that stodgy, conservative Alfred fully supported his younger brother's plan and provided all the necessary funds to carry it out.

John, fluent in French of course, repaired to Issy-les-Moulineaux, a Paris suburb, and got to work. He was convinced that maintaining the best possible weight-to-strength ratios was the key to success, so instead of using wood, he built the world's first airplane made entirely of metal, and instead of the V-engines mounted in most American airplanes, Moisant employed a 50-horsepower Gnôme seven-cylinder rotary. The Gnôme spun with the propeller around a fixed crankshaft and weighed only 176 pounds. Moisant mounted his propulsion system in the front of his aircraft, as did Blériot, but Moisant mounted the propeller behind the motor. To minimize frame weight, Moisant employed steel only for the support tubing; for the body and wings, he chose the new miracle metal, aluminum.

Although it was the third most common substance in the earth's crust, not until 1886 was a commercially feasible electrolytic process developed to extract the metal from aluminum oxide.* In the two subsequent decades, aluminum—light, malleable, corrosion resistant, and in alloys almost as strong as steel—was employed in a dizzying variety of industrial operations. The metal was even used to line the interior facing of the dome in the rotunda of the Library of Congress.

That the metallurgy of aluminum was not sufficiently understood before it was thrown willy-nilly into manufacturing would have dire consequences in subsequent years, but for John Moisant it turned out to be merely an inconvenience. He built his "aluminoplane," *L'Ecrevisse* ("The Crayfish"), then, without bothering to take a lesson, seated himself behind the engine, signaled his mechanic to start the engine, and

* The process was developed in parallel by American Charles Martin Hall and Paul Héroult of France, both obscure and twenty-two at the time, working independently and unknown to each other. Each obtained a patent for what turned out to be the same invention. Like Newton and Leibniz developing calculus, there was some dispute as to how to apportion credit. The technique, now called the Hall–Héroult process, was eventually credited to both men.

lifted off. The apparatus performed wonderfully, perhaps too wonderfully. *L'Ecrevisse* climbed at a steep angle at speeds approaching eighty miles per hour. That was too much even for Moisant, so he cut his engine, causing the aircraft to turn nose down and return to its starting point. Moisant wasn't hurt in the crash, but the airplane was ruined. He immediately started on another but this time took some lessons from Louis Blériot before venturing once more into the skies. His second airplane, *Le Corbeau* ("The Crow"), fared little better than the first. Moisant gave up on that portion of the plan, bought a Blériot, and turned his attention solely to flying.* If aviation hadn't welcomed a new designer in John Moisant, it had, as it would soon learn, acquired a comet.

In a meet in Asbury Park, New Jersey, in August 1910, the Wright Company finally introduced a new airplane. Although the Flyer B, as it was called, contained some improvements over the previous model—the elevator had been moved to the rear and for the first time wheels had been mounted under the skids—the basic wing-warping and control technology remained the same. A racing model was also in the works—the Flyer R, or "Baby Grand." The Asbury Park meet spotlighted the Wright machines' strengths and provided a glimpse into what would be their greatest weaknesses.

Arch Hoxsey and Ralph Johnstone showed the Flyers at their best. Hoxsey took the governor of New Jersey up for a jaunt and on August 19, he and Johnstone flew at night, the first such flights in the United States. In between they soared long and gracefully before cheering crowds.

But on August 10, the first day of the meet, Walter Brookins suffered a mishap that both evoked the death of Thomas Selfridge two years before and provided a grim snapshot of the future. Brookins crashed a Flyer A when photographers crowding the field caused him

* Further examination revealed that *L'Ecrevisse* was fully capable of sustaining flight, which is to say Moisant successfully designed an airplane though he had no training or experience.

to change his descent and then lose control in high winds. Headed directly to the spectators, Brookins swerved at the last moment, missing the grandstand by a foot, and crashed in an alley crowded with program boys, policemen, and National Guardsmen. Those present realized he had put his own life in peril to save others. Carried away semiconscious, Brookins told the National Guard commander, "I did the best I could." All agreed that his flying saved many lives. Ten, however, were caught under the crushed Flyer, one boy suffering a fractured skull and another a broken arm. Brookins himself was first reported as killed but only suffered bruises and a broken nose.[2] Wilbur arrived the following day to try to determine the cause of the calamity. When he heard that his favorite and most trusted aviator had flown in 25-mph winds, he told reporters, "Brookins ought to be hanged for attempting a flight in such circumstances." Still, the accident was said to double admissions sales the following day.[3]

But Wilbur had missed the message of Brookins's crash. The Wright machines could climb, turn gracefully, fly for long distances, and attain high speeds. But in tight situations, where quick maneuvering and complete control of the aircraft were required—the precise sort of flying that was about to predominate in exhibitions and, of course, would always be a prerequisite in war—the Flyers fell short. And in so doing they became unsafe.

In fact, whispering about the safety of Wright aircraft had already begun. Holden Richardson, one of the first naval officers trained as an aviator, flew both Wright and Curtiss machines.

> The Wright plane was furnished with a kind of mixed up control . . . very unnatural. You had to maneuver the bar sideways and you had to move it fore and aft for elevation and then you had a little control mounted on that same thing, so if you wanted to make turns, you could change the incidence of the wing tips, just lower the wing tips. . . . [The Curtiss controls] were definitely better . . . a shoulder yoke control . . . you'd lean left or right to operate your ailerons. The wheel was mounted on a cross-wire so you could

push fore and aft for working the elevators. He didn't use feet except to control the power, the throttle. The Wright machine was mounted on skids and was assisted in take off by means of a falling weight.* Curtiss had enough power to take off right from the sand and gain altitude for maneuvering.[4]

Wilbur and Orville, of course, saw nothing wrong with their systems, particularly as they viewed daredevil flying as simply foolish, so they made no effort to improve their product beyond some minor enhancements. The Baby Grand with its new eight-cylinder motor would be capable of speeds of eighty miles per hour but be no easier to maneuver than previous models—more drag racer than Formula One.

But Curtiss refused to press his advantage. Despite the urgings of Jerome Fanciulli that Charles Hamilton was at best unreliable and that Curtiss needed a real team of his own, Curtiss continued to treat exhibition flying in a more or less ad hoc manner. There was a corporate entity called the Curtiss Exhibition Team but no flyers to man it. Not that there was a shortage of applicants.

After hearing about Arch Hoxsey's exploits, Beckwith Havens was ready to come east. "I thought, 'If Hoxsey can do it, by gosh, the money looks good to me too.' So I wrote to the Wrights and Curtiss and told them I wanted to fly."

The letters did not get a response but Hoxsey then gave Havens an introduction to Augustus Post, another of the larger-than-life figures who dominated early aviation. A balloonist, fixed-wing flyer, and charter member of the Aero Club, Post owned one of the first automobiles in New York City, was a noted singer of ballads, appeared in a vaudeville act, and was a major figure in the development of the Boy Scouts. Distinctive with a singular full beard, in November 1910 he would emerge from a lost week in the Canadian wilderness after a balloon in which he was racing was blown hundreds of miles off

* That, of course, changed when the Wrights introduced the Flyer B.

course. On another occasion, a newspaper reported that "when Mr. Post was learning to fly an aeroplane, he gained distinction at a meet at Sheepshead Bay by jumping out of his grass-skimming craft when it was headed into a fence, grabbing it by one wing and turning it around, and then jumping aboard again for a spin across the field without having turned off the motor."[5]

When he met Havens, Post exclaimed, "You're just what we want! Some new blood in aviation!" He sent Havens to Fanciulli, who hired him in the only position Curtiss had made available. It was not as a pilot. "The first job I had was exhibiting [a Curtiss] airplane in New York. I was the world's first airplane salesman."

While Curtiss dithered, the Wrights' brand of flying continued to predominate. At the Harvard–Boston meet in September, the Wright team decimated Curtiss and Charles Willard, the only aviators in Curtiss aircraft. Brookins, now fully recovered, won for altitude—4,732 feet—and slow lap; Johnstone won for duration, distance, and accuracy. Including appearance fees, Wright aviators won $39,250 compared with $16,500 for Curtiss and Willard, $14,000 of which the Wright team received merely for showing up.

But neither Brookins nor Johnstone was the big winner. That title went to the dashing Englishman Claude Grahame-White. Alternating in a Farman and a Blériot, he won for speed and bomb-throwing accuracy (the first time such an event was included in a major meet) and took in $10,000 for winning a race around Boston Light. In all, Grahame-White officially pocketed $29,600, a sum liberally augmented by the $500 he charged each of the many attendees who wanted to take a flight with him. Grahame-White was everything that Wilbur and Orville loathed—flamboyant, rakish, grossly materialistic, uninterested in science, and an obsessive woman chaser.

But Grahame-White and Charles Hamilton seemed to be where the money was, so the Wrights persevered, making what they considered great concessions to sensationalism but what were in fact merely necessities of basic marketing. On September 29, Walter Brookins flew from Chicago to Springfield, Illinois, 192 miles, a new cross-country record. As had Lena Curtiss, Wilbur followed the flight in a railroad car, cheerleading attending reporters. Within weeks, Grahame-White outdid him. After the Aero Club declined to sanction a planned meet in Baltimore—meaning the promoter did not intend on paying a fee to the Wrights—Grahame-White, strictly in an amateur capacity, flew an infringing Farman biplane twelve miles over Washington, D.C., circled the Washington Monument and the Capitol, and then landed on Executive Avenue near the east gate of the White House. There he was greeted by a contingent of army and navy officers led by Admiral George Dewey, the hero of Manila Bay, and cheered lustily by the hundreds who stood jammed along the narrow street.[6] At roughly the same time, the Burgess Company, where Augustus Herring had made his next stop, began selling biplanes, which their advertisement proclaimed as "designed and built specially for C. Grahame-White," and for which the aviator received a hefty fee.

The Wrights had their own comeback. In October, at a Wright-sponsored meet in St. Louis, with photographers crowded in front of

Arch Hoxsey taking former president Theodore Roosevelt aloft.

his airplane, making it almost impossible for him to taxi, and with moving-picture cameras rolling, Arch Hoxsey took former president Theodore Roosevelt aloft.

These skirmishes were prelude to what promised to be the major battle in late October at the International Aviation Tournament at Belmont Park, the event that had been discussed when the Wrights drafted their agreement with the Aero Club. Belmont promised to be the most important air meet yet to be held on American soil. The event had been conceived by Andrew Freedman as a Wright coronation, and for six months he had been so intimately involved in the planning that he had been named meet chairman. At one point, *Aeronautics* magazine wondered whether it might not be a good idea simply to run the event under the Wright Company's auspices. Although the Wrights' participation officially remained unofficial, in addition to Freedman, Wright Company stockholder August Belmont was chosen as the president of the organizing committee and the venue was, after all, Belmont Park.

In all, $67,300 would be available in prize money. At Freedman's insistence, the Belmont meet was also chosen as the site of the $5,000 1910 Gordon Bennett Cup race. Rumors flew that, given the Wright Company's control of gate receipts, Glenn Curtiss would be forbidden entry, but organizers insisted Curtiss would be invited, and he was.

But Curtiss would not—or could not—defend his Gordon Bennett title. The reason Curtiss declined to enter the race remains a matter of speculation. His biographer claimed that due to the ongoing litigation with Herring, Curtiss, exiled from his factory to a small shop in Hammondsport, simply could not build a machine that had a chance of winning.[7] Certainly the business was in a shambles, so dysfunctional that he was forced to run announcements in trade journals. "All Communications Intended For Glenn H. Curtiss," the half-page ad read, "Should Be Addressed to Aviation Headquarters 1737 Broadway, New York. Jerome S. Fanciulli, Business Representative."

But even so, the hypercompetitive Curtiss had never before shied from a long-odds fight and he had faced a similar situation in Reims a year earlier. Nor is there any record of pressure being applied from either the Aero Club or the Wright Company lawyers, which likely would not have dissuaded him anyway. Whatever his reason, Curtiss chose to allow the most important prize in aviation to go to another flyer by default. And the Wrights were determined that the other flyer would be Walter Brookins in the 80-mph Wright R.*

The Gordon Bennett was not the only prestigious prize to be awarded at the meet. Board member Thomas F. Ryan, a director of Bethlehem Steel, offered $10,000 to the winner of a race from Belmont Park around the Statue of Liberty and back.

The roster of contestants was the most impressive ever: Grahame-White, Latham, Hamilton, Brookins, Hoxsey, Johnstone, Willard, Clifford Harmon, a talented young French aviator named Roland Garros, and Tom Baldwin, who had switched from dirigibles to fixed-wing and brought his own biplane. And one other: the newest flying sensation, a man who after being in the air less than four months had become the rage in Europe, dazzling onlookers with flying that was either brilliant or reckless; no one could ever be sure.

John B. Moisant.

Moisant had burst on the scene at an event in which he had been refused entry. When the French declined to allow "the crazy American kid" to fly in Le Circuit d'Est, the world's first long-distance air race, Moisant packed his friend Garros into the passenger seat of his Blériot and flew thirty-seven miles across Paris, passing directly over the Eiffel Tower, and then landed on the field at Issy-les-Moulineaux, where a quarter-million people had shown up to see the event begin. Moisant later insisted he had performed the stunt because it was the only way he could watch the race.[8] Not satisfied with even that level of shock value, he announced on the spot that he intended to fly from Paris to London and, what was more, he intended to take his mechanic along—the first time anyone would cross the Channel with a passenger.

* There had been rumblings that Orville himself would man the controls but that never seemed in serious consideration.

The mechanic, Albert Fileux, weighed 185 pounds, certain to be too much for the Blériot. Moisant was dismissed as suicidal and Blériot himself begged the American not to force "pauvre Fileux" to accompany him.

But Fileux wanted to go and on August 16, Moisant took off from Issy-les-Moulineaux with only an ordinary compass for navigation. One day and three stops later, Fileux and Moisant, his hands numb from the cold, touched down six miles from Dover. The next morning, the pair left for London, this last leg to be made with a cat given to Moisant by an English engineer, which Moisant named Paree-Londres. But Dover to London was plagued by breakdowns, bad weather, and other delays, all of which allowed suspense to build and Moisant to become an enormous celebrity. Finally, on September 6, he completed the journey. Within days, he had been invited to fly in the upcoming air meet at Belmont, New York.

In press interviews, Moisant, small, trim, as dapper as Latham or

John Moisant with his cat, Paree-Londres, on his shoulder.

Grahame-White, with a face *The New York Times* described as "rather beautiful," constantly stressed his American roots. He intended, he told reporters, to return to the United States to fly on his home turf but noted that he would not participate in a proposed New York to Chicago race unless "he is guaranteed against all interference on the part of the Wright Brothers." Moisant also knew of "a number of European flying men eager to cross the Atlantic to pick up some of the large prizes going begging there, but all are in the same quandary."[9] But with the Belmont meet endorsed by the Aero Club, infringing aircraft were welcome, since the first $20,000 of gate receipts would go to the Wrights.

Moisant stepped off the boat in New York a folk hero. He promptly announced he would enter both the Gordon Bennett and Statue of Liberty races.

But before those races were run, hundreds of thousands were treated to exhibitions of flying that would have defied the imagination just six months before. Wilbur and Orville could not have helped but be pleased. The meet would be a washout for Curtiss while Wright aviators dominated the headlines.

Seven airplanes flew in the rain on opening day, then ten were in the sky at once just two days later. That same day, J. Armstrong Drexel, "Chip," an American flying a Blériot, set an altitude record of 7,183 feet. The press called it the "greatest day's flying seen in the United States since the Wright brothers," an accolade that would not last twenty-four hours.

The following afternoon, in one of the great air duels in history, Ralph Johnstone broke Drexel's record, flying in a "raging snowstorm" above the clouds. For much of the ascent, Hoxsey, Latham, and Count Jacques de Lesseps had kept pace.* Hoxsey and Johnstone were already known as "the stardust twins" for their constant attempts to best the altitude marks of the other. The Wrights had constructed a Flyer

* Count de Lesseps was the second man to fly across the English Channel and the son of the man who conceived of the Suez Canal.

specifically to attain altitudes, featuring elongated wing tips, minimal wing surface, and lightweight, low-horsepower motors.

At about 5,000 feet, Latham's Antoinette suddenly began to plummet, swinging side to side in buffeting air as Latham tried desperately to maintain control. The Antoinette disappeared behind a clump of trees, but Latham miraculously managed to land the craft and emerge uninjured.

Hoxsey and de Lesseps continued to climb, but had to break off at about 7,000 feet because of the wind and frigid weather. But Johnstone kept going, snow and hail whipping across the Flyer and frost fogging his goggles. When he finally returned to earth, it was found that he had soared to 7,303 feet. *The Hartford Courant* reported that "the undemonstrative Wilbur Wright danced with joy when he glanced at the barograph."*[10]

One day after that, Johnstone and Hoxsey "went up in a gale so stiff that for a time they hung over the field immobile in latitude, though they were steadily gaining in altitude, and then began to drift backward."[11] Johnstone was blown fifty miles out over Long Island but "kept climbing until his last drop of gasoline was exhausted." When asked about Johnstone's flight, Wilbur, the same man who had previously declared that Walter Brookins "should be hanged" for flying in conditions far more benign, merely said, "I guess that's the first cross country flight made tail end foremost."

Wilbur's opinion of daredevil pilotry had changed abruptly. He and Orville had initially tried to impose conservative limits on team members, restricting them to simple demonstrations of takeoff, ascending, maneuvering, and landing. In September 1910, Wilbur had written to both Johnstone and Hoxsey before a meet in Detroit. "I am very much in earnest when I say I want no stunts and spectacular frills put on the flights there. If each of you can make a plain flight of ten or fifteen minutes each day keeping always within the inner fence well

* A barograph is a barometer with an attached paper-wrapped drum on which changes in barometric pressure over time are recorded, from which altitude above sea level may then be extrapolated.

away from the grandstand and never more than three feet high, it will be just what we want."[12]

His conversion was likely based on a combination of resignation, pride, and the profit motive. In the first place, exhibition pilots, particularly Johnstone and Hoxsey, simply refused to be held back, and they weren't being paid enough for financial threats to have any bite. And Wilbur and Orville could not have helped but feel a rush of satisfaction watching their creations perform to limits even they would have initially thought impossible. Finally, as Curtiss had demonstrated, what better way to call attention to your product than to show it engaged in one spectacular feat after another? To say nothing of the fact that each of those spectacular feats was funneling thousands in prize money into Wright Company coffers.

The exploits of Johnstone and Hoxsey had set a perfect stage for the Gordon Bennett race, scheduled for the morning of October 29. The Liberty run was initially supposed to take place later the same day, although delays subsequently forced it back to the afternoon of October 30. The favorites in the Gordon Bennett were Claude Grahame-White in a Blériot with a 100-horsepower Gnôme motor and Walter Brookins in the Wright R. The Wrights would have traded all the notoriety of previous days for a victory over Grahame-White, thus making them the heir to Curtiss's 1909 championship.

But if someone was going to beat Grahame-White, it wasn't going to be Brookins. Just after taking off, but before his start could be declared official, four of the eight cylinders on the Baby Grand failed. Brookins tried to control the craft in a 20-mph tailwind but the airplane plunged to the ground not fifty feet from the grandstand. Brookins was thrown from the machine in great pain, his "whole body black and blue, as though he had been beaten with a club," but once again he had escaped with only bruises.[13]

The Wrights were out of the Gordon Bennett, a contest for which they had cared enough to design an airplane specifically. They watched as Grahame-White scorched the twenty-lap, 62.1-mile course in one hour and one minute, beating the "mile-a-minute" mark, faster than anyone had ever flown such a distance. Neither of the two other Americans, Charles Hamilton or Chip Drexel, was considered able to even approach Grahame-White's time and they did not. Hamilton, flying his own creation, the "Hamiltonian," 110 horsepower but utterly unproven, could not complete a lap, and Drexel, in a 50-horsepower Blériot, was simply not a good enough flyer to maneuver a low-power machine to victory in high winds and so quit after seven lackluster laps.*

With Brookins out without having officially started, however, a third spot had opened up on the three-man American team, a spot for a daring aviator to be thrust into the breach to save the honor of America.

The perfect idiom for John B. Moisant.

Peter Young, Hamilton's manager, must have had that very thought because he rushed to the hangars to entreat Moisant to fly, telling him he was America's only chance. Moisant, eating a piece of pie, protested that his airplane had been damaged in an earlier crash and was not yet fully repaired. The controlling mechanism would not allow him to maneuver properly and might even cause a crash. Young told Moisant that he should fly anyway and that he must do so immediately or the deadline to begin would have passed. Moisant, "between mouthfuls of pie," hurried into his aviation clothes and ordered his damaged Blériot out of the hangar.

With literally seconds to spare before the race was closed, Moisant took off. He completed only six laps and with his shoulders and arms quivering from the exertion of controlling the damaged machine, was forced to land so the mechanics could try to make the airplane handle more effectively. Once again just beating the clock, Moisant took off and completed the final fourteen laps. While Grahame-White's time was never in danger—he won by almost an hour—Moisant astounded spectators and his fellow flyers alike by finishing second.

* That at least one of the four flyers in a Curtiss machine had not been chosen by the Aero Club to defend Curtiss's title had caused some outcry, but with Curtiss himself declining to enter, sentiment ran against him.

When Moisant taxied to a halt, Allan Ryan, Thomas F. Ryan's son and chairman of the Aero Corporation, all but dragged Moisant into the clubhouse, where he was toasted with champagne and cheered by Aero Club members. In the newspapers the next day, Moisant's second-place finish was treated almost as a piece of battlefield heroism.

Grahame-White was gracious in victory but his equanimity would not last.

Thomas F. Ryan's Statue of Liberty race began the following afternoon, Sunday, October 30. The event had been conceived in controversy and would be run in controversy, but the true storm would not break until after the flying was done.

To get to the Statue of Liberty from Belmont Park meant flying across Brooklyn, where a direct route would take a flyer immediately over the rooftops of one of the most densely populated areas in the entire United States. There would be no place to land in an emergency; no way to recover if a downdraft pulled the airplane to earth. Engine trouble meant almost certain death for the aviator and likely the same result for some hapless Brooklynites on the ground. The Wrights denounced the flight but even if they had not, no Wright airplane would be flown on a Sunday. Very few remaining flyers were sufficiently brave or sufficiently foolhardy to enter. Grahame-White was one, of course. With the run he had been on, he likely felt a flight to the moon would not present a hazard. Another was Count de Lesseps. Charles Hamilton entered but his 110-horsepower Hamiltonian once again would not start. ("I'm going out and getting myself a Blériot," he said afterward.) The final contestant was John Moisant.

Seventy-five thousand spectators cheered when de Lesseps took to the air just after 3 P.M. and Grahame-White followed three minutes later. Moisant wheeled his Blériot out, climbed aboard, and signaled Albert Fileux to start the motor. When the engine turned over, instead of taxiing, the aircraft spun on the ground and crashed into another airplane. Moisant's rudder had jammed and his Blériot was left with a wing damaged beyond repair.

Disconsolate, Moisant simply sat in his doomed monoplane. His brother Alfred hurried over to find out whether his brother was hurt. When he learned that John was fine, he told him to get out of the wreck. They would buy another craft. They jumped into Alfred's automobile, raced through the staging area, and eventually found a new 50-horsepower Blériot belonging to another French aviator, Alfred Leblanc. Leblanc had crashed a 100-horsepower Blériot during the Gordon Bennett race and was at his hotel in Manhattan recuperating. Alfred called and offered him $10,000 for his airplane. Leblanc accepted.

As the airplane was being prepared, two tiny dots appeared in the west. The first was Grahame-White, who had taken a northern route that would avoid some of the more densely populated areas, and behind him was de Lesseps, who swung to the south where some emergency landing spots were located. Grahame-White completed the 36-mile race in 35:21, got out of the cockpit with great ceremony, and then bowed and waved to the crowd as the band played "God Save the King." De Lesseps landed five minutes later to the strains of "La Marseillaise." Moisant had yet to take off.

The crowd, rather than cheer the winner, began to chant Moisant's name as an airplane he had never so much as set foot in was wheeled out to the starting area. Leaving a glowering Grahame-White to stand and watch, Moisant's newly purchased Blériot left the ground at 4:06.

As many as one million people were along the route: on roads, on rooftops, in boats, or lined along the edge of the harbor. One of the reporters for the *Times,* watching the race at Battery Park, commented on the strange lack of noise from the huge crowd "as each minute speck in the sky 'grew' into a clearly visible man in a flying machine." It was one of the most trenchant descriptions of the public's reaction to early air travel ever put to paper. "The sight, at first uncanny, held them speechless. Cold chills ran down the back. In spite of the fact that they all knew about aeroplanes and that they really do fly, seeing one do it was something like meeting a ghost."[14]

Grahame-White's machine was more powerful, but Moisant simply refused to be denied the prize. He eschewed all caution and headed directly for Bedloe's Island, barely clearing treetops and buildings in the most populated section of the route. As he approached the statue, he ascended to almost three thousand feet, made his turn for home, and then combined a downward glide, a light tailwind, and the same direct route back to the finish. Moisant beat Grahame-White's time by forty-two seconds. Later, when his sister Matilde was asked about John's having chosen a flight path without any chance of an emergency landing, she replied, "My brother doesn't fly to land. He flies to win."[15]

Seconds after Moisant's winning time was announced, Grahame-White was at the judge's table. Not only had they cheated by allowing Moisant his late start, but they had done so for the crassest jingoistic motives. The only fair solution, according to the Englishman, was to allow him to repeat his run, where presumably he too would fly directly at the statue and, with an engine of twice the power, would thereby have no difficulty recording a winning time. The judges deliberated only moments before turning Grahame-White down. The Englishman appealed to the full aviation committee, asking for a rerun the following day. The committee met "long into the night" before upholding the original ruling and denying Grahame-White a second chance.

When asked about the Englishman's refrain that he had been cheated by the colonials, Moisant said simply, "I will race him anywhere at any time under any circumstances on equal terms."[16] Moisant meant, of course, that if *he* had a 100-horsepower machine, Grahame-White would have no chance. The Aero Club jumped on board with an offer to back Moisant to the tune of $100,000.

The Liberty flight made John Moisant not just the story of the meet, but the *American* story. "Moisant, his face red from the fanning of the cold air, shouted too, demanding cheers not for himself, but for America. The band struck into 'The Star-Spangled Banner' and the crowd cheered. It switched to 'Yankee Doodle' and yells greeted it. Then it swung into 'Dixie' and its reception was hysterical. There were tears in the cheers and there were sobs in the shouts of every man, woman, and child who had seen Moisant's return, for something was welling up that made them want to cry for sheer happiness."[17] Quite a turnabout for a man who had been declared a fugitive by this very same country not six months before.

Wilbur Wright joined in the general sentiment. He was so overjoyed to see Grahame-White defeated that he forgot the winner had flown an infringing aircraft. Wilbur reportedly tore off his hat and "gave a yell like a Comanche Indian." He then jumped in the air and told reporters, "That's my opinion, boys."[18] On October 31, the meet's final day, Wilbur got another treat when Ralph Johnstone upped his altitude record to an ethereal 9,714 feet.

Wilbur's effervescence soon diminished, however. On November 3, Orville reported to his partners that in addition to $20,000 they had received for their share of the gate, they had won $15,000 in prize money. The partners voted Wilbur and Orville $10,000 bonuses and declared a dividend of $80,000. But despite the windfall, Wilbur and Orville decided they been shortchanged, that the Aero Corporation owed them an additional $15,000.

"I am going to have the money or have a lawsuit and expose the swindle publicly," Wilbur wrote to Orville.[19] And file a lawsuit he did. What really seemed to bother Wilbur was that prize money, specifically to Grahame-White, had been paid out of gross receipts, and August Belmont, a stockholder, was reimbursed for expenses in preparing the facility before the Wright Company had received its cut.

Allan Ryan, an original stockholder in the Wright Company, characterized the action as "disgraceful" and added, "While the Aero Corporation is trying to advance the science and art of aviation, the Wrights are imbued only with the spirit of commercialism and have little or no interest in real science."[20] Andrew Freedman vehemently opposed the lawsuit and was furious with Wilbur as well. "Ryan and Freedman are hot," was how Wilbur phrased it, "but I intend to have the money collected."[21]

But the courts apparently agreed with Ryan and Freedman. The action was perfunctorily thrown out only weeks later.

The night after the Liberty race, Grahame-White refused to attend the Aero Club banquet. Chip Drexel submitted a letter of resignation to the club and then hosted a dinner of his own attended by, among others, Leblanc, Latham, Clifford Harmon, and Charles Hamilton. Moisant was undeterred and received the club's full backing. Grahame-White refused further comment but canceled his plans to lease a home in New York for the winter.

On December 1, with $100,000 in winnings and a good deal more from endorsements and private flights, Grahame-White sailed for England. Just before he boarded ship, he was served with papers; the Wrights were asking for $50,000 in damages for bringing infringing machines into the country. The suit was problematic because Grahame-White had flown in sanctioned meets, but that he had supplemented his winnings with private activities was not in doubt. Of course, so had a number of other foreign aviators, none of whom the Wrights had chosen to bring similar action against.

The Wrights eventually won the suit but received only $1,700, a pittance considering the fortune Grahame-White had garnered in a mere two months in the United States. Most commentators have considered the verdict a victory for the Wrights, observing that the mere fact of a judgment showed that the courts would protect their patent rights.[22] But the trivial size of the award, the prospect of earning thousands and thousands while losing mere hundreds, would have discouraged very few.

CHAPTER 22

Faster, Steeper, Higher

While John Moisant's victory in the Statue of Liberty race did not change the course of aviation, it did accelerate prevailing trends, which put enormous pressure on designers as well as flyers. Exhibition flying became increasingly audacious and performance limits were tested on every machine in the air. For Glenn Curtiss and the Wrights, whose attention was deflected from the shop to either the courtroom or the boardroom, this presented a significant impediment to remaining competitive.

The Wrights, for example, lacked either the time or the inclination to consider an alternative to wing warping, although European designers were beginning to employ a more efficient and reliable aileron alignment. Curtiss had moved his from the front to the rear strut for superior handling. Within two years, no other airplane would use the Wright technology. Even the Wrights' most sympathetic biographer admitted that after Belmont "it was clear that they had lost their technological edge . . . the inventors of the airplane resigned themselves to a position back in the middle of the pack."[1]

Curtiss watched superiority in motor design pass to the Continent. The rotary Gnôme, which had supplanted Curtiss's V-design in Blériots, Farmans, and Antoinettes, was being increasingly utilized by

American manufacturers.* And, while the biplane favored by both Curtiss and the Wrights remained the sturdier construction, monoplanes, which predominated in Europe, were flying faster and longer. Curtiss had shown up with a monoplane at Belmont for the Gordon Bennett, but the untested machine was never put in the air.

But still, Wilbur and Curtiss continued to battle each other, the puncher stalking the boxer, Wilbur attempting to land a crushing body blow to a weakened opponent and Curtiss, his resources depleted, dodging, feinting, and trying to survive. Curtiss relied almost solely on revenues garnered by the exhibition company; he could not use the Hammondsport factory he had built with his own hands without permission of the receiver until the Herring–Curtiss bankruptcy was resolved.

Wilbur and Curtiss spoke at Belmont, where Curtiss proposed they settle the dispute out of court and asked Wilbur for terms. Wilbur responded in a note of November 5, 1910. Although Wilbur characterized his proposed settlement as "satisfactory in all probability to both factions," it would have reduced Curtiss to a de facto employee of the Wright Company. Wilbur asked $1,000 on every machine Curtiss had ever or would ever manufacture and $100 for each day a Curtiss machine flew in exhibitions.

Curtiss either did not receive or pretended not to receive the note, because on November 14, he wrote to Wilbur again asking for his terms. Wilbur reiterated his offer in a letter in which he referred to "our recent conference." Curtiss replied a week later. "It had been my intention to make you a counter offer, but in thinking the matter over, it has occurred to me that to accept a license—even at no cost to us—might not improve our condition. In fact," he added disingenuously, "it had been my idea that a principal advantage in a deal of this kind would be the assistance it afforded you toward excluding the foreign aviators and those who do use your device."

* Ironically, the American agent for Gnôme, Aeromotion Company, operated out of the Wright building in St. Louis.

Wilbur replied with obvious irritation on November 30. "The negotiation was initiated at your request and now seems similarly closed by you . . . it is well for both parties to revert to the established mode of settlement," meaning the courts. In a letter to Orville, Wilbur demonstrated the conviction that he was playing from strength. "The Curtiss people have evidently given up the license idea. . . . I think they fear that their business is just about played out and that if they could escape the profitable past they could afford to pay license on the small future, but in this also they were disappointed."[2]

But the Wrights had problems of their own. Unlike Curtiss, whose precarious survival emanated from a desiccated capital base, Wilbur and Orville's difficulties were created by expansion.

Soon after the Belmont meet had closed, Orville sailed for Europe to once again assess the state of the German and French affiliates. He was not cheered by what he found. The infringement suits filed with French courts showed no promise of early resolution and the disastrously managed French company licensed to sell Wright aircraft had gone under. As Orville wrote to Wilbur on November 24, the affiliate was "in such bad repute to the government that it could not do business." The bankrupt company had then seen its assets shifted to another manufacturer, Astra, which had also acquired the license to produce Wright aircraft in effect royalty-free. Orville learned from his friend Count de Lambert that Astra had conspired to secure precisely that arrangement. "The entire business in France seems to have been a graft," he wrote to Wilbur.

In Germany, the infringement suit was faring no better than in France, nor was the affiliate. While Orville described the manufacturing facilities and workmanship as "first class," he discovered "a great many machines have been built on which we are receiving no royalties." Orville found the manager of the German operation "entirely incompetent to handle the business," then observed, "He is a bright fellow and a hustler, but lacks judgment." In the end, Orville concluded, "I have about made up my mind to let the European business go. I don't propose to be bothered with it all my life and I see no prospect of its ever amounting to anything unless we send a representative here to stay and watch our interests."[3]

The Wrights were also running into domestic problems, instigated by none other than Charles Hamilton. Wilbur had demanded a $15,000 fee for entering their airplanes in a proposed meet in San Francisco at which star aviators from the United States and Europe would be solicited to compete for prize money that might exceed $100,000. Wilbur had specified that the money would be paid "as a testimonial to the work he and his brother had done in furthering the future of aviation." Israel Ludlow, representing the meet, had all but gained agreement from an excellent lineup, including Latham, Grahame-White, and Moisant, when Hamilton protested. "If we agree to this plan," he observed, "we virtually are acknowledging the validity of the Wright patents and we are prejudicing ourselves in any future suit that may arise. I demand the same guarantee they receive."[4] The other aviators agreed with Hamilton's assessment and for a while it appeared as though the meet might be canceled, but Wilbur stood firm. He eventually got his money and Hamilton did not participate.

In an irony he likely did not appreciate, Wilbur's newfound leverage with promoters came not from having the law on his side but from the quality of his exhibition team. Wright aviators Johnstone, Hoxsey, Brookins, and even newcomer Phil Parmalee had soundly beaten Curtiss flyers at Belmont and, except for Moisant, were now the biggest American headliners around. Hamilton pleased the crowd but rarely won anything. In addition, with aviation entering a more mature and more flamboyant era, the roster of exhibition flyers no longer contained some of the field's most famous names. Curtiss, Blériot, and Paulhan had by then largely restricted their activities to design and manufacture—and in some cases management and legal affairs—and left exhibition work to surrogates. But the surrogates had changed the rules. Selling airplanes for their employers was far less important than making names for themselves and notoriety was best achieved by performing feats of greater and greater daring.

Some flyers, of course—most significantly Hoxsey, Johnstone,

Hamilton, and now John Moisant—had already understood the publicity value of flirting with death, or at least seeming to do so. All except Hamilton insisted privately that they never performed a stunt they were not certain was safe, but pushing their airplanes to the very limit of prudent operation belied those assurances.

The Moisants, as always, had chosen to go their own way. With his brother now one of the most famous men in America, Alfred decided aviation was a coming business. In typical Moisant fashion, Alfred dove in. Only days after the Belmont meet, Alfred capitalized the new Moisant International Aviators, Inc. with $250,000 of his own money and committed another $500,000 to cover anticipated expenses. His immediate plan was to organize a "flying circus," a traveling airborne extravaganza with his brother as the feature attraction. He also planned to establish a complex in Garden City, near the site of the just-concluded meet, to use as a base of operations and home for a flying school.

He began with seven aviators and a distinctly Gallic flavor. Three of the seven were French, including Roland Garros, a fourth was a French-speaking Swiss, and John Moisant was of French lineage. The remaining two were American, one of whom was the peripatetic Charles Hamilton, who would finally have a venue for his Hamiltonian, which he decided to rename the *Black Devil.* Hamilton was drinking more than ever and rarely took to the air without a couple of shots of whiskey. That he didn't die in one of his many crashes amazed his peers.*

Alfred was generous, even profligate, with salaries, promised bonuses, railroad arrangements, and accommodations because he was convinced he had found as valuable a commodity at Belmont as he had in Central America. How could Americans resist paying to see the most incredible phenomenon of the modern world?

It turned out that they could.

* Hamilton was tubercular and likely knew he didn't have all that much time. But he confounded the odds and died in bed, succumbing to pneumonia in 1914.

The Moisant flying circus left New York on November 20 to great hoopla but John and Alfred had succeeded in booking only three mid-sized cities, all in the South. (They eventually added three more.) At each of their stops, press coverage was extensive but paying customers were not.

One of Alfred's miscalculations was in what would constitute a profitable venue. The large air meets he wished to emulate had been held, if not in out-of-the-way places, at least where an interested spectator could not simply wander over and get as good a view from outside the fence as one who had purchased a ticket. In the cities at which the Moisant flying circus performed, however, that was precisely what local devotees could do. Alfred's problem, therefore, was not a lack of enthusiasm for his flyers but a lack of people willing to pay for something they could get for free.

"The Moisant circus is a failure," Wilbur wrote to Orville in early December. "They are losing money steadily and I think will soon wind up their affairs. They took in $600 for a three day show at Chattanooga and only $200 the first day at Memphis." Wilbur added, with obvious satisfaction, "Knabenshue has contracted for Brookins, Hoxsey, and Parmalee at San Francisco at $22,500."[5]

Alfred soldiered on, capital draining as if from a siphon. More than a decade of refusing to admit defeat in El Salvador had not given the Moisant family the feel of when to cut its losses.

With the flying circus occupying so much of his time, the second part of the plan, the Moisant aviation school, didn't get started until the following year. When it did, however, on "1,600 acres unobstructed by a tree or a house," the first two students to sign up guaranteed that the venture would receive wide play in the press and help Alfred recoup some of his losses.

Both were women.

One of the spectators at the Belmont meet had been a magazine feature writer at *Leslie's Illustrated Weekly* named Harriet Quimby. A stunning beauty, tall and sleek, Quimby was described by Matilde Moisant as "the prettiest girl I've ever seen." *Leslie's* planned to devote an entire issue to aviation and Quimby had prevailed on her editor to send her to Jamaica. She had been interested in flying for some time and was chairman of the Ladies Committee of the Model Aero Club of America.

Quimby was thirty-five at the time but regularly lopped five years or more off her age and no one was the wiser. She had been born in rural Michigan in May 1875 but her father failed as a farmer and the family moved west to San Francisco when Harriet was six or seven. Her mother later claimed that the family was of proper New England stock, a fiction that Quimby was all too willing to adopt as she made her way in the world.

Her initial aspiration was the theater—in the census of 1900, Quimby listed herself as an actress—and she pounded the turn-of-the-century pavements with another aspiring actress, Linda Arvidson. Having no luck, Quimby and Arvidson finagled forty dollars to rent a theater to put on a revue, half of which came from San Francisco mayor James Phelan, who fell for a tale of woe from two beautiful young women. Quimby was so striking that a stage photographer shot her for free for the window display and local merchants were persuaded to lend them rugs and furniture. According to Arvidson, they received "good notices, but not enough to put a dent in our careers."[6]

Arvidson continued to try to get work but Quimby abandoned the stage and got herself hired as a feature writer for the San Francisco *Call,* where she penned such articles as "Behind the Scenes with Bernhardt." In another feature, "The Chinese Belle of America," about the arrival of the seventeen-year-old niece of the Chinese consul general, Quimby's opening line exhibited the grandiloquent manner of the day: "When the smoke from the steamer *Gaelic* curled up past Alcatraz, spiraled and settled in hieroglyphics as the heavily laden seahorse from the Orient made fast to her dock, there was something more than the usual stir on deck."[7] She also wrote about art and theater, and freelanced for west coast magazines.

In 1903, Quimby left San Francisco for New York and landed a writing job at *Frank Leslie's Illustrated Weekly.* For the next seven years, in addition to theater reviews, she wrote on everything from businesses that ply their trade underground to the effects of color on human behavior to alligator nests in Florida to the real meaning of stage kisses to fortune-tellers in Egypt. Her pieces were picked up by newspapers across America.

Linda Arvidson remained in the West and in 1905 joined the cast of a play called *Miss Petticoats,* whose company had been stranded in San Francisco. One of the actors was a young man who called himself "Lawrence Griffith," although his real first name was David. Arvidson was fascinated by Griffith, the son of a Confederate colonel who had fought with Stonewall Jackson. The two began seeing each other, but Griffith advised Arvidson never to marry if she intended to remain onstage. In 1906, Arvidson ignored Griffith's advice and did get married—not surprisingly to Griffith himself. The next year, Griffith came east to try his hand as a playwright, Arvidson following soon after. Griffith's playwriting went nowhere and his acting career never took off, either, but he had better luck when he took up film directing. Instead of Lawrence, which Arvidson despised, as a director he used his initials, D.W.

Arvidson and Quimby rekindled their friendship and in 1909, Quimby appeared in a short film directed by Griffith called *Lines of White on a Sullen Sea.* Quimby had a small part as a "fishermaiden"; two of her fellow bit players were Mack Sennett and Mary Pickford.

Quimby did not appear in any more films but did write screenplays for shorts, five of which were filmed by Griffith and produced by the Biograph Company in 1911. Quimby gave her efforts such exotic titles as *The Blind Princess and the Poet, Sunshine Through the Dark,* and *His Mother's Scarf.*

At Belmont, Quimby became friends with both John and Matilde Moisant. When she announced her desire to learn to fly, John encouraged her to do just that. When the school opened, Quimby prevailed on her editor to pay the $750 fee, promising them a rousing story. When Quimby signed up, so did Matilde.

Harriet Quimby might turn out to be the most glamorous aviatrix, but she wouldn't be the first. Glenn Curtiss had also trained a woman pilot, Blanche Stuart Scott. Scott had made news in July 1910 by driving an automobile cross-country and in September, at Jerome Fanciulli's suggestion, she began lessons at Hammondsport. Curtiss tried to restrict her to low, "grass cutting" and training flights, but Scott would not be held back and by November she was flying for Curtiss in exhibitions.

Scott's inclusion on the exhibition circuit was part of a general upgrade also instigated by Fanciulli. Curtiss finally set a more formal structure, with an official roster and terms of pay. Charles Willard and Bud Mars had already been touring unofficially and Curtiss added J. A. D. McCurdy from the AEA. The three were competent enough flyers but no threat to Hoxsey, Johnstone, and Brookins. Without Hamilton, the team had no star power. Then, at an exhibition in Minneapolis in June, Curtiss met a freelance exhibition flyer who might change all that.

Eugene Ely was a farm boy from Iowa who had left at age eighteen for San Francisco. He was fascinated with automobiles and worked at various times as a mechanic, a salesman, and a chauffeur, eventually taking to race-car driving, at which he excelled. As a twenty-year-old, Ely had been acclaimed during the great earthquake for three times driving through fire to ferry patients at Waldeck Hospital to safety. The next year, he married a high school principal's daughter and moved to Oregon, where he discovered that flying was even more appealing and more lucrative than driving. He bought and then repaired an old, wrecked four-cylinder Curtiss machine, taught himself to fly, and with his wife, Mabel, as his manager, hit the circuit. Curtiss signed him up.

Curtiss had a different arrangement with his aviators than the Wrights. "He started us out with twenty-five percent of the take and we paid all our personal expenses," said Beckwith Havens, who joined the team the following year. "We had a minimum charge of $500 for thirty minutes, and if it was a weekend or a holiday, it would be maybe $1,200 or $1,500 for thirty minutes."

Ely didn't actually fly for Curtiss until a meet in Sheepshead Bay in Brooklyn in late August—a big moneymaker for Curtiss—and he fared poorly at Belmont, winning only $100. But two weeks later, he justified Curtiss's decision in a milestone flight.

Curtiss had never lost his fascination for airplanes and water. From the early days of the *Loon,* he had envisioned a true hydroplane. "A new line of thought—or to express it more accurately, the following out of a very old one—was taking my interest and a great part of my time. The experiments I had in mind involved the problem of flying from the water and alighting on the water . . . it was only a question of development, not of pioneering. It was suggested to me by the New York *World* to launch an aeroplane from the deck of a ship at sea and have it fly back to shore carrying messages."[8]

The Hamburg–American Line offered one of their ocean liners for the test. "The ship was fitted with a large platform, erected on the stern, a platform sloping downward, and wide enough to allow an aeroplane set up on it to run down so that it could gather headway for its flight. The plan was to take McCurdy and the aeroplane fifty miles out to sea on the outward voyage from New York, and then launch them from the platform."

But the plan had to be scuttled, first because of bad weather and then when an oil can that had been carelessly left on one of the wings was knocked into the whirling propeller, cracking it. The ship was forced to sail before repairs could be completed.

But a navy captain named Washington Irving Chambers had been at Belmont and he and Curtiss had discussed the potential for naval aviation. Chambers persuaded the navy to offer the cruiser *Birmingham* for the test. Curtiss went to Hampton Roads, Virginia, where the *Birmingham* was docked, and supervised the construction of a fifty-seven-foot, downward-sloping platform over the bow. Eugene Ely was flying in a meet in Baltimore and Curtiss instructed him to take the *Hudson Flyer* to Norfolk.

Curtiss and Ely waited for good weather, but storms set in and persisted for days. Finally, on November 14, Ely insisted on making the try. He waited for sleet to clear and then in rain, wind, and fog, "conditions little short of prohibitory," Ely took off from the *Birmingham*'s deck. The airplane dropped after it cleared the end of the platform, touching the water thirty-seven feet below and sending up a spray that damaged the propeller and drenched Ely, covering his goggles. Ely regained some altitude but found himself enshrouded in fog, unsure of his location or bearing. He first headed out to sea, where he would surely have died—Ely could not swim—but he noticed his error and turned back. When he reached the beach, the fog cleared briefly, just enough for Ely to land "within a few yards of the Hampton Roads Yacht Club house." He had flown five miles in five minutes. Captain Chambers, who had gotten himself appointed as chairman of a board for aeronautical navigation, declared the test even a greater success than he had anticipated and that Ely and Curtiss had proved the feasibility of shipborne aircraft. For his flight, Ely won a prize of $5,000 offered by the Ryan family for the first flight of at least one mile from a ship to land, money Ely got to keep.

It was after the success at Hampton Roads that Curtiss changed his mind about making a deal with Wilbur Wright. He had come up with a better idea. "On November 29, 1910, I sent letters to both Secretary [Jacob] Dickinson of the War Department and to Secretary [George von Lengerke] Meyer of the Navy Department, inviting them to send one or more officers of their respective departments . . . where I would undertake to instruct them in aviation. I made no conditions. I asked for and received no remuneration whatsoever for this service. I consider it an honour to be able to tender my services in this connection."[9] With the honor would come the support of the United States military, heretofore the exclusive province of the Wrights.

With the navy as a tentative ally, there was no thought of delaying until Hammondsport thawed out in the spring. To give himself a warm-weather winter facility and perhaps to get as far as possible away from Herring and the Wrights, Curtiss decided to establish a research base in California. He eventually settled on North Island, a scrubby, two-by-four-mile barrier isle off San Diego. The navy assigned a young lieutenant, Theodore "Spuds" Ellyson, to Curtiss to participate in the development of naval aircraft. Before Ellyson began, Captain Chambers wrote to him. "If I read Mr. Curtiss correctly, he is not too conservative to adopt a good improvement regardless of who owns the patent."[10]

With the splitting off of the exhibition corporation and the promise of support from the navy, Curtiss had at least stabilized his business. His exhibition team would now officially compete with that of the Wrights, whose antagonism became only more pronounced. As Frank Coffyn observed, "We were taught by the Wrights that the Curtiss crowd was just no good at all and we turned up our noses at them. But we found out later on by flying at meets where they were that they were a pretty nice bunch of fellows." While the Wrights' hatred for Curtiss was doubtless reciprocated, there is no record of Curtiss himself ever expressing the same sentiments toward either the Wrights or the men who flew for them.

The Wrights were equally disdainful of the Curtiss aircraft. "They always inferred or hinted," Frank Coffyn said, "that they didn't think the Curtiss planes were any good . . . that they were dangerous to fly."

Then on November 16, at an air show in Denver, Ralph Johnstone was killed.

The headline read, "Johnstone Loses Gamble with Death."[11] Engaged in a stunt called the "spiral glide," in which he began a circular descent, steadily increasing the angle to the ground, "like the swoop of a hawk," a wing tip of the Flyer crumbled, and the craft dropped like a stone from five hundred feet. Johnstone had completed one full revolution from eight hundred feet and was beginning his second when "the middle spur which braces the left side of the lower plane gave way and the wing tips of both upper and lower planes doubled up as if they had been hinged." Johnstone attempted to control the crippled craft "by warping the other wing tip. Then the horrified spectators saw the plane swerve and plunge straight toward the earth." Johnstone still wasn't finished. Although he was "thrown from the seat as the nose of the plane swung downward, he caught one of the wire stays and grasped one of the wood braces of the upper plane with both hands. Then, working with hands and feet, he tried by main strength to warp the planes so that their surfaces might catch the air and check his descent."[12] It appeared for a moment that Johnstone might succeed, but the aircraft turned over and plunged to the ground. Johnstone was buried in the wreckage and when his body was finally extricated, "nearly every bone broken" and carried from the field, the band played ragtime music.

Before that ceremony, however, a more grisly ritual had occurred.

> Scarcely had Johnstone hit the ground before morbid men and women swarmed over the wreckage fighting with each other for souvenirs. One of the wooden stays had gone almost through Johnstone's body. Before doctors or police could reach the scene, one man had torn this splinter from the body and ran away, carrying his trophy, with the aviator's blood still dripping from its ends. The crowd tore away the canvas from over the body and even fought for the gloves that had protected Johnstone's hands from the cold.[13]

Arch Hoxsey was in the air when Johnstone lost control. He descended quickly and landed and he and Walter Brookins hurried to the site of the crash, but there was nothing either of them could do. The flyers knew the thin mountain air was a hazard. The day before he crashed, Johnstone had stated categorically that he "would attempt no tricks because he considered it too dangerous," but then Hoxsey flew "far over the foothills, which seemed to fire Johnstone to outdo his teammate."

Wilbur Wright, in New York, first broke the news to Johnstone's widow and then faced the press. When asked for his reaction, Wilbur said, "I cannot say anything about the accident except to express the grief I feel. The spectacle of the thing as it appears to the onlooker . . . is of no value to me. What I want is a description of how the thing happened from an aviator who saw it. . . . I understand that his left plane [wing] collapsed. When Brookins and Hoxsey report perhaps I can make some analysis of what happened."

Claude Grahame-White did not need to wait for the facts. Interviewed in Philadelphia, Grahame-White said, "Johnstone was one of the most unassuming as well as one of the cleverest aviators I ever met. He was so skillful that I feel sure when the details of the accident are known, it will be found that the machine and not the aviator was at fault." While Grahame-White was hardly averse to jabbing a needle in the Wrights' direction, that the Flyers were unsuitable to exhibition flying had become a constant whisper among aviators other than the Wrights' own. Johnstone was the third American to die in a crash and all three had perished in Wright machines.*

Wilbur questioned both Hoxsey and Brookins at length, trying to determine the cause of the crash. In correspondence between the brothers, their theorizing was exhaustive. But although Brookins had noted to Wilbur, "We could not figure out why Johnstone turned to the right when his left wing took a smaller angle," at no time did either Wilbur or Orville seriously countenance the possibility of a design flaw or that Wright machines might not be reliable in a steep dive.[14] In the end, Wilbur concluded, "On the whole it seems plausible that the trouble began with Johnstone falling off of the seat."[†15]

Johnstone was thirty. In addition to his wife, a German who would return home to Berlin, Johnstone left two small children. Orville sought his widow out on his next trip across the Atlantic to assure her that he and his brother would continue to participate in her support.

* Johnstone was the twenty-sixth overall fatality. Six died in Wright Flyers, four in Blériots, and six in Farmans. The other ten were in a variety of aircraft, including Voisins and Antoinettes. None of the fatalities had occurred in Curtiss machines.

† Flyers in those early days did not employ seat belts or harnesses. Johnstone was not the first to die after falling from an aircraft nor would he be the last. It is astonishing that not one of the great innovators who dominated early flight thought to include such a basic and obvious piece of safety equipment.

On November 23, 1910, just six days after Johnstone, Octave Chanute died as well. In his letter to Orville of November 30, Wilbur simply said, "I am back in New York after a trip west to attend Johnstone's and Chanute's funerals."[16] He noted that Chanute had lived but a few weeks after returning from Europe but made no mention of either personal regret or their previous falling-out. Chanute was never mentioned in their correspondence again.

Chanute was exalted in aviation journals. *Aeronautics* wrote, "The counsel and encouragement which he gave to Wilbur and Orville Wright have been gratefully and gracefully acknowledged by them. . . . It came to them at the time when it was most needed, when they were at the foot of the steepest part of the unblazed trail. It gave them the courage and confidence which were essential to enable them to keep on alone and to emerge at last at the summit triumphant." The article concluded, "Those who knew him will always . . . think of the oft-repeated saying, 'He was more willing to give credit to others than to claim any for himself.'"

In the same issue, Wilbur contributed a laudatory but curiously arm's-length tribute, even referring to himself in the third person.

> By the death of Mr. O. Chanute the world has lost one whose labors had to an unusual degree influenced the course of human progress. If he had not lived, the entire history of progress in flying would have been other than it has been, for he encouraged not only the Wright brothers to persevere in their experiments, but it was due to his missionary trip to France in 1903 that the Voisins, Bleriot, Farman, Delagrange, and Archdeacon were led to undertake a revival of aviation studies in that country, after the failure of the efforts of Ader and the French government in 1897 had left everyone in idle despair.
>
> His writings were so lucid as to provide an intelligent understanding of the nature of the problems of flight to a vast number

> of persons who would probably never have given the matter study otherwise, and not only by published articles, but by personal correspondence and visitation, he inspired and encouraged to the limits of his ability all who were devoted to the work. His private correspondence with experimenters in all parts of the world was of great volume. No one was too humble to receive a share of his time. In patience and goodness of heart he has rarely been surpassed. Few men were more universally respected and loved. [17]

On December 9, at Pau, the scene of Wilbur Wright's triumph just two years before, a Frenchman, Georges Legagneux, flying a Blériot, broke Johnstone's altitude record set at Belmont and in doing so became the first man to exceed 10,000 feet. Chip Drexel had claimed 9,897 feet, but the barograph reading had been disputed by the Aero Club. The dispute became moot in face of Legagneux's 10,499-foot ascent. Legagneux's mark was the first time since Paulhan that the altitude record had slipped from American hands and Hoxsey wanted it back. Two days later, he was given the perfect venue to do so.

Los Angeles decided to stage a follow-up to the wildly successful January meet. The sequel would begin on Christmas Eve, December 24, and run through the New Year. Smaller meets, as the Moisants had found to their chagrin, were generally money losers, and in order to mount a major show one needed the participation and the approval of the Wrights. And the only way to get that was to pay them, and the amount was generally sufficient to threaten the profitability even of a meet that drew tens of thousands.

On December 11, Wilbur agreed to terms. As events unfolded, it seemed that Los Angeles, just up the coast from Curtiss's widely publicized North Island base, would be another immense triumph for the Wright Exhibition Team. On December 26, in front of seventy-five thousand spectators, Arch Hoxsey did reclaim the altitude record, soaring to 11,474 feet, shattering the mark set by Legagneux and almost tripling what Paulhan had done at Dominguez Field only one year earlier. He flew in a 40-mph wind, far stronger than most aviators would chance, and sufficient to wreck Latham's Antoinette monoplane, hurling it against a fence. After he landed, the other flyers carried him on their shoulders in front of the grandstand.

When asked, "Was it windy up there?" Hoxsey replied, "It blew so hard that my machine hardly moved and barely held its own. It was so cold that more than once I thought my carburetor was about to freeze. I made the record because I was determined to keep on going up until I passed Legagneux's record or until the carburetor froze."[18] Three days later, Hoxsey again topped 10,000 feet, flying over Mount Wilson and the recently completed Carnegie Solar Observatory. After the flight, an army lieutenant assigned to observe the proceedings asserted that a thousand biplanes could transport an army of 10,000 men over mountains as high as the Alps.

Hoxsey was fearful that the 11,474-foot mark would not be declared official, and so ascended to 10,575 feet on December 30 to be certain that he had wiped Legagneux from the record books. The following day, to celebrate the coming of the New Year, Hoxsey intended to render any argument moot; a new altitude record, perhaps as high as 12,000 feet, would be the culmination of a bravura performance. In addition to altitude, Hoxsey had won for total duration, more than seventeen hours, and endurance, more than three hours. All three represented new records.

As Hoxsey prepared for his ascent, he learned that John Moisant was dead.

Moisant had been in New Orleans, preparing to take a run at the 1910 Michelin Cup, waiting, as had Wilbur two years earlier, for the end of the year to ensure that his mark would hold. He was flying the same Blériot, now repaired, in which he finished second in the Gordon Bennett, but to accommodate the longer distance he had installed an additional 35-gallon fuel tank just forward of the motor. Although he'd been assured by mechanics that the arrangement was safe, a disproportionate percentage of weight would now be at the

Blériot's nose. More cautious than the public gave him credit for, Moisant wanted to test out the arrangement with the second tank only partially full before he took to the air for as much as eight hours in the official attempt. He decided to fly the craft from the staging area to the airfield where the four-mile course had been laid out.

The morning was cold, with a gusty wind whipping off Lake Pontchartrain. Even for the test flight, Moisant wore so many layers of clothing insulated with newspaper that a friend likened it to a "suit of armor." Moisant couldn't bend his knees enough to get into the airplane so his crew had to lift him.

He ascended only to a few hundred feet, flew to the field, circled it twice, descended to two hundred feet, and then turned to land with the wind behind him. Suddenly, the tail of the aircraft was forced upward by a gust of wind pushing the overweight nose down into a dive. Moisant was thrown from the airplane "as if he had been shot from a gun." The Blériot struck the ground vertically; Moisant was tossed thirty feet. He broke his neck in the fall.

Moisant survived long enough to be placed on a flatbed railroad car, but died before he could be brought to a hospital.

When Hoxsey learned of Moisant's crash, he immediately sent a telegram of condolence to Alfred but, as after Johnstone's death, did not alter his plans to fly. Like Moisant, he took his machine up in strong, swirling winds, although not nearly of the magnitude he had encountered on his record-breaking flights.

He ascended to 7,000 feet, disappeared into the clouds, and "with a thousand field glasses" following him, suddenly and surprisingly re-emerged in descent.

> The biplane came whirring out of the clouds. The crowds cheered again. In the rapid downward spiraling they saw only what they had seen Hoxsey do before these several days, cheating them into gasps of terror only to alight in smiling safety on the ground, when within less than six hundred feet of the ground the twenty-five-

> mile-an-hour wind shot forth treacherous blasts. His machine was caught helplessly in the counter currents. It tumbled over then suddenly slammed to earth.[19]

Hoxsey was killed instantly. His body "was found broken and twisted out of all semblance when the wreckage had been cleared. . . . The steel sprocket which drove the propellers lay across his face, the motor resting upon the right side of his body. Every one of the ribs on that side was shattered. An iron upright, broken by the force of the crash, held the aviators' body impaled upon its jagged point."[20]

Walter Brookins broke down when he saw the wreckage and the other flyers sat stunned. Although all flights were canceled for the day, most spectators remained in the grandstand, many of them sobbing.

Roy Knabenshue said a short time later, "Of all the aviators on the field, he was the one we least expected to see suffer an accident. He was one of the most careful men who has ever flown; he was extremely cautious about the condition of his machine and was always testing it to make sure that it would respond. I cannot explain the accident, but it appears to have been due to the gusty 10 mile an hour wind that swept over the field. Apparently Hoxsey had come down from a calm and rushed into a wind strata about 800 feet above the earth at a terrific pace. The wind caught his machine and before he was able to combat it, the biplane turned over."

Phil Parmalee added, "The indications from the way the aeroplane moved are that Hoxsey made a mighty effort to right himself. If he had had 60 feet more between himself and the earth he might have succeeded. The machine struck almost on its bottom. This indicates that it was being righted even while the aviator was being whirled in a series of somersaults."[21]

Robert Lee, a mechanic, said, "Hoxsey could not bank into the wind as he had expected and that the air threw up one end of the plane and then tipped the whole machine over."

Among those mourning Hoxsey's death was his former passenger Theodore Roosevelt. "I am more grieved than I can say over the tragedy that came to Hoxsey. He was courageous and a splendid type of fellow. I wanted to make the trip in the air with Hoxsey because he was an American aviator and had an American machine. I admired Hoxsey for the skill he had displayed in handling his aeroplane. I felt that it was entirely safe to trust him when I ventured into the air with him. . . . It is important that aviation be carried on. . . . Hoxsey gave his life as a noble sacrifice."

Newspapers announced the following day that Hoxsey's mother, a widow, would receive his $10,000 in winnings at the meet. Wilbur and Orville also paid for the funeral and, as with Johnstone's widow, assured Mrs. Hoxsey that they would continue with their support.

Within hours, America's two most prominent airmen had died. Pictures and stories about aviation's darkest day dominated the front pages. Some surmised that the two crushed bodies would mark the end of daredevil flying.

Instead, it was merely the beginning.

CHAPTER 23

War Birds

Allan Ryan, president of the Aero Club, gave his annual address at the club dinner on January 6, 1911. Harking back to Harry Toulmin's flag-waving defense of the Wright patents, Ryan had a call to patriotism of his own:

> It is my own belief that the future supremacy of this country in the aeronautic field is going to depend very largely upon the harmonious cooperation of the institutions and individuals interested in the great science and it seems to me that the time has arrived to get to work. . . . It is also very important in the future that we give every possible aid and encouragement to worthy inventors and to every branch of scientific development in this country and to that end we should call into association and cooperation with us all those who are seriously working or interested in the field of American aeronautics.[1]

Neither Wilbur nor Orville commented on Ryan's speech, but there would be no move to "association and cooperation" from their end that was not specifically on their terms. Ryan, of course, had been the object of Wilbur's unsuccessful suit to gain an additional $15,000 from the Belmont meet, but the Wrights were also convinced that they would be fools to play in a game where both sides were betting with their money.*

But Wilbur and Orville were also now playing a much weaker hand. The deaths of Hoxsey and Johnstone had more than cost America the services of two of its best aviators; it had also robbed the Wright team of its star draws. No aviator had yet come forward to fill the void, but America thirsted for heroes and the field had opened up. The next major meet was in San Francisco from January 8 to 25, the very event for which the Wrights had stonewalled the promoters into paying them an exorbitant entrance fee, but this time the headlines would be made not by a member of the Wright Exhibition Team but instead a member of Curtiss's.

After Eugene Ely's successful flight from the *Birmingham,* Captain Chambers had become an enthusiastic Curtiss supporter. Helping convince the captain he had made the correct choice, the Wrights had demanded payment for replacement parts Chambers thought should be supplied without charge, and even worse, Orville had sent them to the War Department COD. The invoice had prompted an angry letter from Chambers on December 11. "Dear Sirs. I was surprised this A.M. to learn that the shipment of parts so urgently needed are held at Annapolis by the Express Co to collect the ship charges. I assumed that you would send them under the same conditions as obtained in sending the whole machine. Payment for the parts comes out of our small appropriation for development." Orville wrote back claiming a misunderstanding, an explanation Chambers claimed to accept, but relations between him and the Wrights remained cool from then on.

Later in December, Chambers approached Ely and Curtiss and asked the feasibility of not only taking off from the deck of a warship but landing there as well. Ely was immediately game to try and Cur-

* The suit was still active when Ryan gave his speech. It would be thrown out one week later.

tiss saw the San Francisco meet as the perfect place for Ely to do so. The heavy cruiser *Pennsylvania* was in San Francisco Bay and was ordered to steam to Mare Island Navy Yard to be fitted for the attempt.

Landing on the cruiser presented a unique set of problems. Not only would the surface on which Ely was to alight be moving, but some means would be needed to stop the machine once it had touched down on a surface only forty yards long. The airplane's momentum would thus have to be arrested quickly but not so suddenly that Ely was pitched out, as John Moisant had been in New Orleans. Curtiss devised a system so clever that some variation of the arrangement has been in use ever since.

"The platform was built over the quarterdeck," he wrote,

> about one hundred and twenty-five feet long by thirty feet wide, with a slope toward the stern of some twelve feet. Across this runway we stretched ropes every few feet with a sandbag on each end. These ropes were raised high enough so they could catch in grab-hooks which we placed under the main centerpiece of the aeroplane, so that catching in the ropes the heavy sand bags attached would drag until they brought the machine to a stop. To protect the aviator and to catch him in case he should be pitched out of his seat in landing, heavy awnings were stretched on either side of the runway and at the upper end of it.[2]

With all the inventiveness, Ely's flying would still have to be near perfect. The platform was only four feet wider than the width of the airplane and he would be touching down at approximately forty miles per hour. A miscalculation would mean falling off the side of the ship, or worse, plowing into the crowds of sailors and visitors who would be crowded on the deck.

The first week of the San Francisco meet was subdued, the aviators performing with proficiency but without the escalating brilliance and risk that had attended Johnstone's and Hoxsey's performances. No records were set; no gasp-inducing tricks were attempted; no one tried for high altitude; and there was "a noticeable absence of the celebrated Wright 'spiral.'" "The flights were unspectacular," *Aeronautics* noted. "No doubt the recent death of Hoxsey had its psychological effect upon the aviators and tempered their usual performances."[3] Even the airfield, renamed "Selfridge Field," had the feel of death about it. Still, on January 8, a hundred thousand people paid to see the likes of Brookins, Latham, Willard, and Parmalee soar over the grounds. But as *Aeronautics* also reported, "Considering the poor flights made on that day it is credit to San Francisco's interest in aeronautics that the attendance was good the rest of the meet."

But ten days later, the meet would have its one first. On January 18, shortly before 11 A.M., Ely ascended before seventy-five thousand spectators. He flew across the bay and then to the warship waiting ten miles away. The bridge, deck, and superstructure of the *Pennsylvania* were packed with crew and more than one hundred notable guests who had been shuttled from shore. Standing between the captain of the *Pennsylvania* and the captain's wife was Mabel Ely.

Ely circled the ship once and then came in to land, the wind dangerously at his back, as it had been during John Moisant's fatal crash. After he cut his engines but before he had touched down, an updraft caught the airplane, threatening to cause Ely to miss the line of sandbag-anchored ropes, but he expertly dropped the tail and set the airplane down dead center on the deck about halfway down the platform. The ropes stopped him and to the cheering of both sailors and civilians, he got out of the airplane to be greeted by his wife, the captain, and attending luminaries. Captain Pond invited the Elys for a celebratory lunch during which the airplane was turned around. An hour later, a sated Ely reappeared, took his place at the controls, and completed the second successful takeoff from the deck of a ship. When he landed at Selfridge Field, army and navy personnel hoisted him on their shoulders and carried him before the cheering crowds.

As impressive as Ely's flight was, it did not precipitate a groundswell of support for military aviation from army and navy brass.

Ely's biplane on the deck of the USS Pennsylvania.

Change does not come easily to the military and reluctance among senior officers to divert ample funds to support development had not been diminished. The Wrights' assessment that aviation would linger as a sporting pursuit remained the conventional wisdom and Congress's appropriations to investigate airpower continued to be paltry, as Captain Chambers's letter to the Wrights attested. Captain Chambers, in fact, was not just the head of the aeronautics section—he *was* the aeronautics section. He didn't even have an office, but sat at a desk squeezed between file cabinets at the War Department.[4]

But a number of younger officers had been persuaded that aviation would revolutionize battle tactics, a perspective shared by Curtiss. After his Hudson River flight, Curtiss said publicly, "All the great battles of the future will be fought in the air. I have demonstrated that it is easy to fly over cities and fortifications. It would be perfectly practical to drop enough dynamite or picric acid down on West Point or a city like New York to destroy it utterly."[5] That point of view had begun to be shared by the public. The day after Ely was mobbed by army and navy officers, the San Francisco *Call* ran a front-page article titled, "Tacticians Must Begin to Figure: Fear of Aviators Means That the Rules of Warfare Must Be Revised Entirely."

Even for those isolated members of the military who had considered the utility of aviation, the projected uses of aircraft in battle demanded a fresh perspective. With Baldwin's dirigible and Orville's successful tests at Fort Myer, the army had considered flying machines solely for scouting and surveillance. But bomb-dropping contests had become regular events at exhibitions and at the Sheepshead Bay meet Curtiss had carried an army sharpshooter aloft to discover both if someone could shoot accurately from the air and whether or not the recoil would affect flight. The marksman only hit a target on the ground twice in four passes but the experiment made it yet more difficult not to think of the airplane as a potential weapon.

Whether for scouting or delivering ordnance, aircraft in war would be subject to risks and strains more acute than in peacetime flight. Lacking what would be later referred to as "test pilots," the closest approximation to wartime flying was done at exhibitions. The very sort of outrageous risks taken regularly by Johnstone, Hoxsey, and Hamilton in dives, spirals, or flying in high wind and extremely low to the ground were precisely what was required to determine if an airplane could be effective in combat. And foolhardy flying or not, if aviators could not successfully pull off high-risk maneuvers, it meant that ultimately the fault would be with the aircraft. That was a fundamental truth of combat that both Wilbur and Orville failed to grasp.

This is not to imply that the Wrights did not try to improve their product. They produced specialized versions of the Flyer to climb to altitude, attain high speed, or travel for great distances. Their notebooks and letters are filled with the most detailed specifications and descriptions of every inch of their machines. Their correspondence is replete with suggestions, proposals, or questions about solving problems or improving performance in what they had built. Wilbur's investigations of Johnstone's crash and then Hoxsey's were minute and exhaustive. Not an angle of incidence or point of resistance or innocuous mechanical process did not regularly come under their intensely critical gaze.

But while focusing on details of a machine whose essential design they never questioned, as if it were 1903 and they were still in North Carolina, they missed the larger picture: that the very rudiments of aircraft technology were not only bound to evolve but were in fact already evolving. Wilbur remained a stunning theoretician and Orville a superb craftsman. To regain their preeminence, they needed only to return to what had first gotten them to Kitty Hawk: approaching the problem as if it were entirely new, with no past designs to burden their thinking. Wilbur was still more than capable of great intellectual leaps but to achieve them would require a reprioritization of his time. But he had in large part ceased to be a scientist or an engineer and was now almost entirely a business executive, a role for which he was uniquely unsuited.

So while Curtiss continued to seek fresh applications for existing technology in order to create new products, the Wrights, having designed a product they were convinced might need refinement but not recasting, focused their energies on sales. The officers assigned to Wilbur and Orville were taught to fly Wright machines and taught very well; those assigned to Curtiss participated in development, testing, frequent failure, but often ultimate success.

One of Curtiss's visions was an airplane that could take off and land on water, a true hydroplane. Development of such a craft occupied Curtiss and his team in the first months at North Island. More than fifty versions failed before he got one to work. "Those of us who did not know Mr. Curtiss well," Spuds Ellyson observed, "wondered that he did not give up in despair. Since that time we have learned that anything he says he can do, he always accomplishes, as he always works out the problem in his mind before making any statement. . . . It was never a case of 'do this' or 'do that' to his amateur or his regular mechanics, but always, 'What do you think of making this change?' He was always willing to listen to any argument but generally managed to convince you his plan was best."[6]

Belying Grover Loening's assertion that Curtiss was only a promoter, Augustus Post described Curtiss's inspiration for the draft design. "During the period when he was planning a new series of experiments, Mr. Curtiss, accompanied by Mrs. Curtiss, attended a New York theatre in which there was being presented a play much talked about just then. The curtain went up on the first act, and the noted aviator was apparently enjoying the show when, just as the scene was developing one of its most interesting climaxes, he turned to Mrs. Curtiss and said: 'I've got it.' On the theatre program he had sketched what ultimately became the design of the hydroaeroplane."[7]

On January 26, 1911, that design reached fruition. A Curtiss aircraft, buoyed by two pontoons and a redesigned "deflector" front assembly to prevent water from being forced over the top of the pontoon, successfully rose from the waters off North Island. Curtiss himself made three short flights and then after each, landed successfully on the water. Five days later, Curtiss had an improved version with a single pontoon, flat-bottomed and covered with waterproofed canvas. The float was twelve feet long, two feet wide, and one foot deep, with a sharp upsweep from the underside at the bow and a sharp down-

Curtiss piloting his flying boat at sixty miles per hour.

sweep from the top side at the stern. He once again took off successfully, then landed, settling on the water "like a duck." Curtiss had not removed the wheels but rather attached the float independently and he would soon modify the design to create the world's first amphibious airplane.

For those flights and a subsequent one later in February in which the hydroplane was lifted from the water to the deck of a warship—demonstrating that no special platform was needed for a ship to carry an aircraft—Glenn Curtiss spurred further innovation and became known as "the father of naval aviation." Ironically, the Wrights would also benefit from Curtiss's innovations. In March 1911, Wilbur and Orville offered to train one aviator if the navy bought a Wright airplane for $5,000. In July, after a fresh round of appropriations by Congress, the Wright Company made the sale.

Curtiss's flights over water came in the middle of a quite favorable run. At a meet in San Diego that opened the day after San Francisco closed, only Curtiss machines were entered and Curtiss himself flew and "showed that the Curtiss machine was certainly capable of all the air gymnastics the Wright machines had been executing." Lieutenant Ellyson flew publicly for the first time; he crashed but walked away unhurt and eager to go up again. Another Curtiss crew gave an exhibition in Havana, Cuba, where McCurdy flew across the island and around Morro Castle. But the best news for Curtiss came in early February when the receiver in the Herring–Curtiss bankruptcy announced that the Hammondsport plant had been sold back to Curtiss, its original owner, for $18,000. Curtiss had been using the plant on a temporary basis with the receiver's permission for some months, so the sale-back gave the newly incorporated Curtiss Aeroplane and Motor Company a manufacturing facility, allowing Curtiss to abandon plans to totally relocate to California.

Herring was a party to Curtiss's other lawsuit as well, of course, as a codefendant, and the Wrights were having as much trouble pinning him down as had Curtiss. Herring had been scheduled on a number of occasions to give a deposition, only to offer a series of excuses at the last minute in pleas for more time. At one point, Orville wrote to Wilbur, "Herring put in a plea for an extension . . . on account of his being sick. . . . I presume he will be asking for another but I have instructed Toulmin to fight any further extension." But the Wrights, who urgently needed as quick a resolution to the suit as possible and had hoped for a trial that summer, sat in frustration as the presiding judge continued to grant Herring's and Curtiss's requests.* As Orville wrote in a telling passage to Toulmin in June, "Curtiss has been busy since his return from the West in getting business and not in getting ready for this trial. Delay is money to him, and his only hope."

Wilbur had spent virtually no time in 1910 designing aircraft and 1911 promised to be the same.[8] The attorney handling the infringement suit in France against Blériot, Farman, and the rest asked urgently for one of the brothers to come to testify. Wilbur and Orville had agreed to alternate, and so in March Wilbur sailed for Europe, intending to be gone perhaps a month. Instead, shuttling between France, Germany, and Britain, he would not return until August.

Wilbur had friends in France, to be sure, but among the general population he had become anathema for impugning the integrity of men the French saw as heroes and pioneers in their own right. Certainly, Wilbur never had much need of trappings of any sort but he had enjoyed the accolades, the visits to the best homes, and dinners with the elite of French society, none of which would occur on this trip.

Still, initially the journey seemed well considered. After Wilbur gave testimony in Paris, the "substitute," the aeronautics expert ap-

* According to law, after the plaintiff had completed deposed testimony, which the Wrights had by March, the defendant had four months to reply, after which, if the judge agreed to move forward, a trial date would be set. Motions from either side could delay the process further and, with matters so technical, ultimate resolution might be many months or even years away.

pointed by the court to aid with technical matters, issued an opinion that seemed to agree with the Wrights almost entirely.*

Despite the ruling, significant problems remained, once again centering on leadership in the French subsidiary. "I have been pretty much over the CGNA accounts and I find that the trouble over here has been more the result of bad management than rascality though the latter might not be entirely lacking." CGNA had been effectively acquired by Astra, which Wilbur described as "the best robber in the pile." Although bookkeeping and supervision were in fact shoddy, the principal problem seemed to have been what Wilbur described as "totally unreliable motors" that were depressing sales for French-made machines.

Back home, although heartened by what seemed total victory across the Atlantic, much of the Wright Company's affairs were in a surprising state of disarray. The source was once again management—in this case, their own. In an April 23 letter to Wilbur, Orville wrote:

> Our exhibition department is in a rather demoralized condition just at present.... When Knabenshue started out after business, he came back completely discouraged. He found that the Curtiss people have been out, while we were fooling around, securing our business. They got the Grand Forks job away from us. The Curtiss outfit are taking work at one half to two-thirds of our prices. Kna-

* Wilbur was at first dissatisfied, feeling the substitute "gave us bushels of beautifully colored husks and gave the others the kernel." The expert had agreed that the Wrights had founded the flying art; that the patent was valid; that the details had not been revealed before the patent had been applied for; and that they had discovered "the method of control that enabled man to fly." He did however conclude that the Wrights had "not sufficiently claimed the *independent* command of wings and rudder" and therefore the French manufacturers had not infringed. Later, however, Wilbur realized the question of infringement had been left open but was more favorable to him than to the defendants. So strong was the ruling that he assumed Blériot, Farman, and the others would move to settle rather than continue to a final judgment.

> benshue was very much opposed to cutting prices at all, and was in favor of taking less work at higher prices, leaving the cheaper work to Curtiss. I told him he must take work away from Curtiss, whether we made any money on it or not. That he should not allow Curtiss to make any money this year.[9]

Although Orville would not so acknowledge, the origin of Knabenshue's poor morale was not simply the need to acquiesce to cut-rate contracts; the Wrights had proved to be overbearing employers. In a number of letters from June 1910 until the end of the year, Knabenshue had been chided severely for everything from entering into agreements that didn't comport specifically to Wright dictates to being told not to bring his wife and daughter with him to air meets. In March 1911, Knabenshue sent the Wrights a letter written on company stationery. Referring to his expiring employment contract, he wrote, "It states that I am to have entire charge of this department. During this season I received considerable interference on the part of several members of your organization, and this same interference resulted directly in the loss to the Company of a great many thousands of dollars." Although other members of the company, notably Frank Russell, had occasionally stuck their noses in, the two members who had interfered the most were, of course, Wilbur and Orville. And since he had not received a renewal, Knabenshue added, "In view of the foregoing, I wish to tender my resignation to take effect at the expiration of the current contract."

After some dithering and dickering, Knabenshue was talked out of quitting and on March 27 was presented with a contract extension at favorable terms with a specification that only Wilbur and Orville could give him instructions. Knabenshue continued to refuse. "I beg to state that the proposition as submitted by you is not in accordance with the verbal agreement with Mr. Wilbur Wright and I therefore respectfully decline." He clarified his refusal three days later. "As long as I receive proper support from the Wright Company and that I have the business of securing and signing all exhibition contracts, I will continue to operate under the conditions named in your letter of March 27."

A week later, Orville capitulated. He agreed to allow Knabenshue to sign contracts "after having first secured our approval" but retained the right "to withdraw this privilege at any time should your signing of contracts be unsatisfactory to our Company." After securing this tepid endorsement, Knabenshue grudgingly agreed to stay on. One week afterward, Orville described Knabenshue as "demoralized."

In that same April 23 letter, Orville related a remarkable exchange with Glenn Curtiss. Curtiss had come to Dayton to meet with Orville "to see what arrangements could be made to stop all the other people excepting those in his outfit and ours. Willard and three or four others have left Curtiss. It was these that he especially wanted us to prosecute!"*

Then, according to Orville, Curtiss made a surprising admission concerning the upcoming New York hearing on the infringement case. "He would like to have his case disposed of in some way so that he will not have to go on the stand. He says he has a very poor memory, and that although he always tries to tell the truth, he cannot always remember exactly what he said before, and that the lawyers would probably make it very embarrassing for him!"

It is difficult to know what to make of the statement. That Orville is not telling the truth is extremely unlikely given both his own propensities and that he was disclosing the information to his brother. So if Curtiss *did* say it, why? In no other instance does Curtiss lament a bad memory. Quite the reverse. And if he was dissembling to Orville, the most likely explanation is not that he feared he would lie inadvertently on the witness stand but rather that he feared to be forced to do so intentionally. And the most likely incident about which he would

* Willard and J. A. D. McCurdy formed a partnership to both mount their own exhibition team and to manufacture a "headless biplane" where "no ailerons or plane warping will be used for stability but the ribs will extend back of the rear beams considerably and be warped."

feel the need to lie is the 1906 meeting with the Wrights at which the brothers had insisted they had disclosed vital data on the mechanics of flight that Curtiss had pirated. Which suggests that, whether or not Curtiss believed that he had developed a new technology in ailerons, he was not as innocent of the Wrights' accusations as he pretended.

Knabenshue was not the only member of the exhibition team to chafe under the Wrights' puritanical, parsimonious rule. Their two most proficient remaining flyers, one of whom was their former protégé Walter Brookins, were in open rebellion. As early as the Baltimore meet, just after Belmont, he had complained of not being allowed to fly the best machines, as if he were blamed for the crash of the Baby Grand at Long Island that prevented the Wrights from claiming the Gordon Bennett trophy. After Hoxsey's death, Brookins's estrangement became more pronounced.

On May 21, Orville wrote to Wilbur, "Russell and Knabenshue have been having a great deal of trouble with Brookins and Parmalee. The trouble with Parmalee comes from his associating with Brookins. We would be better off if we were rid of Brookins. I have never in my life seen such a swelled head as he has developed. As a matter of fact, I think something is wrong with the machinery inside of it; his whole manner is so entirely changed from what it was a year ago. He spends his whole time talking of his superiority, and of the small amount he is paid for his services." That Brookins's "swelled head" might have been caused by watching two of his closest friends plunge to their deaths for $50 while the Wrights made $1,000 per day for their services apparently never entered Orville's thinking. As with Chanute and many others, Walter Brookins had been transformed virtually overnight from an intimate, a boy they had watched grow up, a student in their sister's class, and a pilot who had risked his life to fly their planes, to a greedy ingrate.

Brookins and Parmalee flew with Frank Coffyn and some newly trained replacements but the results were not good, at least financially. Orville wrote a number of letters to Wilbur in early June complaining of the paucity of revenues realized by participating in small meets. Later in the month, Brookins announced that he was giving up flying. Orville learned of Brookins's resignation in the newspapers, and decided that a minor mishap at a meet in Quincy, Illinois, had prompted the action. "He bought an undeveloped orange farm and some mining stock. He announces that he is going to devote his time to these!"

Whatever the personality issues, Brookins would have been a great loss, even more so if Parmalee went as well. At San Francisco, Parmalee alone had salvaged the honor of the Wright team with a splendid three-hour, forty-minute endurance flight, longer than any American had ever continuously stayed in the air. Coffyn, as he noted, was extremely cautious and none of the new flyers had the skill or panache to capture the imagination as had Johnstone or Hoxsey. Even with Brookins and Parmalee, for the first three months of the 1911 season, the exhibition team cleared only $8,000. An additional $5,300 was owed from an exhibition in Columbus, Ohio, which was never collected despite a lawsuit to compel payment. Orville blamed foreign flyers for depressing the prices and, of course, those aviators flew infringing machines. The Wrights had initiated suit against Curtiss, Paulhan, and Grahame-White but, for reasons they never made clear, they had held off in filing similar actions against others—for example, the Moisant aviators.

With what seemed to be a highly favorable decision in the French courts, Freedman demanded that change. He wrote to Orville, "The field here is developing so largely and the future to me to be so important that the necessity of fully protecting and assuring yourselves of your rights and your patents appears to me to be more important than ever. . . . There appears, from what I see in the papers, to be a good many infringements now being worked, both in manufacture and patents, and I believe in these matters we should take as strong a policy as possible to protect ourselves." Freedman suggested waiting until June before initiating more actions, by which time he assumed Wilbur would have returned from Europe, but when Wilbur decided to remain, they went ahead without him. In the August issue of *Aeronautics* was an article, "Wright Company to Start Wholesale Suits."

Wilbur's decision to remain in France and Germany was unilateral. In at least three letters to Orville he expressed a desire to attempt to get the European businesses into shape, "if I am not needed in America." Wilbur's opinion of German business practices was no more favorable than of the French. He described the conduct of the subsidiary and other of its associates as a "bare-faced fraud" designed to steal profits from their American partners by circumventing the licensing fees. In America, Wilbur insisted, such conduct would "come under the laws relating to criminal conspiracy . . . and would be an indictable offense."*

His frustration was compounded by an inability to control problems with the American company and the pending legal actions. After chiding Orville for writing only "two letters in two months," on May 26, Wilbur lamented, "I do not understand why I hear nothing about our American law suits. I instructed Toulmin under no circumstances to grant White an extension of time. His time [to respond] should have expired on the 12th of May, but I have no news. Also Curtiss's

* In that same letter, from Berlin on May 6, Wilbur spoke of Walter Rathenau, a director of Allgemeine Elektricitäts-Gesellschaft (AEG), an electrical engineering company founded by his father. Rathenau had advocated the development of a German aircraft industry since 1907 and was an early supporter of the Wrights. Wilbur nonetheless accused him of being party to the fraud. "The story of his transactions," he wrote, "is exceedingly interesting, especially if told in court; and I feel certain that, like all Jews, he lacks courage for an open fight, however much he may bluster with those poor idiots who are afraid of him." In a letter of June 6, Wilbur specifically said that Rathenau had swindled him, and insisted in a letter to Katharine that he would have Rathenau and "his dummies" kicked off the board. But Rathenau, as it turned out, lacked neither courage nor honor. He became one of the most respected men in Germany during the war and one of the most respected men in all of Europe in its aftermath. He was named foreign minister of the Weimar Republic, a position he took despite repeated and credible threats against his life. After he was assassinated in 1922 by right-wing extremists, hundreds of thousands of Germans of all religions and political persuasions lined the streets of Berlin to pay their respects as his casket was wheeled by.

time should expire the first of June but nothing seems to be going on." Wilbur complained about Toulmin's performance as "simply throwing away money." But Wilbur's harshest comments were reserved for Frank Russell. "If he gets smart on your hands, 'fire' him. He is not in charge of anything but the factory and the selling departments. We are bossing the legal and exhibition departments ourselves." Then, in a deeply revealing dictum, Wilbur concluded, "If he says anything about being under me only, as distinguished from being under you, let him know in short order who is boss."

Then Toulmin came under fire again. "Please do not let Toulmin allow any delay in our cases against Curtiss, White, and Paulhan. Each three months of delay costs us at least $50,000. Impress it upon him that every moment is precious. We will never be in good position until we can get injunctions again and every month passed without an injunction means thousands of dollars of loss. Each day counts! Make him hurry matters."

What these 1911 letters reveal is not simply the strain under which Wilbur was functioning but also the pressure he was putting on his brother. Orville's letters discussed problems but never did he order Wilbur to take one course of action or another and never did he imply that Wilbur was the cause. In Wilbur's letters, as in the exchange after Thomas Selfridge's death, the opposite is true. Wilbur, in fact, often challenged Orville to "measure up," as if his brother could resurrect Johnstone and Hoxsey for the exhibition business or make the judicial process move at a suitable pace. Orville never discussed how he felt about these demands, the compulsion to perform from his older brother, but in one year Wilbur would be dead, and the lack of resolution of these very issues would be cited by Orville himself as the reason.

As for Wilbur, despite his spending almost half the year in Europe, in theory to provide the sort of on-site management that was sorely lacking in the French and German companies, it was not at all clear whether his presence made any difference at all. All that his extended absence seemed to achieve was to exhaust him and leave him every bit as perturbed and discouraged as when he left. Even the French decision, which had seemed so promising, did not result in the rush to obtain Wright licenses that Wilbur, Orville, and Freedman had assumed. For this, Wilbur placed the blame on Henry Peartree, the lawyer who had shepherded the case through French courts. Late in May, as "the settlement [got] farther and farther away," Wilbur grumbled, "I will not waste my time with him now, but will let matters rest a while and take the negotiation up elsewhere." But it was hardly Peartree's fault. As Blériot, Farman, and the other defendants were well aware but Wilbur only learned in May, an appeal would likely continue the case until 1913.

Returning home would provide no respite. When Wilbur stepped off the boat in August 1911, he found himself facing an acute threat to the ability to generate income from licensing that emanated not from a conglomeration of small manufacturers but rather from a group of men as wealthy and as powerful as those who sat on the Wright Company's board.

CHAPTER 24

Owning the Sky

Like most Americans, Harold Fowler McCormick was enamored of aviation. But unlike most Americans, if Harold wanted to see an air show in his home city of Chicago, he could stage it himself. And if he wanted it to be the biggest, most opulent air show the world had ever seen, he could do that, too. Harold Fowler McCormick was the youngest son of Cyrus McCormick, chairman of the board of International Harvester, and thus a scion of one of the richest families in America. To add even more heft to his bank balance, Harold, not yet forty, was married to the former Edith Rockefeller, daughter of John D.

McCormick's idea, hatched in spring 1911, was to recruit midwestern Brahmins to join him in sponsoring an air show that would dwarf all that came before. The very best American and international aviators would be invited to participate. The meet would be staged on the bank of Lake Michigan, where the crowds might exceed a half million. The International Aviation Meet Association, which he established to run the event, would be initially capitalized at $200,000, with more in reserve if needed. At least $80,000 in prize money would be up for grabs and the association would also be generous with appearance fees, expenses for overseas flyers, and amenities for spectators. Before a single flyer had agreed to appear, McCormick and his associates had exceeded all records for funding an air meet.

The Wright flyers were among those asked to participate, of course, and as soon as word reached Dayton, Knabenshue was dispatched to engage in licensing negotiations. Knabenshue was told to ask for the standard 20 percent of the total of prize money and appearance fees. As with San Francisco, the Wrights assumed the committee would grouse, take the proposal under consideration, attempt to negotiate a lower amount, and then ultimately agree to terms. Orville wrote to Harry Toulmin in May, "Of course [the promoters] will not do this, nor will they be able to get the foreigners over without a license from us. The foreigners will shy of America, unless they have assurance from us that they will not be prosecuted."[1]

But the McCormicks were used to making terms, not acquiescing to them, and the committee rejected the Wright proposal out of hand. Knabenshue wrote to Orville, "I then asked the Committee if I was to understand that the Committee refused to pay the Wright Company a license and the reply was made by Mr. McGann [a committee lawyer] that 'it looks like it.'" Knabenshue then asked the committee to abandon the meet, which they refused to do. "There are a number of lawyers on the Committee," Knabenshue added, "and the situation had evidently been thrashed out before I arrived." The members had also decided that if the Wright Company brought suit against individuals, "the Committee would protect the aviators by cash bond or otherwise."

McCormick's committee had a counteroffer: Wilbur and Orville could join as competitors, just like everyone else. "These men expressed themselves as believing that the Wright Company had everything to gain by entering its machines and participating in the contests and winning such praises that might be awarded to them and, on the contrary, had everything to lose by precipitating lawsuits in connection with this meet as there would be a great amount of adverse criticism that such action, if taken, would be considered unsportsmanlike, unfair, ill-timed, and out of place."

Lest there be any doubt of the committee's resolve, one of their attorneys leveled an ultimatum of his own. "Mr. McGann told me that the Wright Company could bring suit if they saw fit, and in case they did, these members—all wealthy men—would finance whatever the costs would be to fight against such action and *to make every effort to prevent a final adjudication of the Wright Bros. patents.*"[2] McGann did not stop there. "The publicity committee is composed of the heads of the various newspapers in this city and that if the Wright Company should bring any action against the Association or any member of the meet, these newspapers will publish all facts in the case and do everything within their power to embarrass the Wright Company in such proceedings." Knabenshue added, "Personally, I believe this to be true."

Orville eventually met twice with McCormick, lamenting that without the licensing fees the Wrights actually lost money with their exhibition team "as a result of people remaining in this country who were brought over at the expense of the promoters of the [Belmont] meet and who would not have come at all except for the fact that the meet was licensed." Orville even had Frank Coffyn take McCormick aloft for a short spin. Despite McCormick's apparent sympathy to Orville's plight, there would be no change in policy. "The facts of the case," Orville wrote to Wilbur, "are that they do not want to pay anything for a license and they expect our men to come for the prizes they can win." Orville was also negotiating with the sponsors of a Boston meet who heard of the Chicago negotiations and refused to pay license fees as well. He asked Wilbur to "begin the circulation of the report among the European aviators that we now intend to go hard after every one of them that comes to this country, so that the promoters of the Chicago and Boston meets will have difficulty negotiating with the foreign men." Then Orville knuckled under and entered the Wright team as competitors only, securing a small appearance fee to save face.

Whether because of the Wright threat or for other reasons, only one foreign aviator crossed the Atlantic for Chicago, although a number of foreign flyers already in the United States entered the meet. The most notable of those was Thomas Sopwith from England, who came with a Wright and a Blériot, oblivious to the ruling in the French court that his second airplane infringed Wright patents.* But to some extent, lack of European competitors worked in the meet's favor. Most of the prominent names were either members of the Wright, Curtiss, or Moisant exhibition teams or were independents who flew their airplanes, so the Chicago meet added a layer of team competition that further stoked public interest.

That the Moisant team was still in existence was due to either the perseverance or pigheadedness of Alfred, depending how one chose to view a man who continued to pour capital into a venture that had only lost him money. After his brother's death, he simply pushed harder. He bought out the equipment of a small manufacturer that had gone broke, rented a factory, and, using a modified Blériot design, began turning out Moisant monoplanes. His French and Swiss aviators continued flying circus exhibitions in the South, almost always with more spectators watching from outside the fence than in. Occasionally, ticket sales allowed Alfred to approach break-even, but generally they fell short. Popularity, however, wasn't a problem; the diminutive Roland Garros proved a particular draw, maneuvering his Moisant with a fine touch that elicited screams from the crowd.

Alfred saw opportunity in the wake of Ely's flight from the *Pennsylvania,* when Congress appropriated sufficient funds to create an incipient market for military sales. In early February, the Moisant aviators, none of whom was American, flew a successful test scout mission for the United States Army. That was followed by a genuine reconnaissance over Mexico, observing both sides in the ongoing civil war. It wasn't precisely live action, since the flight had been announced in advance and the parties had agreed to a brief cease-fire. Alfred then offered seven airplanes, with pilots, to the Signal Corps for scouting purposes. The army did engage airplanes, but they chose Curtiss's instead of Moisant's. It was typical of Alfred's leap-first approach to business that he believed

* Sopwith, at age twenty-four, would found his own manufacturing company the following year. The most famous of his products would be the "Camel," which saw extensive service in both World War I and the *Peanuts* comic strip.

the War Department would abandon its ongoing relationships with the Wrights and Curtiss to make its largest purchase ever from him.

Undeterred that his old employer had already landed the deal, the irrepressible Charles Hamilton, now foisting his particular brand of insubordination on Alfred, took off in his *Black Devil* and flew an unofficial reconnaissance over Juarez, a war zone in which no cease-fire had been ordered. Government soldiers were fascinated so no one shot at Hamilton, who took the opportunity to buzz a fort and cause a terrified soldier to dive into the river. Hamilton followed that stunt by attempting to break his contract with Alfred during a subsequent Mexican tour, then trying to steal his airplane, which had been impounded, for which he was thrown in jail for three days before bribing his way out and hotfooting it back across the Rio Grande, where he and Alfred filed suit against each other.

Alfred survived Hamilton but whether he could survive his own profligacy was another issue. After a disastrous three-month whistle-stop tour where once again many watched his aviators but few paid, he doubled the capitalization of his company to $1 million, sold stock, then purchased land and built the complex in Garden City. The presence of two women among the students at the flying school brought him what was by now his familiar combination of great notoriety and a trickle of revenue. On August 1, when Harriet Quimby passed the test given by the Aero Club and won license #37, and Matilde followed twelve days later for license #44, Alfred had at least succeeded in making the Moisant flight school as well known as any in America. Success by his aviators in Chicago flying Moisant monoplanes might therefore provide an actual spur to revenues. Alfred was also cheered by the recent addition to his team of Chicago native St. Croix Johnstone, whose daring in the air was reminiscent of Hoxsey or Ralph Johnstone (to whom he was not related) and did precisely the sort of flying that the hundreds of thousands who were expected to line the lakefront would thirst for. Within weeks of joining the Moisant team, Johnstone had set an American record for duration, staying in the air for four hours while covering 176 miles on a measured course.

Harriet Quimby in her trademark purple flying suit.

The Wrights had also come to Chicago with a good deal of optimism. The exhibition team had added new members to supplement mainstays like Frank Coffyn and Parmalee, who had not been dismissed after all, but they could also pin hope on independents flying Wright machines. One was Walter Brookins, who seemed not as prepared to become an orange rancher as he had thought. Another was newly licensed Calbraith Perry Rodgers, who had been taught by Orville at Dayton only weeks before but who seemed the sort of natural flyer who might well have a spectacular debut in Chicago.

But Glenn Curtiss had a new sensation of his own, an aviator beside whom all these others paled. Curtiss, it seemed, in a stroke of immense good fortune, had stumbled on quite possibly the greatest flyer who ever lived.

Jerome Fanciulli had eventually persuaded Curtiss to give Lincoln Beachey a place on the exhibition team, and at first Beachey seemed a competent but not spectacular flyer—certainly nothing like the "Boy Aeronaut" who had displayed such skill in the undercarriage of a dirigible. He first flew for Curtiss at Los Angeles in December 1910, and then performed well in the novice class at the San Francisco meet in January 1911. The following week, Beachey was part of the Curtiss team that flew in Cuba, although McCurdy got all the headlines. In Tampa on March 1, Beachey made a flight at night in a Curtiss biplane equipped with two acetylene headlamps—Blériot's invention—on the biplane's front assembly. He made a second flight without the lamps and was almost killed when he was forced to fly through the smoke of smudge fires lit to mark the airfield and his machine ran into an obstruction while landing. Miraculously, and in a harbinger of future events, Beachey walked away from the crash.

Later in March, Curtiss set up a monthlong training school in Pinehurst, North Carolina, to coincide with equestrian season and sent Beachey to run it. The school made quite a splash among Carolina society and Beachey became a local celebrity by taking up a series of noteworthy passengers, including the winner of the local golf tournament and a visiting Japanese naval officer, "a hero of the siege of Port Arthur." In an unfortunate and unintended preview, newspapers reported that "Commander Saito was enthusiastic over his experience and expressed his faith in the aeroplane for naval purposes in time of war."[3] By mid-April, Beachey was again flying exhibitions, and soon began to exhibit glimmers of the virtuoso antics to come.

The first week of May, Beachey was a member of the three-man team Fanciulli sent to an exhibition at the Benning Race Track at the eastern border of Washington, D.C. Reporters had not forgotten the man who had flown a dirigible around the Capitol five years earlier. "I guess I am about the only private individual who has ever stopped Congressional legislation," Beachey said in an interview. "I alighted in the square on the east front of the Capitol, and when I stepped out of the machine I found [Speaker] Uncle Joe Cannon had declared a recess of the House out to look at the balloon, and I answered questions for an hour before they would let me fly back. . . . I also called on President Roosevelt but he was out in Georgetown so I missed him."

Two days later, he did it again. "In a hitherto unattempted and unscheduled feat, without parallel in the history of aviation," a page-one story read, "Lincoln Beachey, one of the pluckiest little aviators which the profession has yet produced, yesterday afternoon darted away from the aviation field at the Benning race track, flew over the thickly populated section of the city, and circled the United States Capitol."[4] The flight was made in swirling, hazardous winds and Beachey added a number of spiral dives to a spectacular ten-mile loop around the city as thousands stood gaping in the streets. "Five years ago I satisfied a strong desire to circle the Capitol in a dirigible," Beachey said afterward, "and since that time I always wanted to perform the same feat in an aeroplane. The Capitol loomed in the distance and I could not withstand the temptation."

Fanciulli lost no time in promoting Beachey's flight. The licensed Curtiss agent, the National Aviation Company, took large ads in Washington newspapers that read, "Buy a Curtiss Aeroplane. The kind that flew over Washington yesterday, three thousand feet above the Capitol. The Curtiss machine is without a blot on its record. It has never had a serious accident. It is the swiftest, safest, and most easily controlled machine in the world." A second advertisement appeared immediately underneath. "LEARN TO FLY. Fame and Fortunes for Aviators. Good Pilots Find Immediate Employment at Big Salaries."[5]

During that same meet, Beachey added what would become one of the most popular events at air shows and one that spectators would actually have to pay in order to see, a race between an airplane and an automobile. Charles Hamilton had pioneered such a contest the year before but in the coming months Beachey and champion driver Barney Oldfield would make the event their own. President Taft witnessed the contest at Benning, which Beachey narrowly won, and declared it "the most exciting thing I ever saw."

After Washington, Beachey tried a number of difficult and oddball stunts. In mid-May in New Haven, Connecticut, he dropped baseballs from three hundred feet while the Yale catcher moved underneath trying to snag them. The balls fell too wide for the catcher to get to them and they eventually gave up.

During this period, Beachey also made a major improvement in the design of Curtiss airplanes, albeit totally by accident. As Beckwith Havens related, "Beachey was flying one day and hit the fence and broke his front controller [elevator]. Even though he didn't have front control, he flew anyhow and did some wonderful flying. So I thought there's something about this . . . he's got no front control. . . . I'll take my front control off. The mechanic [Lou Krantz] said, 'No. Not unless Curtiss tells me to.' But [later] we were a day ahead for a meet and I said, 'Lou, here's my chance to take my front control off.' He said, 'All right, on one condition. I'll set the thing up the day before and you come out and fly it before the crowd is here.' So I did and it was just like you'd been shackled all your life and suddenly you tore off your shackles. Oh, it could fly! It was just a bad mistake having those two controls because they were just fighting each other."[6] Shortly thereafter, the "headless biplane" became standard for Curtiss machines. The Wrights, of course, had moved their elevators to the rear in the Flyer B the previous year.

In late June 1911, Beachey suddenly announced that he would fly over Niagara Falls. No one had ever dared brave the falls previously; the winds were swirling and treacherous and the spray could easily disable the engine. Even Curtiss, who generally balked at nothing, tried to dissuade Beachey from undertaking a flight that seemed certain to end in death. Beachey was undeterred. On June 26, 150,000 people came to watch an aviator attempt the impossible. *The New York Times* reported, "Sweeping down from immense height in a shower of rain . . . Beachey . . . passed over Horseshoe Falls, under the steel arch

Lincoln Beachey's Flight under Niagara Falls Bridge. —(Copyright 1911, by Photo Specialty Co.)

Lincoln Beachey flying under a bridge span at Niagara Falls.

bridge, on down the Gorge almost to the Whirlpool Rapids, then rose . . . and, shaving the wooded cliff, landed safely and unconcerned on the Canadian side." Not content merely to overcome an obstacle thought insurmountable, Beachey slowed at the brink of the falls before plunging straight down, then skimmed along "less than fifteen feet from the tumbling water . . . missing the top of the gorge by only a few feet."

What stunned the crowd most was that even when the airplane was buffeted by the wind and spray, at no time did Beachey seem anything but in total control. The closing line of the *Times* article was "Beachey will repeat the flight tomorrow."*

Praise for Beachey's daring and skill rang out from every corner of the nation. Only *Collier's* magazine, owned by Robert Collier, Wilbur and Orville's close friend and member of the Wright Company board, was critical, although it took more than a year to be so. Henry Wood-

* The next day, the wind approached gale force. Beachey did not pass under the bridge and was lucky to escape with his life.

house, in a 1912 article, attacked the circus atmosphere that surrounded aviation and the unnecessary risks taken by aviators, themes Wilbur had harped on except in relation to his own flyers. Woodhouse asserted, "Even more reckless was the feat of Lincoln Beachey last year when he 'did' the Niagara Falls in his aeroplane. He was flying in the neighborhood of the falls when he thought of taking a trip under the suspension bridge. He did not know that the atmospheric conditions about any bridge are supposed to be more or less impossible. Five times he went down the gorge, intending to shoot under the arch, five times he had to jump over the bridge to avoid mishaps. The sixth time he knew the conditions of the air under the bridge and shot through the arch like a dart, so close to the water that sprays drenched his plane. Needless to say, had his motor stopped it would have been certain death for Beachey." The article was notable not just for the gross inaccuracies in describing Beachey's flight but for the timing—it was published just when the patent suit against Curtiss had been submitted for judgment—and the lack of mention of all the aviators who had died in Wright Flyers.

In an era of revolving-door celebrities, the Niagara Falls run had vaulted Beachey into the forefront of public consciousness. Always with a nose for publicity, he began to fly more spectacularly, adding a series of spins, dives, and corkscrews to his repertoire, all to the delight of crowds large enough that his appearances actually made money for promoters.

Beachey's signature maneuver, one that not a single other pilot could master, was the "Dip of Death," in which he flew thousands of feet aloft and then plunged straight down, sometimes with his hands off the controls and held out to his sides. Only when he was so near the ground that a horrible crash seemed inevitable did Beachey pull out of the dive and glide to a perfect, controlled landing. The Dip was reminiscent of the way in which Ralph Johnstone and Arch Hoxsey had died, and other aviators were astounded that Beachey could maintain control where even the best of them could not. He claimed to have discovered the trick unwittingly, although separating fact from embellishment in Beachey's public statements was a near impossibility.

"I was high above the clouds," he told reporters. "I felt like an angel. And in a twinkling death seemed to creep upon me and reach out and touch me with a bony fingertip. My motor has stopped dead!" From there, Beachey said that he began to "drop, drop, drop with dazzling speed." He turned the nose down in order to "die calmly." But near the ground, he eased the biplane out of the dive and was as surprised as anyone to land it safely. It was, he observed, "the forerunner of all that people have been pleased to call my 'air deviltry.'"

"Beachey was a weird character," Beckwith Havens observed. "He was a little bit of a fellow, very short, with a pugnacious jaw, and not afraid of anything, especially people."

As moody and distant in private as he was flamboyant in public, Beachey neither smoked nor drank. "He couldn't drink," Havens noted. "One glass of champagne and he'd be tight." Beachey's only vice was women and in that he indulged with enthusiasm and regularity, not the least inhibited by the inconvenience of a wife he thought he had left in San Francisco. "We used to have excitement with him because he was running away from his wife and she was always trying to catch up with him and get some of his money. He was making a lot of money. But Beachey was so afraid of this wife of his . . . that she'd get some of his money . . . that he'd get a safety deposit box in the various towns where we were and just put it in those boxes. And then forget where they were. When he died, I think there were these boxes all over the country."

Beachey's wife finally divorced him in 1914, on grounds of "abandonment and cruelty," and was granted an unspecified but likely substantial financial settlement.

In early August Curtiss scored a coup, and once again Beachey enabled him to maximize its impact. Gimbel Brothers had offered $5,000 to the winner of a race from New York to Philadelphia with the requirement that the winning aviator must pass over the Gimbel stores in each city. The race took place on August 5, one week before the opening of the Chicago meet, and three flyers were scheduled to compete, all in Curtiss machines: Beachey, Hugh Robinson, and, marking his return to the Curtiss fold, Charles Hamilton. That Curtiss allowed Hamilton to fly for him after the legal and financial wrangles with the semi-mad flyer is a testament to either a forgiving nature or stupidity. Either way, on race day the winds were strong with an ominous sky to the west and Hamilton begged off, publicly claiming the conditions were unsafe and he had not had an opportunity to test-fly the Curtiss airplane. But safety and Charles Hamilton were two terms never used in mutual description; far more likely is that Hamilton demanded money at the last instant and for once Curtiss refused to pay. But Eugene Ely, who had watched the notoriety he had achieved get buried in a tide of Beachey publicity, immediately volunteered to go in Hamilton's stead.

Beachey took off first, leaving Governors Island just after two thirty in the afternoon, followed by Ely and then Robinson. The three airplanes headed north, circled the Gimbel department store at Greeley Square, and then turned south. Ely's engine gave out at the halfway point but Robinson and Beachey, each making one stop to refuel, made it to the end. Many thousands watched from roads and rooftops along the route and 100,000 people were jammed into downtown Philadelphia at the finish. Beachey was the winner, with an elapsed time for the 112-mile course of 2 hours, 2 minutes, 25 seconds. He was greeted by a young woman in "a purple hat and purple and white gown" named Mae Wood, a Curtiss student, who "extended congratulations."

Beachey and Robinson had both flown through storm clouds and were drenched and frozen from the strong winds, but Beachey seemed little the worse for it. "It was my longest cross country flight," he said, "but it was so easy that I do not see why I could not fly from here to Chicago after I get something to eat."[7]

Beachey took the train to Chicago instead, but when he arrived four days later he was pleased to find himself the number one attraction for the greatest gathering of aviators and airplanes ever assembled.

Attendance from the first day to the last was everything Harold McCormick and his partners could have hoped for. Newspaper photographs show visitors literally jammed along the lakefront, hundreds of thousands each day. On opening day, twenty-five airplanes flew over downtown Chicago, as many as ten at once. The Wright team had a promising opening with Art Welsh (who, unbeknownst to the Wrights, was actually a Russian-born Jew named Laibel Welcher) setting a new record by flying more than two hours with a passenger. As always, Wright machines would fare superbly in duration tests. Another Wright team member, Howard Gill, won the day's honors for altitude, reaching 4,590 feet.[8]

The second and third days of the meet each featured a plethora of thrills for the avalanche of spectators who witnessed flying that sometimes began at 8:30 A.M. and did not end until 7:30 P.M. The *Chicago Daily Tribune* reported, "Hundreds of thousands of people dammed the usually swift current in Michigan Avenue yesterday. The vertical sides on the west were banked as high as the highest cornice with solid masses of humanity as intent as the awed throng below in following the aviators circling in the air."[9] Unless they arrived early, Chicagoans who had purchased tickets, a small percentage of the total assemblage, found it difficult if not impossible to reach their seats in the grandstand.

Lincoln Beachey, christened "the fancy diver," won a tight twenty-mile biplane race from Englishman Earle Ovington with a local boy, Jimmie Ward, finishing a close third in a contest newspapers declared "the greatest ever witnessed over an aviation course." Wright aviator Oscar Brindley remained in the air so long, two and a half hours, that he received a relieved cheer when he finally landed at dusk.

What made the meet unique was that with more planes in the air than had ever been seen in America and aviators trying desperately to outdo one another, the meet had not had a single accident or mishap.

That changed on day four.

"A wealthy Pittsburgh amateur" named William R. "Billy" Badger had entered the meet in a Baldwin biplane; Cap't Tom was by then manufacturing machines based on the Curtiss design. Badger had just finished learning to fly at Baldwin's flight school and had received his certificate only two weeks before. Chicago was his first public exhibition and Badger arrived determined to make a name for himself. If Lincoln Beachey had taken aviation by storm, why couldn't he? For three days, Badger entertained spectators with a series of dives and spirals that garnered him the accolades he sought. Late in the afternoon of August 15, he decided to try a trick that only one man had completed successfully. He took his airplane to five hundred feet and turned it straight to the ground. At fifty feet, he attempted to pull out of the dive "when his machine crumpled like a pigeon shot while on the wing."[10] Badger was crushed under the wreckage and died soon afterward. He was the first aviator killed trying to emulate Beachey's "Dip." There would be many more.

Two hours later, St. Croix Johnstone, flying a Moisant over the lake about a mile from shore, started a corkscrew dive of his own when, at about eight hundred feet, "his spidery monoplane tipped a bit, shot downward with a sickening swoop, overturning just before it splashed in the water." Later reports said one of the monoplane's wings snapped from the torque of the dive. Hugh Robinson, flying a Curtiss hydroplane, landed on the water and cruised to mark the spot where Johnstone's monoplane, barely visible, was bobbing upside down.

> When I reached the wreckage, the ripples were still on the water. Above the water the tail of the machine had been torn to bits by the fall. I worked the hydro-aeroplane into the wreckage and then scouted all around. I cut in circles, hoping that Johnstone had started swimming. I knew if I found him I could carry him on my planes until the launches came. I couldn't get sight of him, however. It was full ten minutes before the launches and pleasure boats

arrived. I was satisfied by that time that Johnstone was dead beneath the wreckage.[11]

Robinson then took off, which the crowd took as a sign that Johnstone was safe. A cheer went up, which buoyed Johnstone's wife, who was waiting by the mooring at the foot of Van Buren Street. Officials tried to keep the news that Johnstone had drowned from her, but she eventually guessed the truth and collapsed.

In the wake of two deaths in two hours, Harold McCormick issued a statement. "This has been a bad day for us. I can't find words to express my sorrow over the death of the two men. I think, however, that the committee has done all in its power to make the conditions of the events as safe as possible." Still, the committee tightened the rules so that "all recklessness will be eliminated from the meet." The committee also noted that the deaths were "part of the sacrifice necessary to the advancement of aviation . . . such events must mark the progress toward the goal of safe, practicable flying; that a postponement of further experimentation and encouragement of flying would effect nothing but delay without a reduction of the fatalities that must occur before the goal is reached."[12] The day after Badger and Johnstone died, the crowds increased.

The Wrights would provide McCormick with another complication. Although Orville had acquiesced to the committee's demands and entered Wright aviators without condition or license, on August 9, when Wilbur walked down the gangplank of the White Star liner *Oceanic* in New York after six grinding, debilitating months in Europe, the equation seems to have changed. (To that point, the Wrights had almost always traveled on German ships, but the infringement suit in Germany had not been going well.)

With Orville at his side, he told the reporters who met him at the dock that he was not certain whether he would enter the Wright exhibition team in the unlicensed Chicago meet—ignoring the fact that Orville already had—and claimed to have little use for exhibitions in general. "I am more concerned in what the average man can do than I am in what the daredevil or simpleton can do with an aeroplane."[13]

Within forty-eight hours, Orville was on his way to Chicago with a new set of instructions. Before he left, he sent an urgent telegram to Toulmin. "Chicago holding pirate meet. Organizers have personally conspired with pirate aviators by guaranteeing aviators that no license would be taken. Interesting and important case. We must act promptly and vigorously. Please meet me at Chicago Monday." On August 16, Toulmin did act, filing suit against McCormick and the other promoters for patent infringement and asking a percentage of the proceeds of the meet.

Of all the Wrights' legal actions, this one seemed the most ill-considered. The defendants were wealthy, powerful, and influential men being sued in their backyard. Orville's initial willingness to enter Wright aviators would work against them as well. What was more, seeking a share of the proceeds was pointless. The meet had $142,000 in receipts against $195,000 in expenses, leaving only red ink for the Wrights. To get paid, they would need to sue the committee members as individuals, which provided an even less likely chance of success.

The losses didn't faze McCormick or his associates. It had never been their intention to make money on the show—they had enough of that already. Harold McCormick wanted only to propel his city into the spotlight of world aviation and in that he was most certainly successful. Nothing that had come before or would be staged in the future—even subsequent events in Chicago—could match the 1911 meet for sheer grandeur. When the meet closed on August 20 with a cannon shot, Tom Sopwith, the leading money winner at $14,020, flew McCormick in a lazy circle over Lake Michigan and returned him to the landing field as the announced crowd of 350,000 cheered.

Calbraith Rodgers also had a brilliant meet. Outsized for a flyer at six feet three and weighing more than two hundred pounds, Rodgers was a grand-nephew of both Commodore Oliver Hazard Perry, hero of the War of 1812, and Commodore Matthew Calbraith Perry, who had helped open Japan to American shipping in 1854. Where the

Wrights generally required student aviators to spend weeks learning to operate a Flyer safely, Rodgers had demonstrated complete control of the aircraft after ninety minutes. He received his aviator's license on August 7, only five days before the Chicago meet opened.

Rodgers was perfect to capture the imagination of the crowd. Wearing a constant rakish grin with a cigar protruding pugnaciously from one corner, he was wealthy, fearless, charismatic . . . and deaf. He had contracted scarlet fever as a child, and lost all the hearing in one ear and almost all in the other. Where many flyers used the sound of the motor to help them judge the attitude of the airplane, Rodgers was forced to rely on vibration alone.

Like Sopwith, Rodgers flew constantly in Chicago, winning the grand prize for endurance and finishing third in prize money. (If Rodgers had flown for the Wright team instead of as an independent, he would have lost the prize because he would not have been allowed to fly on Sunday.) Rodgers, like so many others in the burgeoning field of aviation, had arrived at an air show as an unknown and left as a star.

But no one was going to upstage Lincoln Beachey. Even after the meet had officially closed, he found a way to etch the last, indelible impression on the nine-day event.

Beachey wanted the altitude record desperately. The official mark at that time was 11,150 feet, held by a captain in the French Army Corps. Two days earlier, Oscar Brindley in a Wright biplane seemed to have ascended to 11,726 feet, but his barograph was faulty and he was found to have actually gone only slightly more than half that height. Beachey had been ascending higher each day, but there was no way for him to clear 10,000 feet and have enough fuel to return safely to land, so he decided the only way to set a record was to use all his fuel on the way up. That would leave him in the thin, freezing air with no way down but to "volpane"—glide—left totally to the mercy of crosswinds and updrafts. At 5:30 P.M. on August 20, the "megaphone men" announced to the grandstand that Lincoln Beachey would do precisely that. As with Niagara Falls, the decision seemed suicidal; no one had ever attempted to descend without power from anywhere approaching that height.

Beachey "ascended steadily, first in circles around the borders of Grant Park and then in wide sweeps that swung him out over the city and then over the lake."[14] With the sky totally clear, Beachey was never out of eyeshot of the ground. His plane was reduced to a speck but then began to quickly grow larger. Beachey descended in tightening spirals. "One great circle carried him several hundred yards out over the lake and curved back over Michigan Avenue. His third circle was more nearly around the flying course and his fourth and fifth narrowed as he neared the earth. At the north end of the field he seemed almost to shoot downward." As he neared the ground, spectators could see that his propeller was not turning. At about 7:30 P.M., after more than a two-mile, fifteen-minute glide, Beachey landed the Curtiss machine not ten yards from where he had taken off. After careful examination and testing of his barograph, it was determined that Beachey had ascended to 11,642 feet above Lake Michigan. Curtiss, who had watched the entire flight, told reporters, "That's nothing. He frequently throws off his engine when he is at great height . . . his control of the machine is wonderful." Glenn Curtiss and Orville Wright did not agree on much, but each man said that Lincoln Beachey was the finest aviator he had ever seen.

George F. Campbell Wood, secretary of the Aero Club, writing in *Aircraft* magazine, said that Beachey's flight for the altitude record was "without question, one of the finest performances in the annals of aeronautic competition, and this is not saying little at a time when wonderful air feats are the order of the day." Then, in a passage remarkably prescient for a world not yet at war, Wood noted, "As to Beachey—believers in 'safe and sane' flying would naturally feel prejudiced against a man who would fly over the falls and down the gorge at Niagara, but the man compels one's unstinted admiration by his admirable control, and his precision and accuracy give a glimpse of what the future may have in store for all of us."[15]

CHAPTER 25

The Wages of Righteousness

On August 10, the day after Wilbur returned home from Europe, he attended an executive committee meeting of the Wright Company with Orville, whom afterward he dispatched to Chicago to sue Harold McCormick. Wilbur then returned to Dayton. He would never again pilot a Wright airplane nor participate except cursorily in one's development. Defending his monopoly, defeating those whom he saw as his enemies, had become every bit as much an obsession as defending his father from Milton's enemies in the church. Whatever experimenting in which the Wright Company would engage, whatever training of aviators or relations with the army or navy, would be under Orville's direction. Wilbur was still the Wright Company president and Orville a vice president. That Wilbur, without whose genius there would have been no Wright Company, had turned entirely to business affairs and the Wright Company's various lawsuits demonstrated that all other considerations had become secondary.

In pursuing damages over technology, the Wrights had rendered themselves anachronisms. Their lack of moderation was equally self-defeating. Wilbur and Orville thought anyone who did not see things their way was either ignorant or duplicitous; anyone who overtly disagreed with them was either a liar or a cheat. The fact that the performance of their competitors improved while Wright airplanes remained substantially unchanged was, according to the brothers, only because the rest of the aviation community were a bunch of craven patent infringers.

That they were beset by problems on all sides increased their isolation. Even without the Chicago meet, the exhibition business was one long headache with receipts almost never justifying the expense. And then, after all the fuss, the Wright team did not fare well in Chicago, their early successes more than eclipsed by the likes of Beachey and Sopwith. Whatever notoriety Wright airplanes did achieve was garnered by independents, most notably Cal Rodgers. Other meets yielded equally unsatisfying results. In September, Orville wrote to Wilbur of the team's travails and said, "We won't be in it next year."[1]

Manufacturing was also not running smoothly. Frank Russell, the Algers' nephew, was proving to be imperious and not particularly competent and was constantly at odds with Charlie Taylor. In April 1912, Wilbur would write that in a meeting, Russell "immediately assumed a look of a dog about to be whipped. I suspect he is up to some scheme that he is rather ashamed of."[2] Russell would eventually be dismissed by Orville and replaced by Grover Loening. Loening was a brilliant hire. Still in his early twenties, his loyalty to the Wrights unquestioned, Loening had published late in 1911 *Monoplanes and Biplanes: Their Design, Construction, and Operation. The Application of Aerodynamic Theory, with a Complete Description and Comparison of the Notable Types,* a comprehensive and authoritative treatise 340 pages long, with 278 illustrations. But Loening remained in the position only one year, after which the Wright Company would again lack adequate management.

Licensing was another problem area. Although a number of exhibition flyers and many promoters paid the Wrights royalties, albeit never what the brothers thought they deserved, the only significant contract was with the Burgess Company & Curtis, a Massachusetts concern that paid the Wrights $1,000 per aircraft. The problem was that the basic principles of aviation had become so commonly known that they had spawned legions of manufacturers and almost none of them bothered to purchase licenses from the Wrights.

Even worse, there was an abundance of information readily available to allow an interested amateur to build his own airplane. Trade magazines regularly contained long, detailed articles on how to build a Curtiss airplane, or a Blériot, or a Wright. *Aeronautics* counted 759 machines built in 1911, only 200 of which were products of "aeroplane manufacturers," such as Wright, Curtiss, or Moisant.[3] In the space of four months, for example, trade journals contained detailed descriptions, schematic drawings, and/or how-to-build instructions for, among others, the Curtiss biplane, the Valkerie monoplane, the McCurdy headless biplane, the Nieuport monoplane, the Willard headless biplane, the Kirkbride all-steel biplane, the Burgess–Curtis "Baby," the two-seat Deperdussin monoplane, the Queen monoplane, and even the Wright Model B.*

The journals also contained instructions for building a dizzying array of components including lubricators, turnbuckles, "gyromotors," carburetors, propellers, laminating presses, pressure equalizers for ailerons, clutches, stabilizers, and a plethora of construction aids. For those components that could not be easily built, there was no shortage of manufacturers happy to provide motors, radiators, wire wheels, aeronautical cloth, bamboo framing, and magnetos cheaply, on credit, or delivered to your door. The notion that even with complete success in the courts a monopoly could be imposed on an industry so anarchic, where innovation had such a brief half-life, was almost comical.

Although Wilbur continued the fight with unbroken ferocity, he was beginning to despair of the business he had been so desperate to establish. "My position for the past six months," he wrote in a long, bitter, and remarkably frank letter to Orville on June 30, 1911, "has been that if I could get free from business with the money we already have in hand I would do it rather than continue in business at a con-

* The monoplane was clearly the future and few designers bothered with two-surface technology. Of those pusher biplanes that were produced, most were "headless."

siderable profit. Only two things lead me to put up with responsibilities and annoyances for a moment. First, the obligations we are under to the people who put money into our business, and second, the reluctance a man naturally feels to allow a lot of scoundrels and thieves to steal his patents, subject him to all kinds of troubles, or even try to cheat him out of his patents entirely."

There is little doubt as to whom Wilbur is most referring. He was determined to vanquish Curtiss, to ruin him. His focus had become so personal, so obsessive, that the substantive issues on which the feud had begun were forgotten. Wilbur never seemed to grasp that his crusade to destroy his nemesis could destroy him as well.

Not that Curtiss alone was the source of his anger. "I do not feel we are in debt to either the French or German companies. We have had not a square deal from either of them. . . . I hate to see the French infringers wreck our business and abuse us and then go unscathed. And I hate to see these Rathenaus succeed in their knavish plans without a scratch on their faces. But so far as making money is concerned I am going to quit worrying myself to death in order to get more than I have already got."

But he did not quit. Wilbur remained home in Dayton less than two weeks before returning to to New York for *Wright Company v. Herring–Curtiss Company.*

A letter of triumph to Orville on September 18, 1911, after an exchange involving a Curtiss witness, epitomized Wilbur's growing monomania. The incident occurred during Harry Toulmin's questioning of Augustus Post, who was near the completion of five days on the witness stand. Toulmin was "no good at cross examination," according to Wilbur, but "just before the end, Post, of his accord, dug a hole, jumped into it and under direction of his own attorney, floundered around till he absolutely ruined his value to the defense."

As Wilbur related the events, lawyers for the defense intended to continue to emphasize "the bold statement that regardless of all theories, the machine in the test with the fixed tail at Hammondsport did not swerve from a straight path nor turn on a vertical axis, although

Curtiss worked the balancing planes [ailerons] to the limit and caused the machine to tilt to a great degree and restored it to position again several times during the flight" and that, during these flights, Curtiss "*never at any time for any cause* moved his rudder even though he lost lateral balance and regained it again during such flights," and that "the rudder was merely a means of turning right or left," and finally "that he knew by practical experience that there was no co-relation of any kind between the results of moving the wing tips and rudder." Here of course was the crux of Curtiss's defense, that the Wrights' patent was limited to a three-axis system of control, whereas with ailerons instead of warping, the rudder was not needed to maintain lateral stability. In fact, Curtiss or his aviators had demonstrated as much many times.

Post, according to Wilbur, appeared initially "to be a much more foxy and capable witness than I expected and always evaded answering the questions Toulmin asked him by beginning to answer about something he had not been asked. He had Toulmin completely beaten." But then Post made his "fatal error." He "accidentally said that in his experience if the balancing planes were turned as to tilt the machine making the left wing rise and the other fall, the machine would swerve and turn to the right in a saucer shaped course *without any movement of the rudder whatever.*" Wilbur wasn't present for this exchange and "Toulmin never noticed that [Post] had betrayed himself."

Wilbur pored over the transcript that night and instructed Toulmin to do nothing, confident that Emerson Newell, Curtiss's attorney, would raise the issue the next day. "Sure enough," Wilbur exulted, "he did so." Post responded that to correct for the effect, Curtiss would in fact sometimes "*turn his rudder* toward the high wing . . . thus flatly contradicting his assertions he had previously made over and over again that he *never* moved his rudder."

While certainly this admission does contradict Curtiss's statement, Wilbur's sense of victory is overdone. In order to demonstrate that the three-axis system was necessary, the rudder would *always* need to be turned to maintain stability in a bank, not just occasionally. Otherwise the necessity to employ the rudder in specific instances might have been the result of a shift in wind or change of pressure, which Wilbur more than anyone would have known. The evidence remained that Curtiss's system of ailerons was, for the majority of the time, sufficient to maintain stability without employing the rudder. Wilbur was so elated that Curtiss was caught in what he saw as a lie that the lack of real significance eluded him.

While the trial proceeded, Orville decided to return to Kitty Hawk.

The one genuine innovation to come out of the Wright camp since wing warping was a system of automatic stabilization and it was Orville's. The first man to discuss automatic stability had been Herring. He had postulated vaguely that a system could be based on gyroscopes, but as with virtually all of his ideas, nothing had ever found its way onto an actual airplane. Langley and the dihedral proponents had also advocated automatic stability, but theirs was built into a wing design that came at the expense of maneuverability.

Orville's notion was to employ a pendulum and vane that would sense a change in any of the three axes of attitude and engage the wing-warping controls using canisters of compressed air. Orville had been working on it for three years but his concept was still largely theoretical and untested, even in prototype. On the trip to Kitty Hawk, he intended to mount the apparatus on a glider. Before he left, Wilbur wrote and instructed him to file an injunction against Walter Brookins to prevent him from flying in exhibitions without paying a licensing fee. He also instructed Orville to try to determine exactly how much money Tom Sopwith had won in Chicago so that a lawsuit for damages might be pursued.

Orville arrived in North Carolina at the beginning of October and remained a bit more than three weeks. His stay was oddly unproductive. While he did establish a record for remaining in the air unpowered—nine minutes and forty-five seconds, which was not matched for ten years—he never tested his automatic stabilizer and suffered two crashes from which he was lucky to walk away unscathed.

In the end, Orville did little more than experiment with an outmoded technology, doomed to obsolescence before he began.

But obsolescence doesn't come all at once. There were still triumphs to be had for the Flyer and the greatest was to be by Cal Rodgers. As soon as the Chicago meet concluded, the nation's largest aviator announced that he intended to win aviation's largest prize—$50,000—for the first man to fly from the Atlantic to the Pacific in less than thirty days.

William Randolph Hearst had first offered the prize in October 1910, which at the time seemed like nothing but a ploy to hype his newspapers. To win, a flyer would have to cover twenty times the distance that Glenn Curtiss had in his Albany-to-New York flight the previous May and no airplane was remotely up to the task. Hearst got a good deal of publicity for the offer, which distressed him not at all, and was even given a medal by the Aeronautical Society for his vision, all the while hanging on to his $50,000. But after Chicago, flying across the United States did not seem so ridiculous. During the very weeks that Beachey, Rodgers, and the rest were flying before hundreds of thousands over Lake Michigan, another Huffman Prairie–trained Wright aviator, Harry Atwood, set a record of 1,266 miles on a twelve-day, eleven-stop journey from St. Louis to New York. The month before, Atwood had flown from Boston to Washington, D.C., landing his Flyer on the White House lawn.

But a cross-country flight would involve complex, extremely expensive logistics. Airplanes couldn't fly very far in 1911 and they broke down and crashed often. To succeed, an aviator would need not only a run of extraordinary luck, but an entire support team carrying fuel, spare parts, and possibly a backup airplane mirroring his progress on the ground. With automotive technology almost as formative as aeronautics, the only way to reliably keep the support staff positioned properly was by rail, and since no one knew how much or little progress the airplane might make at any given time, that meant a private train.

Rodgers was wealthy but not that wealthy. To defray costs, his business manager approached the Armour meatpacking company to ask for sponsorship. Armour agreed. In return for supplying the train and paying Rodgers for each mile he flew, Rodgers agreed to use the trip to promote the company's new grape drink, "Vin Fiz." He renamed his specially made Wright EX model *Vin Fiz,* and the private train was dubbed the "Vin Fiz Special."* Armour had the Vin Fiz logo painted on the front and rear stabilizers and the words on the underside of the wings and gave Rodgers a bottle of the vile-tasting stuff to carry with him on the journey.†

As he prepared for the flight, Rodgers told a reporter, "It's important, because everything else I've done before was not important." On September 17, the third anniversary of Tom Selfridge's death, Rodgers took off with great fanfare from Sheepshead Bay in Brooklyn and landed in Middletown, New York, for the night. While taking off the next morning, the airplane's wing clipped a tree and Rodgers crashed. He wasn't seriously hurt but the *Vin Fiz* was almost totally wrecked and had to be rebuilt. Rodgers called Charlie Taylor, who had become so disgusted at working with Frank Russell that he had moved his family to California and was planning on following them there. Taylor agreed to help and when he told a stunned Orville he was leaving, Orville persuaded him to call his departure a "leave of absence."‡ Rodgers paid Taylor a per diem and Taylor remained for five weeks, making repairs and adjustments.

Taylor earned his money. On September 21, Rodgers was off again, only to crash again. And so it went. Rodgers crashed at least five times, had an engine explode twice, frequently became lost in the vast plains without a compass, survived a death spiral over the desert, and was almost electrocuted in a thunderstorm. In the train below were his

* "EX" stood for "exhibition" and its design was derived from the Wright R, the "Baby Grand" that Walter Brookins had failed to race at Belmont.

† "Tastes like a cross between sludge and horse slop," one reviewer noted. The formula was evidently improved later.

‡ "He is accompanying Rodgers to the coast!" he wrote to Wilbur on September 22.

wife and his mother, who loathed each other and were not shy about showing it, even when Rodgers was with them on the ground.

The thirty-day limit came and went—Hearst would never be forced to pay out the money—but Rodgers never quit. As tales of his perseverance were reported in the newspapers, he became a national phenomenon, hundreds and then thousands gathering at each of his landing spots. On November 6, Rodgers flew by Mount Wilson and landed at Pasadena. Even then, his travails were not over. Taking off for the short hop to the Pacific Ocean, Rodgers crashed yet again and was knocked unconscious and sent to the hospital with a concussion. His airplane was wrecked. By the next day, he was sitting up in bed, smoking a cigar, and vowing to complete the race, which he did in early December at Long Beach, when he taxied into the surf of the Pacific Ocean before a cheering crowd of fifty thousand. Hearst offered him a cup in lieu of the prize money. Rodgers refused the offer, adding some choice words for reporters about Hearst's parsimony.

Cal Rodgers draped with an American flag and flowers upon his arrival in Pasadena, California.

While Rodgers's flight was gratifying to Wilbur and Orville, it did not deter them from their focus. In November, the brothers obtained a Curtiss airplane and brought it to Dayton for tests. They decided, not surprisingly, that the Curtiss was a poor imitation of the Flyer. Milton wrote in his dairy, "The boys try a Curtiss machine and break it." A few days later, he added, "Wilbur went out to try a Curtiss machine. It was hard to fly with." It was Wilbur Wright's final flight, at the controls of his rival's machine.

In late November, the Wrights submitted a deposition in the Herring–Curtiss case and in early December responded to similar depositions by Herring, Curtiss, and George Spratt, the young physician with whom they had developed such a close friendship at Kitty Hawk. To Spratt, who claimed that only certain aspects of the Wright system had been developed independently, the brothers were generous. Since he was "an excellent companion, the most wonderful raconteur we ever met, and an earnest student of birds and of the principles of flight," his contentions must only have been lapses of memory. Of Herring, their reply was sneering, dismissive, and dead on the mark. "He speaks of having made certain 'discoveries' regarding the superior lifting qualities of arched surfaces, but though we are familiar with the literature of the subject and with a great number of living experimenters, we have never anywhere found anyone who attributed either of these 'discoveries' to Mr. Herring, except Mr. Herring himself in his present affidavit."[4]

But Wilbur and Orville saved their most withering vitriol for Curtiss. They opened, "The present affidavit of Mr. Curtiss is a most remarkable one and of itself constitutes an impeachment of his powers of correct observation and shows his incompetence to give expert testimony as to what actually occurs in his machine." The Wrights based their statement on their study of the Curtiss machine they obtained. But nowhere was it made clear what age the airplane was, what model, and whether or not it had been altered or repaired to Curtiss's specifications. So, when Curtiss testified, "At present our balancing surfaces are flat," which by then they were, as ample photographs and drawings in trade magazines would confirm, the Wrights insisted that the surfaces were arched. Arched ailerons would, according to the Wrights, become lifting surfaces, although why that would be more significant for application to their patent was unclear. The Wrights' strategy seemed to be aimed more at so undermining Curtiss as an authority (a drumbeat that Grover Loening would later pick up) that the court would find it inconceivable that he could have developed a groundbreaking innovation on his own.

On another occasion, Curtiss had asserted that "there was no appreciable turning tendency" when the weight of the passengers was unevenly distributed across the center line of the aircraft. The Wrights countered that the statement was "as if Mr. Curtiss should say, 'When I am in flight there is no appreciable attraction of gravity.' Such a statement would not establish the fact that gravity had ceased to exist, but only that Mr. Curtiss was an incompetent or willfully blind observer."

At first blush, the ad hominem approach might have seemed odd. Curtiss, after all, was a world-renowned pioneer and innovator and no one outside the Wrights' intimate inner circle would have suggested he was a fraud. A string of experts, including Paul Beck and Theodore Ellyson, military officers whose veracity was beyond question, had confirmed all of Curtiss's assertions. But the trial was being played out before a judge who had demonstrated both a lack of scientific sophistication and a predisposition toward monopoly interests. Still, while Wilbur and Orville were waiting for the judicial system to finally, after endless delays, smite their enemy, the enemy continued to build and innovate, increasing both his profits and his reputation.

In December, the Wrights won a skirmish in the courts but not against Curtiss. In the infringement case against Claude Grahame-White, Judge Learned Hand, in district court, ruled that the British aviator could not fly in the United States unless he used a Wright machine and paid royalties and even then not without permission of the Wrights. The decision was narrowly drawn, however, not applicable to the broader case against Curtiss. Hand also ruled that White was liable for damages for the hundreds of thousands he had earned since November 1910, but that award was reduced to a paltry $1,700. And the courts could take from the Wrights as well. Herring–Curtiss was again adjourned until at least February and probably longer.

Through the court battles, Curtiss successfully pushed his business forward. Although land-based aircraft continued to sell briskly, Curtiss's new product focus had turned almost exclusively to waterborne aviation. His first major success was the *Triad,* an amphibious "flying boat" developed in 1911 to fulfill a contract with the navy. The specifications: "A hydroaeroplane, capable of rising from or landing on either the land or the water, capable of attaining a speed of at least fifty-five miles an hour, with a fuel supply for four hours' flight. To carry two people and be so fitted that either person could control the machine." Curtiss fashioned a biplane and mounted floats in the center and one on each of the wing tips. Spuds Ellyson successfully flew the *Triad* from Keuka Lake in June, and the navy purchased two of the craft.* Curtiss later fashioned a launch system in which a cable was stretched on a downward incline from the boat deck to bow to allow the machine to be launched from a battleship. In January 1912, he introduced the first true hydroplane, the two-engine *Flying Fish.* Unlike the *Triad,* which employed only pontoons, the *Flying Fish* had a stepped hull that rested on the water, essentially a hydrofoil that actually produced lift as the aircraft gained speed moving through the water. Foreign navies found the hydroplane irresistible; Russia purchased two and Japan three, the first foray into naval aviation for the erstwhile combatants of 1905.

Although others, including Orville Wright, experimented with mounting floats under their aircraft, Curtiss was the acknowledged leader in the field. Only he, as one commentator put it, "thought from the water up, rather than from the air down."[5] Due almost exclusively to his efforts, the United States, which had been supplanted as the

* The ailerons, as can be readily discerned from the many photographs and schematics of the craft, were flat and not arched.

Glenn Curtiss and Theodore Ellyson at the controls of an A1.

leader in land-based aviation by the French, Germans, and even the Russians, still held the lead on the water. In addition to possessing the most advanced designs, Curtiss's training of military aviators such as Ellyson and John Towers gave aviation a cadre of young, talented officers for naval planning that was lacking in other countries.*

Although military leaders only contemplated using aircraft for communication and reconnaissance, bomb-dropping contests had become a part of almost every air meet and the use of the airplane as an offensive weapon of war seemed imminent. Here too, Curtiss more than the Wrights seemed to sense the future. Despite trying to sell airplanes to the army and navy, Wilbur and Orville had not substantially moved from their belief that aviation would be primarily a sporting pursuit, perhaps with commercial applications down the road. Curtiss's innovations, on the other hand, would all be applicable to the

* The navy had assigned Lieutenant John Rodgers, Calbraith Rodgers's brother, to the Wrights for training as well, but Rodgers spent most of his time learning on the Flyer, not on hydroplanes.

use of airplanes as a means of attack. In November 1911, Secretary of the Navy George von Lengerke Meyer contributed an article to *Aircraft* magazine in which he praised Curtiss, did not mention the Wrights, and predicted that within a year the navy would purchase large numbers of aircraft that could be launched from warships by means of the cable system. The prospect of Curtiss securing the bulk of those orders put that much more pressure on the Wrights to conclude their infringement suit soon and successfully.

Training aviators was another ongoing source of revenue for Curtiss as well as the Wrights. In 1911, the Wrights opened a new training center in Long Island and Curtiss opened a second winter facility in Miami. He billed his schools as the only ones where a student could learn to fly both "a standard aeroplane and a hydroaeroplane."

On the exhibition circuit, Curtiss's aviators fared a good deal better than the Wrights' and not just because of Beachey. Jerome Fanciulli proved more aggressive than Roy Knabenshue and Curtiss flyers barnstormed on a regular schedule, performing in smaller cities such as Wilkes-Barre, Wichita, Joplin, Fort Wayne, and Little Rock, maintaining a steady if unspectacular income stream for both the team members and Curtiss.

The Wrights watched their enemy grow richer and more established while waiting for the court case to inch forward. Their urgings to Toulmin and their other attorneys to fight any further delays came to naught. In December 1911, the AEA was awarded a patent for a device that "maintains or restores lateral balance of a machine having rigid supporting surfaces by means distinct from the supporting surfaces themselves," in other words, ailerons mounted on the struts between the wings. The patent was distinct from "supporting surfaces made flexible for the purpose of warping the extremities to preserve balance." The AEA transferred this patent to Curtiss. Curtiss also obtained a patent for the shoulder harness that he used to control the ailerons, although the mechanism was not very different from the hip cradle the Wrights had initially employed.

The Wrights were furious but publicly brushed the new patent off as unimportant. Wilbur wrote a letter to Roy Knabenshue in January 1912 responding to Knabenshue's complaint that the Wright patent was providing no protection in exhibitions. Wilbur first noted that the Wrights had prevented Grahame-White and Tom Sopwith from competing in the United States—Judge Hand had issued restraining orders within days of the Curtiss patent acceptance—then insisted that the Curtiss patent "amounts to nothing at all and does not get around our 1906 patent."* Wilbur tried to gloat about Curtiss's discomfort at the trial. "I think that if you could have seen his face and his actions when recently on the witness stand you would not take much stock in his confidence in winning this suit."

Curtiss ironically was now fighting on both sides of the street. In another letter to the Wrights, Knabenshue recounted a conversation at North Island. "The funny part of the whole affair is that he has secured a patent and is very much upset on account of the many infringers who insist on copying his machine and using his principle." An announcement in *Aeronautics* stated, "Mr. Curtiss wishes to inform the public that he is not acquiescent in the general use of his inventions upon patents that will eventually issue." Curtiss made some effort to enforce his patents but did not have any more success than Wilbur and Orville.

By the end of 1911, Wilbur's frustration had begun to gnaw at his health. He had by his own admission worked harder and for longer hours pursuing the case against Glenn Curtiss than he had developing the Wright Flyer. He drove himself to exhaustion traveling around the country, meeting with lawyers and giving depositions, and grew so thin as to appear cadaverous. Family members began to express concern about the crushing pace he insisted on maintaining.

In January 1912, Wilbur wrote a singular letter to the Hungarian anthropologist Guillaume de Hevésy.[6] "During the past three months, most of my time has been taken up with lawsuits," he began. After

* Knabenshue was by then running his own promotion company but still managing Parmalee and Turpin and using Wright airplanes under license.

expressing a hope that he could be "freed from this kind of work," and that it was "more pleasant to go to Kitty Hawk for experiments than to worry over lawsuits," Wilbur told Hevésy that he'd "hoped in 1906 to sell our invention to governments for enough money to satisfy our needs and then devote our time to science, but the jealousy of certain persons blocked this plan and compelled us to rely on our patents and commercial exploitation." Then Wilbur made an extraordinary assertion. "When we think what we might have accomplished if we had been able to devote [the past five years] to experiments, we feel very sad."[7]

There is little question that the patent wars were devastating American aviation. By January 1912, France boasted 800 aviators a day making flights to only 90 in the United States.[8] As early as July 1911, *Aeronautics* ran an editorial whose opening line read, "What is the matter with aviation in America?" The journal lamented that "in three short years" after the "epoch-making flights of the Wright brothers in France and at Fort Myer [that] electrified the world," America had "changed places from the head to the foot of the procession." The magazine blamed a combination of a fear of innovation, an unwillingness to spend money, and a desire by the government to sit on the sidelines and wait to see what Europe came up with. Nowhere did the editorial mention that America's two greatest designers were either spending a good part of their time (Curtiss) or all of their time (Wilbur Wright) trying to best each other in the courtroom.

And for the Wrights, the litigation went well beyond Glenn Curtiss. Two weeks before his letter to Guillaume de Hevésy, Wilbur had been in New York, testifying in the refiled lawsuit to try to pry out of the Aero Club the $15,000 the Wrights had decided they had been shortchanged at Belmont, an action that his attorney in the matter observed involved "a considerable loss of time."[9] Then there were the actions against Paulhan, Sopwith, Grahame-White, and the Chicago organizers; the threatened actions against Brookins; and countless others. Five days before Wilbur testified in New York in the Aero

Club case, he and Orville were required to give depositions in one of a number of cases in which the Wrights were *defendants.*[*] The array of legal actions to be tracked and overseen would have taxed an entire law firm but Wilbur insisted on going it essentially alone. He did take time out from the legal wrangling to announce the new automatic stabilizing device, an invention that the newspapers then credited to him and not Orville.

At the end of January, Wilbur conferred with signal corps officers at Augusta, Georgia, and then returned to Dayton, supposedly to help craft a higher-powered, six-cylinder engine that would allow a military aircraft to carry two men, a wireless, and "measuring equipment" for reconnaissance flights. But within a week he was back in New York, attending the annual Aero Club dinner at the request of the club's new president, Wright Company board member Robert Collier. In addition to trying to get the $15,000, the Wrights had been engaged in an ongoing battle with the club about licensing at air meets, especially another Chicago meet scheduled for that August, but Collier persuaded Wilbur that the dinner was the perfect place to lobby the guest of honor, President William Howard Taft, for higher appropriations for aviation. The event would also be the venue at which the first annual Aero Club award for the most important advancement in aviation of the previous year was presented.[†] Wilbur, who would have had every reason to believe that Collier, a close friend, had urged him to come to surprise him with the honor, sat stoically near President Taft at the head table as the winner was announced.

* These generally involved other inventors who believed that the Wrights had appropriated *their* ideas. All were frivolous and none resulted in anything but total victory for the Wrights.

† The award was later christened the Collier trophy, which still exists. It is now given annually by the National Aeronautic Association, presented to those who have made "the greatest achievement in aeronautics or astronautics in America, with respect to improving the performance, efficiency, and safety of air or space vehicles, the value of which has been thoroughly demonstrated by actual use during the preceding year."

It was Glenn H. Curtiss for the hydroplane. The only small consolation for Wilbur was that Curtiss was in California and not present to accept in person. By January 31, Wilbur was back in Dayton.

Orville had been working feverishly to catch up to Curtiss in hydroplane development but was finding the design parameters more difficult than he had anticipated. On January 8, 1912, he wrote to Russell Alger that the wooden models he had built carried too much weight, which he attributed to the white lead paint they had used.* Alger, who had to some degree replaced Wilbur as a design partner, replied that "aluminum pontoons are the thing" because "while they bend and sometimes break the frames inside, they don't leak." Although by early February, Frank Coffyn would have great success flying a Wright hydroplane around New York City, Curtiss by then had already improved his original design and Coffyn's performance was not sufficient to draw the navy away from its commitment to the *Triad* and the *Flying Fish*.

For virtually the entire month of February and well into March, Wilbur and Orville gave testimony in the Herring–Curtiss suit but were at least allowed to do so in Dayton. Orville wrote to Russell Alger on March 12 that "the prospects of victory look very good to us, but of course law is a rather uncertain thing." In the midst of his testimony, the Wrights learned that their German patent had been nullified on the grounds that the processes for which the patent was sought had already been made public. The court based its decision on a speech by Octave Chanute and Wilbur's article in the Western Society of Engineers journal.

The battle with the Aero Club went on. The Wrights were convinced that other than Collier, the members of the club's board were their enemies. Orville wrote to Alger at the end of March after Wilbur failed to exact licensing concessions during extensive meetings in New York. "The Aero Club of America from the beginning has done

* Orville also informed Alger that the Wrights "had decided to give a 75% discount from the daily royalties on the machines used for exhibition purposes until we are able to secure an adjudication of the patent, that will enable us to enjoin infringers."

everything it could to our injury," and other than Collier, "the rest of them . . . have done all the damage they could in the past three or four years, and now when they find that we have the upper hand, they are eager to make some contract to do away with what advantages we now have."[10]

Alger, unaccustomed to the Wrights' vitriol and convictions of persecution, was taken aback. "Do you not think that possibly you exaggerate a little the Aero Club's attitude to you?" he wrote back. "I don't think they have been by any means altogether wise in their manner of negotiating, but at the same time I do think that they are not necessarily out to intentionally injure you in any way." Alger pointed out that the club had agreed to put 30 percent of all prize money claimed at unlicensed meets in escrow to be paid to the Wrights if they won their lawsuit. He also mentioned that he would like to purchase the new Wright six-cylinder Model C when it was completed and asked for a price. Orville offered the machine at the standard 10 percent discount for directors, to which Alger replied, "I think if the other Directors are entitled to 10% I ought to be entitled to more, as certainly I have done what I could personally for the company." Orville did not reply.

The Model C was completed in April and delivered in May. In addition to the larger motor, the C featured a number of new features that met the army's specifications that it carry two people with the largest possible field of observation for both, allow the controls to be used by either operator from either seat, ascend two thousand feet in ten minutes with a 450-pound load plus fuel, stay airborne for four hours, have an independent starting and landing system, travel at forty-five miles per hour, and land in a plowed field. The only feature lacking was the automatic stabilizer. It was not in the specifications but, seeing that it had been announced publicly, the army had asked if it might be included. Orville replied that the system would not be completed in time for the official performance tests, which were scheduled for late May at the army's training center in College Park, Maryland. The Wrights assigned Art Welsh to fly the plane for the tests and the army assigned a talented young flyer, Lieutenant Leighton Hazelhurst.

With *Wright v. Herring–Curtiss* still undecided, Wilbur penned what amounted to editorials defending the Wrights' position, the same as he had done in defending his father. Called "What Mouillard Did" and "What Clément Ader Did," referring to a French aviation pioneer who had been credited with achieving heavier-than-air flight, Wilbur's writings demonstrated why neither of these men had precursed his discovery of wing warping or the attainment of powered flight.

At the beginning of April, Wilbur wrote to one of his lawyers to excuse himself for overlooking a bill; he had been so busy with lawsuits that his desk hadn't been cleaned in two months. By mid-month, he was back in New York, negotiating with the Aero Club. With the Wright Exhibition Team no longer flying, the only sources of exhibition revenue for the Wright Company were either a piece of the prize money or licensing fees for allowing a meet to take place. Wilbur wanted both. The Aero Club remained willing to set money aside and in some cases pay the Wrights some monies in advance, but balked at the 20 or 30 percent that Wilbur was demanding. But in his letter to Orville dated April 24, 1912, he said he hoped "to get a definite settlement of Aero Club license today."

He did not, however, and two days later Wilbur left for Boston. Whether or not he ate tainted clam broth or was exposed in some other manner, by the time he returned to Dayton, he was feeling ill. No one in the family took much notice at first but Wilbur developed a fever and on May 2, D. B. Conklin, a Wright family physician, diagnosed Wilbur as having typhoid fever.[11] The next day, his fever became worse but Milton wrote, "Nothing else ailed him. He suffered nothing."

Wilbur Wright wrote his final letter on May 4, 1912, not to a loved one, a friend, or a fellow aviator, but rather to Frederick W. Fish, an attorney on the patent case. In it, Wilbur excoriated Fish for a letter he had written to Harry Toulmin proposing an adjournment until autumn. "I fear Mr. Toulmin has not made it plain to you why it is so important that the case should be heard this spring. He looks at the matter from a lawyer's point of view while I am compelled to consider our lawsuit as a feature of our general business."

Wilbur then issued a sad valedictory. "Unnecessary delays by stipulation of counsel have already destroyed fully three fourths of the value of our patent. The opportunities of the last two years will not return again. At the present moment almost innumerable competitors are entering the field, and for the first time are producing machines that will really fly. These machines are being put on the market at one half less than the price which we have been selling our machines for." Toulmin seemed to have become a particular source of Wilbur's irritation. "Owing to some unfortunate features in the statement of the claims of the patent, if there is much further delay, means will be found of evading these claims, so that even a decision in our favor might not give us a monopoly. . . . Under these conditions, I told Mr. Toulmin more than a year ago that under no conditions would I consent to further delays by stipulation of counsel and that all applications for delay must be passed on by the Court itself." If the letter was answered, the reply has been lost.

For the next week, Wilbur's condition was little changed. On some days he would be marginally better, on others marginally worse. During this period, his illness was considered by his doctors to be serious but not necessarily a threat to his life.

But typhoid had claimed many lives and a victim might well know the end was coming before family or doctors. On May 10, Wilbur summoned his personal lawyer to take instructions for his will. He left $1,000 to his father, $50,000 each to Reuchlin, Lorin, and Katharine, and the remainder, approximately $126,000, to Orville. He made no specific bequests to charity but Milton said later that that was because he trusted Orville to do what he would have wished without being told.

Six days later, when Wilbur's illness continued to linger but not worsen, Orville left for College Park to deliver the Wright C for the army tests. On May 18, Art Welsh took the airplane up for the first time in an unofficial trial. He reported in his log, "Climbed one thousand feet with passenger in the four minutes before engine stopped." Welsh continued flying the machine for the next two weeks, coaxing improved performance out of it as he became more experienced.

Orville had told Katharine to keep him informed and at 2 A.M. on May 17, she telegraphed that while Wilbur was "slightly more delirious" and his "general condition unimproved," Orville should "pay no attention to any of the alarming reports that may be sent out." She then wished him well on the trials and closed that the doctor was "splendid." But the next morning, she telegraphed again to suggest that while "nothing [was] immediately alarming," Orville should make plans to return home. That same day, Wilbur was put on opiates and spent most of his time only vaguely conscious. Orville returned to Dayton on May 20 to find his brother unaware of his presence. On May 22, a specialist from Cincinnati arrived and Wilbur rallied slightly. On May 24, Milton pronounced him "in nearly every respect

Orville leading the funeral procession for his brother.

better." His improvement continued such that two days later, Orville was able to take a niece for an outing to Miami City. But that night, Sunday, May 26, Wilbur began his final slide. By Tuesday, the doctors had given up hope and at 3:15 A.M. on May 30, 1912, one of the most important and iconic figures in American history died peacefully in his bed, with his father, brothers, and sister by his side.

Milton wrote in his diary, "A short life, full of consequences. An unfailing intellect, imperturbable temper, great self-reliance and as great modesty, seeing the right clearly, pursuing it steadily, he lived and died." Wilbur Wright was a complex man, flawed to be sure, but Milton's assessment did not contain one word that wasn't true.

CHAPTER 26

The Romance of Death

Where Wilbur Wright had died in bed, many others in aviation did not.

One of Curtiss's strongest selling points, as the National Aviation Company noted in their ad, was that "the Curtiss machine is without a blot on its record. It has never had a serious accident." That changed on September 1, 1911.

John J. Frisbie had been one of the original members of the Moisant flying circus, the other American besides Hamilton to go on tour. At forty-six, Frisbie was the oldest of the Moisant aviators by a good twenty years and just about the oldest exhibition flyer in general. He had enjoyed solid if unspectacular success and been one of the Moisant aviators in Chicago, where he had earned a solid if unspectacular $2,000. Unique on the team, he flew not a Moisant machine but rather a Curtiss 50-horsepower biplane.

After Chicago, unbeknownst to Alfred, Frisbie had booked himself a series of one-man shows, the first of which was a county fair in Norton, Kansas. Frisbie flew for three days with no incident but on the fourth, his engine stalled forty feet off the ground and the biplane fell to the earth. The crash was minor, as were Frisbie's injuries, but no experienced mechanic was present to check the airplane out so Frisbie decided not to take to the air for his scheduled second flight. "The spectators hooted and shouted 'fakir' and refused to listen to explanations. Frisbie announced that rather than have the big crowd go away with the impression that he was not willing to do his best, he would attempt a flight."[1]

He took off without difficulty but at about one hundred feet the ailerons evidently malfunctioned when Frisbie attempted a turn and the biplane started downward. Frisbie fought for control but one wing clipped the top of a barn and the airplane crashed with Frisbie pinned underneath. He died an hour later. Frisbie's wife and young daughter were in the crowd, sitting among those whose taunts had sent the aviator to his death. Although Curtiss would never have permitted the airplane to take off again without being thoroughly checked, in newspapers across the nation Frisbie was reported to have been a member of the Curtiss team. Although he didn't know Frisbie, Curtiss felt sufficiently responsible for this first fatality in one of his airplanes to organize a benefit for his widow that raised five thousand dollars.

The second fatality was not nearly so long in coming.

Lincoln Beachey's exploits caught the fascination of the public like none who had preceded him. Even Hamilton, whose flamboyance was legendary, had never generated the same clamor to pay to see him fly. Hoxsey and Johnstone had come the closest, but their exploits tended to be restricted to height and distance. Beachey did *stunts.* He controlled an airplane as none had before. And the airplane he controlled was, as every article about him pointed out, a Curtiss. The name Curtiss therefore became synonymous with the most daring exhibition flying, a reputation the erstwhile speed demon on land and in the air enthusiastically embraced. Whereas owning a Wright airplane connoted solid, conservative flying, owning a Curtiss meant flying in the machine Beachey flew.

October 2, 1911, was typical. Beachey drew 20,000 people to see him fly in Dubuque, Iowa, a city whose entire population was only 57,000. It was Dubuque's first exhibition and Beachey gave them quite a show.

> When his plane left the ground at 4 o'clock the rain was pelting down. Through it Beachey traveled to the south end of the park, then turned and followed back above the race course. On the turn, he made one of his famous dips so successfully that for a moment the machine appeared to be literally turning upside down. On righting, it glided along above the track 50 feet in the air to the north end of the park, there mounted to about 150 feet and then with a sudden turn, came swooping down toward the crowd. As they scattered in a panic it glided off again 50 feet above their heads. The descent a few minutes later was made near the starting place.
>
> Beachey wasn't done.
>
> The second flight, a race with five motorcycles, proved the thrilling event of the meet. The plane sped around the course five times at the rate of 54 miles an hour, and came in at the finish 200 yards in the lead of the motorcycle riders. On crossing above the goal, instead of descending as the crowd had expected, Beachey took advantage of the rain and the low-hanging clouds to make an ascent above them. The plane mounted up into the air in big corkscrew spirals through the rain and straight into a cloud, out of it into another, and out again and into still another. The third disappearance lasted a full minute. Then suddenly as it had gone, the machine came volplaning toward the ground at a sharp angle. Within 60 feet of the earth it began to drop slowly, and as it touched the earth sped along a short distance to the place in which it was to be stored for the night.[2]

What the public did not see was that away from the spotlight, Beachey worked relentlessly to perfect his craft. In 1911, for example, a tailspin meant almost certain death, since no aviator had found a means to recover once the aircraft began spiraling toward the ground.

Convinced he could solve the problem, Beachey flew his Curtiss biplane to five thousand feet and then intentionally threw it into a tailspin. Trying different techniques as he spun downward, he eventually kicked the rudder hard against the spin, and the plane leveled out. (He likely would have been killed in a flexible-winged Wright.) He repeated the maneuver another eleven times to be certain it was no quirk. Then, rather than take credit for the service he had performed for other flyers, Beachey simply incorporated the move into his already stunning repertoire and called it, as he did in Dubuque, "the Corkscrew Twist."[3]

But the public Beachey was all that mattered and other exhibition flyers felt that they had little choice but to try to match his audacity. If an aviator attempted to complete a booking without a death-defying trick, both the crowds and the promoters would feel cheated and the aviator risked not being paid. And of course these aviators were proud, competitive men and the acclaim Beachey received rankled them. So "doing a Beachey" became shorthand among the exhibitionists for attempting a trick that was excessively risky and no trick was riskier than the Dip of Death. It had become Beachey's trademark maneuver.

Obviously, the steeper the angle to the ground, the more exciting and the more dangerous the stunt. One of the only flyers who could even approach Beachey's near vertical was Eugene Ely. His wife, Mabel, hated the Dip, but it had become almost an obligatory part of his exhibition repertoire.

On October 19, 1911, Ely was flying at a racetrack at the Georgia State Fair in Macon. Eight thousand people had paid to see the man famed for landing an airplane on the deck of a warship. On his second flight of the day, Ely took his airplane to three thousand feet and, as he was completing a circle of the field, "made a dip, seemingly to startle the thousands beneath him."

As reported in the San Francisco *Call,* "The machine shot down with tremendous velocity and the crowd applauded, thinking the aviator would rise as he had many times before. But Ely seem[ed] to lose his grip on the lever and the machine continued its downward plunge." Showing remarkable presence of mind, Ely actually jumped from the airplane just before it struck the ground but the force of the fall was too much. When officials of the fair reached him, Ely was still conscious. "I lost control," he is reported to have said. "I know I am going to die." And he did, moments later.*

As had become almost customary, spectators rushed to the crash to fight for souvenirs "as police fought in vain to keep them back. In a few minutes the field was cleared of every bit of wreckage. Ely's collar, tie, gloves, and cap similarly disappeared."[4] Spectators combed through the wreckage late into the night, looking for souvenirs.

Mabel Ely, also her husband's business partner, was not with Ely but en route to meet him after attending to business matters in New York. It was the first time since he had begun flying that she was absent. Mabel's mother was quoted as insisting, "This never would have happened if Mabel had been with him," because she never let him do anything that wasn't safe. Mabel had a different explanation for the accident. She wrote a letter to Beachey after her husband's death. "God punish you, Lincoln Beachey. Gene would be with me now if he had not seen you fly."†

In the wake of Ely's crash came the predictable spate of lamentation. The death of "one of the very greatest of American aviators," the editor of *Aircraft* magazine wrote, "brings up the question of whether exhibition flying is a benefit or a detriment to the progress of aerial flight." After a discussion of all the reasons flying should be conducted with the utmost care and without risk, he concluded that "carelessness upon the part of the expert and non-experience upon the part of the

* Whether or not this bit of dialogue is true is unclear. Ely was quite possibly already dead when rescuers reached him.

† Some recent literature suggests Mabel Ely goaded her husband into his foolhardy flying with taunts accusing him of being "not as good as Beachey," but this seems preposterous. Mabel Ely was her husband's biggest supporter and they were as close as any couple could be.

novice are two bad factors which have caused so many fatal accidents" and both "should be guarded against to the utmost limit."

This editorial and many like it missed the point entirely. In exhibitions, in private, and especially in battle, the limits of aircraft performance were going to be tested and retested. By the time of Ely's death, few doubted that aviation would have decisive military applications. In the same issue of the *Call,* another item reported "The Chinese Army Equipped with Airships."

Even without military interest, there was no way an invention with the dramatic allure of the airplane would not continue to spur death-defying acts. So with each fatality—and Ely's was the hundred-and-first since Tom Selfridge had died at Fort Myer—the public clamor for extreme flying increased.

In November 1911, the Wrights, as Orville had predicted, gave up. Although exhibition flyers such as Phil Parmalee would continue to be identified as "Wright aviators," Wilbur and Orville officially disbanded their team and turned their energies almost exclusively toward the courtroom.

Curtiss also had a loose arrangement with aviators flying his aircraft, although for publicity purposes he promoted the affiliation, especially with Beachey. At the same time, he tried to disavow the more disagreeable aspects of exhibition flying. He penned an article for *The New York Times* on December 31, 1911, in which he emphatically and unconvincingly disputed the notion that spectators came to meets to see spectacular crashes.

But the possibility of those spectacular crashes continued to be the big draw. For the next eighteen months, Beachey performed impossible maneuvers and tempted fate across America and in the process became perhaps the most famous man in the United States. In a nation of 76 million, before radio and television, where only the tiniest percentage of Americans had ever seen or heard Presidents Roosevelt, Taft, or Wilson, by the time Beachey's career ended as many as 20 million people had witnessed his matchless artistry. Spectators often exceeded 100,000 and twice in Chicago topped a half million; Beachey regularly earned more in a day than most Americans made in a year. His skill was so unerring, so exceptional, that he was dubbed "the Man Who Owns the Sky."

But Beachey had no illusions about the source of his popularity. When asked to describe his appeal, he replied, "People come to see me die."

Or to see pretenders die. In January 1912, before he had ever flown as a professional, a Yale graduate named Rutherford Page was being billed as "the second Lincoln Beachey." Page had recently completed six weeks at Curtiss's aviation school in San Diego, trained by Curtiss himself, where he had flown brilliantly. He was granted his aviation license three days before the opening of the third Los Angeles Air Meet, which was where Page decided to begin his exhibition career.[5]

Before adoring crowds that cheered his every move, it seemed as if Page might well live up to the hoopla. He promised that he would push Beachey to the limit and then best him in a short handicap race; when Beachey performed a series of stunts, Page swore he would "beat Beachey or break my fool neck," and then duplicated the "dips and sharp turns" in a flight "even more daring" than Beachey's. When he landed, Curtiss warned him that Beachey's maneuvers were dangerous and took years to learn. Page laughed and told Curtiss he was "all to the good."[6]

Beachey was not about to lose the spotlight to a rookie. His flying was "simply marvelous. He executed right handed and left handed spirals that were not dreamed of a year ago. With his 75 H.P. Curtiss motor and trim little machine, he left the ground and very quickly mounted high in the air. Having gained the altitude desired, he came down in small spirals that were certainly not more than three hundred feet in diameter and probably less. During these spirals he at times took his hands off the controlling wheel and even stood up."

Page decided that the best place to supplant the champion was the five-mile "free for all" race on January 22, in which Beachey was entered. Page took his Curtiss biplane up in a stiff wind, flew out over a ravine, and then attempted to "turn on a pivot" back to the starting point at a treacherous spot whose constant crosscurrents prompted aviators to call it "Death Curve."

While four thousand spectators looked on, Page's aircraft suddenly turned nose down and plunged to the ground. Upon impact, the engine broke loose and landed on the young aviator, crushing his skull. Page died instantly. So that spectators would be prevented from rushing the fallen airplane to fight for souvenirs, the wreckage was burned on the spot.

As was customary, the remainder of the day's events were canceled, but the next day the crowds were back. Beachey, in his Curtiss, and Phil Parmalee in a Wright dominated the events, winning for speed and endurance. On January 28, Beachey made a stunning announcement. A "new girl aviator, Miss Florence Walker of Seattle," whom Beachey had trained, would fly at the meet and do as well as any man. In the early afternoon, Miss Walker, short and solidly built, dressed in a long skirt and opera cape, appeared as promised and took her seat in Beachey's Curtiss biplane. Then, "with broken silk garters flying and a 35 mile gale playing havoc with the draperies," the woman "performed today what probably were the greatest aviation feats ever seen on Dominguez Field." She "ascended to a great height, tilted the machine almost perpendicular, and dived back to the windswept course. The only mishap was when the wind blew off a silk garter." Then Miss Walker sent her craft round Death Curve "at 60 miles an hour, and not more than 25 feet from the ground."[7] When the plane landed, Florence Walker removed hat and wig to reveal the familiar form of Lincoln Beachey. The thousands of onlookers, oblivious that Rutherford Page had lost his life at the very spot that Beachey had pulled his stunt, cheered wildly.

Aeronautics declared the meet "a howling success from a show standpoint, a fair success financially, and disappointing from a sporting point of view. It was a veritable circus in the air." *Aircraft* magazine agreed, characterizing the meet as "a great success." Rutherford Page was not mentioned.

Ten weeks later, Cal Rodgers was in Long Beach, California, where the town was planning to erect a monument to commemorate his cross-country flight. From late March until early April, Rodgers performed exhibitions, often taking passengers aloft to soar over the Pacific Ocean. Rodgers had become known for his reckless flying, ignoring friends who urged him to be more cautious. "The air is nothing to me now," he said to reporters. "I've conquered it. I have never been afraid when I go up."

On April 3, before a crowd estimated at seven thousand, Rodgers took off in his Wright B, "circling through the air over the city, performing thrilling manoeuvres," then engaged in a series of "Texas Tommy" figures, wild aerial gyrations that had gotten their name from a raffish dance begun at a "Negro cabaret" in San Francisco in 1910. At one point, "Seeing a flock of seagulls disporting themselves among a great swarm of sardines just over the breakers, Rodgers turned and dived down into them, scattering the birds in all directions." The crowd cheered. "Highly elated with the outcome of his dive," Rodgers had gained altitude and headed out to sea when suddenly he went into a steep descent. Initially, he relaxed his hands on the levers, as if he had gone into the dive intentionally, but he was then seen desperately trying to pull them back. The airplane did not respond and Rodgers "crashed into the surf and was crushed beneath the engine."[8] He perished within moments. When there was no attempt to keep spectators away from the site, some swarmed over the wreckage fighting for souvenirs even before Rodgers had died. When he examined the remains of the airplane, Rodgers's mechanic, Frank Shafer, found "the body of a seagull tightly wedged between the tail and the rudder of his aeroplane."[9] The gull had rendered the rudder immovable and snapped the control wire when Rodgers tried to pull out of the dive.

In the wake of Rodgers's death, Walter Brookins assembled a group of aviators at the Hotel Manhattan in New York to found the "Safe and Sane" flyers' club. All members pledged not to attempt extreme stunts, particularly the Dip of Death. Brookins "pointed out that of the early airmen . . . the Wrights, Curtiss, Grahame-White, and Paulhan are still alive and happy, a group that took up aviation immediately after the pioneers who gained their fame has now become nearly extinct." Those who died, according to Brookins "were almost always the trick riders and daredevils of the sport." Although Brookins tried to recruit Tom Baldwin, Curtiss, and flyers known for conservatism, such as Frank Coffyn, his effort went nowhere. The money was in tricks and most flyers were more than willing to risk their lives rather than their livelihoods.

Despite Orville's grousing about his association with the traitorous Brookins, the Wrights were content to allow Phil Parmalee to continue to fly under their aegis. He had been joined on the circuit by his friend and another Wright-trained flyer, J. Clifford Turpin. Just weeks after Brookins's aborted organizing effort, Parmalee and Turpin were flying at an exhibition in Seattle. On May 30, the very day Wilbur Wright died, Turpin, in a Wright B, was coming in to land, "careening down the airfield ... at 50 mph," when an "unknown man rushed across the track and would have been beheaded by the machine but for the quick action of the aviator."[10] Turpin turned away from the landing strip toward the packed grandstand but could not gain enough altitude to clear the crowd. He cut his engines, trying to bring down

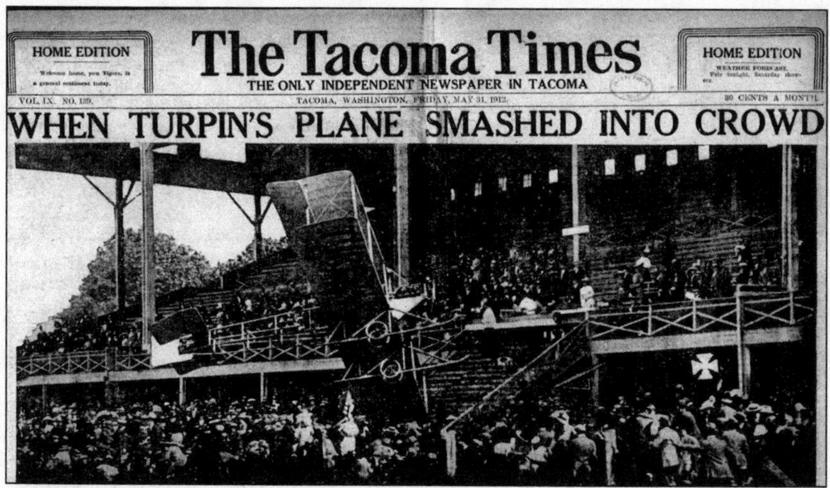

HOME EDITION

Welcome home, you Tigers, is a general sentiment today.

The Tacoma Times

THE ONLY INDEPENDENT NEWSPAPER IN TACOMA

HOME EDITION

WEATHER FORECAST. Fair tonight, Saturday showers.

VOL. IX. NO. 139. TACOMA, WASHINGTON, FRIDAY, MAY 31, 1912. 30 CENTS A MONTH

WHEN TURPIN'S PLANE SMASHED INTO CROWD

Clifford Turpin just before crashing into the crowd in Seattle.

the airplane short of the spectators, but crashed into the lower tier of boxes, killing two spectators, one of them a ten-year-old boy, and injuring fifteen more. According to the Chicago *Day Book,* a "heavily jeweled woman's hand was found in the wreckage."[11]

Although everyone assured him that the accident was unavoidable, Turpin was distraught. Still, he and Parmalee refused to cancel the tour. They moved on to Yakima, where two days later in high wind, Parmalee took his seat at the controls. With Turpin's accident so fresh, the promoters asked him to postpone the flight until the wind abated. Parmalee, known for safe and prudent flying, is reported to have "laughed at the persistent and fatal misfortune that had dogged aviators for the week and climbed to his seat." At about four hundred feet, he passed the rim of Moxie Canyon, seemed to have been hit by a side gust of wind, and went into a vertical dive from which he could not pull out. His body was found by local farmers and pulled from under the wreckage.

After Arch Hoxsey had crashed, Parmalee had told reporters, "There goes another. It won't be long before it gets all of us. We ourselves do not realize the chances we take. Even if a warping wire were to break, we would fall like a stone. When a man gets into this business, he knows what he is up against and must be prepared to take the final chance."[12]

Turpin, recovering from injuries suffered in his own crash, nonetheless insisted on taking charge of Parmalee's body. "It's the way of the game," he insisted. Parmalee had weeks before been betrothed to Turpin's sister and both men were about to quit flying with their hides intact. "We'd been at it two years and a half," Turpin explained, "and that's more than most." Parmalee had recently told his fiancée that he believed his good luck in avoiding injury was about to run out. After Parmalee's death, Turpin vowed never to fly again.

Orville Wright remained at home in Dayton after Wilbur's death, spending most of his time with Katharine, but the performance tests for the Wright C continued without him at College Park. Orville received telegraphed reports on this newest version of the Flyer, which he had worked on for more than a year and newspapers had reported was "regarded by the late Wilbur Wright as the best craft he and his brother had ever built."[13] By June 11, the machine had met the speed and endurance criteria handily and all that was left was to climb to two thousand feet in less than ten minutes carrying 450 pounds of dead weight in addition to gasoline, oil, and water. Just before 6:30 P.M., Art Welsh took his place at the controls with Lieutenant Hazelhurst at his side.

Welsh took off and circled. He must have doubted the machine's ability to make the climb because instead of attempting it straightaway, he took the C to about 250 feet, signaled the army officers and other spectators on the ground that he was ready, then began a dive to gain speed and create momentum once he turned upward. But he never did. The airplane seemed to quiver when it reached the horizontal about thirty feet above the ground and then pitched forward and crashed, killing both men instantly.

Orville received reports from the officers present and knew what had happened. He wrote to J. William Kabitzke, another Wright aviator, that Welsh died as a result of making his dive at too sharp an angle, which was "so unlike Mr. Welsh, who had always displayed so much caution."* After a careful examination of the wreck and hearing the testimony of eyewitnesses, the army's investigators agreed.

Katharine accompanied Orville to Washington for Welsh's and Hazelhurst's funerals. Welsh, né Welcher, was buried at Adas Israel Cemetery in Anacostia, Virginia, in a Jewish ceremony, which was completely foreign to both the Wrights and the army officers in attendance. Katharine observed that "all of his family and all of his wife's

* Kabitzke graduated from the Wright school the day before Wilbur died. That October, during a two-hour endurance test of the Wright C at College Park, he would be thrown from the craft after plummeting two thousand feet but miraculously escape injury. He later became head of the Wright school himself and lived until 1944.

family show their Jewish traits much more than Mr. Welsh did." The following day, Hazelhurst was interred at Arlington. Hazelhurst's pallbearers included Spuds Ellyson, Paul Beck, Benjamin Foulois, Hap Arnold, and Charles deForest Chandler, who, although no one knew it at the time, represented an honor roll of the future of American military aviation.

Attending two more funerals just two weeks after Wilbur's did not add to Orville and Katharine's grief. Rather, as she wrote to Milton, "The change has done us both a great deal of good. I am sleeping fairly well now. We are both tired but feeling better than we did."

Curtiss was not spared tragedy during the Wrights' run of misfortune. Julia Clark, who had been fascinated by the flying at the 1911 Chicago meet, traveled to San Diego and refused to leave until Glenn Curtiss personally taught her to fly. Curtiss, whose experience with Blanche Stuart Scott had not convinced him that women should be in the air, finally acceded. Clark showed sufficient aptitude to become the third woman to obtain an aviator's license, after which she immediately announced her intention to join an exhibition tour. Curtiss didn't think she was ready and told her to practice more before joining the circuit. Clark wouldn't hear of it.

Six days after Welsh crashed, on June 17, 1912, during her first flight at an exhibition in Springfield, Illinois, Julia Clark flew into a tree and was killed instantly. She was the first American woman to die in a crash and aviation's 146th fatality.

In the 1,369 days since Thomas Selfridge had been killed at Fort Myer, an aviator had died roughly every ten days.

Two weeks later, on July 1, at a meet in Boston, Harriet Quimby took off for a flight around Boston Harbor with William Willard, the exhibition's organizer and Charles Willard's father, in the passenger seat.

Quimby had become every bit the star she had aspired to be onstage. On April 16, she had made headlines around the world when, dressed in her trademark one-piece, hooded purple aviation suit—which "by an ingenious device can be converted into a traditional walking skirt"—she became the first woman to fly across the English Channel. She left Dover at 5:30 A.M. in her Blériot two-seater, disappeared into the fog, emerged thirty minutes later, flew over the French coast, made two circles over Boulogne, and then landed at the tiny village of Hardelot. (After she landed, the Armour Company wasted little time in signing her up to replace Cal Rodgers as the face of Vin Fiz. The logo for the drink was changed from a bunch of grapes to an attractive young woman in a purple flying suit and goggles.)

At the Boston meet, Quimby was flying the Blériot monoplane painted "pure white." After circling the lighthouse at about seven thousand feet, she flew past the field at approximately eighty miles per hour, and then circled back to land a quarter mile farther on. For reasons never fully explained, the craft pitched violently forward at fifteen hundred feet. First Willard then Quimby were ejected. Five thousand spectators watched the two turn over and over before landing in the shallows. Both bodies were described as "terribly crushed." The Blériot recovered its equilibrium after its occupants were ejected, "gliding off gracefully into the wind," and settled into the water, where it was recovered substantially undamaged.[14]

After the crash, there was some question as to whether Quimby and Willard had been belted in. Glenn Martin, another aviator, claimed there had been no restraints in Quimby's Blériot. "If they had been strapped in, the accident would not have happened," he said. But others claimed that she had buckled a broad strap across a space less than a foot in front of her, and from behind and on either side, hollow tubing ran to a vertical mast on the fuselage to which support wires fastened. "How Miss Quimby could have been thrown from her seat without herself unbuckling the strap is a mystery, especially since the tubing converged to a point directly in front."[15]

Blanche Stuart Scott provided the most apt testimonial. She had been circling the harbor at five hundred feet and witnessed the fall. Although distraught at the death of a friend and fellow pilot, when asked if Quimby's death would cause her to reconsider flying, Scott replied, "Certainly not." She added later, "All aviators get it sooner or later. If they stay in the game it is only a question of time before something goes wrong and they are killed. We all realize that. All aviators are fatalists; they realize that what is to be will be."*

André Haupert, who had taught Quimby to fly at the Moisant school, had a different take. "You ask me if aviation is safe. My answer is that it is safe for the man who is safe. You take Sopwith and Grahame-White. They are not killed. But they do not go out in a machine if they are not certain of its soundness and they make no specialty of spectacular flights."

Lincoln Beachey was also asked to comment. "They were going 80 to 100 miles an hour. Miss Quimby was coming down from some 5,000 feet with full power on. She was a light, delicate woman and it could easily have happened that the terrific rush of air was too much for her and that she became weakened and unable to control her levers." Beachey eventually retracted those remarks and said instead, "What caused this and other accidents similar, no one will ever know." Later examination of the wreckage revealed that a cable to the rudder fouled in the lever that controlled the warping mechanism on the Blériot, which might have caused the craft to pitch forward.

Beachey remained an enigma. Held sufficiently responsible in the press for the deaths of fellow aviators to be labeled the "Pacemaker for Death," he had also become perhaps the nation's leading advocate for aircraft safety. He tried constantly to dissuade other flyers from attempting stunts that were beyond their ability to complete safely. He always wore a shoulder harness, made certain to scrupulously check every airplane in which he flew before each ascent, and was always recommending improvements in equipment to increase safety. On more than one occasion, he mercilessly excoriated the War Department for refusing to invest in aviation and accused the generals of killing young flyers by requiring them to go aloft in second-rate airplanes.

* But Scott, in the end, did not "get it." She quit flying in 1916, went to Hollywood as a screenwriter, and lived until 1970.

But Beachey continued to embrace the outrageous as well. At the 1912 Chicago air meet in August, he once again bragged that he had trained a female pilot, this time a Frenchwoman, one Clarice Lavaseur, and, sure enough, a short, dowdy woman with rouged cheeks, dressed in a long skirt and coat and large hat, took the controls of Beachey's plane.* Ascending unsteadily, Lavaseur appeared as if she would never survive. Dipping erratically then ascending, then diving toward the crowd of one hundred thousand now-scattering spectators, Lavaseur eventually made her way to Michigan Avenue, where the plane lost altitude until the wheels were literally bouncing off the roofs of automobiles. "Police reported cases of watchers toppling out of automobiles in the paddock." At one point, the out-of-control aircraft seemed certain to ram a ferry on Lake Michigan. Passengers on a launch all ran to one side to watch and tipped the boat over, necessitating a rescue in Lake Michigan.[16] Eventually the woman found a way to land the plane directly in front of the center of the grandstand. As they had in Los Angeles, the stunned crowd suddenly erupted in cheers and applause when Beachey whipped off the hat and wig underneath and stood before them.

As Beachey was careening about, Beckwith Havens was having an incident of his own. He had been cajoled to go aloft with a film company director in a small hydroplane built for one person. He took off at the lakeside, did a lap in the air, and then landed on the water. But the plane lacked the power for a water takeoff with the weight of two passengers, so Havens persuaded the director to jump overboard close to the shore. The director was unfazed but the police didn't take kindly to Havens ditching his passenger.

"Next thing, a police launch was alongside and they had me by the collar and hauled me up in front of hundreds of thousands of people. Lincoln Beachey had a trick he used to pull at the shows. He'd come out dressed as a woman and take off and fly as if he was crazy, all over

* The state of national news at the time was not such that Beachey's similar stunt earlier in the year at Los Angeles would have been known by more than a handful of people in Chicago.

the place, and everybody'd be screaming and yelling. He saw what was happening while he was doing this act so he took a dive at me, just over my head . . . very amusing."

Once again, spectacle coexisted with death. Eight days earlier, Wright aviator Howard Gill had been killed in a midair collision at the opening of the meet.

CHAPTER 27

A Reluctant Steward

Milton Wright estimated that within two days of Wilbur's passing, more than one thousand telegrams were received at the Wright home, including one from Glenn Curtiss. On June 1, twenty-five thousand people filed past his coffin at Dayton's First Presbyterian Church before Wilbur was taken for a private graveside service and buried in the family plot in Woodland Cemetery. President Taft said that Wilbur "deserves to stand with Edison and Bell," comparisons that were also made in a great many newspapers.

Aeronautics wrote, "Strange as it may seem, few have commented on him as a Man, though his work has been lauded to the skies. He was generally misunderstood; he realized this but apparently cared little of what the world thought of him. This is unfortunate. Those who knew him best were scarcely able to pierce the veil which seemed to surround his intricate nature. Suffice to say, however, that the better one knew him, the more he was loved. The world never obtained the proper perspective." *The New York Times* added, "Wilbur Wright was not a martyr. His life, if it means anything, shows that a man can carry a great work to success, not only without credit from his fellows, but with supreme indifference to their opinion."

Most but not all of the eulogies mentioned Wilbur as one half of a team and few implied that his contribution was greater or more significant than Orville's. Nowhere was it noted that Wilbur was president of the Wright Company while Orville served as one of either two or three vice presidents, depending on the year. But the disparity of the brothers' standing in the business was made clear in Andrew Freedman's condolence letter to Orville. "While my association with [Wilbur] was more intimate than with yourself, I trust you will appreciate the feeling I must naturally have for you as his brother, co-laborer, partner, and successor." Freedman added that a board of directors resolved "that in the death of Mr. Wright, this company has suffered the irreparable loss of its chief inspiration and guiding spirit," phrasing that doubtless caused Orville conflicting emotions.

Orville traveled to New York for a board meeting after the Welsh and Hazelhurst funerals and was elected as the new Wright Company president. It was an unlikely marriage, as Grover Loening understood. "Orville was good at business, I thought, in that very few people could put anything over on him, but he certainly did not have any 'big business' ideas or any great ambition to expand. He seemed to be lacking in push."[1]

Once again, Orville was a victim of comparison. Wright Company treasurer Alpheus Barnes told Grover Loening, "Ever Since Orville succeeded [Wilbur] as president, we really have no boss. He takes forever to make a decision . . . nothing like the quick-acting, quicker-thinking Wilbur. Maybe the breakup of the team has had a bad effect."[2] Tom Crouch added, "Wilbur had not been especially fond of management, but he had worked at it, driven by an ambition that would not permit failure. . . . Orville had almost none of his brother's restless ambition nor the energy and drive to succeed that came with it. . . . The thought of attending a board meeting, let alone presiding at one, was abhorrent to him. Moreover, with the single exception of Robert Collier, he felt little other than contempt for the rich New Yorkers whom Wilbur had regarded as friends and associates."[3] Still, as Orville and Katharine saw it, Wilbur had been killed by the "scoundrels and thieves" who refused to acknowledge the Wrights' invention, and they would expend whatever energy necessary to avenge their brother. "Orville sued Curtiss for revenge and prestige," Grover Loening stated flatly.

In that quest, Orville began with a disappointment. As a result of Wilbur's death, Curtiss's lawyers requested yet another adjournment of *Wright Company v. Herring–Curtiss,* this until the fall term, a move Orville opposed but the judge granted. In an attempt to speed up the process, Wright lawyers decided to suspend the lawsuit against the Aero Club and fold it in with Herring–Curtiss, which made the trial in Buffalo before Judge Hazel the one that would determine the course of American aviation. Judge Hazel, who had been so sympathetic to the Wright cause, also seemed less likely to allow the case to drag on interminably.

Curtiss would try to keep stalling regardless; he had nothing to gain by allowing the trial to go forward. For him, the best legal outcome was to be allowed simply to continue to do what he was already doing—building and selling airplanes. Every week that passed, the Curtiss Aeroplane Company grew richer and, perhaps of greater importance, more entrenched with the military, especially the navy. Orville, however, could only gain by bringing the trial to a positive resolution and, as Wilbur had noted in his letter to Frederick Fish, every postponement decreased the value of their patent.

Each time the Curtiss legal team came back, there was a different reason for the delay; the need for further testimony, a desire to refine their brief, even misunderstandings as to the scope of their defense. By November, however, their options had run out and on the eighteenth of that month, the trial in *Wright v. Herring–Curtiss* was finally completed before Judge Hazel in Buffalo.

During this process, Orville showed that he had no intention of being a mere figurehead, nor would he be a pushover. When Freedman telegraphed to tell him that "the annual meeting of the Wright Company has been called for the thirteenth of November at the offices of the company, and I think it would be well that you are here at that time," Orville replied, "I have decided not to come to New York until after the trial at Buffalo, which begins Monday." His reasons were good—he thought it better that he be able to report to the board about the trial—but he was also telling Freedman that as president of the company he would set the calendar, not be a slave to it.

Orville also demonstrated that, despite all the criticism, he might be a more measured chief executive than his brother. Wilbur had pursued the suit against the Aero Club for the Belmont meet receipts of $15,000 with the same unflinching commitment as he had everything else. At first, Orville continued the quest, even in the face of adverse rulings in court. Eventually, however, he began to resist attorney Pliny Williamson's advice to continue appeal after appeal. On June 29, Williamson informed Orville that Wilbur had authorized the case be taken to the court of appeals if necessary, and Orville agreed to let his brother's decision stand. But one month later, when Williamson noted that "in addition to lawyers' fees, there are court costs which go to the opposing party when the moving party is defeated," Orville began to wonder if he would be throwing good money after bad. He also expressed surprise that Wilbur would have approved such a course. Williamson, who was receiving hefty fees, assured Orville that Wilbur had been adamant about continuing the case, even wanting to file a second action, and that "there were certain reasons, which I do not care to write in a letter but which I will give you when I see you." Orville reluctantly allowed the case to go forward, but in December he called a halt to the second action. Although he didn't hold out much hope for a favorable decision, he agreed to allow the appeal to run its course since so much money had already been spent. Then, in a sentence Wilbur never would have written, he told Williamson, "But if we cannot win on our present case, I think we had better abandon the claim."

As the legal proceedings inched forward, Curtiss conducted himself as if they did not exist. His factory hummed along in a process of almost continuous expansion and his various lines of business all achieved unprecedented profits. In June, the Curtiss school in Hammondsport broke all records by conducting 240 training flights in a single day. In July, Curtiss produced the true flying boat, "not an aeroplane with boats attached, but a bona fide, dyed-in-the-wool, honest-and-truly motor boat with wings and is an improvement on the experimental flying boat."[4] It was the most advanced craft ever built; included a collapsible waterproof hood to protect the operator from spray and was "so strongly built that it can be beached with safety even in a high surf." Almost immediately, Curtiss sold models in France, Germany, Russia, and Japan, and orders came in "faster than the machines could be built." It also did not hurt publicity that Curtiss aviator Hugh Robinson took off from Keuka Lake and flew a physician to the other side to tend a young boy who had fallen from a balcony and broken his hip, a story that was picked up by newspapers across America.

Hydroplanes had become immensely popular and any number were being designed and thrown on the market, including by the Wright Company, but the Curtiss models were invariably superior. In August, confident that the trial would not take place as scheduled, he sailed for Europe to help overseas sales while the Wright Company opened a hydroplane school in Glen Head, New York.

Before he left, American aviation saw progress of a different sort. In July, the army tested a special airplane-mounted, air-cooled machine gun invented by Lieutenant Colonel Isaac Lewis of the army's Coast Artillery Corps, which was capable of firing up to six hundred rounds per minute.* A Wright B was used since the Wright C had yet to pass its performance tests.

Curtiss had to deal with crisis as well. In November 1912, Jerome Fanciulli, whose energy and exceptional business instincts had both propelled the Curtiss Exhibition Team to preeminence and created a marketing and sales powerhouse, left to head up "Aquaero," a subsidiary of the Electric Boat Company of New London, Connecticut. Fanciulli intended to "inject new life into the aeroplane business" with

* The Lewis gun would become a favored weapon of the British army in World War I.

a series of radical design improvements in flying boats. Anticipating an increase in government funding, Fanciulli set up shop in Washington, D.C., intending to manufacture airplanes for both commercial and military use.* Replacing Fanciulli would be extremely difficult and in the end Curtiss didn't try.

Fanciulli's departure was particularly ill-timed as at that moment Curtiss was facing a vital decision. He had received overtures from a number of foreign nations, including Russia and France, offering facilities and other incentives to relocate within their borders in the event he lost the case. France especially would have had appeal. They might have overstated their role in pioneering aviation but there was no doubt that by the end of 1912 they were leading it. On December 11, for example, Roland Garros set a new altitude record of 19,027 feet, almost doubling Beachey's Chicago mark in sixteen months. Curtiss refused to commit to any of the offers but neither did he unequivocally turn them down.

He was in California, at North Island, when the decision came down on February 21, 1912. To the surprise of no one, except perhaps Curtiss himself, Judge Hazel ruled completely and unambiguously for the Wrights. Citing a number of precedents, although oddly not *Westinghouse,* Hazel wrote, "Having attained success where others failed, they may rightly be considered pioneer inventors in the aeroplane art. Their concept was practical and their combination of old and new elements meritoriously advanced the operativeness of aeroplanes of this type from which astonishing flights have resulted." The concept of pioneering, broad in itself, was applied more broadly still. "And even if the patentees were not strictly pioneers, in the sense of producing an apparatus novel in its entirety, they nevertheless strikingly surpassed their predecessors in devising means for restoring lateral balance, and are entitled to a liberal construction of their claims in controversy, and

* Fanciulli had made an uncharacteristic error. The large government appropriations he was anticipating didn't materialize until the United States entered World War I, by which time he had left aviation for the automobile business, where he remained for the rest of his career. He worked well into his eighties and died in 1986, age ninety-eight.

to the application of a range of equivalents that will include an aeroplane appropriating substantially the same instrumentalities and the same principle of operation."

Hazel then agreed with the Wright claim that "the same principle of operation" seemed to apply to any method of restoring lateral balance. Even Augustus Post's admission that on some occasions he had used the rudder in conjunction with the ailerons was interpreted by Judge Hazel as invalidating Curtiss's defense.[5]

"The defendants," the judge concluded:

> have embodied in their aeroplane the various elements of the claims in suit. While it is true, as pointed out herein, that the defendants have constructed their machine somewhat differently from the complainant's, and do not at all times and on all occasions operate the same on the Wright principle, yet the changes they have made in their construction relate to the form only. They have constructed their machine so that it is capable of restoring equilibrium in substantially the same way as is complainant's machine, and the evidence is that on occasions, depending upon aerial conditions or other disturbing causes, they use the vertical rudder, not only to steer their machine, but to assist the ailerons in restoring balance.[6]

Having chosen sweeping acceptance, Judge Hazel showed little patience for detail.

> It is unnecessary to further answer the arguments advanced at the bar bearing on the defense of noninfringement, as to do so would extend this opinion beyond reasonable length. Everything relating to the testimony and the criticisms thereon has not been fully treated, yet the material features have been sufficiently elaborated. The questions of law in the case are important; but the questions of fact are controlling, and in view of the novelty of the claims and their scope, the question of infringement is resolved adversely to

the defendants as to the claims which are the subject of this controversy.

Curtiss's only victory seemed simply a postponement of the inevitable but it would prove to be a good deal more. "A decree may be entered, with costs, in favor of the Wright Company, as prayed in the bill; but, because of the importance of the litigation and of the questions involved, a supersedeas will be allowed, upon condition that an appeal be diligently prosecuted."

As Curtiss promised to do just that, from a practical standpoint the decision would have no immediate effect other than to cost Curtiss $10,000 for his bond. Still, most of those who were convinced they would soon have to deal with Orville, hat in hand, praised the decision. The most amusing comment came from the former president of the Aeronautical Society, whose organization only six months before had insisted the Wright claims were groundless. "The decision by Judge Hazel is to be highly commended for the conscientious and painstaking effort to arrive at sound conclusions and there is no question but that from the evidence adduced before the court, his decision would have been reached by any other equally conscientious judge."[7]

Former Curtiss intimate Thomas Baldwin deftly turned with the prevailing winds. "I cannot see why it would harm anybody to pay the Wright Company a reasonable royalty. I have always been of the opinion and do know that if it had not been for the Wright brothers, none of us would have been flying. . . . I think we all owe to them a loyal support at this point."

From his correspondence as well as his public pronouncements there is no doubt that Curtiss believed he was a victim of injustice. Two months before the decision, he had written to Washington Irving Chambers, "[The Wright brothers'] success in actual flying led them to try to make their patent cover things it was not intended to cover, and their exploitation as the first to fly has been used in an effort to get the court to enlarge the scope of their patent. The lawyers have tried to show we copied their machine, purposely making slight changes to avoid infringing their patent and they now claim our rudder is in no sense a rudder but simply a vane used for counteracting the turning effect, as in their machines."[8]

Curtiss never seemed to grasp the notion of pioneer patents; either his lawyers had been negligent in not informing their client of the most important change in patent law in a century, or they had so informed him and Curtiss refused to acknowledge that such a restrictive measure could actually exist. In either case, Curtiss quite clearly felt himself not only heroic in standing up to a couple of bullies but also a defender of other persecuted opponents of the Wrights. "Had we not taken this stand, the Wright Co. would have been in the position to enjoin all manufacturers and the whole industry would have been monopolized. Not only warping machines, but aileron construction and the Farman construction would have been controlled; in fact, any machine that could fly, including hydroplanes would come under jurisdiction of the Wright patent, so that the trade certainly owes us something."

Orville wasn't present when the decision he had awaited for four years was published; he had sailed to Europe with Katharine earlier in February to deal with the patent issues there. In Germany, lawyers were appealing the decision effectively disallowing the Wright patent, and in France, despite favorable rulings, the Wright claims had yet to be enforced as a final decision was repeatedly postponed pending further expert evaluation. The first stop, however, was in England, where Orville formally, at long last, established a British subsidiary, of which he was named chairman of the board. That turned out to be the only good news they would get. In Leipzig, five days after Judge Hazel's decision in Buffalo, the German supreme court upheld the earlier decision and ruled that the Wright patent was unenforceable except where the three-axis system was employed specifically as described.* The French court ruled in their favor, that wing warping and the rud-

* One month later, Germany's Harlan manufacturing company unveiled the world's first bomb-dropping apparatus linked to a bombsight.

der need only "co-exist," but once again granted a motion to stay the judgment while the decision was evaluated by another panel of experts.

Curtiss leapt on the rulings, discussing them, oddly, as if Wilbur were still alive. "Recent cable reports give the impression that the Wrights had won sweeping decisions in the European courts, whereas the German decisions only uphold the Wright claims for the use, in combination, of the wing warp and vertical rudder, but refuse the claims on these devices working independently; and also deny that the Wright patent in any way covers ailerons. . . . In all machines now manufactured, including those made by the Wrights, the wing warping and vertical rudder are used independently." He claimed, inaccurately, that the French decision was largely the same.

Orville and Katharine sailed home in mid-March. Europe might be a loss but final victory in the United States seemed within their grasp. Unless the circuit court defied the odds and threw out all Judge Hazel's reasoning in Curtiss's appeal, they had every reason to believe any remaining impediments to monopoly would be smashed.

They were home less than a week when disaster struck Dayton. A series of winter storms over frozen ground caused the Great Miami River to overflow its banks and swamp an inadequate series of levees, leaving parts of the downtown under as much as twenty feet of water. Fires from broken gas lines broke out across the city. Hundreds died, thousands of homes were destroyed, and damage estimates were put at $100 million.

Although the Wright factory was largely unharmed and some early concerns about Milton's safety were quickly assuaged, all the records of Wilbur and Orville's experiments as well as irreplaceable photographs and glass-plate negatives were stored in the shed behind the house on Hawthorn Street. Fortunately for the Wright family and history, the most important materials were on the second floor, which the floodwaters stopped just short of reaching. In the end, the Wrights suffered only a modest loss of their personal possessions and almost nothing vital to the business. Even the 1903 airplane, stored in a flooded shed, could be salvaged after cleaning. Within two weeks, the factory had reopened and three weeks after that Orville was experimenting on the Great Miami River with what he called the Wright Company's first true hydroplane, the CH, which was in truth merely a Model C with a pontoon slapped on.

But just before Orville was prepared to introduce the CH, Curtiss unveiled his latest design, the first-ever tractor hydroplane, built specifically for Wright adversary Harold Fowler McCormick. Curtiss was innovating at such a pace that he said designating his models would be meaningless. The CH, a clumsy, badly performing craft that never met the navy's performance criteria, was rendered obsolete before it ever left the water.

Tractors were beginning to supplant pushers across the industry; largely because of the crashes of the Wright C, the army would soon stipulate that all land-based aircraft must have front-mounted engines. Wing design was also in flux. Monoplanes had appeal to designers for sport flying, but for exhibitions—or in war—monoplanes had yet to demonstrate sufficient strength to hold up under the increased stress. Curtiss was actively experimenting in both technologies; Orville was not.

Orville was also proving to be an ineffective manager. Grover Loening had just begun at the Wright factory in mid-1913 and, despite the fact that he adored Orville personally, he was distressed at what he saw. "Factory organization was pretty rough. Orville would delay making a decision and drive us all nuts trying not to disobey his orders on the one hand and yet not knowing what to do."

A large part of the problem was that Orville remained consumed with Curtiss. He and Katharine made no secret that they held him responsible for Wilbur's death. Frank Russell, whom Orville had recently fired, had witnessed Wilbur's descent. "The last two years of Mr. Wilbur Wright's life were devoted entirely to his fight with Curtiss on patent matters. . . . Throughout the formative period, when we built the first airplanes, started the first exhibition business in this country, Orville Wright did all of the work, because Wilbur Wright had to devote himself, if you please, to patent suits. Wilbur Wright died of typhoid fever because he worked himself to death fighting a patent suit."[9] Loening added, "Orville and Katharine had preying on their minds and characters the one great hate and obsession, the patent fight with Curtiss. It was a constant subject of conversation, and the effort of Curtiss and his group to take credit away from the Wrights was a bitter thing to stand for . . . it monopolized Orville's attention and discouraged any attempt to incorporate the latest technical advances into the design of Wright aircraft."[10]

This lack of attention to the product manifested itself most acutely in the Wright C, which was described as "obsolete . . . slow, tail-heavy, and unstable." The C was plagued with crashes but characteristically Orville resisted any suggestion of flaws in the design and insisted pilot error was to blame. Meanwhile, "the death toll continued to mount" among military flyers in Wright aircraft.[11] Two were killed in a Wright B in September 1912, another in a B in July 1913, and four more in C's later that year.

Orville convinced himself that his automatic stabilizer was the answer. At the expense of his obligations as an executive and manager, he threw himself into perfecting the apparatus and then tested it in secret. In addition to providing the solution to the crashes plaguing the C's, Orville was determined to win the Aero Club prize for 1913 and wrest it away from Curtiss, who had won for 1912 as well as 1911. In October 1913, Orville was granted a patent for the design, and by the following month he was confident that the device was ready to be unveiled to the world. But he didn't schedule a public test until the last day of the year. As Wilbur had with the Michelin trophy, choosing December 31 would ensure that no one, especially Curtiss, could then best him for the Aero Club prize by unveiling some other improvement. The demonstration "would be a particularly sweet moment . . . a way to use the invention to triumph over Curtiss."[12]

And a triumph it was. Orville made seventeen flights in Dayton that day before three Aero Club representatives, one of whom was Grover Loening. During the last flight, Orville made seven successive turns with his hands off the controls. The Aero Club members were suitably wowed; Orville would have his trophy. No reporters had been present but four days later, Orville cabled a description of the device to the *Daily Mail* that was reprinted in *The New York Times*. In accompanying remarks, Orville proclaimed with great satisfaction that "we have invented an automatic stabilizer which will revolutionize flight." His new invention would, for the first time, make "flying as nearly fool-proof as anything can be" and thus "aerial transportation as safe as any other mode of travel." He promised to market the device by spring and "expressed the belief that the aeroplane would be in general use for commercial transportation within a very short time." Finally, he asserted that the crashes that had plagued aviation, by which he meant specifically his airplanes, had been caused by pilot error, which would now be eliminated by the automatic stabilizer.[13] The *Daily Mail* called the invention "a contribution to the art of flying only second in importance to the invention of the powered airplane."

As satisfying as winning the Aero Club trophy was, it paled before the news Orville would receive two weeks later.

CHAPTER 28

A Wisp of Victory

On January 13, 1914, the three judges of the United States Court of Appeals for the Second Circuit issued a perfunctory and unanimous opinion, only three paragraphs long, affirming the district court ruling in *Wright v. Herring–Curtiss.* It opened, "A machine that infringes part of the time is an infringement, although it may at other times be so operated as not to infringe." The judges went on: "As we are in full accord with the reasoning by which Judge Hazel (and Judge Hand) reached the conclusions that the patent in suit is a valid one, that the patentees may fairly be considered pioneers in the practical art of flying with heavier-than-air machines, and that the claims should have a liberal interpretation, it seems unnecessary to add anything to what has been already written." And finally, "The decree is affirmed, with costs."[1]

Curtiss had at long last been crushed. He was left only with the option of appealing to the Supreme Court, but with monopoly rights at their zenith in American jurisprudence and only a dismissive appellate opinion on which to base his action, he seemed to have no chance.

The appeals court decision liberated Orville, banished his doubts, exorcised his demons. "I knew in my own mind from the start that there was only one decision which the court could honestly reach," he told reporters. "We took special pains to present our case fairly and at the same time get before the court all of the evidence, and I am not surprised at the result." Although he would not yet talk of what specific actions the Wright Company would take, the monopoly he and Wilbur had so long sought now seemed his. All that was needed was to wait the roughly thirty days for the judgment to be filed. He wrote to Russell Alger on January 24, "These broad claims cover every machine of which I have any knowledge, flown either here or abroad. I am expecting to see you next Wednesday at the Executive Committee meeting at New York, when we will take up the matter of bringing action to stop further infringement."

But Orville's view of how to do that differed from the New York financiers with whom he shared both the board of directors and mutual antipathy. They wanted to move ahead ruthlessly, eviscerate all competition, and either put other firms out of business or make them subsidiaries of the Wright Company. The means to achieve that end were certainly available. The Wright Company could now demand royalties and damages of whatever amount it chose for every machine that had ever been sold by any company, except Burgess–Curtis.

But Orville refused. Whether he did so because of disinclination, a sense of fairness, fatigue, or some other reason cannot be determined with certainty but it is possible to get a hint of his thinking in an interview he granted to *The New York Times* in late January. The paper proclaimed that "for the first time" since Kitty Hawk, Orville had "ended a policy of silence" and told "the frank and full story of what it had cost he and Wilbur in money, industry, and patience to launch the aeroplane as a patented and protected device."[2]

Orville first decried patent laws that "made it impossible for any inventor without vast financial resources to obtain the fruits of his invention" and said that he would advise any young inventor to "absolutely withhold all knowledge of his invention from the public, and from the patent office as well, until he has obtained $200,000 in backing to be used in fighting through the tedious court processes."

As to the matter of most concern to everyone else involved in aviation, Orville revealed that he intended to ask 20 percent of the purchase price for every airplane sold by every manufacturer in the United States and Europe, the same percentage Wilbur had set before his death. Most airplanes sold for at least $5,000 (some twice that), and even using an extremely conservative estimate of 1,000 airplanes a year, for just 1914, at the 25 to 1 ratio of 2010 to 1910 dollars, the Wright Company would have cleared at minimum the equivalent of $25 million in royalties alone. Again following Wilbur's dictates, Orville also reserved the right to ask that every manufacturer pay an equal royalty on every airplane sold since 1906—which was every airplane ever sold—in order to secure a Wright license. He insisted his fee structure was not an "act of harshness but an act of great benefit to aerial navigation." Needless to say, other manufacturers saw things differently.

Having established that he *could* demand damages from everyone in the business, Orville detailed what he *would* do: He would adopt "a policy of leniency. . . . Innocent purchasers of aeroplanes which were infringements would be protected and aeroplane manufacturers who had built machines without deliberately knowing they were infringing would be dealt with lightly." Thus, while licenses and the 20 percent royalty would be required for future sales, no retroactive compensation would be sought.

But not for Curtiss. Glenn Curtiss alone would be required to pay every last penny of royalties for every airplane he had ever sold, a sum certain to once and for all break the man responsible for Wilbur's premature death.

Orville gave his reasons for singling out one man. "The death of my brother Wilbur is a thing we must definitely charge to our long struggle, and I am sure that anyone who has not carried on a patent fight, with its endless mazes of delays, could not possibly understand what Wilbur went through. The delays were what worried him to his death. It wasn't as if we were fighting a stand-up foe in a square give-and-take fight. We were fighting foes whose strategy was played in the dark."

Orville had an example of just how duplicitous his archenemy was. "When I lay in the hospital at Fort Myer after the fall in which I was severely injured, three gentlemen asked to look over our wrecked machine in its hangar. An appointment was made for them, but they did not appear and the aeroplane was crated up. Later, when the guards were at dinner, one of the visitors took the parts of the machine out of its crate and measured each part. Later we found an aeroplane on the market duplicating the measurements of our own exactly."

This version of the events after Selfridge's funeral was utterly fanciful. Not only did the testimony of those present not support any of Orville's assertions, but even the Wrights' previous accusations were at odds with what Orville was now alleging. And of course Curtiss was not even in Washington. Orville went on to present equally mythical versions of Curtiss's visit to Dayton in 1906 and their interactions since. His contention that "every improvement on which we filed patent papers we found quickly added to the machines of our competitors," meaning Curtiss, was blatantly false as well. If anything, the Wrights had taken to appropriating Curtiss's designs, particularly in flying boats. All of Orville's indictments led to the final damning conclusion. "All of this worried Wilbur first into a case of chronic nervousness, and then into a physical fatigue which made him an easy prey for the attack of typhoid that caused his death."

Curtiss was therefore being singled out because his lies, treachery, theft, refusal to play fair, and deceit in court had caused Wilbur's death. Only by freeing other purchasers and manufacturers from the penalty being assessed Wilbur's murderer could that point be made.

Orville's partners were furious. In their world, when the marketplace presented an opportunity, it was seized, not deferred—and it certainly wasn't deferred to satisfy a personal vendetta. Orville's strategy would make them a good deal of money, it was true, but not nearly as much as would be made in a true monopoly. There is no record of the conversations in the executive committee meetings but they were sufficiently acrimonious that by early March Orville was undertaking to buy out all the investors in the Wright Company and become sole owner. His partners would haggle about terms but not one of them demurred.*

Curtiss was in Europe on a sales tour when the devastating decision was handed down. He cut short his visit and sailed for home. The court's ruling not only threatened his business and his future in aviation, but might well cut short his latest project, the ultimate exploitation of the flying boat and the crowning achievement of his career.

On March 31, 1913, Lord Northcliffe offered a £10,000 prize ($50,000) for the first crossing of the Atlantic in seventy-two consecutive hours from any point in the United States or Canada and any point in Great Britain or Ireland in either direction.† Changing aircraft would not be permitted and all landings for repairs or to take on fuel must be made on the water. He published the announcement in the *Daily Mail* on April 1 and opened the competition to all nationalities. Wilbur Wright's old pupil, Count de Lambert, said the trip was feasible and that moreover, within ten years, the same crossing would be made in a single summer's day. He said the two greatest obstacles to success were maintaining course out of the sight of ships and not smashing up when landing on the waves to refuel.

Orville Wright scoffed that the journey was not possible at the current state of the art, which Northcliffe, an old friend and supporter, did not appreciate. Rodman Wanamaker, who had paid Augustus Herring $5,000 to exhibit the *Reims Racer* in the window of his New

* Robert Collier, Orville's only friend among the stockholders, was in Europe and did not reply to Orville's solicitation for some weeks. By the time he returned, he and Orville agreed that he should keep his shares.

† In 1910, Walter Wellman, a journalist and adventurer, had attempted to cross the Atlantic in an airship after failing to soar to the North Pole, but his engine had failed after thirty-eight hours and he crashed into the water near Bermuda, where he was rescued. From that point on, the feat was considered impossible until the development of the hydroplane.

York store, decided the trip was indeed possible and that it should be made by an American. Privately, he solicited Curtiss to begin planning a design and offered to fund the project.

Curtiss accepted eagerly but told only a few intimates at the plant of Wanamaker's plan. He realized the aircraft would have to be larger and sturdier than anything he had built in the past and that meant a larger, more powerful motor. He worked all summer on the design of what would be called the "H-1," all the while releasing two advanced models of flying boats, one of which seated four.

By late autumn, the possibility of a transatlantic crossing began to be speculated on regularly in the trade journals, and Curtiss admitted "he had interest," without indicating just how intense his interest was. A number of French aviators, including Roland Garros, were also purportedly in the process of designing the appropriate aircraft, as were two other consortiums in the United States. Orville Wright continued to think the idea ridiculous.

In late December, just weeks before the court of appeals ruling, Curtiss admitted he was in fact tinkering with the design of a transatlantic flying boat and that he had fabricated a 200-horsepower motor to power the craft. He still made no mention of Wanamaker's participation or that the effort had been ongoing for six months.

From the moment the ruling did come down, Curtiss made it clear he did not intend to go quietly. On January 16, his plant manager claimed that Curtiss had "three other means of control," two of which did not infringe the Wright patent, and said that production at Hammondsport would go on as before. The next day, Curtiss—by Marconi wireless—informed the American press that he intended to pursue the case to the Supreme Court and that in the interim, construction of the transatlantic flying boat would proceed.

Orville jumped into the fray a few days later, reversing his position on the feasibility of the crossing and claiming that with Harry Atwood, he was now studying the transatlantic flight problem himself and the Wright Company might well undertake the crossing. He estimated that a Wright airplane might succeed in traversing the ocean in twenty-five hours.

On February 5, in an address at the Aero Club dinner—the same dinner at which Orville was awarded the Collier trophy for his automatic stabilizer—Rodman Wanamaker revealed the full extent of the transatlantic project and his role in it.* "Mr. Wanamaker, in commenting on the proposed flight, declared that its accomplishment had been a cherished vision of his for years." The motive was altruistic. "His purpose, he said, was in the interest of world peace and by this he explained that a trip over the ocean in one flight would awaken the world to the tremendous importance of aviation in warfare." Finally, he "asked for the cooperation of all persons interested in seeing America first to conquer the air routes between the United States and Europe."

Wanamaker's subtext could not have been more clear: Not only did Curtiss have a wealthy and powerful new benefactor, but to interfere with Curtiss—or to ask for money to allow the project to go forward—would be an act of greed and barbarity, and unpatriotic to boot.

Orville, of course, could parry Wanamaker by building his own transatlantic aircraft, but, despite his pronouncements to the press, he had nothing even in the planning stage that could begin to achieve the goal. By the time Orville gave his interview in late February, he once more insisted "he did not take the matter of making a flight across the Atlantic seriously," and then asserted, "I cannot do so and neither can any other aeroplane manufacturer who will speak frankly." Curtiss's claims to be building such a craft for the Atlantic crossing were "insincere," simply a dodge to avoid the judgment of the courts. Orville demanded that Wanamaker cease aiding Curtiss with money or anything else. As with McCormick, Orville underestimated the degree to which men of great wealth refused to be pushed around. Wanamaker sent his "personal representative" to inform Orville that his "determi-

* Orville was not present at the Aero Club event. He chose to attend a Rotary Club dinner in Dayton instead.

nation to keep Curtiss from building aeroplanes until he takes out a license from the Wrights would have no effect on the relations between Mr. Wanamaker and Mr. Curtiss" and "that the preparations for the expedition would be continued exactly as if no decision had been rendered by the Court of Appeals."[3] Curtiss added that the proof of his sincerity was that payment for the machine was due only after it had demonstrated it could carry the load necessary for the flight.

Curtiss, to Orville's astonishment, was on the attack again. Curtiss next replied to Orville's assertions that he was responsible for the death of Wilbur Wright, categorizing them as "insinuations . . . I cannot believe Mr. Wright or any sane man ever made." But he had other, more substantive intrigues in store. In the first, one of his new associates was about to take Orville's vaunted new automatic stabilizer and toss it on the scrap heap.

In 1912, Elmer Sperry, who had invented the gyrocompass and then developed a means to stabilize ships using gyroscopes, wrote to Curtiss suggesting that gyroscopic stabilization might be adapted for aviation.* Curtiss wrote back, "Recent accidents have caused people to appreciate the dangers of aviation. In some cases, accidents could perhaps have been prevented had the machine been equipped with this device."[4] Curtiss agreed to supply the aircraft; Sperry sent his son Lawrence to Curtiss for flying lessons. Soon afterward Lawrence set to work on the gyroscopic stabilizer. One year later, he was ready. Using two gyroscopes, his device would sense shifts in any of the three axes of flight and make corrections to maintain optimal stability. Gyroscopic stabilizers were as much of an advancement over Orville's vane and pendulum system as ailerons had been over wing warping. On June 14, 1914, Sperry demonstrated his device in France, a triumphant flight in which Sperry, in a Curtiss biplane, took his hands from

* A gyroscope uses a wheel within a frame that spins about an axis like a top. The angular momentum of the wheel causes it to remain oriented in one direction regardless of changes in the orientation of the frame. A gyrocompass uses this spinning-wheel effect rather than magnetism to determine true rather than magnetic north.

the controls and stood up while his mechanic crawled seven feet out onto one wing. The machine held attitude perfectly. Thus Orville had less than six months to celebrate his triumph before being left behind once again.

Another of Curtiss's counterattacks involved proving that while the Wrights might have been the first to achieve a successful flight, they were not the first to produce a machine *capable* of flight, and thus the breadth that their patent had been granted was undeserved. To demonstrate this seemingly indemonstrable assertion, Curtiss solicited the Smithsonian Institution. Remnants of Langley's aerodromes were still crated away in their warehouse. Curtiss claimed that Langley had been correct in that the launching mechanism was all that was wrong with the craft, so Curtiss proposed to repair the doomed aerodrome and then fly it on Keuka Lake.

Just one week after the appeals court decision, Curtiss put Lincoln Beachey up to request the artifacts in order to rebuild the aerodrome and fly it. Beachey famously observed, "You can fly a kitchen table if the motor is strong enough." Charles D. Walcott, who had succeeded his close friend Langley as secretary, expressed interest, at least in allowing a duplicate to be built, and offered Beachey whatever help he needed. In fact, Walcott had been hoping for just such an opportunity to rehabilitate one of the Smithsonian's most famed and controversial figures. But for reasons that would later become clear, Beachey never followed up, so a few weeks later Curtiss asked on his own. The trustees initially turned him down but by April Walcott had prevailed. Curtiss had the aerodrome and in Charles Walcott, Orville had a new and enduring enemy.

Curtiss worked on the *Langley,* as the machine was now known, for six weeks. In late May, the newly "restored" aerodrome flew 150 feet on Keuka Lake and longer flights were made in the fall. That flight and the longer ones that followed provided fodder for the last, great skirmish in the Curtiss–Wright feud.

Curtiss and his supporters insisted that his effort with the *Langley* was honest and straightforward and that all modifications were made in public and without artifice. The flight at the end of May was achieved with the addition of pontoons, it was true, but that was only because Keuka Lake was the only feasible launching spot and Curtiss wished to avoid the catapult launch that he believed had done in Langley in 1903. Every other piece on the craft was either original or fashioned to be identical to the original. Charles Manly asserted that the motor was the same as the one he had fashioned.

Orville Wright countered that he had a witness who would prove that Curtiss produced a craft that bore only a superficial resemblance to the one that had plunged into the Potomac and almost drowned Charles Manly. Griffith Brewer, a British pioneer balloonist who had met Wilbur Wright at Pau and became one of both brothers' closest friends, had proposed in early 1914 coming once more to America and writing a history of aviation. He was also the Wrights' British lawyer and had often been a guest of the Wright family in Dayton. Orville suggested that Brewer first travel to Hammondsport as a journalist and observe Curtiss's machinations with the *Langley* firsthand.

Brewer arrived after the initial test at the end of May and what he saw confirmed Orville's suspicions. Curtiss had replaced Manly's motor with one of his own; the wings of the aerodrome seemed to differ in every key measurement; the wing structure was reinforced more effectively; the steering mechanism was changed; and Curtiss had installed his own wheel-turning system. The redesigned *Langley* flew, not surprisingly, quite a bit more effectively than the original model.

Brewer informed Orville, who fumed while the Smithsonian trumpeted the "triumph." None too pleased with Orville by then, the trade journals were eager to echo the Smithsonian's praise. *Aeronautics* ran an article under the headline "Original Langley Machine Flies," followed by a detailed description of the new aerodrome, a schematic, and then a glowing tribute to Langley, which included the spurious claims that other pioneers, such as Blériot, had based their designs on his. The implication, obviously, was that the Wright brothers had produced an airplane with some but not all of the features that would enable powered flight. Just to make certain no one missed the point, in its description of the craft *Aeronautics* noted, "No changes have been made in the balance or general design of the machine. It has, however, been equipped with three shallow pontoons to keep it afloat on the water." *The New York Times,* which had been so mocking of Langley's debacle, ran a full-page article on page one of its Sunday magazine on May 31 under the headline "Flies with Langley's Aeroplane and Vindicates Him." Even worse for Orville was the *Times*'s assertion that Langley "established the principles developed so successfully after the inventor's death."

When Orville heard Griffith Brewer's tale of seeming skulduggery two weeks later, he persuaded Brewer to submit his own article to the *Times.* Brewer did so and on June 21 "Langley Flier Tests: Pertinent Questions as to Their Efficacy and Results" ran on page eight of the newspaper. Brewer insisted that Langley's machine was not built strongly enough, was inefficient in lift, had propellers that would not adequately power the craft, had no means of lateral stability, and, if it ever did succeed in becoming airborne, which was extremely doubtful, would have been upset by the smallest gust of wind. Only by essentially remaking the machine was Curtiss successful in getting it to fly.

Brewer's article achieved the desired result and produced a storm of condemnation for Curtiss's methods, although a number of respected publications, such as *Scientific American,* stood by both the methodology and the results. Curtiss added that the modifications to which Brewer referred were only made after the initial successful test and then in full view of both the reporters and aviation experts who had gathered at Hammondsport. The experiment with the *Langley* was to have two phases and each had been approved by Charles Walcott. The first, to determine whether the aerodrome was capable of flight, had been completed before Brewer arrived. The modifications were made for the second phase: to investigate the feasibility of tandem-winged aircraft. To that end, the Langley machine had been altered for maximum efficiency. What Griffith Brewer saw as deceit was simply an incomplete understanding of the facts.

Orville refused to back down; so did Curtiss and Walcott. That dispute, like all disputes between Curtiss and the Wrights, has never been resolved. All that is undeniable is that in flying the *Langley,* Curtiss was motivated by more than scientific curiosity, and in defending the Wrights, Brewer had never shown himself to be an objective judge.* The most tangible upshot was Orville's response to Walcott's perceived treachery: He initiated a feud with the Smithsonian that lasted thirty years.

While remaking Langley's aerodrome, Curtiss did not pause in his development of the transatlantic flying boat, now christened the *America.* He obtained two pilots: a British lieutenant named John Cyril Porte and a navy flyer named John Towers, who had worked with him from his first days in San Diego. By summer, the *America* was ready. Takeoff would be from Newfoundland and landfall in Ireland. Navy destroyers would be stationed every one hundred miles along the route. Curtiss estimated the flight could be made sometime in August, or September at the latest.

The overall effect of the *America* and the *Langley* was to keep Curtiss and his innovative aircraft in the headlines while the only noteworthy event for the Wright Company was the withdrawal of the C after yet another army flyer met his death, in February 1914. Orville continued to blame pilot error but the army's board of investigation concluded what everyone but Orville had known all along: The design of the C was flawed, which no automatic stabilizer would change, and the machine was a death trap.

That Curtiss was increasingly seen as not only an innovator but the true father of American aviation did not increase the Wright Com-

* Brewer also explained away the death of Charles Rolls, the cofounder of Rolls-Royce, in a French-built Wright Flyer in Britain in 1910 by asserting that the machine crashed because the tail frame, which broke off, had not been built to Wright standards. In fact, Rolls had been attempting a "daring maneuver," a dive and twist, which strained the Wright design and would later cause difficulties for Wright exhibition flyers.

pany's popularity. Prospects were so poor, even with the court ruling, that Grover Loening quit after just one year to seek his fortunes elsewhere.

Moreover, Orville was showing signs of wearing down; Curtiss was not. He pressed on with his counterattack. For his final gambit, he was aided by a man who had mounted quite an effective counterattack of his own.

In 1911, Henry Ford had finally prevailed over George Selden and John R. Hazel. With only one year to run on the Selden patent, a federal appeals court ruled that Selden's patent was invalid as it relied on the Brayton engine, state of the art when Selden first filed in 1876 but hopelessly primitive by the time the patent was granted in 1895. It had never been used to construct a motorcar.

Ford was now both very rich and very committed to seeing that the patent laws were not used to stifle innovation. It is uncertain when he and Curtiss first met, but there is a photograph of them together taken in Hammondsport in 1913. At some point he clearly offered to help Curtiss find a means to end-run Judge Hazel's decision. After the appeals court ruling, Curtiss took Ford up on it.

Curtiss hired Ford's lawyer, W. Benton Crisp, a former judge who had formulated the strategy that had bested Selden in appeals court. Crisp advised Curtiss not to waste his time appealing to the Supreme Court; the justices rarely accepted patent cases and the appellate ruling left little room to continue the case successfully. Rather, he should exploit the very aspects of the Wright patent that had been successfully used against him. Judge Hazel's opinion had discounted Curtiss's claim that all three parts of his stabilizing apparatus—two ailerons and rudder—were not used in conjunction. But in doing so, Hazel had tacitly admitted that all three *must* be used in conjunction to uphold the Wright patent. Curtiss should design his aircraft so that no question could exist that all three were not employed at the same time.

Curtiss saw immediately how to solve the problem. He installed a locking mechanism that required that the ailerons be used independently; they could not be engaged simultaneously. In fact, this was a distinction without a difference; a pilot alternating between left and right ailerons would produce the same effect as employing them together. But that argument would have to be made in court. Orville was thus left with three choices: He could focus only on damages from previous sales and allow Curtiss to build new machines without a license; he could file suit all over again to prove Curtiss was still infringing; or he could enter into two new, expensive rounds of litigation simultaneously. None of these alternatives was especially palatable.

Orville, by this time the sole stockholder in the Wright Company except for a small percentage owned by Robert Collier, chose the second. Curtiss could not be allowed to manufacture unlicensed airplanes—or any airplanes. In November 1914, the Wright Company filed suit against the Curtiss Aeroplane Company, alleging that "despite earlier decrees and judgments in favor of the Wright Company, the Curtiss Aeroplane Company is continuing to manufacture, use, and sell flying machines which infringe the Wright patent."

The patent wars, it seemed, were not yet over.

CHAPTER 29

The Grip of the Spotlight

In May 1913, Lincoln Beachey announced that he would never fly again. He had been hinting at his retirement for two months but waited to make the formal announcement in an address to the Olympic Club in his hometown of San Francisco.

"You could not make me enter an aeroplane at the point of a revolver," he is reported to have said. "I am done. They call me the Master Birdman, but there was just one thing which drew crowds to my exhibitions—a morbid desire to see something happen. They all predicted that I would be killed and none wanted to miss the sight."[1] Beachey then read off the names of twenty-four flyers who had been killed and said, "Those boys were like brothers to me." His rendition of Mabel Ely's indictment was less damning than in the letter reported elsewhere: "Eugene would be with me now if he had never seen you fly."

Beachey was a sufficiently complex figure that his real motivation is difficult to gauge. Most of those he mentioned as close friends were men he either rarely spoke to or hardly knew. While doubtless an ad hoc fraternity of exhibition flyers had grown up around the daring and danger, Beachey had always been noteworthy for holding himself aloof. But something had prompted him to give up flying, and as later events would make plain, it had not been fear.

In any event, within weeks Beachey's retirement speech had lengthened into a newspaper feature article written under his byline but quite possibly penned by the publicist whom Beachey kept on constant call.

Many of the lines from the speech in San Francisco were repeated. "They call me the Master Birdman, but people come to see me die." He insisted once more he had no fear for himself, only for others.

> In Chicago, the mother of Horace Kearney begged me not to teach him any more of my tricks. Three months later he was dead. Charlie Walsh's wife pleaded with me to have the young flyer cut out my spirals. But he said I was jealous, and that if I did them he must also to get the big money. Two weeks later, while he was in the midst of a dead reverse spiral a little wire snapped and he was dead when they picked him up. So it was with John Frisbie, Rutherford Page, Phil Parmalee, Billy Badger, Eugene Ely, Cal Rodgers, and Cromwell Dixon, all fine boys. Death has left me alone because I was a good servant to him.

Once again, separating fact from exaggeration is impossible. What was more, many of those whom Beachey listed as dying trying to emulate him were victims of either accidents or other causes, like Cal Rodgers's bird strike. But Beachey was undeniably the most reckless and the most popular of the exhibition flyers and his departure cast a pall over the entire enterprise. Curtiss and some of the independents continued to make out, but many flyers found themselves booked into smaller venues for decreased money.

Beachey sought other avenues to exploit his fame. There has been speculation that he went into real estate, but no record exists of any transaction with his name on it. By the summer of 1913, he had found his way into vaudeville. He began as a headliner, playing at such venues as Proctor's Fifth Avenue Theatre in New York, where he would "entertain with views of his many perilous flights and a talk on the profession of flying." But hearing someone talk about risking death is not the same as watching him do it, and Beachey had soon drifted off the top of the bill.

Being in the limelight for so long, Beachey must have chafed at being reduced to a mediocrity. To make matters worse, his cherished American altitude record was surpassed in July, when a previously unknown aviator named Frank Burnside ascended to 12,950 feet. To know for certain is impossible, but it would not be difficult to imagine Beachey searching for an excuse to get back in the air.

A Frenchman named Adolphe Pégoud gave it to him.

Pégoud was among the second generation of French flyers who were taking advantage of the intense interest by both government and manufacturers in expanding the limits of aviation to prepare for the war that seemed more certain with every passing month. In August 1913, Pégoud became the first man to parachute from an airplane in flight, jumping safely from nine hundred feet, a feat whose military application was all too apparent.* The following month, he performed the most elusive feat in aviation, one that many considered impossible.

The one trick Beachey had been unable to do, that no one was able to do, was a loop. In addition to the challenges for the pilot, a loop was thought to put untenable strain on the support structure.† And at the time, airplane motors were fed fuel by gravity and so might stall when upside down. Rotary motors, such as the Gnôme, would in theory solve the stalling problem but still no one could successfully negotiate an aerial somersault without side-slipping or loss of control.

On September 1, 1913, Adolphe Pégoud did. Taking a Blériot XI to three thousand feet, Pégoud tried four times before finally complet-

* Airplanes were so plentiful in France by that time that no one cared at all that Pégoud let the driverless craft crash and be smashed to bits.

† Aviators no longer fell out of aircraft. Seat belts and shoulder restraints had become standard for any sort of serious flying.

ing a successful loop. The following day, before a military board of experts, he duplicated the feat.[2]

News of Pégoud's achievement splashed across the front pages of American newspapers. "Flies Upside Down for Quarter of a Mile," the *New York Times* headline read. Just below: "Experts Say Pégoud's Feat Is Epoch-Making Experiment in Aeronautics." The most significant practical effect of Pégoud's loop was in demonstrating that aircraft had become a good deal more stable and were more solidly constructed than commonly believed. Thus the ability to maneuver, particularly against other aircraft, was heightened. To the public, however, the loop was simply another barrier that had been smashed by those intrepid charioteers of the skies.

Soon after word of Pégoud's achievement reached America, Beachey—still at Proctor's but now described as a "novelty"—was asked what he thought. Beachey replied that he had no doubt he could have performed the trick had he remained in aviation. It took three weeks of giving similar answers before Beachey had had enough. He was off to Hammondsport and there announced his return to flying. He added that Glenn Curtiss had agreed to build him an aircraft strong and powerful enough to match Pégoud's achievement, a 100-horsepower motor on a biplane with only a twenty-five-foot wingspan.

Beachey had a good rationale when asked to justify his return. "In a year, aviation has changed from a dangerous pursuit to a serious business. The development of the flying boat means much to the world; wonderful speed combined with comfort and safety. I believe there is work for me to do that is worth any man's doing." He did admit that "perhaps it is the competitive spirit that is helping to urge me back into the game."[3]

Curtiss set to work and on October 7, Beachey tried out the new design. The test flight was not announced but word got around that Beachey might loop and a large crowd gathered at the open field where he was due to fly near Bath, New York, five miles south of

Hammondsport. Four of the early arrivals were two naval officers and their dates, sisters Ruth and Dorothy Hildreth, daughters of a New York City hotel owner and president of the American Wine Growers Association. To get a better view, the naval officers helped the Hildreth girls onto the roof of a barn, where they perched on the top.

Beachey took off and flew over the barn, dipping his wings to acknowledge the officers' salutes. It was reported later to have been Beachey's first flight since quitting in May but he had often flown Curtiss's hydroplanes from Keuka Lake while in Hammondsport.

The new airplane was powerful and compact but far too heavy to hold a loop. As Beachey flew for a second pass over the barn, the airplane suddenly dipped and one wing clipped the roof. The officers ducked away but despite their efforts to pull the women with them, both were swept off. Ruth Hildreth was killed instantly when her head struck the sharp corner of an automobile parked below; Dorothy Hildreth suffered fractures of an arm and a leg and her chest was crushed. She survived but carried the wounds for the rest of her life. Beachey flew into the nearby woods and crashed but miraculously walked away from the wreck with only minor bruises. He was distraught and checked himself in to a hospital more to deal with emotional distress than with physical injuries. It was first reported that Beachey claimed his foot slipped on a lever but subsequent accounts had him encountering a sudden downdraft, which the weight of the aircraft did not allow him to overcome. While he was flying, a thief broke in to Mrs. Mott's rooming house and robbed him of six thousand dollars.

Beachey was fully exonerated by a coroner's jury but he was badly shaken and once again contemplated retirement. But letters both from other aviators and ordinary Americans poured in from across the nation urging him not to again give up flying. He likely would not have in any case. Because of Beachey's reputation, no one suggested Curtiss had designed a flawed aircraft. He set to fixing the defects in the machine and five weeks later, on November 18, Beachey performed America's first loop at North Island and within two months he had not only set a record with seven, but had added a corkscrew twist—the controlled tailspin—that no other flyer could master. By the time the appeals court had ruled for the Wright Company in January 1914, Beachey had again been acknowledged as the world's greatest flyer and this time nothing was going to deter him from continuing to occupy that mountaintop.

After the decision Beachey remained a Curtiss loyalist only briefly. Soon after his request to the Smithsonian to rehabilitate the Langley aerodrome, Beachey began to distance himself. In February, when Lieutenant Henry Post was killed because a wing on his Wright C crumpled, Beachey was lacerating in his criticism but directed his wrath at the government for using "old equipment" that would "probably be patched up with a few new wires and some cloth," not at the Wright Company for selling the army a machine that could not be flown safely.

In March, Beachey broke with Curtiss entirely. He announced that from then on he would fly machines that he built himself, and then he sailed for Europe to purchase two motors and study the newest designs in aircraft. One design that would intrigue him was the speedy new Morane–Saulnier monoplane, which Roland Garros was flying to great acclaim in exhibitions.

Before he left, he became the first exhibition flyer to apply for a Wright license. "I was astonished at the liberality of Orville Wright," he said as he embarked on the *Carmania*. "I was offered the very reasonable terms of $25 per day royalty for exhibition flights where admission fees are charged and $1,000 for each machine I build. The control of the situation by the Wrights means the end of the old hoodoo days of high death rates and an abundant crop of accident stories."[4] In fact, given the performance of the Wright C, it would likely mean just the opposite.

During the same interview, Beachey expressed skepticism about Curtiss's transatlantic flight. "I am really sorry to see schemes flaunted before the public that are on their face absurd and impossible." Orville could not have said it better. Curtiss, who once again exhibited stunning social tone-deafness, replied in a letter to Beachey that he must have been misquoted, because "I cannot think of any reason why you should 'knock' our transatlantic scheme."[5]

When Beachey returned from Europe at the end of April, he was more popular than ever. For the remainder of the year, he toured the nation, visiting cities and towns, regularly playing to crowds of fifty thousand or more. He flew his own Gnôme-powered biplane with BEACHEY painted across the top of the wings, readily visible to spectators when he flew upside down or in a loop. But he also introduced tricks such as the "tail slide," where he cut his engine and actually descended one thousand feet *backward* before starting it up and heading forward again. At New York's Brighton Beach, during a race with Barney Oldfield, Beachey "turned somersaults, dropped thousands of feet, flew upside down, and floundered about in the clear air until the spectators were dizzy."[6] He flew inside loops, outside loops, added spirals, corkscrews, and rolls. Unlike before his retirement, he had no challengers; no one thought to emulate Beachey's preternatural control of an invention only ten years old. For the remainder of 1914, it is quite possible that Lincoln Beachey did the finest flying the world has ever seen.

But as great as Beachey's show was, it wasn't the only one. By June it appeared that Curtiss's *America* was not an absurd notion at all but was actually prepared to undertake the transatlantic flight.

The craft itself was a stunning feat of engineering, with a span of 72 feet on the top wing and 46 on the bottom, a total of 500 square feet of wing surface. Front to back, the *America* was 32 feet, fashioned of white cedar, and weighed 2½ tons, 690 pounds of which were two 100-horsepower engines fed by tanks that could hold 1,500 gallons of fuel. A third motor was added in July for added lift. The hull contained four watertight compartments and the skin was varnished Japanese silk painted brilliant red to be visible at sea. A foot pedal operated the ailerons, which were fitted with the locking device to ensure that they operated upward only, another way to circumvent the Wright patent.

The *America* was christened at Hammondsport on June 22 with a bottle of champagne that for a time refused to break, and a successful

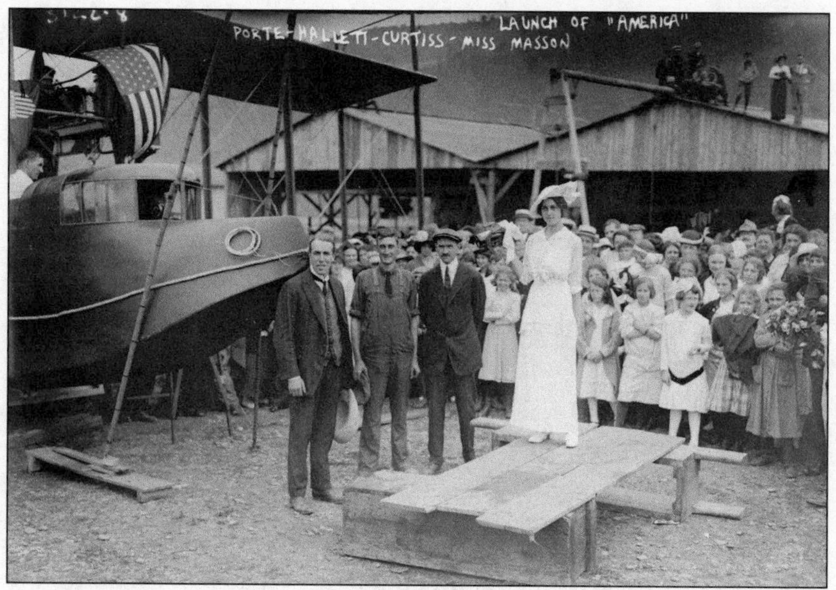

John Cyril Porte, George Hallett, Glenn Curtiss, and Katherine Masson at the launch of America.

test was run the next day. Tests continued through July, and although many bugs were found and many refinements were made, the basic design seemed sound. Lieutenant Porte pronounced the *America* the "finest flying craft I ever sat in" and both Curtiss and Rodman Wanamaker expressed confidence in a successful outcome.

Beachey remained critical. In June, while in the hospital after a crash in Hartford, Connecticut, caused by a stall in the Gnôme, "propped up on pillows," he expressed his doubts. "I came over on the *Lusitania* with Porte and he didn't seem very enthusiastic about the flight. . . . It looks like a risky business to me. Lieutenant Porte should be training for the dash. He should be taking short trips every day. It will be a great strain on him and his assistant to run the engine for twenty-four hours." Beachey added that by flying the Langley aerodrome, Curtiss had not improved his chances of overturning the Wright patent victory.[7]

In July, with the *America* in the final stages of preparedness, a group of aviation experts, including Beachey, Charles Manly, Grover Loening, Elmer Sperry, Thomas Baldwin, and Robert Peary, were asked if they thought the flying boat would make it. Beachey reiterated that transatlantic air travel remained "unfeasible," but Elmer Sperry thought the flight might well be a success, as did, of all people, Grover Loening. Alan Hawley, president of the Aero Club, was certain that if the *America* didn't succeed, the next Curtiss machine would. Peary agreed. Baldwin rated the chances at even money, and Manly thought only "bad luck" would cause a failure. Conspicuous by his absence among the luminaries was Orville Wright.[8]

But in August 1914, when the flight had been scheduled, Europe was no longer concerned with breaking distance records. John Cyril Porte had been mobilized, as had many of the flyers who had stunned the world in exhibitions. Many would not survive. The question of whether Glenn Curtiss had built an aircraft capable of spanning the Atlantic, along with the plans of millions of others, would have to be postponed.

CHAPTER 30

The Death of Innocence

Initially, the war in Europe had remarkably little impact on American aviation. Although it was apparent from the early days of the fighting that airplanes would play a key role in reconnaissance and even in combat, there was only a faint stir in Congress to increase appropriations. The general sentiment was that fortress America need not worry about a conflict that could never reach American shores.

Between those shores, as giant armies settled into trenches across the Atlantic to begin the greatest war of attrition in history, Orville Wright continued his quixotic pursuit of final victory in court, Glenn Curtiss continued to experiment and innovate, and Lincoln Beachey continued his grand tour of America. In San Francisco, plans for a world's fair beginning in February 1915 continued even though much of the world would not be able to attend.

The city had begun preparations for the event, fortuitously dubbed the "Panama–Pacific International Exposition," in 1911, only five years removed from the great earthquake, when President Taft had proclaimed San Francisco the host for a celebration of the completion of the Panama Canal and the four hundredth anniversary of the discovery of the Pacific Ocean. The exposition was considered vital to the city's rebirth and the organizers spared no expense in creating the most opulent, irresistible event of its kind in history.

The Panama–Pacific would occupy 635 acres and be filled with enough modern marvels to leave even the most sophisticated adult goggle-eyed. At the east end of the grounds was "the Zone," sixty-five acres filled with rides, games, food from around the world, concessions, performers, and exhibits, including replicas of Yellowstone Park and the Grand Canyon—to scale, of course—and a five-acre working model of the Panama Canal. The actual Liberty Bell was on display, on loan from Philadelphia, and the news of the day was churned out automatically on an immense Underwood typewriter. States, counties, and industrial firms exhibited their wares and their wonders. There was a "Street of Fun," hula dancers, midgets, a railway, a submarine ride, and a compartment on a swing arm that sent those inside swinging to and fro over the grounds.

At the Palace of Transportation, the Ford Motor Company would set up an assembly line that turned out an automobile every ten minutes for three hours every afternoon except Sunday. More than four thousand cars would be produced during the fair's ten months. A wood and steel building called the Palace of Machinery was more than three hundred yards long, one hundred yards wide, and forty yards high. The entire complement of United States army and navy personnel could have stood at attention under its roof. Mabel Normand and Roscoe "Fatty" Arbuckle, two major stars of the silent screen, would be filmed touring the fair by the Keystone Film Company.

The effect on visitors would be electric, literally as well as figuratively. The General Electric Illuminating Engineering Laboratory was engaged to put on perhaps the greatest display of lighting ever seen. William D'Arcy Ryan, the director, who had previously lit Niagara Falls to a brilliance of 1,115,000,000 candles, would outdo himself in San Francisco. One historian later wrote, "When he presented his plans before the architects, designers, and color artists who were involved in preparation for the Exposition, his proposals seemed so fantastic that there was scarcely a detail which was not opposed." The centerpiece of Ryan's plan was a forty-three-story "Tower of Jewels," which would be decorated with more than one hundred thousand pieces of polished stained-glass "novogems," imported from Vienna, strung on wires, each backed by a tiny mirror. Twenty colored spotlights, hidden from spectators' view, would illuminate the tower each night. Edwin Markham, a local poet, would announce after seeing the General Electric display, "I have tonight seen the greatest revelation of beauty that was ever seen on the earth."

No event of this kind, the organizers knew, would be complete without an air show. In the spirit of the event, the organizers wanted something bigger and more astounding than any air meet ever held and struck on the idea of a round-the-world race to be held under the fair's auspices. An international commission would be appointed, with representatives from Britain, France, Germany, Russia, Japan, and British Columbia. First in line to express interest in participating was native son Lincoln Beachey, who was never asked how he could fly around the world without crossing the unfeasible Atlantic. To give potential customers a sense of what might be to come, in January 1914 Beachey flew through the entrance of the unfinished Palace of Machinery, circled, and then flew out again, the first and only indoor flight in history. "All I yearn for now is to fly underground," he said afterward.[1]

The coming of war put an end to the round-the-world race; the next idea was for a race across the country, but that could not be arranged, either. Finally, the organizers settled on a spectacular air show, which Beachey eagerly agreed to headline. In addition to watching Beachey's aerobatics, for fifty cents a fair visitor would be able to ride in a tractor biplane, sitting behind the propeller while the pilot soared, dipped, and banked over the Pacific Ocean.

In the meantime, Beachey continued his spectacular run. In late September, "solely to impress Washington with the possibilities of flight," Beachey gave a stunning exhibition over the capital that was witnessed by President Woodrow Wilson and many members of Congress.

Curtiss's *America,* now again called simply the H-1, was not totally abandoned with the coming of war. At Porte's behest, the British navy purchased both models of the H-1 and eventually employed them with great success in submarine detection. The design became standard and is credited with sparking the development of the British flying-boat industry.

The emigration of the *America* to Britain did not decrease Orville's interest. On January 5, 1915, he wrote to Griffith Brewer and asked him to check on rumors that the flying boat's ailerons were actually being operated in violation of the court's edict. "I have been told (but cannot remember who told me) that the *America,* while at Hammondsport, had all of the cables and pulleys necessary to operate the ailerons simultaneously and in opposite directions as they were used in earlier Curtiss machines, but the cables to the underside of the flaps were disconnected." Orville asked Brewer to try to see the craft for himself and inspect it to check the cable work. Brewer replied "that it would be impossible to obtain the information as to the construction and arrangement of the two machines sold to the British Navy, because owing to the state of war and to the machines being owned by the War Department, the mere enquiry as to the construction of the machines owned by the government might be regarded as a criminal act."

Orville pressed on, giving depositions and writing the occasional article, but more and more he slipped into the background as the industry moved forward in the face of the European war. The Wright Company's advertisements in trade journals shrunk to a quarter page, were buried in the interior, and sported bland, understated copy. The text of one simply explained that "the new Wright aeroplanes . . . now embody the improvements that have been suggested by the experiments quietly conducted during the past ten years."[2] Curtiss's ads, in contrast, were full-page, in large font, and were often on the cover or just inside.

The war took an immediate toll on aviators who just months before had flown together as friends. Roland Garros was reported killed when he flew "headfirst into a German airship." The report would prove false, but Garros would die in 1918, shot down just one month before the war ended. Adolphe Pégoud would die in combat as well, killed by a former student who afterward flew over the French lines and dropped a wreath.

The Wright Company had no machine capable of impacting the war in the skies but in September 1914, Curtiss introduced his "Model J" tractor biplane, the forerunner of JN-4, the "Jenny," one of the most successful airplanes in history.*

One year earlier, on the same European trip that he had first met John Porte, Curtiss had visited Tom Sopwith's factory. The two shared a mutual antipathy of the Wrights and both had been flyers who had turned to design and manufacture. Sopwith was building tractors, which would soon be the only design the army would accept. Curtiss and Sopwith exchanged ideas and Curtiss, with Sopwith's blessing, hired B. Douglas Thomas to join his company as a designer. Unlike either of the Wrights, Curtiss understood that he could not be his company's sole designer in perpetuity.

Thomas designed both the J and its more powerful cousin, the N. Curtiss took the best features of each and designed the "JN," the fourth incarnation of which was the Jenny, which was rolled out in 1916. From the first, the Jenny series was used almost exclusively as a trainer and was the airplane in which 95 percent of American pilots in the war years learned to fly.

But in early 1915, Americans remained blissfully ignorant that its native sons would ever need to fly in anger in Europe's war, and as the moment approached for the opening of the Panama–Pacific Exposition, millions planned to visit the fair's wonders. On February 20, President Wilson threw a switch in Washington, D.C., and the fair

* The Jenny was featured on the nation's first air mail stamp, issued in May 1918, which depicted an indigo airplane amid a red background and cost twenty-four cents. The "inverted Jenny," in which the image of the airplane was mistakenly printed upside down on only one sheet, is among the world's rarest stamps and is valued at approximately $1 million. A block of four, still attached, sold at auction in 2005 for $3 million.

Amy Beachey atop the Tower of Jewels, watching her son fly.

was officially under way. Beachey flew over the midway, causing the entire throng of opening-day visitors to crane their necks to watch. Four days later, Beachey performed his thousandth loop, as well as "two entirely new and death defying stunts," while his mother watched 435 feet up at the top of the Tower of Jewels. She "cried out only once," when Beachey wrote "1000" a mile up in the sky.

With all the stunning exhibits, Beachey remained the unquestioned star of the fair. It became almost impossible for him to outdo himself. On March 14, he decided to try. Fifty thousand people crammed into the grandstand or jostled for position along the railing. As many as two hundred thousand more crowded along the bay front outside the fairgrounds. They had come to see Beachey for the first time attempt the Dip of Death in a monoplane.

Beachey had used the Morane–Saulnier design, powered with an 80-horsepower Gnôme motor that would allow the airplane to reach 100 miles per hour. To make the machine light and strong, he used aluminum in the body and wings, and instead of struts, Beachey's airfoils would be braced by a series of support wires from the top and bottom of the fuselage to the wing surface.

Beachey made three flights that March 14. The first ended prematurely when he had to land and retune the engine. In the second, according to a correspondent for *Aeronautics,* "He shot straight up into the air, climbing to about 5,000 feet before leveling off. He made a trip over San Francisco, then turned around and crossed the bay to Sausalito, after which he made three or four excellent loops, and glided down to the Grounds at a slow angle and landed safely. The monoplane was a beautiful sight in the air, having graceful lines, and very fast." Thirty minutes later, "Beachey went up approximately 4,000 feet, made several loops, and then circled up until he had gained approximately 5,000 or 6,000 feet altitude, made another loop and then started for the ground perpendicularly."[3]

The dive was perfect. But while aluminum's weight-to-strength ratio is greater than steel in withstanding pressure, it is also highly ductile, which means it folds easily. "When Beachey started to level out, approximately 500 feet from the ground, one wing simply folded straight back and exploded like a prefire of the motor. It was not long before the other did the same thing." Helpless, Beachey plunged into San Francisco Bay.

Although he hit the water at high speed, Beachey did not die from the impact or even lose consciousness. He had broken his leg in the crash but was otherwise unhurt. As he sunk into forty feet of water, he clawed desperately at his harness and the tangle of cables and detritus. While Beachey tried to free himself from the wreckage so that he could float to the surface, divers were dispatched from waiting ships. They attempted frantically to locate the plane in the murky waters and attach a grappling hook. But the fuselage was only brought to the surface forty minutes later. In the end, the greatest aviator America has ever seen died of drowning.

Beachey's death in March 1915 marked the end of the exhibition era. Europe was at war and the taste for watching pilots die performing stunts seemed to fade in America, when so many young men were dying for more important reasons across the Atlantic.

That same year saw the end of the participation of the Wright brothers in the advancement of powered flight. In October, after months of negotiation, Orville Wright left the industry he and his brother had been so responsible for creating. He sold his holdings in the Wright Company, including its patents, to a consortium of Wall Street investors. He was titularly retained as "chief aeronautical engineer" at $25,000 per year, but he had in fact retired. With Orville no longer an executive of the Wright Company, changes were made. When the Wright Model K hydroplane and the Model L military scout were introduced in late 1915, stability was achieved by ailerons, not wing warping.

EPILOGUE

Orville made a great deal of money on the sale—an estimated $1.5 million—and, financially secure, he immediately created friction with the new owners by doing little to earn his $25,000 annual fee. The arrangement was soon terminated.

The new Wright Company fared poorly. The K and L models were failures and just one year after the sale, the company merged with Glenn Martin and the Simplex Automobile Company. The merged Wright–Martin Company did not last long; Glenn Martin left in 1917 to once again start up his own company and the remaining entity was reorganized as the Wright Aeronautical Company in 1919.

Orville's departure effectively ended the patent wars. Although the litigation continued, it was largely of its own momentum and bore little resemblance to the ferocious legal wrangling of previous years. Even the formality of a lawsuit vanished with America's entry into the war in 1917. To ensure that the very best American airplanes were available for the war effort, a board was created, headed by W. Benton Crisp, to draft a cross-licensing arrangement that would allow any manufacturer to use any patented process for a modest fixed fee. But the battle between the Wrights and Curtiss had taken its toll. Not a single American airplane design was deemed worthy to be adapted to combat flying. Only after the war was done and Europe was decimated did American aviation once again attain a prominent place in world markets.

Orville set up a workshop in Dayton and tinkered. He came up with a few workable ideas, such as the split flap, but never again would Orville Wright be in the news as anything other than an elder statesman. He did lend his name to the Dayton–Wright Company, a concern established by close Ohio friends to produce airplanes during the war. But they had no designs so resorted to copying the de Havilland 4 from Britain. The American version was so poorly made that it earned the nickname "flaming coffin."[1]

Orville had never been comfortable in the public eye—be it Wilbur or Curtiss, he seemed always to feel unfavorably compared with someone—and so he began a retreat into reclusiveness. The exception was his perpetuation of the feud with the Smithsonian. Charles Walcott had escalated the dispute by ordering the Langley aerodrome restored to its original design and then exhibited with a plaque that read "The first man-carrying aeroplane in the history of the world capable of sustained free flight." Orville stewed until 1925 and then announced that he would send the 1903 Flyer, fully restored, to the Science Museum in London. Walcott died in 1927 with the Flyer still on this side of the Atlantic but the new secretary, astrophysicist Charles Abbott, a former Langley assistant, offered only to modify the language on the aerodrome exhibit, not eliminate it. The following year, after completing most of the restoration himself, Orville did precisely what he had threatened to do and the 1903 Wright Flyer became a centerpiece of the London museum. And there it would remain until the Second World War had ended and Orville Wright was dead.*

Although he was often asked to comment on the progress of avia-

* During the war the Flyer was stored in a secret underground vault outside London along with many treasures of the British Empire.

tion or trotted out to appear with other luminaries, Orville, bitter and vengeful, continued to withdraw into himself. His longtime secretary, Mabel Beck, zealously and jealously guarded his isolation. Beck was almost universally disliked, including by Wright family members. Orville's niece Ivonette said, "She felt the power of her position and seemed to want to alienate everyone from Orville in order to have his full attention."[2] But Orville needed little help; his animus, even to those closest to him, grew to extraordinary proportions. When beloved Katharine, with whom he had been inseparable for three decades, finally decided to marry in 1926, he accused her of disloyalty, of abandoning him, and refused to attend her wedding. When Katharine lay dying three years later, he had to be dragged by his brother Lorin to her bedside.[3]

Katharine's death seemed to cut Orville's last link to society. In 1930, a writer for *The New Yorker* came to Dayton for an interview. "He found 'a gray man . . . dressed in gray clothes. Not only have his hair and his mustache taken on that tone, but [also] his curiously flat face . . . a timid man whose misery at meeting you is so keen that, in common decency, you leave as soon as you can.'"[4]

Orville continued to meander between his home and his workshop for the better part of two decades. He was awarded multiple honors and admitted to a variety of associations but was mostly only a face in a photograph. He suffered a heart attack, his second, on January 27, 1948, as he was entering his office in Dayton. He died three days later and was buried in the family plot at Woodland Cemetery. There are three graves in his row: Orville is on one side, Wilbur on the other, and Katharine is between them.

For all his achievements and notoriety, it is difficult to view Orville Wright as anything but a sad and lonely man who never found his calling—and perhaps never even sought it—and who died without ever making one genuine friend.

The war was a boon to Curtiss, even before America's entry spurred the cross-license patent pool. Orders came in from Great Britain in such volume that the War Office advanced him $600,000 against future deliveries, funds with which Curtiss opened a second factory in Buffalo. In 1916, he took in a group of financiers, as had the Wrights six years earlier, but Curtiss's partners were not at cross-purposes with the man they had bought out. The two factories hummed along, turning out trainers and hydroplanes, more than 10,000 before the war's end. When the *Lusitania* was sunk, Congress, so pecuniary to that point, suddenly appropriated $640 million for aviation. With part of that appropriation, the navy commissioned Curtiss to design and build a long-range flying boat that could traverse the Atlantic and then carry sufficient ordnance to fly missions against German U-boats. Opinion in Britain and France was that such an aircraft could not be built, but Curtiss had no doubts. He submitted two plans, one for a three-engine craft and another for five. Both airplanes would be huge—the cable-braced tail section alone (a Curtiss innovation) was twice the size of a single-seat airplane. Eventually the three-engine design was chosen and, instead of producing the entire craft under its direct supervision, the navy gave Curtiss full control. The craft was designated the "Navy-Curtiss (NC)-1."

Curtiss came up with the initial design but by this time he employed an entire engineering department to put his ideas to paper and test them out. Former Curtiss pupil Holden Richardson, who had risen to commander and was a senior officer in naval aviation, had as much to do with the finished product as Curtiss himself. Components were fabricated at various locations and assembled at another new Curtiss facility in Garden City, New York. During its first test flight in September 1918, the NC-1 rose from the water off Rockaway Beach with five passengers. It would eventually carry as many as fifty-one. But then the war ended and the contract was canceled.

Largely at the behest of Assistant Secretary of the Navy Franklin D. Roosevelt, the project was revived. Lord Northcliffe had also renewed his £10,000 prize. On May 16, 1919, three flying boats took off from Newfoundland bound for the Azores: the NC-1, and two improved models, the NC-3, and NC-4.[5] The plan was to refuel, then continue on to Lisbon and then to Plymouth. The four-engine NC-4 made it, the other two did not. Both went down in heavy fog two hundred miles from their destination. The NC-1 sank but its crew was rescued by a passing Greek freighter. The commander of the NC-3, former Curtiss student John Towers, rigged a mast and sail to the craft—it really was a "flying boat"—and sailed it to the Azores. The NC-4 landed in Lisbon on May 27 and in Plymouth four days later, the first aircraft to fly across the Atlantic Ocean. But the accolades were short-lived. Two weeks later, Royal Naval Air Force pilots John Alcock and Arthur Brown flew from Newfoundland to Ireland in sixteen hours to claim both the honor and £10,000 for completing the first nonstop flight across the Atlantic.

The NC-4 was Curtiss's finale in aviation. The following year, he liquidated his interests and then retired and moved to Florida, leaving behind an extraordinary record. The list of his inventions and achievements is immense and includes the seaplane, retractable landing gear, twist-grip throttles for motorcycles, dual controls, the enclosed cockpit, tricycle landing gear, the step pontoon, the watertight compartment, the airboat, and a number of machines to manufacture airplane components. He created the first civilian flying school and the first military flying school, conducted both the first simulated bombing run and first use of firearms from an aircraft, and delivered the first radio communication from the skies.

The Wright–Curtiss feud persists to the present day as a proxy war—historians of early flight tend to deify one and demonize the other. Either the Wrights were brilliant visionaries and honest toilers attempting to ward off the incursions of those, particularly Curtiss, who stole their ideas and even perhaps improved on them, but refused to acknowledge their debt in word or banknote; or Wilbur and Orville were rapacious misanthropes who were all too happy to stop progress in its tracks by stifling brilliant innovators, particularly Curtiss, all to stuff their pockets with more money than they could spend in ten lifetimes.

Both descriptions contain grains of truth but each is mostly beside the point. Whether Curtiss would have discovered the secrets of flight if he had not journeyed to Dayton in September 1906 is also not relevant to the larger issue. Curtiss may not have been an intuitive genius but he was an inveterate innovator; he may have been incapable of a great breakthrough, but he would constantly improve any resultant product. Wilbur Wright was a visionary architect, but Glenn Curtiss was a master builder. One can dispute who was more vital but progress unquestionably demands both. By attempting to neuter Curtiss, even if their accusations were correct, the Wrights stifled the development of American aviation.

That is, of course, the irony of the patent system. Without patent protection, a competitor can simply replicate an invention and undercut the inventor's price—which necessarily includes all the time and expense of research and development—so the incentive to experiment and create will be severely inhibited. But if innovators such as Glenn Curtiss cannot build on the progress of others without paying exorbitantly for the privilege, the incentive to continue to experiment and create is similarly inhibited. Finding the proper balance remains difficult. Although pioneer patents have passed from jurisprudence, the patent system remains as difficult to administer as it was in the Wrights' time as the plethora of suits among Internet providers and device makers will attest.

Curtiss did not arrive in Florida as the stereotypical retiree. He almost immediately purchased 220,000 acres in Dade County and formed a syndicate that developed the cities of Hialeah, including the racetrack, Miami Springs, and Opa-Locka, intended as a planned community with Arabian Nights architecture. The current Miami International Airport was begun during that period as Curtiss Field.

In 1918, however, a failure to tie up loose ends almost a decade earlier left Curtiss vulnerable to another of his enemies and that vulnerability was quickly exploited. Augustus Herring arose once more from aviation's scrap heap to claim that the dissolution of Herring–

Curtiss had been the result of a deceitful act by Curtiss against his innocent and well-meaning partner. Curtiss, it seems, had neglected to have his old company legally dissolved after the bankruptcy. Herring called a stockholders' meeting at which he was the only stockholder present and then resurrected the company, at least on paper, with him as president and a board of directors of cronies. The company then refiled Herring's previous suit against Curtiss and the other original board members on the grounds that they had connived to cheat Herring out of his stock after obtaining his designs and ideas, and then used those designs and ideas to make a good deal of money. That there had been no designs or ideas was once again omitted from Herring's brief.

The trial took five years to come to a verdict and it was in Curtiss's favor. Curtiss, by then busily developing land in Florida, thought that would be the end of it, but Herring was nothing if not persevering. He appealed, but in 1926, while the appeal was pending, Herring suffered a series of strokes and died. His heirs, however, demonstrated that they were equally persevering and pressed the claim on their father's behalf. And incredibly, they were successful. In 1928, an appeals court judge in Buffalo ruled that Curtiss had committed "malfeasance and misfeasance" in cheating Herring out of royalties. Curtiss vowed to continue to fight. He didn't have much use for the Wrights, but he loathed Herring.

In July 1930, Curtiss was once more called to Buffalo, due to testify in an appeal of the verdict, when he was struck with appendicitis while visiting Hammondsport. Surgery was performed on July 11 in Buffalo and for two weeks, Curtiss's convalescence was excellent. But on July 23, he unexpectedly lapsed into a coma and the next day he was dead at age fifty-two of a pulmonary embolism.

Herring's heirs pressed on and in the end, the greatest fabulist in aviation history won out. With both principals dead, the Curtiss estate settled with the Herring estate for an estimated $500,000.[6]

Curtiss might have been spared watching his money being handed over to the Herring family, but he was very much alive in June 1929 to see the Wright Aeronautical Company merge with the Curtiss Aeroplane and Motor Company to form Curtiss-Wright, the largest aviation holding company in America, with assets of more than $70 million. Seven companies affiliated with Curtiss and two with Wright were included in the deal. Neither the Wright nor Curtiss families participated in the transaction beyond lending their names to the new corporation.* Nonetheless, the industry that the Wrights and Curtiss begat has become one of the most successful in history. In commercial aviation alone, thousands of aircraft carry millions of passengers billions of miles each year.

As the saga of early flight becomes more distant, it gains rather than loses fascination. Air travel is now so commonplace, has been so widely experienced, that those who risked their lives every time they took an airplane aloft, who flew in open aircraft totally exposed to the elements and without seat restraints, who took their machines to great heights in freezing cold or in pelting rain, who died and watched their friends die pushing up against the limits of performance, have become almost mythical figures. They were that, of course, but they were also simply young and eager men and women embracing a new technology with the breathless zeal of youth. The fear of death would dissuade them no more than it did the first climber to summit Everest without extra oxygen or the first diver to swim among sharks without a cage.

But every bit as poignant as the deaths of the many men and women who braved those early airplanes and perished in spectacular fashion is the tragic enigma that was Wilbur Wright. Wilbur seemed as determined to hurtle to his own destruction as Ely or Beachey or Cal Rodgers. But where Beachey, Ely, and Rodgers died doing what they loved, Wilbur died doing something he hated.

He was driven forward to pursue his aspirations to monopoly with almost religious zeal, and therein perhaps lies a hint to the apparent contradiction between Wilbur's unflagging insistence that he and Or-

* Curtiss-Wright remains in business and is traded on the New York Stock Exchange.

ville toiled only for the betterment of humanity and the Wrights' obssessive focus on profiteering.

In St. Louis to visit the 1904 exposition at which Roy Knabenshue piloted the *California Arrow* to glory if not to riches was a forty-year-old German intellectual named Max Weber. Well thought of in Germany but virtually unknown in America, Weber was to become a titan, brilliant in every discipline, a transcendent philosopher who would blur the lines between sociology, economics, and political theory and be credited as one of the founders of what today is called "social science." During his stay in St. Louis, he was working on a series of essays that would be published the following year in German and become his most famous work, *Die Protestantische Ethik und der Geist des Kapitalismus*—or, *The Protestant Ethic and the Spirit of Capitalism.*

Weber's essential thesis was that "ascetic Protestantism," with its emphasis on the notion that hard work was an activity ordained by God, supported the belief that the manifestation of the fruits of hard work—profit—was indicative of maximum piety. Lest Weber be misunderstood, he emphasized that there was a distinction between financial success as an indication of godliness and simple greed, that amassing money for its own sake has nothing to do with either religion or capitalism. But genuine hard work for profit was seen by the righteous Protestant as a calling for those who sought to please God by their adherence to His dictates and those who would frustrate such an ambition were evil and sinful.

Weber's construct inspired immense controversy when it was published and continues to do so today but *Protestant Ethic* has nonetheless been as influential as anything ever written in the social sciences short of Marx's *Kapital* and Tocqueville's *Democracy in America.*

While Protestant capitalists did not go about waving copies of Weber's essay in the pursuit of wealth—it wasn't even translated into English until 1930—the essential argument does seem suited to the Wrights, particularly Wilbur, who brought an ecclesiastical view of human affairs to his forays into both science and business. It was an ethos ideally suited to the former and stunningly unsuited to the latter, and explains Wilbur's rigidity and his strict delineations between good and evil. That Wilbur believed he was doing God's work and toiling for the betterment of humanity by pursuing monopoly wealth seems congruent to both his public behavior and his private correspondence, particularly his insistence that he had little use for personal gain.

Whatever the explanation, the demons that caused Wilbur Wright to abandon science, to eschew innovation, to embark on a hopeless crusade to vanquish foes both real and imagined, robbed him of decades of his life and America and the world of one of its exceptional intellects. That the tragedy of Wilbur's fall was self-generated makes the irony only that much more cruel.

NOTES

All letters except those noted are from the Wilbur and Orville Wright Papers, Manuscript Division, Library of Congress.

Abbreviations are as follows:

Aeronautics—*Aeronautics* Magazine
AF—Andrew Freedman
Aircraft—*Aircraft* Magazine
GHC—Glenn Hammond Curtiss
HAT—Harry A. Toulmin
KW—Katharine Wright
MW—Milton Wright
NYT—*New York Times*
OC—Octave Chanute
OW—Orville Wright
WW—Wilbur Wright

CHAPTER 1. FULCRUM

1. Quoted in John D. Anderson, Jr., *A History of Aerodynamics and Its Impact on Flying Machines* (New York: Cambridge University Press, 1999), p. 6.
2. Chanute's biography is taken from a memorial article in the *Transactions of the American Society of Civil Engineers* 74 (December 1911), pp. 483–89.
3. Mouillard to Chanute, January 5, 1896, http://invention.psychology.msstate.edu/inventors/i/Chanute/library/Chanute_Mouillard/Chanute-Mouillard.html.

CHAPTER 2. HIGHWAY IN THE SKY

1. The most complete treatment of Herring's early life and his role in aeronautics before 1900 is in Tom D. Crouch, *A Dream of Wings* (New York: Norton, 1981).

2. Quoted in ibid., p. 147.
3. *Chicago Daily Tribune,* May 13, 1896, p. 2.

CHAPTER 3. MEN IN THE DUNES

1. Chanute, "Experiments in flying," *McClure's Magazine,* June 15, 1900, pp. 127–33.
2. Chanute, "Recent 'Experiments in Gliding Flight,'" *Aeronautical Annual* 3 (1897), p. 49.
3. Ibid.
4. Crouch, *Dream,* p. 199.
5. *Boston Daily Globe,* September 14, 1896, p. 10. The article did, however, refer to him as "F. T. Herring."
6. *Aeronautical Annual* 3 (1897), p. 53.
7. Crouch, *Dream,* p. 205.
8. *Chicago Times-Herald,* September 8, 1897, p. 2.

CHAPTER 4. TO KITTY HAWK

1. WW to Smithsonian Institution, May 30, 1899.
2. The most comprehensive treatment of the schism, and indeed of all of Wilbur and Orville's early life, is provided by Tom D. Crouch, *The Bishop's Boys* (New York: Norton, 1989).
3. Crouch, *Bishop,* pp. 60, 62.
4. Ibid., pp. 81, 86.
5. Ibid., p. 92.
6. *Aeronautical Annual* 2 (1896), pp. 23–25.
7. WW to OC, May 13, 1900.
8. Crouch, *Bishop,* p. 182.
9. OW to KW, September 26, 1900.
10. OC to WW, November 29, 1900.

CHAPTER 5. SOPHOMORE SLUMP

1. *Journal of the Western Society of Engineers* 2 (1897), p. 27.
2. OW to KW, July 28, 1901. Space constraints prevent the ten-page letter from being reprinted here, but Orville's account of the mosquito wars is hilarious and should be read in its entirety.
3. OW to WW, August 6, 1902.
4. Quoted in Rena Faye Subotnik and Herbert J. Walberg, *The Scientific Basis of Education Productivity* (Washington, D.C.: Information Age, 2006), p. 41.
5. Crouch, *Bishop,* p. 238.

CHAPTER 6. GAS BAG

1. *National Magazine* 28 (July 1908), pp. 457–60. This article, written by Thomas F. Baldwin [*sic*], contains Baldwin's usual combination of fact, hyperbole, and outright fantasy. With all the bluster, however, Baldwin's documented record of innovation and achievement is undeniable and guarantees him the place in aviation history he would have claimed for himself.
2. Gary F. Kurtz, "'Navigating the Upper Strata' and the Quest for Dirigibility," *California History* 58, No. 4 (Winter 1979/1980), pp. 334–47.
3. *Aircraft,* March 1910, p. 23.
4. *The Curtiss Aviation Book* (New York: Frederick A. Stokes, 1912), p. 29. The book was ghostwritten for Curtiss by Augustus Post, who also included some sections under his own name. As with most of the accounts of the period, liberties were often taken with specifics but the basic facts seemed generally accurate.
5. C. R. Roseberry, *Glenn Curtiss: Pioneer of Flight* (Garden City, N.Y.: Doubleday, 1972), p.12.
6. *Curtiss Aviation Book,* pp. 19–20.
7. WW to OC, January 19, 1902.
8. Roy Knabenshue, "Chauffeur of the Skies," quoted in Robert Hedin, *The Zeppelin Reader* (Iowa City: University of Iowa Press, 1998), p. 23.
9. *Albuquerque Evening Citizen,* August 23, 1905, p. 6.
10. Roseberry, *Curtiss,* p. 44.
11. *Los Angeles Herald,* September 27, 1905, p. 1.
12. *NYT,* September 24, 1906, p. 12.
13. *NYT,* June 26, 1907, p. 6.

CHAPTER 7. WHERE NO MAN HAD GONE BEFORE

1. Although Thomas Baldwin also realized that an airship propeller would need a different configuration from that of a ship, he thought air and water had essentially the same properties. And Baldwin never went through anything like the rigorous process to find the optimum specifications that the Wrights undertook.
2. WW to OC, June 6, 1901.
3. Italics added in both quotes. The dispute was never resolved, eventually precipitating anger and wounded feelings on both sides. In any event, this exchange can be seen as the beginning of the change in the relationship between the two men.
4. *NYT,* October 8, 1903, p. 1.
5. *NYT,* October 9, 1903, p. 16.
6. *Washington Times,* October 8, 1903, p. 2. Washington, D.C., newspapers were generally kinder, running the story off the front page.
7. *NYT,* December 9, 1903, p. 1.
8. Quoted in Crouch, *Dream,* p. 292.

CHAPTER 8. PATENT PIONEERING

1. Wilbur's statement: "On the morning of December 17, between 10:30 and noon, four flights were made, two by Orville Wright and two by Wilbur Wright. The starts were all made from a point on the level near our camp in Dare County, North Carolina. The wind at the time of the flights had a velocity of twenty-seven miles an hour. The flight was made directly against the wind. Each time the machine started from the level ground by its own power, with no assistance from gravity or other sources whatever. After a run of about eight inches on the ground it arose from the track, and under the direction of the operator climbed upward on an inclined course till a height eight or ten feet from the ground was reached, after which the course was kept as near horizontal as the wind gusts and the limited skill of the operator would permit. The flyer made its way forward with a speed of ten miles an hour over the ground and of thirty to thirty-five miles an hour through the air. The flight was short. The succeeding flights rapidly increased in length, and at the fourth trial a flight of fifty-nine seconds was made, in which the machine flew a little more than a half mile through the air and a distance of more than 852 feet over the ground. All of the experiments have been conducted at our own expense, without assistance from any individual or institution."
2. WW to OC, January 4, 1904.
3. Wilbur was later quite open about seeking a monopoly on flying machines. It has been suggested that it was Herring's letter that prompted Wilbur and Orville to file for a patent, but Herring's proposal only reinforced their thinking. In another indication that the Wrights' commercial intentions predated Herring's "offer," the day before the letter was posted, *The New York Times* reported offhandedly that "[t]he inventors of the airship which is said to have made several successful flights in North Carolina, near Kitty Hawk, are anxious to sell the use of their device to the government." The *Times* cited no source and surely there was a good deal of misleading, exaggerated, and even ludicrous reporting in the weeks after Wilbur and Orville took flight. Still, this item is sufficiently congruent with later events to be persuasive.
4. HAT to WW, January 19, 1904.
5. Toulmin's precise phrasing: "We wish it to be understood, however, that our invention is not limited to this particular construction, since any construction whereby the angular relations of the lateral margins of the aeroplanes may be varied in opposite directions with respect to the normal planes of said aeroplanes comes within the scope of our invention. . . . Moreover, although we prefer to so construct the apparatus that the movements of the lateral margins on the opposite sides of the machine are equal in extent and opposite in direction, yet our invention is not limited to a construction producing this result, since it may be desirable under certain circumstances to move the lateral margins on

one side of the machine in the manner just described without moving the lateral margins on the other side of the machine to an equal extent in the opposite direction."

6. OC to Patrick Alexander, January 18, 1904; OC to WW, January 20, 1904.
7. OC to WW, January 14, 1904.
8. WW to OC, January 18, 1904.

CHAPTER 9. THE VAGARIES OF THE MARKETPLACE

1. Foster to OW, November 22, 1905.

CHAPTER 10. THE INEXORABLE PROGRESSION OF KNOWLEDGE

1. GHC to OW and WW, June 22, 1906.
2. *National Magazine* 28 (July 1908), p. 462.

CHAPTER 12. LANGLEY'S LEGACY

1. *National Geographic* 14, No. 6 (June 1903).
2. WW to OW, July 2, 1907.
3. WW to OC, July 21, 1907.
4. OW to WW, July 11, 1907. At this point, Flint and the Wrights had yet to formalize an agreement.
5. WW to OW, August 9, 1907.

CHAPTER 13. CLOSING FAST

1. The Bells had two daughters. Mabel Bell had also given birth to two boys, neither of whom survived his first year.
2. One of those accounts was a deposition Curtiss later gave in his patent infringement suit with the Wrights. While his veracity might be questioned in a document in which he was defending himself, the Wrights also seemed to accept that ailerons were Bell's idea.
3. Santos-Dumont and a glider designer, Robert Esnault-Peletrie, had both used similar devices.

CHAPTER 14. VINDICATION

1. Marvin W. McFarland, ed., *The Papers of Wilbur and Orville Wright* (New York: McGraw-Hill, 1963), p. 883.
2. KW to WW, July 2, 1908.

3. Claim 14 reads, "A flying-machine comprising superposed connected aeroplanes, means for moving the opposite lateral portions of said aeroplanes to different angles to the normal planes thereof, a vertical rudder, means for moving said vertical rudder toward that side of the machine presenting the smaller angle of incidence and the least resistance to the atmosphere, and a horizontal rudder provided with means for presenting its upper or under surface to the resistance of the atmosphere, substantially as described." But Orville, in a letter to Wilbur, later expressed concern that the wording of Claim 14 did not cover Curtiss's aircraft.

CHAPTER 15. ORVILLE AND SELFRIDGE

1. The other two were Benjamin Foulois and Frank Lahm, both of whom would eventually retire from the Army Air Corps as generals.
2. AEA Bulletins, from October 5, 1908, to December 28, 1908.
3. Bell to McCurdy, October 22, 1908.
4. *Boston Daily Globe,* September 18, 1908, p. 1.

CHAPTER 16. THE TOAST OF FRANCE

1. WW to OW, October 18, 1908.
2. Roseberry, *Curtiss,* p. 152.
3. Ibid., pp. 157, 238.
4. Ibid.
5. Crouch, *Bishop,* p. 387.
6. *Aeronautics,* July 1909, p. 13.

CHAPTER 17. TRADING PUNCHES

1. WW to MW, January 1, 1909.
2. *Hartford Courant,* July 26, 1909, p. 1.
3. *Boston Daily Globe,* July 26, 1909, p. 1.
4. Crouch, *Bishop,* p. 399.
5. *Boston Daily Globe,* July 27, 1909, p. 3.
6. OW to WW, August 19, 1909.
7. *Curtiss Aviation Book,* p. 65.
8. Ibid., pp. 65–66.
9. *NYT,* August 23, 1909, p. 1.
10. *NYT,* August 29, 1909, p. 2.
11. The speed of Curtiss's flight remained imprecise, ranging between 45.73 and 47.06 miles per hour, depending on which of the "official" times one accepted. In any case, it remained short of Orville's 47.4 miles per hour at Fort Myer.

12. OW to WW, September 2, 1909.
13. OW to WW, September 28, 1909.
14. WW to OW, August 21, 1909.
15. *Boston Daily Globe,* September 23, 1909, p.11. The nature of the "information" was never revealed. Given Wilbur's acerbic wit, he might well have been referring to the 1906 meeting on which he had largely based his infringement suit.
16. Ibid., p. 12.
17. Grover C. Loening, *Our Wings Grow Faster* (Garden City, N.Y.: Doubleday Doran, 1935), p. 43.
18. Ibid., p. 7.
19. Ibid., p. 11.
20. Roseberry, *Curtiss,* p. 218.
21. *Boston Daily Globe,* October 5, 1909, p. 1.

CHAPTER 18. BEST-LAID PLANS

1. *Los Angeles Herald,* November 8, 1909, p. 1.
2. *Los Angeles Herald,* December 1, 1909, p. 1.
3. *Aeronautics,* February 1910, pp. 18–19.
4. HAT to WW and OW, January 5, 1910.
5. Herbert A. Johnson, "The Wright Patent Wars and Early American Aviation," *Journal of Air Law and Commerce* (Winter 2004).
6. *New-York Tribune,* June 1, 1900, pp. 1–2, emphasis added. The yacht, the *Enquirer,* valued at $25,000, was sold to the government for $80,000.
7. Ibid., May 17, 1900.
8. Strictly speaking, Hazel was ruling on a demurrer filed by the defendants seeking dismissal of the suit—in essence, an appeal. Hazel was concurring with another judge. The principle, however, stands regardless and Hazel would demonstrate his point of view in subsequent cases.
9. *NYT,* September 16, 1909, p. 1.
10. To label the legal strategy that of Wilbur and Orville alone would be a mistake. While they had significant input into what the lawyers did and there is every indication they approved of what would soon be seen as a ham-fisted, public-be-damned approach to protecting their patents, the lawyers were now representing a good deal more than the interests of the inventors.
11. *NYT,* January 6, 1910, p. 4.
12. Ibid.
13. *NYT,* January 19, 1910, p. 1.
14. *NYT,* January 11, 1910, p. 1.
15. *Boston Daily Globe,* January 11, 1910, p. 5.
16. *Aeronautics,* March 1910, p. 80.

17. *NYT,* January 21, 1910, p. 1.
18. San Francisco *Call,* January 22, 1910, p. 10.

CHAPTER 19. BOWING TO THE INEVITABLE

1. AF to WW, January 28, 1910.
2. WW to OC, January 3, 1910. He had written, "Your letter of the 23rd December was received, and we were all glad to know that you were well. We, that is Orville and I, are expecting to be present at the dinner in your honor at Boston on the 12th where naturally we will have the pleasure of meeting you."
3. WW to OC, January 20, 1910.
4. OC to WW, January 23, 1910.
5. WW to OC, April 28, 1910.
6. *Salt Lake Herald,* February 1, 1910, p. 1.
7. *NYT,* March 4, 1910, p. 4.
8. *Aeronautics,* March 1910, p. 90.
9. *Boston Daily Globe,* March 15, 1910, p. 1.
10. *NYT,* April 12, 1910, p. 6.
11. *Boston Daily Globe,* March 13, 1910, p. 1.
12. Andrew Freedman had negotiated the arrangement with Philip Dodge, president of the Mergenthaler Linotype Company and on the board of the Aero Club.

CHAPTER 20. TEAM SPORTS

1. *Curtiss Aviation Book,* pp. 90, 93.
2. *Curtiss Aviation Book,* pp. 91–92.
3. *NYT,* May 30, 1910, p. 1.
4. Roseberry, *Curtiss,* p. 275.
5. Byron Newton to AF, May 29, 1910.
6. AF to WW, June 1, 1910.
7. AF to WW, July 8, 1910.
8. WW to AF, July 21, 1910.
9. *Boston Daily Globe,* August 5, 1910, p. 1.

CHAPTER 21. MAVERICKS

1. Doris L. Rich, *The Magnificent Moisants* (Washington, D.C.: Smithsonian Institution Press, 1998), p. 13.
2. *New-York Tribune,* August 11, 1910, p. 1.
3. *Aeronautics,* August 1910, p. 88.

4. Holden Richardson interview, Columbia Oral History Project.
5. *NYT,* February 12, 1912, p. 11.
6. *Washington Times,* October 14, 1910, p. 1.
7. Roseberry, *Curtiss,* p. 293.
8. Rich, *Moisants,* pp. 40–41.
9. *NYT,* August 20, 1910, p. 1.
10. *Hartford Courant,* October 26, 1910, p. 1.
11. *Boston Daily Globe,* November 18, 1910, p. 1.
12. WW to Archibald Hoxsey, September 9, 1910.
13. *NYT,* October 30, 1910, p. 1.
14. *NYT,* October 31, 1910, p. 2.
15. Rich, *Moisants,* p. 69.
16. *Boston Daily Globe,* November 1, 1910, p. 1.
17. *NYT,* October 31, 1910, p. 1.
18. Quoted in Rich, *Moisants,* p. 68.
19. WW to OW, November 30, 1910.
20. *Aeronautics,* January 1911, p. 28.
21. WW to OW, December 9, 1910.
22. See Crouch, *Bishop.*

CHAPTER 22. FASTER, STEEPER, HIGHER

1. See Crouch, *Bishop,* p. 433.
2. WW to OW, December 16, 1910.
3. OW to WW, November 24, 1910.
4. *NYT,* November 5, 1910, p. 3.
5. WW to OW, December 9, 1910.
6. Linda Arvidson Griffith, *When the Movies Were Young* (New York: Benjamin Blom, 1925), p. 10.
7. San Francisco *Call,* November 10, 1901, p. 20.
8. *Curtiss Aviation Book,* p. 116.
9. Ibid., pp. 118–19.
10. Roseberry, *Curtiss,* p. 311.
11. *Boston Daily Globe,* November 18, 1910, p. 1.
12. Ibid.
13. *Richmond Times-Dispatch,* November 1910, p. 1.
14. Walter Brookins to WW, January 10, 1911.
15. WW to OW, December 9, 1910.
16. WW to OW, November 30, 1910. This is the same letter in which Wilbur closed complaining of the Belmont "swindlers" and vowing to sue to get an additional $15,000.

17. *Aeronautics,* January 1911, pp. 3–5.
18. *NYT,* December 27, 1910.
19. New York *World,* January 1, 1911, p. 1.
20. *NYT,* January 1, 1911, p. 2.
21. San Francisco *Call,* January 2, 1911.

CHAPTER 23. WAR BIRDS

1. *Aircraft,* February 1911, p. 432.
2. *Curtiss Aviation Book,* p. 120.
3. *Aeronautics,* March 1911, p. 95.
4. Roseberry, *Curtiss,* p. 308.
5. Quoted in ibid., p. 279.
6. Ibid., p. 313.
7. *Curtiss Aviation Book,* p. 123.
8. Much of the technical work Wilbur did was theorizing with Orville in their exchanges of letters when one of them was traveling.
9. OW to WW, April 23, 1911.

CHAPTER 24. OWNING THE SKY

1. OW to HAT, May 11, 1911.
2. Knabenshue to OW, emphasis added, July 7, 1911.
3. *NYT,* April 5, 1911, p. 11.
4. *Washington Herald,* May 6, 1911, p. 3.
5. Ibid.
6. Beckwith Havens interview, Columbia Oral History Project.
7. *NYT,* August 8, 1911, pp. 1–2.
8. *Chicago Daily Tribune,* August 13, 1911, p. 1.
9. Ibid., August 14, 1911, p. 3.
10. Ibid., August 16, 1911, p. 1.
11. *Aeronautics,* September 1911, p. 92.
12. *Chicago Daily Tribune,* August 16, 1911, p. 1.
13. New York *Sun,* August 10, 1911, p. 7.
14. *Chicago Daily Tribune,* August 21, 1911, p. 1.
15. *Aircraft,* September 1911, p. 229.

CHAPTER 25. THE WAGES OF RIGHTEOUSNESS

1. OW to WW, September 22, 1911.
2. WW to OW, April 24, 1912.

3. *Aeronautics,* January 1912, p. 1.
4. *Wilbur and Orville Wright Papers,* http://memory.loc.gov/cgi-bin/ampage?collId=mwright&fileName=04/04127/mwright04127.db&recNum=0&itemLink=D?wright:125:./temp/~ammem_eOAX:.
5. *Aircraft,* January 1912, p. 367.
6. Hevésy's given name was Wilhelm, but he went under the French equivalent.
7. WW to Guillaume de Hevésy, January 25, 1912.
8. *NYT,* January 28, 1912, p. 2.
9. Pliny Williamson to WW, January 26, 1912.
10. OW to Russell Alger, March 27, 1912.
11. Most of the day-to-day account of Wilbur's illness comes from Milton Wright's diary, reproduced in *Papers,* pp. 1042–46.

CHAPTER 26. THE ROMANCE OF DEATH

1. *New-York Tribune,* September 2, 1911, p. 1.
2. *Aero and Hydro,* October 7, 1911, p. 10.
3. National Aviation Hall of Fame, http://www.nationalaviation.org/beachey-lincoln/.
4. San Francisco *Call,* October 20, 1911, p. 1.
5. Page's flights at the Los Angeles meet are described in *Aeronautics,* February 1912, the San Francisco *Call,* January 23, 1912, p. 1, and *NYT,* January 23, 1912, p. 1.
6. *Aeronautics,* February 1912, p. 63.
7. San Francisco *Call,* January 28, 1912.
8. San Francisco *Call,* April 4, 1912.
9. *Aeronautics,* July 1912, p. 39. Rodgers was thus the first victim of bird strike.
10. San Francisco *Call,* May 31, 1912, p. 1.
11. Chicago *Day Book,* May 31, 1912, p. 5.
12. San Francisco *Call,* June 2, 1912, p. 33.
13. *NYT,* June 12, 1912, p. 3.
14. *NYT,* July 2, 1912, p. 1.
15. *NYT,* July 3, 1912, p. 7.
16. *Chicago Daily Tribune,* September 23, 1912, p. 3.

CHAPTER 27. A RELUCTANT STEWARD

1. Loening, *Our Wings Grow Faster,* p. 44.
2. Grover C. Loening, *Takeoff into Greatness* (New York: Putnam, 1968), p. 54.
3. Crouch, *Bishop,* pp. 455–56.
4. *Aeronautics,* July 1912.

5. Hazel actually used the testimony of Charles Willard and Lieutenant Thomas Milling instead of Post's. Willard testified that he sometimes used the rudder; Milling claimed to have done so almost always.
6. 204 F. 597, D.C.N.Y., 1913, February 21, 1913.
7. *Aeronautics,* March 1913.
8. Quoted in Roseberry, *Curtiss,* p. 341.
9. Pooling of Patents: Hearing on H.R. 4523 Before the House Comm. on Patents, 74th Cong. 115 (1936).
10. Loening, *Our Wings Grow Faster,* p. 45; Crouch, *Bishop,* p. 455.
11. Crouch, *Bishop,* pp. 457–58.
12. Ibid., p. 459.
13. *NYT,* January 5, 1914, p. 7.

CHAPTER 28. A WISP OF VICTORY

1. 211 F. 654, CA 2, 1914. The judges were Alfred C. Coxe, Emile Lacombe, and Henry Ward, all longtime members of the court and all appointed by probusiness presidents.
2. *NYT,* January 27, 1914, p. 1.
3. *NYT,* January 28, 1914.
4. Roseberry, *Curtiss,* p. 327.

CHAPTER 29. THE GRIP OF THE SPOTLIGHT

1. *NYT,* May 13, 1913, p. 6.
2. It was later learned that twelve days earlier, Peter Nesterov, a captain in the Russian army, had flown a loop as well.
3. *New-York Tribune,* September 29, 1913, p. 1.
4. *NYT,* March 26, 1914, p. 10.
5. Roseberry, *Curtiss,* p. 371.
6. *New-York Tribune,* May 23, 1914, p. 20.
7. *Hartford Courant,* June 15, 1914, p. 12.
8. Ibid., July 13, 1914, p. 13.

CHAPTER 30. THE DEATH OF INNOCENCE

1. *Philadelphia Inquirer,* January 9, 1914.
2. *Aeronautics,* July 1914.
3. Ibid., April 15, 1915, p. 42.

EPILOGUE

1. Crouch, *Bishop,* p. 470.
2. Ibid., p. 476.
3. Tom Crouch comes just short of blaming Katharine for the rift. "Orville believed that he and his sister were bound by a firm understanding—they were the sole survivors. Through it all, from Milton's early church difficulties to the patent wars, they had avoided any entangling personal relationships outside the family circle. . . . In this family, such informal agreements had the force of law." Crouch, *Bishop,* p. 482.
4. Quoted in Crouch, *Bishop,* p. 472.
5. The War Department would not let any of the participants compete for the money since the flight was under the auspices of the United States government.
6. Roseberry, *Curtiss,* p. 479.

SELECTED BIBLIOGRAPHY

BOOKS AND ARTICLES

Anderson, John D., Jr. *A History of Aerodynamics and Its Impact on Flying Machines.* New York: Cambridge University Press, 1999.

Brady, Tim, ed. *The American Aviation Experience: A History.* Carbondale: Southern Illinois University Press, 2000.

Crouch, Tom D. *The Bishop's Boys: A Life of Wilbur and Orville Wright.* New York: Norton, 1989.

———*A Dream of Wings: Americans and the Airplane, 1875–1905.* New York: Norton, 1981.

Curtiss, Glenn Hammond, and Augustus Post. *The Curtiss Aviation Book.* New York: Frederick A. Stokes, 1912.

Goddard, Stephen B. *Race to the Sky: The Wright Brothers Versus the United States Government.* Jefferson, N.C.: McFarland, 2003.

Grahame-White, Claude. *The Aeroplane: Past, Present, and Future.* New York: Harry Harper, 1911.

Greenleaf, William, and David L. Lewis. *Monopoly on Wheels: Henry Ford and the Selden Automobile Patent.* Detroit: Wayne State University Press, 2011.

Griffith, Linda Arvidson. *When the Movies Were Young.* New York: Benjamin Blom, 1925.

Harp, Stephen L. *Marketing Michelin: Advertising and Cultural Identity in Twentieth-Century France.* Baltimore: Johns Hopkins University Press, 2001.

Hatch, Alden. *Glenn Curtiss: Pioneer of Aviation.* 1942; reprint, Guilford, Conn.: Lyons Press, 2007.

Hedin, Robert. *The Zeppelin Reader: Stories, Poems, and Songs from the Age of Airships.* Iowa City: University of Iowa Press, 1998.

Herlihy, David V. *Bicycle: The History.* New Haven, Conn.: Yale University Press, 2004.

Hobbs, Leonard S. *The Wright Brothers' Engines and Their Design.* Washington, D.C.: Military Bookshop, 2011.

Hoffman, Paul. *Wings of Madness: Alberto Santos-Dumont and the Invention of Flight.* New York: Hyperion, 2003.

Howard, Fred. *Wilbur and Orville: A Biography of the Wright Brothers.* New York: Knopf, 1987.

Johnson, Herbert A. "The Wright Patent Wars and Early American Aviation," *Journal of Air Law and Commerce,* Winter 2004.

Kelly, Fred C. *The Wright Brothers: A Biography.* Mineola, N.Y.: Dover, 1989.

Kurtz, Gary F. "'Navigating the Upper Strata' and the Quest for Dirigibility." *California History* 58, No. 4 (Winter 1979/1980).

Lebow, Eileen F. *Before Amelia: Women Pilots in the Early Days of Aviation.* Washington, D.C.: Brassey's, 2002.

Loening, Grover C. *Our Wings Grow Faster.* Garden City, N.Y.: Doubleday Doran, 1935.

——— *Takeoff into Greatness: How American Aviation Grew So Big So Fast.* New York: Putnam, 1968.

Ludlow, Israel. *Navigating the Air: A Scientific Statement of the Progress of Aëronautical Science Up to the Present Time.* New York: Aero Club of America, 1907.

Marrero, Frank. *Lincoln Beachey: The Man Who Owned the Sky.* San Francisco: Scottwall, 1997.

McFarland, Marvin W., ed. *The Papers of Wilbur and Orville Wright.* New York: McGraw-Hill, 1963.

Mortimer, Gavin. *Chasing Icarus: The Seventeen Days in 1910 That Forever Changed American Aviation.* New York: Walker, 2010.

Pattillo, Donald M. *Pushing the Envelope: The American Aircraft Industry.* Ann Arbor: University of Michigan Press, 2001.

Pauley, Kenneth E., and Dominguez Rancho Adobe Museum. *The 1910 Los Angeles International Air Meet.* Mount Pleasant, S.C.: Arcadia, 2009.

Pottage, Alain, and Brad Sherman. *Figures of Invention: A History of Modern Patent Law.* New York: Oxford University Press, 2010.

Rich, Doris L. *The Magnificent Moisants: Champions of Early Flight.* Washington, D.C.: Smithsonian Institution Press, 1998.

Roseberry, C. R. *Glenn Curtiss: Pioneer of Flight.* Garden City, N.Y.: Doubleday, 1972.

Schoonover, Thomas David. *The United States in Central America, 1860–1911: Episodes of Social Imperialism and Imperial Rivalry in the World System.* Durham, N.C.: Duke University Press, 1991.

Schwartz, Rosalie. *Flying Down to Rio: Hollywood, Tourists, and Yankee Clippers.* College Station: Texas A&M University Press, 2004.

Scott, Phil. *Then & Now: How Airplanes Got This Way.* Batavia, Ohio: Sporty's Pilot Shop, 2012.

Shulman, Seth. *Unlocking the Sky: Glenn Hammond Curtiss and the Race to Invent the Airplane.* New York: HarperCollins, 2002.

Smith, Robert A. *A Social History of the Bicycle, Its Early Life and Times in America.* New York: American Heritage Press, 1972.

Spenser, Jay. *The Airplane: How Ideas Gave Us Wings.* New York: Collins, 2008.

Subotnik, Rena Faye, and Herbert J. Walberg. *The Scientific Basis of Education Productivity.* Washington, D.C.: Information Age, 2006.

Tobin, James. *To Conquer the Air: The Wright Brothers and the Great Race for Flight.* New York: Simon & Schuster, 2004.

Weber, Max. *The Protestant Ethic and the Spirit of Capitalism: And Other Writings.* New York: Penguin, 2002.

Wright, Wilbur, Orville Wright, and Fred C. Kelly (ed.). *Miracle at Kitty Hawk: The Letters of Wilbur and Orville Wright.* New York: Da Capo, 2002.

WEBSITES

Alexander Graham Bell Family Papers. Manuscript Division, Library of Congress, Washington, D.C. http://memory.loc.gov/ammem/bellhtml/bellhome.html.

Chronicling America. National Endowment for the Humanities and the Library of Congress, Washington, D.C. http://chroniclingamerica.loc.gov/.

The Hudson–Fulton Celebration and New York City. Fordham University. http://www.fordham.edu/academics/colleges_graduate_s/undergraduate_colleg/fordham_college_at_l/special_programs/honors_program/hudsonfulton_celebra/.

Wilbur and Orville Wright Papers. Manuscript Division, Library of Congress, Washington, D.C. http://memory.loc.gov/ammem/wrighthtml/wrighthome.html.

Wright Brothers Aeroplane Company. http://www.wright-brothers.org.

PERIODICALS

Aero and Hydro: America's Aviation Weekly. Vols. 1–5, 1909–13. Chicago: E. Percy Noël.

Aeronautics. Vols. 1–17, 1908–15. New York: E. L. Jones, by the Aeronautics Press.

Aircraft. Vols. 1–5, 1910–15. New York: Lawson.

Everybody's Magazine. Vol. 20, January 1909. New York: North American.

The Horseless Age. Vol. 7, May 1900. New York: Horseless Age.

Munsey's Magazine. Vol. 45, September 1911. New York: Frank A. Munsey.

National Geographic. Vol. 14, June 1903. Washington, D.C.: National Geographic Society.

National Magazine. Vol. 28, July 1908. Boston: Chappelle.

Popular Science. Vol. 110, April 1927. New York: Popular Science Publishing.

Transactions of the American Society of Civil Engineers. Vol. 74, 1911. Chicago: American Society of Civil Engineers.

OTHER

The Aeronautical Annual: Devoted to the Encouragement of Experiment with Aerial Machines and to the Advancement of the Science Aerodynamics. Vols. 1–3, 1894–96. Boston: W. B. Clarke.

Columbia Oral History Project: Beckwith Havens, Hillary Beachey, Holden Richardson, Matilde Moisant.

INDEX

ABOUT THE AUTHOR

LAWRENCE GOLDSTONE is the author or co-author of fourteen books, and a recipient of the New American Writing Award. His writing has appeared in the *Boston Globe, Los Angeles Times, Chicago Tribune, Miami Herald,* and other periodicals. He has also been a teacher, lecturer, senior member of a Wall Street trading firm, taxi driver, actor, quiz show contestant, and policy analyst at the Hudson Institute. He lives in Sagaponack, New York, with his wife and daughter.

ABOUT THE TYPE

This book was set in Caslon, a typeface first designed in 1722 by William Caslon (1692–1766). Its widespread use by most English printers in the early eighteenth century soon supplanted the Dutch typefaces that had formerly prevailed. The roman is considered a "workhorse" typeface due to its pleasant, open appearance, while the italic is exceedingly decorative.